General Motors
Cadillac DeVille and Seville
Automotive Repair Manual

**by Bob Henderson
and John H Haynes**

Member of the Guild of Motoring Writers

Models covered:

Cadillac DeVille (1994 thru 2002)
Cadillac Seville (1992 thru 2002)

ABCDE
FGHIJ
KLMNO
PQR

Haynes Publishing Group
Sparkford Nr Yeovil
Somerset BA22 7JJ England

Haynes North America, Inc
861 Lawrence Drive
Newbury Park
California 91320 USA

Acknowledgements

Wiring diagrams originated exclusively for Haynes North America, Inc. by Valley Forge Technical Information Services. Technical writers who contributed to this project include Rob Maddox, Mike Stubblefield, John Wegmann and Larry Warren. Technical consultants include Jamie Sarté, Jr. and Brad Conn.

© **Haynes North America, Inc. 2003**

With permission from J.H. Haynes & Co. Ltd.

A book in the Haynes Automotive Repair Manual Series

Printed in the U.S.A.

ISBN 1 56392 483 8

Library of Congress Control Number 2002115734

Contents

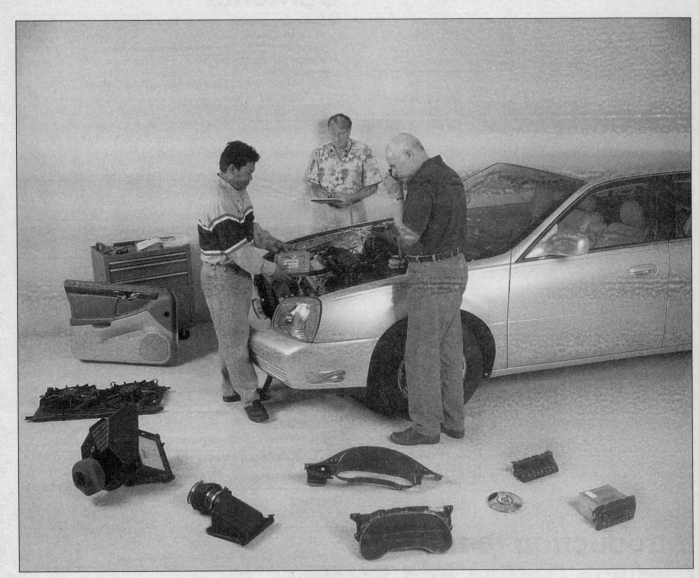

Haynes mechanic, author and photographer with a 2000 Cadillac DeVille

About this manual

Its purpose

The purpose of this manual is to help you get the best value from your vehicle. It can do so in several ways. It can help you decide what work must be done, even if you choose to have it done by a dealer service department or a repair shop; it provides information and procedures for routine maintenance and servicing; and it offers diagnostic and repair procedures to follow when trouble occurs.

We hope you use the manual to tackle the work yourself. For many simpler jobs, doing it yourself may be quicker than arranging an appointment to get the vehicle into a shop and making the trips to leave it and pick it up. More importantly, a lot of money can be saved by avoiding the expense the shop must pass on to you to cover its labor and overhead costs. An added benefit is the sense of satisfaction and accomplishment that you feel after doing the job yourself.

Using the manual

The manual is divided into Chapters. Each Chapter is divided into numbered Sections, which are headed in bold type between horizontal lines. Each Section consists of consecutively numbered paragraphs.

At the beginning of each numbered Section you will be referred to any illustrations which apply to the procedures in that Section. The reference numbers used in illustration captions pinpoint the pertinent Section and the Step within that Section. That is, illustration 3.2 means the illustration refers to Section 3 and Step (or paragraph) 2 within that Section.

Procedures, once described in the text, are not normally repeated. When it's necessary to refer to another Chapter, the reference will be given as Chapter and Section number. Cross references given without use of the word "Chapter" apply to Sections and/or paragraphs in the same Chapter. For example, "see Section 8" means in the same Chapter.

References to the left or right side of the vehicle assume you are sitting in the driver's seat, facing forward.

Even though we have prepared this manual with extreme care, neither the publisher nor the author can accept responsibility for any errors in, or omissions from, the information given.

NOTE

A **Note** provides information necessary to properly complete a procedure or information which will make the procedure easier to understand.

CAUTION

A **Caution** provides a special procedure or special steps which must be taken while completing the procedure where the Caution is found. Not heeding a Caution can result in damage to the assembly being worked on.

WARNING

A **Warning** provides a special procedure or special steps which must be taken while completing the procedure where the Warning is found. Not heeding a Warning can result in personal injury.

Introduction to the Cadillac DeVille and Seville

Cadillac DeVille and Seville models are all four-door sedans.

1992 models came equipped with 4.9L V8 engines. 1993 and 1994 models were available with either a 4.9L V8 engine or a 4.6L V8 engine. All 1995 and later models had the 4.6L V8 engine. All models are equipped with fuel injection.

The transversely mounted engine transmits power to the front wheels through a four-speed automatic transaxle via independent driveaxles.

Suspension is independent in the front, utilizing MacPherson struts and lower control arms to locate the knuckle assembly at each wheel. The rear suspension on 1992 Seville models uses a transverse composite leaf spring, lower control arms and suspension knuckles supported by strut-type shock absorbers. The rear suspension on 1993 through 1997 Seville models and 1994 through 1999 DeVille models features upper and lower control arms, coil springs, toe links and telescopic shock absorbers. 1999 and later Seville models and 2000 and later DeVille models use trailing-type control arms, toe links, coil springs and shock absorbers

The rack-and-pinion steering unit is mounted behind the engine with power-assist as standard equipment.

The brakes are disc at the front and rear, with power assist standard. An Anti-lock Braking System (ABS) is standard equipment on all models.

Vehicle identification numbers

Vehicle Identification Number (VIN)

This very important identification number is stamped on a plate attached to the left side of the dashboard and is visible through the driver's side of the windshield (see illustration). The VIN also appears on the Vehicle Certificate of Title and Registration. It contains information such as where and when the vehicle was manufactured, the model year and the body style.

VIN engine and model year codes

Two particularly important pieces of information found in the VIN are the engine code and the model year code. Counting from the left, the engine code letter designation is the 8th digit and the model year code letter designation is the 10th digit.

On the models covered by this manual the engine codes are:

1992
    B 4.9L V8
1993 and 1994
    B 4.9L V8
    9, Y........................ 4.6L V8
1995 through 2002
    9, Y........................ 4.6L V8

On the models covered by this manual the model year codes are:

N	1992
P	1993
R	1994
S	1995
T	1996
V	1997
W	1998
X	1999
Y	2000
1	2001
2	2002

The Vehicle Identification Number (VIN) is on a plate attached to the top of the dashboard on the driver's side of the vehicle - it can be seen through the windshield

The Vehicle Certification label is located on the end of the driver's side door

The engine identification number can be seen from below the vehicle (4.6L V8 shown, 4.9L V8 similar)

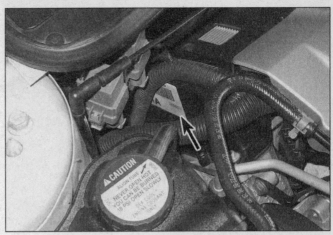

The engine unit number label is on the right valve cover

Vehicle Certification label

The Vehicle Certification Plate (VC label) is affixed to the rear of the left front door **(see illustration)**. The plate contains the name of the manufacturer, the month and year of production, the Gross Vehicle Weight Rating (GVWR) and the certification statement.

Engine identification number

The engine ID number is located on a tag at the left hand side at the rear of the engine block **(see illustration)**. The engine unit number label is on the rear (firewall) side valve cover **(see illustration)**.

Service parts identification label

This label is located inside the trunk on the spare tire cover. It lists the VIN number, wheelbase, paint number, options and other information specific to your vehicle. Always refer to this label when ordering parts.

Transaxle identification number

The transaxle identification number is located on the rear side of the transaxle case **(see illustration)**.

Vehicle Emissions Control Information label

The Vehicle Emissions Control Information label is under the hood, often attached to the left shock tower (see Chapter 6 for more information and an illustration of the label).

The transaxle identification number tag can be seen from below the vehicle

Buying parts

Replacement parts are available from many sources, which generally fall into one of two categories - authorized dealer parts departments and independent retail auto parts stores. Our advice concerning these parts is as follows:

Retail auto parts stores: Good auto parts stores will stock frequently needed components which wear out relatively fast, such as clutch components, exhaust systems, brake parts, tune-up parts, etc. These stores often supply new or reconditioned parts on an exchange basis, which can save a considerable amount of money. Discount auto parts stores are often very good places to buy materials and parts needed for general vehicle maintenance such as oil, grease, filters, spark plugs, belts, touch-up paint, bulbs, etc. They also usually sell tools and general accessories, have convenient hours, charge lower prices and can often be found not far from home.

Authorized dealer parts department: This is the best source for parts which are unique to the vehicle and not generally available elsewhere (such as major engine parts, transmission parts, trim pieces, etc.).

Warranty information: If the vehicle is still covered under warranty, be sure that any replacement parts purchased - regardless of the source - do not invalidate the warranty!

To be sure of obtaining the correct parts, have engine and chassis numbers available and, if possible, take the old parts along for positive identification.

Maintenance techniques, tools and working facilities

Maintenance techniques

There are a number of techniques involved in maintenance and repair that will be referred to throughout this manual. Application of these techniques will enable the home mechanic to be more efficient, better organized and capable of performing the various tasks properly, which will ensure that the repair job is thorough and complete.

Fasteners

Fasteners are nuts, bolts, studs and screws used to hold two or more parts together. There are a few things to keep in mind when working with fasteners. Almost all of them use a locking device of some type, either a lockwasher, locknut, locking tab or thread adhesive. All threaded fasteners should be clean and straight, with undamaged threads and undamaged corners on the hex head where the wrench fits. Develop the habit of replacing all damaged nuts and bolts with new ones. Special locknuts with nylon or fiber inserts can only be used once. If they are removed, they lose their locking ability and must be replaced with new ones.

Rusted nuts and bolts should be treated with a penetrating fluid to ease removal and prevent breakage. Some mechanics use turpentine in a spout-type oil can, which works quite well. After applying the rust penetrant, let it work for a few minutes before trying to loosen the nut or bolt. Badly rusted fasteners may have to be chiseled or sawed off or removed with a special nut breaker, available at tool stores.

If a bolt or stud breaks off in an assembly, it can be drilled and removed with a special tool commonly available for this purpose.

Most automotive machine shops can perform this task, as well as other repair procedures, such as the repair of threaded holes that have been stripped out.

Flat washers and lockwashers, when removed from an assembly, should always be replaced exactly as removed. Replace any damaged washers with new ones. Never use a lockwasher on any soft metal surface (such as aluminum), thin sheet metal or plastic.

Grade 1 or 2   Grade 5   Grade 8

Bolt strength marking (standard/SAE/USS; bottom - metric)

Grade	Identification	Grade	Identification
Hex Nut Grade 5	3 Dots	Hex Nut Property Class 9	Arabic 9
Hex Nut Grade 8	6 Dots	Hex Nut Property Class 10	Arabic 10

Standard hex nut strength markings

Metric hex nut strength markings

Class 10.9   Class 9.8   Class 8.8

Metric stud strength markings

00-1 HAYNES

Fastener sizes

For a number of reasons, automobile manufacturers are making wider and wider use of metric fasteners. Therefore, it is important to be able to tell the difference between standard (sometimes called U.S. or SAE) and metric hardware, since they cannot be interchanged.

All bolts, whether standard or metric, are sized according to diameter, thread pitch and length. For example, a standard 1/2 - 13 x 1 bolt is 1/2 inch in diameter, has 13 threads per inch and is 1 inch long. An M12 - 1.75 x 25 metric bolt is 12 mm in diameter, has a thread pitch of 1.75 mm (the distance between threads) and is 25 mm long. The two bolts are nearly identical, and easily confused, but they are not interchangeable.

In addition to the differences in diameter, thread pitch and length, metric and standard bolts can also be distinguished by examining the bolt heads. To begin with, the distance across the flats on a standard bolt head is measured in inches, while the same dimension on a metric bolt is sized in millimeters (the same is true for nuts). As a result, a standard wrench should not be used on a metric bolt and a metric wrench should not be used on a standard bolt. Also, most standard bolts have slashes radiating out from the center of the head to denote the grade or strength of the bolt, which is an indication of the amount of torque that can be applied to it. The greater the number of slashes, the greater the strength of the bolt. Grades 0 through 5 are commonly used on automobiles. Metric bolts have a property class (grade) number, rather than a slash, molded into their heads to indicate bolt strength. In this case, the higher the number, the stronger the bolt. Property class numbers 8.8, 9.8 and 10.9 are commonly used on automobiles.

Strength markings can also be used to distinguish standard hex nuts from metric hex nuts. Many standard nuts have dots stamped into one side, while metric nuts are marked with a number. The greater the number of dots, or the higher the number, the greater the strength of the nut.

Metric studs are also marked on their ends according to property class (grade). Larger studs are numbered (the same as metric bolts), while smaller studs carry a geometric code to denote grade.

It should be noted that many fasteners, especially Grades 0 through 2, have no distinguishing marks on them. When such is the case, the only way to determine whether it is standard or metric is to measure the thread pitch or compare it to a known fastener of the same size.

Standard fasteners are often referred to as SAE, as opposed to metric. However, it should be noted that SAE technically refers to a non-metric fine thread fastener only. Coarse thread non-metric fasteners are referred to as USS sizes.

Since fasteners of the same size (both standard and metric) may have different strength ratings, be sure to reinstall any bolts, studs or nuts removed from your vehicle in their original locations. Also, when replacing a fastener with a new one, make sure that the new one has a strength rating equal to or greater than the original.

Metric thread sizes

	Ft-lbs	Nm
M-6	6 to 9	9 to 12
M-8	14 to 21	19 to 28
M-10	28 to 40	38 to 54
M-12	50 to 71	68 to 96
M-14	80 to 140	109 to 154

Pipe thread sizes

	Ft-lbs	Nm
1/8	5 to 8	7 to 10
1/4	12 to 18	17 to 24
3/8	22 to 33	30 to 44
1/2	25 to 35	34 to 47

U.S. thread sizes

	Ft-lbs	Nm
1/4 - 20	6 to 9	9 to 12
5/16 - 18	12 to 18	17 to 24
5/16 - 24	14 to 20	19 to 27
3/8 - 16	22 to 32	30 to 43
3/8 - 24	27 to 38	37 to 51
7/16 - 14	40 to 55	55 to 74
7/16 - 20	40 to 60	55 to 81
1/2 - 13	55 to 80	75 to 108

Standard (SAE and USS) bolt dimensions/grade marks

G   Grade marks (bolt strength)
L   Length (in inches)
T   Thread pitch (number of threads per inch)
D   Nominal diameter (in inches)

Metric bolt dimensions/grade marks

P   Property class (bolt strength)
L   Length (in millimeters)
T   Thread pitch (distance between threads in millimeters)
D   Diameter

Tightening sequences and procedures

Most threaded fasteners should be tightened to a specific torque value (torque is the twisting force applied to a threaded component such as a nut or bolt). Overtightening the fastener can weaken it and cause it to break, while undertightening can cause it to eventually come loose. Bolts, screws and studs, depending on the material they are made of and their thread diameters, have specific torque values, many of which are noted in the Specifications at the beginning of each Chapter. Be sure to follow the torque recommendations closely. For fasteners not assigned a specific torque, a general torque value chart is presented here as a guide. These torque values are for dry (unlubricated) fasteners threaded into steel or cast iron (not aluminum). As was previously mentioned, the size and grade of a fastener determine the amount of torque that can safely be applied to it. The figures listed here are approximate for Grade 2 and Grade 3 fasteners. Higher grades can tolerate higher torque values.

Fasteners laid out in a pattern, such as cylinder head bolts, oil pan bolts, differential cover bolts, etc., must be loosened or tightened in sequence to avoid warping the com-

Micrometer set

Dial indicator set

ponent. This sequence will normally be shown in the appropriate Chapter. If a specific pattern is not given, the following procedures can be used to prevent warping.

Initially, the bolts or nuts should be assembled finger-tight only. Next, they should be tightened one full turn each, in a criss-cross or diagonal pattern. After each one has been tightened one full turn, return to the first one and tighten them all one-half turn, following the same pattern. Finally, tighten each of them one-quarter turn at a time until each fastener has been tightened to the proper torque. To loosen and remove the fasteners, the procedure would be reversed.

Component disassembly

Component disassembly should be done with care and purpose to help ensure that the parts go back together properly. Always keep track of the sequence in which parts are removed. Make note of special characteristics or marks on parts that can be installed more than one way, such as a grooved thrust washer on a shaft. It is a good idea to lay the disassembled parts out on a clean surface in the order that they were removed. It may also be helpful to make sketches or take instant photos of components before removal.

When removing fasteners from a component, keep track of their locations. Sometimes threading a bolt back in a part, or putting the washers and nut back on a stud, can prevent mix-ups later. If nuts and bolts cannot be returned to their original locations, they should be kept in a compartmented box or a series of small boxes. A cupcake or muffin tin is ideal for this purpose, since each cavity can hold the bolts and nuts from a particular area (i.e. oil pan bolts, valve cover bolts, engine mount bolts, etc.). A pan of this type is especially helpful when working on assemblies with very small parts, such as the carburetor, alternator, valve train or interior dash and trim pieces. The cavities can be marked with paint or tape to identify the contents.

Whenever wiring looms, harnesses or connectors are separated, it is a good idea to identify the two halves with numbered pieces of masking tape so they can be easily reconnected.

Gasket sealing surfaces

Throughout any vehicle, gaskets are used to seal the mating surfaces between two parts and keep lubricants, fluids, vacuum or pressure contained in an assembly.

Many times these gaskets are coated with a liquid or paste-type gasket sealing compound before assembly. Age, heat and pressure can sometimes cause the two parts to stick together so tightly that they are very difficult to separate. Often, the assembly can be loosened by striking it with a soft-face hammer near the mating surfaces. A regular hammer can be used if a block of wood is placed between the hammer and the part. Do not hammer on cast parts or parts that could be easily damaged. With any particularly stubborn part, always recheck to make sure that every fastener has been removed.

Avoid using a screwdriver or bar to pry apart an assembly, as they can easily mar the gasket sealing surfaces of the parts, which must remain smooth. If prying is absolutely necessary, use an old broom handle, but keep in mind that extra clean up will be necessary if the wood splinters.

After the parts are separated, the old gasket must be carefully removed and the gasket surfaces cleaned. If you're working on cast iron or aluminum parts, stubborn gasket material can be soaked with rust penetrant or treated with a special chemical to soften it so it can be easily scraped off. **Caution:** *Never use gasket removal solutions or caustic chemicals on plastic or other composite components.* A scraper can be fashioned from a piece of copper tubing by flattening and sharpening one end. Copper is recommended because it is usually softer than the surfaces to be scraped, which reduces the chance of gouging the part. Some gaskets can be removed with a wire brush, but regardless of the method used, the mating surfaces must be left clean and smooth. If for some reason the gasket surface is gouged, then a gasket sealer thick enough to fill scratches will have to be used during reassembly of the components. For most applications, a non-drying (or semi-drying) gasket sealer should be used.

Hose removal tips

Warning: *If the vehicle is equipped with air conditioning, do not disconnect any of the A/C hoses without first having the system depressurized by a dealer service department or a service station.*

Hose removal precautions closely parallel gasket removal precautions. Avoid scratching or gouging the surface that the hose mates against or the connection may leak. This is especially true for radiator hoses. Because of various chemical reactions, the rubber in hoses can bond itself to the metal spigot that the hose fits over. To remove a hose, first loosen the hose clamps that secure it to the spigot. Then, with slip-joint pliers, grab the hose at the clamp and rotate it around the spigot. Work it back and forth until it is completely free, then pull it off. Silicone or other lubricants will ease removal if they can be applied between the hose and the outside of the spigot. Apply the same lubricant to the inside of the hose and the outside of the spigot to simplify installation.

As a last resort (and if the hose is to be replaced with a new one anyway), the rubber can be slit with a knife and the hose peeled from the spigot. If this must be done, be careful that the metal connection is not damaged.

If a hose clamp is broken or damaged, do not reuse it. Wire-type clamps usually weaken with age, so it is a good idea to replace them with screw-type clamps whenever a hose is removed.

Tools

A selection of good tools is a basic requirement for anyone who plans to maintain and repair his or her own vehicle. For the owner who has few tools, the initial investment might seem high, but when compared to the spiraling costs of professional auto maintenance and repair, it is a wise one.

To help the owner decide which tools are needed to perform the tasks detailed in this manual, the following tool lists are offered: *Maintenance and minor repair, Repair/overhaul* and *Special.*

The newcomer to practical mechanics should start off with the *maintenance and*

Dial caliper

Hand-operated vacuum pump

Timing light

Compression gauge with spark plug hole adapter

Damper/steering wheel puller

General purpose puller

Hydraulic lifter removal tool

Valve spring compressor

Valve spring compressor

Ridge reamer

Piston ring groove cleaning tool

Ring removal/installation tool

Ring compressor

Cylinder hone

Brake hold-down spring tool

Brake cylinder hone

Clutch plate alignment tool

Tap and die set

minor repair tool kit, which is adequate for the simpler jobs performed on a vehicle. Then, as confidence and experience grow, the owner can tackle more difficult tasks, buying additional tools as they are needed. Eventually the basic kit will be expanded into the *repair and overhaul* tool set. Over a period of time, the experienced do-it-yourselfer will assemble a tool set complete enough for most repair and overhaul procedures and will add tools from the special category when it is felt that the expense is justified by the frequency of use.

Maintenance and minor repair tool kit

The tools in this list should be considered the minimum required for performance of routine maintenance, servicing and minor repair work. We recommend the purchase of combination wrenches (box-end and open-end combined in one wrench). While more expensive than open end wrenches, they offer the advantages of both types of wrench.

Combination wrench set (1/4-inch to
  1 inch or 6 mm to 19 mm)
Adjustable wrench, 8 inch
Spark plug wrench with rubber insert
Spark plug gap adjusting tool
Feeler gauge set
Brake bleeder wrench
Standard screwdriver (5/16-inch x
  6 inch)

Phillips screwdriver (No. 2 x 6 inch)
Combination pliers - 6 inch
Hacksaw and assortment of blades
Tire pressure gauge
Grease gun
Oil can
Fine emery cloth
Wire brush
Battery post and cable cleaning tool
Oil filter wrench
Funnel (medium size)
Safety goggles
Jackstands (2)
Drain pan

Note: *If basic tune-ups are going to be part of routine maintenance, it will be necessary to purchase a good quality stroboscopic timing light and combination tachometer/dwell meter. Although they are included in the list of special tools, it is mentioned here because they are absolutely necessary for tuning most vehicles properly.*

Repair and overhaul tool set

These tools are essential for anyone who plans to perform major repairs and are in addition to those in the maintenance and minor repair tool kit. Included is a comprehensive set of sockets which, though expensive, are invaluable because of their versatility, especially when various extensions and drives are available. We recommend the 1/2-inch drive over the 3/8-inch drive. Although the larger drive is bulky and more expensive,

it has the capacity of accepting a very wide range of large sockets. Ideally, however, the mechanic should have a 3/8-inch drive set and a 1/2-inch drive set.

Socket set(s)
Reversible ratchet
Extension - 10 inch
Universal joint
Torque wrench (same size drive as
  sockets)
Ball peen hammer - 8 ounce
Soft-face hammer (plastic/rubber)
Standard screwdriver (1/4-inch x 6 inch)
Standard screwdriver (stubby -
  5/16-inch)
Phillips screwdriver (No. 3 x 8 inch)
Phillips screwdriver (stubby - No. 2)
Pliers - vise grip
Pliers - lineman's
Pliers - needle nose
Pliers - snap-ring (internal and external)
Cold chisel - 1/2-inch
Scribe
Scraper (made from flattened copper
  tubing)
Centerpunch
Pin punches (1/16, 1/8, 3/16-inch)
Steel rule/straightedge - 12 inch
Allen wrench set (1/8 to 3/8-inch or
  4 mm to 10 mm)
A selection of files
Wire brush (large)
Jackstands (second set)
Jack (scissor or hydraulic type)

Note: *Another tool which is often useful is an electric drill with a chuck capacity of 3/8-inch and a set of good quality drill bits.*

Special tools

The tools in this list include those which are not used regularly, are expensive to buy, or which need to be used in accordance with their manufacturer's instructions. Unless these tools will be used frequently, it is not very economical to purchase many of them. A consideration would be to split the cost and use between yourself and a friend or friends. In addition, most of these tools can be obtained from a tool rental shop on a temporary basis.

This list primarily contains only those tools and instruments widely available to the public, and not those special tools produced by the vehicle manufacturer for distribution to dealer service departments. Occasionally, references to the manufacturer's special tools are included in the text of this manual. Generally, an alternative method of doing the job without the special tool is offered. However, sometimes there is no alternative to their use. Where this is the case, and the tool cannot be purchased or borrowed, the work should be turned over to the dealer service department or an automotive repair shop.

Valve spring compressor
Piston ring groove cleaning tool
Piston ring compressor
Piston ring installation tool
Cylinder compression gauge
Cylinder ridge reamer
Cylinder surfacing hone
Cylinder bore gauge
Micrometers and/or dial calipers
Hydraulic lifter removal tool
Balljoint separator
Universal-type puller
Impact screwdriver
Dial indicator set
Stroboscopic timing light (inductive pick-up)
Hand operated vacuum/pressure pump
Tachometer/dwell meter
Universal electrical multimeter
Cable hoist
Brake spring removal and installation tools
Floor jack

Buying tools

For the do-it-yourselfer who is just starting to get involved in vehicle maintenance and repair, there are a number of options available when purchasing tools. If maintenance and minor repair is the extent of the work to be done, the purchase of individual tools is satisfactory. If, on the other hand, extensive work is planned, it would be a good idea to purchase a modest tool set from one of the large retail chain stores. A set can usually be bought at a substantial savings over the individual tool prices, and they often

come with a tool box. As additional tools are needed, add-on sets, individual tools and a larger tool box can be purchased to expand the tool selection. Building a tool set gradually allows the cost of the tools to be spread over a longer period of time and gives the mechanic the freedom to choose only those tools that will actually be used.

Tool stores will often be the only source of some of the special tools that are needed, but regardless of where tools are bought, try to avoid cheap ones, especially when buying screwdrivers and sockets, because they won't last very long. The expense involved in replacing cheap tools will eventually be greater than the initial cost of quality tools.

Care and maintenance of tools

Good tools are expensive, so it makes sense to treat them with respect. Keep them clean and in usable condition and store them properly when not in use. Always wipe off any dirt, grease or metal chips before putting them away. Never leave tools lying around in the work area. Upon completion of a job, always check closely under the hood for tools that may have been left there so they won't get lost during a test drive.

Some tools, such as screwdrivers, pliers, wrenches and sockets, can be hung on a panel mounted on the garage or workshop wall, while others should be kept in a tool box or tray. Measuring instruments, gauges, meters, etc. must be carefully stored where they cannot be damaged by weather or impact from other tools.

When tools are used with care and stored properly, they will last a very long time. Even with the best of care, though, tools will wear out if used frequently. When a tool is damaged or worn out, replace it. Subsequent jobs will be safer and more enjoyable if you do.

How to repair damaged threads

Sometimes, the internal threads of a nut or bolt hole can become stripped, usually from overtightening. Stripping threads is an all-too-common occurrence, especially when working with aluminum parts, because aluminum is so soft that it easily strips out.

Usually, external or internal threads are only partially stripped. After they've been cleaned up with a tap or die, they'll still work. Sometimes, however, threads are badly damaged. When this happens, you've got three choices:

1) *Drill and tap the hole to the next suitable oversize and install a larger diameter bolt, screw or stud.*
2) *Drill and tap the hole to accept a threaded plug, then drill and tap the plug to the original screw size. You can also buy a plug already threaded to the original size. Then you simply drill a hole to the specified size, then run the threaded*

plug into the hole with a bolt and jam nut. Once the plug is fully seated, remove the jam nut and bolt.
3) *The third method uses a patented thread repair kit like Heli-Coil or Slimsert. These easy-to-use kits are designed to repair damaged threads in straight-through holes and blind holes. Both are available as kits which can handle a variety of sizes and thread patterns. Drill the hole, then tap it with the special included tap. Install the Heli-Coil and the hole is back to its original diameter and thread pitch.*

Regardless of which method you use, be sure to proceed calmly and carefully. A little impatience or carelessness during one of these relatively simple procedures can ruin your whole day's work and cost you a bundle if you wreck an expensive part.

Working facilities

Not to be overlooked when discussing tools is the workshop. If anything more than routine maintenance is to be carried out, some sort of suitable work area is essential.

It is understood, and appreciated, that many home mechanics do not have a good workshop or garage available, and end up removing an engine or doing major repairs outside. It is recommended, however, that the overhaul or repair be completed under the cover of a roof.

A clean, flat workbench or table of comfortable working height is an absolute necessity. The workbench should be equipped with a vise that has a jaw opening of at least four inches.

As mentioned previously, some clean, dry storage space is also required for tools, as well as the lubricants, fluids, cleaning solvents, etc. which soon become necessary.

Sometimes waste oil and fluids, drained from the engine or cooling system during normal maintenance or repairs, present a disposal problem. To avoid pouring them on the ground or into a sewage system, pour the used fluids into large containers, seal them with caps and take them to an authorized disposal site or recycling center. Plastic jugs, such as old antifreeze containers, are ideal for this purpose.

Always keep a supply of old newspapers and clean rags available. Old towels are excellent for mopping up spills. Many mechanics use rolls of paper towels for most work because they are readily available and disposable. To help keep the area under the vehicle clean, a large cardboard box can be cut open and flattened to protect the garage or shop floor.

Whenever working over a painted surface, such as when leaning over a fender to service something under the hood, always cover it with an old blanket or bedspread to protect the finish. Vinyl covered pads, made especially for this purpose, are available at auto parts stores.

Jacking and towing

Jacking

Warning: *The jack supplied with the vehicle should only be used for raising the vehicle when changing a tire or placing jackstands under the frame. Never work under the vehicle or start the engine while the jack is being used as the only means of support.*

The vehicle must be on a level surface with the wheels blocked and the transaxle in Park. Apply the parking brake if the front of the vehicle must be raised. Make sure no one is in the vehicle as it's being raised with the jack.

Remove the jack, lug nut wrench and spare tire (if needed) from the vehicle. If a tire is being replaced, use the lug wrench to remove the wheel cover. **Warning:** *Wheel covers may have sharp edges - be very careful not to cut yourself.* Loosen the lug nuts one-half turn, but leave them in place until the tire is raised off the ground. Position the jack under the vehicle at the indicated jacking point. There's a front and rear jacking point on each side of the vehicle **(see illustration)**.

Turn the jack handle clockwise until the tire clears the ground. Remove the lug nuts, pull the tire off and install the spare. Reinstall the lug nuts with the beveled edges facing in and tighten them snugly. Don't attempt to tighten them completely until the vehicle is lowered or it could slip off the jack.

Turn the jack handle counterclockwise to lower the vehicle. Remove the jack and tighten the lug nuts in a criss-cross pattern. If possible, tighten the nuts with a torque wrench (see Chapter 1 for the torque figures).

If you don't have access to a torque wrench, have the nuts checked by a service station or repair shop as soon as possible.

Stow the tire, jack and wrench and unblock the wheels.

Towing

As a general rule, these vehicles should be towed with the front (drive) wheels off the ground. If absolutely necessary, the vehicle can be towed with the rear end raised and the front wheels on the ground for distances up to 500 miles provided speed does not exceed 55 mph. These vehicles should not be towed with all four wheels on the ground. A wheel lift type tow truck or a car carrier type tow truck must be used; never have the vehicle towed with a sling type tow truck. Tie-down chains must be attached to the main structural members of the vehicle, not the bumpers or brackets.

Be sure to release the parking brake. If the vehicle is being towed with the front wheels on the ground, place the transaxle in Neutral. Also, the ignition key must be in the OFF (not LOCK) position, since the steering lock mechanism isn't strong enough to hold the front wheels straight while towing. The tow truck operator will attach a purpose-built steering wheel holder suitable for towing conditions.

Safety is a major consideration when towing and all applicable state and local laws must be obeyed. A safety chain must be used at all times. Remember that power steering and brakes won't work with the engine off.

The head of the jack must engage securely on the rocker panel flange at either the front or rear of the vehicle

Booster battery (jump) starting

Observe these precautions when using a booster battery to start a vehicle:

a) *Before connecting the booster battery, make sure the ignition switch is in the OFF position.*
b) *Turn off the lights, heater and other electrical loads.*
c) *Your eyes should be shielded. Safety goggles are a good idea.*
d) *Make sure the booster battery is the same voltage as the dead one in the vehicle.*
e) *The two vehicles MUST NOT TOUCH each other!*
f) *Make sure the transaxle is in Neutral (manual) or Park (automatic).*
g) *If the booster battery is not a maintenance-free type, remove the vent caps and lay a cloth over the vent holes.*

On some models the battery is located inside the vehicle, under the rear seat. Due to the lack of accessibility, a remote positive battery connection is provided inside the engine compartment for jump-starting **(see illustration)**.

Connect the red-colored jumper cable to the positive (+) terminal of the booster battery and the other end to the positive (+) terminal of the dead battery or the remote positive terminal inside the engine compartment. Then connect one end of the black colored jumper cable to the negative (-) terminal of the booster battery and other end of the cable to a good ground, such as a bolt or bracket.

Start the engine using the booster battery then, with the engine running at idle speed disconnect the jumper cables in the reverse order of connection.

On models with a remotely mounted battery, a remote positive terminal is located in the engine compartment, under a cover on the fuse/relay box

Make the booster battery cable connections in the numerical order shown (note that the negative cable of the booster battery is NOT attached to the negative terminal of the dead battery)

DECIMALS to MILLIMETERS

Decimal	mm	Decimal	mm
0.001	0.0254	0.500	12.7000
0.002	0.0508	0.510	12.9540
0.003	0.0762	0.520	13.2080
0.004	0.1016	0.530	13.4620
0.005	0.1270	0.540	13.7160
0.006	0.1524	0.550	13.9700
0.007	0.1778	0.560	14.2240
0.008	0.2032	0.570	14.4780
0.009	0.2286	0.580	14.7320
		0.590	14.9860
0.010	0.2540		
0.020	0.5080		
0.030	0.7620		
0.040	1.0160	0.600	15.2400
0.050	1.2700	0.610	15.4940
0.060	1.5240	0.620	15.7480
0.070	1.7780	0.630	16.0020
0.080	2.0320	0.640	16.2560
0.090	2.2860	0.650	16.5100
		0.660	16.7640
0.100	2.5400	0.670	17.0180
0.110	2.7940	0.680	17.2720
0.120	3.0480	0.690	17.5260
0.130	3.3020		
0.140	3.5560		
0.150	3.8100		
0.160	4.0640	0.700	17.7800
0.170	4.3180	0.710	18.0340
0.180	4.5720	0.720	18.2880
0.190	4.8260	0.730	18.5420
		0.740	18.7960
0.200	5.0800	0.750	19.0500
0.210	5.3340	0.760	19.3040
0.220	5.5880	0.770	19.5580
0.230	5.8420	0.780	19.8120
0.240	6.0960	0.790	20.0660
0.250	6.3500		
0.260	6.6040		
0.270	6.8580	0.800	20.3200
0.280	7.1120	0.810	20.5740
0.290	7.3660	0.820	20.8280
		0.830	21.0820
0.300	7.6200	0.840	21.3360
0.310	7.8740	0.850	21.5900
0.320	8.1280	0.860	21.8440
0.330	8.3820	0.870	22.0980
0.340	8.6360	0.880	22.3520
0.350	8.8900	0.890	22.6060
0.360	9.1440		
0.370	9.3980		
0.380	9.6520		
0.390	9.9060		
		0.900	22.8600
0.400	10.1600	0.910	23.1140
0.410	10.4140	0.920	23.3680
0.420	10.6680	0.930	23.6220
0.430	10.9220	0.940	23.8760
0.440	11.1760	0.950	24.1300
0.450	11.4300	0.960	24.3840
0.460	11.6840	0.970	24.6380
0.470	11.9380	0.980	24.8920
0.480	12.1920	0.990	25.1460
0.490	12.4460	1.000	25.4000

FRACTIONS to DECIMALS to MILLIMETERS

Fraction	Decimal	mm	Fraction	Decimal	mm
1/64	0.0156	0.3969	33/64	0.5156	13.0969
1/32	0.0312	0.7938	17/32	0.5312	13.4938
3/64	0.0469	1.1906	35/64	0.5469	13.8906
1/16	0.0625	1.5875	9/16	0.5625	14.2875
5/64	0.0781	1.9844	37/64	0.5781	14.6844
3/32	0.0938	2.3812	19/32	0.5938	15.0812
7/64	0.1094	2.7781	39/64	0.6094	15.4781
1/8	0.1250	3.1750	5/8	0.6250	15.8750
9/64	0.1406	3.5719	41/64	0.6406	16.2719
5/32	0.1562	3.9688	21/32	0.6562	16.6688
11/64	0.1719	4.3656	43/64	0.6719	17.0656
3/16	0.1875	4.7625	11/16	0.6875	17.4625
13/64	0.2031	5.1594	45/64	0.7031	17.8594
7/32	0.2188	5.5562	23/32	0.7188	18.2562
15/64	0.2344	5.9531	47/64	0.7344	18.6531
1/4	0.2500	6.3500	3/4	0.7500	19.0500
17/64	0.2656	6.7469	49/64	0.7656	19.4469
9/32	0.2812	7.1438	25/32	0.7812	19.8438
19/64	0.2969	7.5406	51/64	0.7969	20.2406
5/16	0.3125	7.9375	13/16	0.8125	20.6375
21/64	0.3281	8.3344	53/64	0.8281	21.0344
11/32	0.3438	8.7312	27/32	0.8438	21.4312
23/64	0.3594	9.1281	55/64	0.8594	21.8281
3/8	0.3750	9.5250	7/8	0.8750	22.2250
25/64	0.3906	9.9219	57/64	0.8906	22.6219
13/32	0.4062	10.3188	29/32	0.9062	23.0188
27/64	0.4219	10.7156	59/64	0.9219	23.4156
7/16	0.4375	11.1125	15/16	0.9375	23.8125
29/64	0.4531	11.5094	61/64	0.9531	24.2094
15/32	0.4688	11.9062	31/32	0.9688	24.6062
31/64	0.4844	12.3031	63/64	0.9844	25.0031
1/2	0.5000	12.7000	1	1.0000	25.4000

Conversion factors

Length (distance)

Inches (in)	X	25.4	= Millimeters (mm)	X 0.0394	= Inches (in)
Feet (ft)	X	0.305	= Meters (m)	X 3.281	= Feet (ft)
Miles	X	1.609	= Kilometers (km)	X 0.621	= Miles

Volume (capacity)

Cubic inches (cu in; in³)	X	16.387	= Cubic centimeters (cc; cm³)	X 0.061	= Cubic inches (cu in; in³)
Imperial pints (Imp pt)	X	0.568	= Liters (l)	X 1.76	= Imperial pints (Imp pt)
Imperial quarts (Imp qt)	X	1.137	= Liters (l)	X 0.88	= Imperial quarts (Imp qt)
Imperial quarts (Imp qt)	X	1.201	= US quarts (US qt)	X 0.833	= Imperial quarts (Imp qt)
US quarts (US qt)	X	0.946	= Liters (l)	X 1.057	= US quarts (US qt)
Imperial gallons (Imp gal)	X	4.546	= Liters (l)	X 0.22	= Imperial gallons (Imp gal)
Imperial gallons (Imp gal)	X	1.201	= US gallons (US gal)	X 0.833	= Imperial gallons (Imp gal)
US gallons (US gal)	X	3.785	= Liters (l)	X 0.264	= US gallons (US gal)

Mass (weight)

Ounces (oz)	X	28.35	= Grams (g)	X 0.035	= Ounces (oz)
Pounds (lb)	X	0.454	= Kilograms (kg)	X 2.205	= Pounds (lb)

Force

Ounces-force (ozf; oz)	X	0.278	= Newtons (N)	X 3.6	= Ounces-force (ozf; oz)
Pounds-force (lbf; lb)	X	4.448	= Newtons (N)	X 0.225	= Pounds-force (lbf; lb)
Newtons (N)	X	0.1	= Kilograms-force (kgf; kg)	X 9.81	= Newtons (N)

Pressure

Pounds-force per square inch (psi; lbf/in²; lb/in²)	X	0.070	= Kilograms-force per square centimeter (kgf/cm²; kg/cm²)	X 14.223	= Pounds-force per square inch (psi; lbf/in²; lb/in²)
Pounds-force per square inch (psi; lbf/in²; lb/in²)	X	0.068	= Atmospheres (atm)	X 14.696	= Pounds-force per square inch (psi; lbf/in²; lb/in²)
Pounds-force per square inch (psi; lbf/in²; lb/in²)	X	0.069	= Bars	X 14.5	= Pounds-force per square inch (psi; lbf/in²; lb/in²)
Pounds-force per square inch (psi; lbf/in²; lb/in²)	X	6.895	= Kilopascals (kPa)	X 0.145	= Pounds-force per square inch (psi; lbf/in²; lb/in²)
Kilopascals (kPa)	X	0.01	= Kilograms-force per square centimeter (kgf/cm²; kg/cm²)	X 98.1	= Kilopascals (kPa)

Torque (moment of force)

Pounds-force inches (lbf in; lb in)	X	1.152	= Kilograms-force centimeter (kgf cm; kg cm)	X 0.868	= Pounds-force inches (lbf in; lb in)
Pounds-force inches (lbf in; lb in)	X	0.113	= Newton meters (Nm)	X 8.85	= Pounds-force inches (lbf in; lb in)
Pounds-force inches (lbf in; lb in)	X	0.083	= Pounds-force feet (lbf ft; lb ft)	X 12	= Pounds-force inches (lbf in; lb in)
Pounds-force feet (lbf ft; lb ft)	X	0.138	= Kilograms-force meters (kgf m; kg m)	X 7.233	= Pounds-force feet (lbf ft; lb ft)
Pounds-force feet (lbf ft; lb ft)	X	1.356	= Newton meters (Nm)	X 0.738	= Pounds-force feet (lbf ft; lb ft)
Newton meters (Nm)	X	0.102	= Kilograms-force meters (kgf m; kg m)	X 9.804	= Newton meters (Nm)

Vacuum

Inches mercury (in. Hg)	X	3.377	= Kilopascals (kPa)	X 0.2961	= Inches mercury
Inches mercury (in. Hg)	X	25.4	= Millimeters mercury (mm Hg)	X 0.0394	= Inches mercury

Power

Horsepower (hp)	X	745.7	= Watts (W)	X 0.0013	= Horsepower (hp)

Velocity (speed)

Miles per hour (miles/hr; mph)	X	1.609	= Kilometers per hour (km/hr; kph)	X 0.621	= Miles per hour (miles/hr; mph)

Fuel consumption*

Miles per gallon, Imperial (mpg)	X	0.354	= Kilometers per liter (km/l)	X 2.825	= Miles per gallon, Imperial (mpg)
Miles per gallon, US (mpg)	X	0.425	= Kilometers per liter (km/l)	X 2.352	= Miles per gallon, US (mpg)

Temperature

Degrees Fahrenheit = (°C x 1.8) + 32

Degrees Celsius (Degrees Centigrade; °C) = (°F - 32) x 0.56

It is common practice to convert from miles per gallon (mpg) to liters/100 kilometers (l/100km), where mpg (Imperial) x l/100 km = 282 and mpg (US) x l/100 km = 235

Safety first!

Regardless of how enthusiastic you may be about getting on with the job at hand, take the time to ensure that your safety is not jeopardized. A moment's lack of attention can result in an accident, as can failure to observe certain simple safety precautions. The possibility of an accident will always exist, and the following points should not be considered a comprehensive list of all dangers. Rather, they are intended to make you aware of the risks and to encourage a safety conscious approach to all work you carry out on your vehicle.

Essential DOs and DON'Ts

DON'T rely on a jack when working under the vehicle. Always use approved jackstands to support the weight of the vehicle and place them under the recommended lift or support points.

DON'T attempt to loosen extremely tight fasteners (i.e. wheel lug nuts) while the vehicle is on a jack - it may fall.

DON'T start the engine without first making sure that the transmission is in Neutral (or Park where applicable) and the parking brake is set.

DON'T remove the radiator cap from a hot cooling system - let it cool or cover it with a cloth and release the pressure gradually.

DON'T attempt to drain the engine oil until you are sure it has cooled to the point that it will not burn you.

DON'T touch any part of the engine or exhaust system until it has cooled sufficiently to avoid burns.

DON'T siphon toxic liquids such as gasoline, antifreeze and brake fluid by mouth, or allow them to remain on your skin.

DON'T inhale brake lining dust - it is potentially hazardous (see *Asbestos* below).

DON'T allow spilled oil or grease to remain on the floor - wipe it up before someone slips on it.

DON'T use loose fitting wrenches or other tools which may slip and cause injury.

DON'T push on wrenches when loosening or tightening nuts or bolts. Always try to pull the wrench toward you. If the situation calls for pushing the wrench away, push with an open hand to avoid scraped knuckles if the wrench should slip.

DON'T attempt to lift a heavy component alone - get someone to help you.

DON'T rush or take unsafe shortcuts to finish a job.

DON'T allow children or animals in or around the vehicle while you are working on it.

DO wear eye protection when using power tools such as a drill, sander, bench grinder, etc. and when working under a vehicle.

DO keep loose clothing and long hair well out of the way of moving parts.

DO make sure that any hoist used has a safe working load rating adequate for the job.

DO get someone to check on you periodically when working alone on a vehicle.

DO carry out work in a logical sequence and make sure that everything is correctly assembled and tightened.

DO keep chemicals and fluids tightly capped and out of the reach of children and pets.

DO remember that your vehicle's safety affects that of yourself and others. If in doubt on any point, get professional advice.

Asbestos

Certain friction, insulating, sealing, and other products - such as brake linings, brake bands, clutch linings, torque converters, gaskets, etc. - may contain asbestos. Extreme care must be taken to avoid inhalation of dust from such products, since it is hazardous to health. If in doubt, assume that they do contain asbestos.

Fire

Remember at all times that gasoline is highly flammable. Never smoke or have any kind of open flame around when working on a vehicle. But the risk does not end there. A spark caused by an electrical short circuit, by two metal surfaces contacting each other, or even by static electricity built up in your body under certain conditions, can ignite gasoline vapors, which in a confined space are highly explosive. Do not, under any circumstances, use gasoline for cleaning parts. Use an approved safety solvent.

Always disconnect the battery ground (-) cable at the battery before working on any part of the fuel system or electrical system. Never risk spilling fuel on a hot engine or exhaust component. It is strongly recommended that a fire extinguisher suitable for use on fuel and electrical fires be kept handy in the garage or workshop at all times. Never try to extinguish a fuel or electrical fire with water.

Fumes

Certain fumes are highly toxic and can quickly cause unconsciousness and even death if inhaled to any extent. Gasoline vapor falls into this category, as do the vapors from some cleaning solvents. Any draining or pouring of such volatile fluids should be done in a well ventilated area.

When using cleaning fluids and solvents, read the instructions on the container carefully. Never use materials from unmarked containers.

Never run the engine in an enclosed space, such as a garage. Exhaust fumes contain carbon monoxide, which is extremely poisonous. If you need to run the engine, always do so in the open air, or at least have the rear of the vehicle outside the work area.

If you are fortunate enough to have the use of an inspection pit, never drain or pour gasoline and never run the engine while the vehicle is over the pit. The fumes, being heavier than air, will concentrate in the pit with possibly lethal results.

The battery

Never create a spark or allow a bare light bulb near a battery. They normally give off a certain amount of hydrogen gas, which is highly explosive.

Always disconnect the battery ground (-) cable at the battery before working on the fuel or electrical systems.

If possible, loosen the filler caps or cover when charging the battery from an external source (this does not apply to sealed or maintenance-free batteries). Do not charge at an excessive rate or the battery may burst.

Take care when adding water to a non maintenance-free battery and when carrying a battery. The electrolyte, even when diluted, is very corrosive and should not be allowed to contact clothing or skin.

Always wear eye protection when cleaning the battery to prevent the caustic deposits from entering your eyes.

Household current

When using an electric power tool, inspection light, etc., which operates on household current, always make sure that the tool is correctly connected to its plug and that, where necessary, it is properly grounded. Do not use such items in damp conditions and, again, do not create a spark or apply excessive heat in the vicinity of fuel or fuel vapor.

Secondary ignition system voltage

A severe electric shock can result from touching certain parts of the ignition system (such as the spark plug wires) when the engine is running or being cranked, particularly if components are damp or the insulation is defective. In the case of an electronic ignition system, the secondary system voltage is much higher and could prove fatal.

Automotive chemicals and lubricants

A number of automotive chemicals and lubricants are available for use during vehicle maintenance and repair. They include a wide variety of products ranging from cleaning solvents and degreasers to lubricants and protective sprays for rubber, plastic and vinyl.

Cleaners

Carburetor cleaner and choke cleaner is a strong solvent for gum, varnish and carbon. Most carburetor cleaners leave a dry-type lubricant film which will not harden or gum up. Because of this film it is not recommended for use on electrical components.

Brake system cleaner is used to remove brake dust, grease and brake fluid from the brake system, where clean surfaces are absolutely necessary. It leaves no residue and often eliminates brake squeal caused by contaminants.

Electrical cleaner removes oxidation, corrosion and carbon deposits from electrical contacts, restoring full current flow. It can also be used to clean spark plugs, carburetor jets, voltage regulators and other parts where an oil-free surface is desired.

Demoisturants remove water and moisture from electrical components such as alternators, voltage regulators, electrical connectors and fuse blocks. They are non-conductive and non-corrosive.

Degreasers are heavy-duty solvents used to remove grease from the outside of the engine and from chassis components. They can be sprayed or brushed on and, depending on the type, are rinsed off either with water or solvent.

Lubricants

Motor oil is the lubricant formulated for use in engines. It normally contains a wide variety of additives to prevent corrosion and reduce foaming and wear. Motor oil comes in various weights (viscosity ratings) from 0 to 50. The recommended weight of the oil depends on the season, temperature and the demands on the engine. Light oil is used in cold climates and under light load conditions. Heavy oil is used in hot climates and where high loads are encountered. Multi-viscosity oils are designed to have characteristics of both light and heavy oils and are available in a number of weights from 5W-20 to 20W-50.

Gear oil is designed to be used in differentials, manual transmissions and other areas where high-temperature lubrication is required.

Chassis and wheel bearing grease is a heavy grease used where increased loads and friction are encountered, such as for wheel bearings, balljoints, tie-rod ends and universal joints.

High-temperature wheel bearing grease is designed to withstand the extreme temperatures encountered by wheel bearings in disc brake equipped vehicles. It usually contains molybdenum disulfide (moly), which is a dry-type lubricant.

White grease is a heavy grease for metal-to-metal applications where water is a problem. White grease stays soft under both low and high temperatures (usually from -100 to +190-degrees F), and will not wash off or dilute in the presence of water.

Assembly lube is a special extreme pressure lubricant, usually containing moly, used to lubricate high-load parts (such as main and rod bearings and cam lobes) for initial start-up of a new engine. The assembly lube lubricates the parts without being squeezed out or washed away until the engine oiling system begins to function.

Silicone lubricants are used to protect rubber, plastic, vinyl and nylon parts.

Graphite lubricants are used where oils cannot be used due to contamination problems, such as in locks. The dry graphite will lubricate metal parts while remaining uncontaminated by dirt, water, oil or acids. It is electrically conductive and will not foul electrical contacts in locks such as the ignition switch.

Moly penetrants loosen and lubricate frozen, rusted and corroded fasteners and prevent future rusting or freezing.

Heat-sink grease is a special electrically non-conductive grease that is used for mounting electronic ignition modules where it is essential that heat is transferred away from the module.

Sealants

RTV sealant is one of the most widely used gasket compounds. Made from silicone, RTV is air curing, it seals, bonds, waterproofs, fills surface irregularities, remains flexible, doesn't shrink, is relatively easy to remove, and is used as a supplementary sealer with almost all low and medium temperature gaskets.

Anaerobic sealant is much like RTV in that it can be used either to seal gaskets or to form gaskets by itself. It remains flexible, is solvent resistant and fills surface imperfections. The difference between an anaerobic sealant and an RTV-type sealant is in the curing. RTV cures when exposed to air, while an anaerobic sealant cures only in the absence of air. This means that an anaerobic sealant cures only after the assembly of parts, sealing them together.

Thread and pipe sealant is used for sealing hydraulic and pneumatic fittings and vacuum lines. It is usually made from a Teflon compound, and comes in a spray, a paint-on liquid and as a wrap-around tape.

Chemicals

Anti-seize compound prevents seizing, galling, cold welding, rust and corrosion in fasteners. High-temperature ant-seize, usually made with copper and graphite lubricants, is used for exhaust system and exhaust manifold bolts.

Anaerobic locking compounds are used to keep fasteners from vibrating or working loose and cure only after installation, in the absence of air. Medium strength locking compound is used for small nuts, bolts and screws that may be removed later. High-strength locking compound is for large nuts, bolts and studs which aren't removed on a regular basis.

Oil additives range from viscosity index improvers to chemical treatments that claim to reduce internal engine friction. It should be noted that most oil manufacturers caution against using additives with their oils.

Gas additives perform several functions, depending on their chemical makeup. They usually contain solvents that help dissolve gum and varnish that build up on carburetor, fuel injection and intake parts. They also serve to break down carbon deposits that form on the inside surfaces of the combustion chambers. Some additives contain upper cylinder lubricants for valves and piston rings, and others contain chemicals to remove condensation from the gas tank.

Miscellaneous

Brake fluid is specially formulated hydraulic fluid that can withstand the heat and pressure encountered in brake systems. Care must be taken so this fluid does not come in contact with painted surfaces or plastics. An opened container should always be resealed to prevent contamination by water or dirt.

Weatherstrip adhesive is used to bond weatherstripping around doors, windows and trunk lids. It is sometimes used to attach trim pieces.

Undercoating is a petroleum-based, tar-like substance that is designed to protect metal surfaces on the underside of the vehicle from corrosion. It also acts as a sound-deadening agent by insulating the bottom of the vehicle.

Waxes and polishes are used to help protect painted and plated surfaces from the weather. Different types of paint may require the use of different types of wax and polish. Some polishes utilize a chemical or abrasive cleaner to help remove the top layer of oxidized (dull) paint on older vehicles. In recent years many non-wax polishes that contain a wide variety of chemicals such as polymers and silicones have been introduced. These non-wax polishes are usually easier to apply and last longer than conventional waxes and polishes.

Troubleshooting

Contents

This section provides an easy reference guide to the more common problems which may occur during the operation of your vehicle. Various symptoms and their possible causes are grouped under headings denoting components or systems, such as Engine, Cooling system, etc. They also refer to the Chapter and/or Section that deals with the problem.

Remember that successful troubleshooting isn't a mysterious art practiced only by professional mechanics. It's simply the result of knowledge combined with an intelligent, systematic approach to a problem. Always use a process of elimination, starting with the simplest solution and working through to the most complex - and never overlook the obvious. Anyone can run the gas tank dry or leave the lights on overnight, so don't assume that you're exempt from such oversights.

Finally, always establish a clear idea why a problem has occurred and take steps to ensure that it doesn't happen again. If the electrical system fails because of a poor connection, check all other connections in the system to make sure they don't fail as well. If a particular fuse continues to blow, find out why - don't just go on replacing fuses. Remember, failure of a small component can often be indicative of potential failure or incorrect functioning of a more important component or system.

Engine and performance

1 Engine will not rotate when attempting to start

1 Battery terminal connections loose or corroded (Chapter 1).
2 Battery discharged or faulty (Chapter 1).
3 Automatic transaxle not completely engaged in Park (Chapter 7).
4 Broken, loose or disconnected wiring in the starting circuit (Chapters 5 and 12).
5 Starter motor pinion jammed in flywheel ring gear (Chapter 5).
6 Starter solenoid faulty (Chapter 5).
7 Starter motor faulty (Chapter 5).
8 Ignition switch faulty (Chapter 12).
9 Neutral start switch faulty (Chapter 7).
10 Starter pinion or driveplate teeth worn or broken (Chapter 5).
11 PASS-Key theft deterrent system malfunctioning. **Note:** *Sometimes the receptor in the ignition key lock cylinder becomes dirty and won't "read" the resistance value of the key. This problem can sometimes be rectified by spraying some electrical contact cleaner into the lock cylinder and allowing it to dry.*

2 Engine rotates but will not start

1 Fuel tank empty.
2 Battery discharged (engine rotates slowly) (Chapter 5).
3 No fuel pressure (Chapter 4).
4 Ignition components damp or damaged (Chapter 5).
5 Worn, faulty or incorrectly gapped spark plugs (Chapter 1).
6 Broken, loose or disconnected wiring in the starting circuit (Chapter 5).
7 Broken, loose or disconnected wires at the ignition coil(s) or faulty coil(s) (Chapter 5).

3 Engine hard to start when cold

1 Battery discharged or low (Chapter 1).
2 Fuel system malfunctioning (Chapter 4).
3 Emissions or engine control system malfunctioning (Chapter 6).

4 Engine hard to start when hot

1 Air filter clogged (Chapter 1).
2 Fuel not reaching the fuel injection system (Chapter 4).
3 Corroded battery connections, especially ground (Chapter 1).
4 Emissions or engine control system malfunctioning (Chapter 6).

5 Starter motor noisy or excessively rough in engagement

1 Pinion or driveplate gear teeth worn or broken (Chapter 5).
2 Starter motor mounting bolts loose or missing (Chapter 5).

6 Engine starts but stops immediately

1 Loose or faulty electrical connections at coil pack or alternator (Chapter 5).
2 Insufficient fuel reaching the fuel injectors (Chapter 4).
3 Vacuum leak at the gasket between the intake manifold/plenum and throttle body (Chapters 1 and 4).
4 Restricted exhaust system (most likely the catalytic converter) (Chapters 4 and 6).

7 Oil puddle under engine

1 Oil pan gasket and/or oil pan drain bolt seal leaking (Chapters 1 and 2).
2 Oil pressure sending unit leaking (Chapter 2).
3 Valve cover gaskets leaking (Chapter 2).
4 Engine oil seals leaking (Chapter 2).
5 Timing chain cover sealant or sealing flange leaking (Chapter 2).

8 Engine lopes while idling or idles erratically

1 Vacuum leakage (Chapter 4).
2 Leaking EGR valve or plugged PCV valve (Chapters 1 and 6).
3 Air filter clogged (Chapter 1).
4 Fuel pump not delivering sufficient fuel to the fuel injection system (Chapter 4).
5 Leaking head gasket (Chapter 2).
6 Timing chain worn (Chapter 2).
7 Camshaft lobes worn (Chapter 2).

9 Engine misses at idle speed

1 Spark plugs worn or not gapped properly (Chapter 1).
2 Faulty spark plug wires (Chapter 1).
3 Vacuum leaks (Chapters 1 and 4).
4 Incorrect ignition timing (Chapter 5).
5 Uneven or low compression (Chapter 2C).

10 Engine misses throughout driving speed range

1 Fuel filter clogged and/or impurities in the fuel system (Chapters 1 and 4).

2 Low fuel output at the injector (Chapter 4).
3 Faulty or incorrectly gapped spark plugs (Chapter 1).
4 Incorrect ignition timing (Chapter 5).
5 Leaking spark plug wires (Chapter 1).
6 Faulty emission system components (Chapter 6).
7 Low or uneven cylinder compression pressures (Chapter 2).
8 Weak or faulty ignition system (Chapter 5).
9 Vacuum leak in fuel injection system, intake manifold or vacuum hoses (Chapter 4).

11 Engine stumbles on acceleration

1 Spark plugs fouled (Chapter 1).
2 Fuel injection system needs adjustment or repair (Chapter 4).
3 Fuel filter clogged (Chapter 1).
4 Incorrect ignition timing (Chapter 5).
5 Intake manifold air leak (Chapter 4).

12 Engine surges while holding accelerator steady

1 Intake air leak (Chapter 4).
2 Fuel pump faulty (Chapter 4).
3 Loose fuel injector harness connections (Chapter 4).
4 Defective ECM (Chapter 6).

13 Engine stalls

1 Idle speed incorrect (Chapters 1 and 4).
2 Fuel filter clogged and/or water and impurities in the fuel system (Chapters 1 and 4).
3 Ignition components damp or damaged (Chapter 5).
4 Faulty emissions system components (Chapter 6).
5 Faulty or incorrectly gapped spark plugs (Chapter 1).
6 Faulty spark plug wires (Chapter 1).
7 Vacuum leak in the intake manifold or vacuum hoses (Chapter 4).

14 Engine lacks power

1 Incorrect ignition timing (Chapter 5).
2 Faulty or incorrectly gapped spark plugs (Chapter 1).
3 Fuel injection system malfunctioning (Chapter 4).
4 Faulty coil(s) (Chapter 5).
5 Brakes binding (Chapter 1).
6 Automatic transaxle fluid level incorrect (Chapter 1).
7 Fuel filter clogged and/or impurities in the fuel system (Chapter 1).
8 Emission control system not functioning properly (Chapter 6).

9   Low or uneven cylinder compression pressures (Chapter 2).
10   Restricted exhaust system (most likely the catalytic converter (Chapters 4 and 6).

15   Engine backfires

1   Emissions system not functioning properly (Chapter 6).
2   Ignition timing incorrect (Chapter 5).
3   Faulty secondary ignition system (Chapter 5).
4   Fuel injection system malfunctioning (Chapter 4).
5   Vacuum leak at fuel injectors, intake manifold or vacuum hoses (Chapter 4).
6   Valves sticking (Chapter 2).

16   Pinging or knocking engine sounds during acceleration or uphill

1   Incorrect grade of fuel.
2   Ignition timing incorrect (Chapter 5).
3   Fuel injection system malfunctioning Chapter 4).
4   Improper or damaged spark plugs or wires (Chapter 1).
5   Worn or damaged ignition components (Chapter 5).
6   Faulty emissions system (Chapter 6).
7   Vacuum leak (Chapter 4).

17   Engine runs with oil pressure light on

1   Low oil level (Chapter 1).
2   Short in wiring circuit (Chapter 12).
3   Faulty oil pressure sender (Chapter 2).
4   Oil viscosity too low or oil diluted.
5   Worn engine bearings and/or oil pump (Chapter 2).

18   Engine diesels (continues to run) after switching off

1   Excessive engine operating temperature (Chapter 3).
2   Excessive carbon deposits on valves and pistons.

Engine electrical system

19   Battery will not hold a charge

1   Alternator drivebelt defective or not adjusted properly (Chapter 1).
2   Battery terminals loose or corroded (Chapter 1).
3   Alternator not charging properly (Chapter 5).
4   Loose, broken or faulty wiring in the charging circuit (Chapter 5).
5   Short in vehicle wiring (Chapters 5 and 12).
6   Internally defective battery (Chapters 1 and 5).

20   Voltage warning light fails to go out

1   Faulty alternator or charging circuit (Chapter 5).
2   Alternator drivebelt defective or out of adjustment (Chapter 1).
3   Alternator voltage regulator inoperative (Chapter 5).

21   Voltage warning light fails to come on when key is turned on

1   Warning light bulb defective (Chapter 12).
2   Fault in the printed circuit, dash wiring or bulb holder (Chapter 12).

Fuel system

22   Excessive fuel consumption

1   Dirty or clogged air filter element (Chapter 1).
2   Incorrectly set ignition timing (Chapter 5).
3   Emissions system not functioning properly (Chapter 6).
4   Fuel injection system malfunctioning (Chapter 4).
5   Low tire pressure or incorrect tire size (Chapter 1).

23   Fuel leakage and/or fuel odor

1   Leak in a fuel feed or vent line (Chapter 4).
2   Tank overfilled.
3   Evaporative emissions control canister defective (Chapters 1 and 6).
4   Fuel injector seals faulty (Chapter 4).

Cooling system

24   Overheating

1   Insufficient coolant in system (Chapter 1).
2   Water pump drivebelt defective or out of adjustment (Chapter 1).
3   Radiator core blocked or grille restricted (Chapter 3).
4   Thermostat faulty (Chapter 3).
5   Electric cooling fan blades broken or cracked (Chapter 3).
6   Radiator cap or expansion tank cap not maintaining proper pressure (Chapter 3).
7   Ignition timing incorrect (Chapter 5).

25   Overcooling

Incorrect (opening temperature too low) or faulty thermostat (Chapter 3).

26   External coolant leakage

1   Deteriorated/damaged hoses or loose clamps (Chapters 1 and 3).
2   Water pump seal defective (Chapters 1 and 3).
3   Leakage from radiator core or header tank (Chapter 3).
4   Engine drain or water jacket core plugs leaking (Chapter 2).

27   Internal coolant leakage

1   Leaking cylinder head gasket (Chapter 2).
2   Cracked cylinder bore or cylinder head (Chapter 2).

28   Coolant loss

1   Too much coolant in system (Chapter 1).
2   Coolant boiling away because of overheating (Chapter 3).
3   Internal or external leakage (Chapter 3).
4   Faulty radiator cap (Chapter 3).

29   Poor coolant circulation

1   Inoperative water pump (Chapter 3).
2   Restriction in cooling system (Chapters 1 and 3).
3   Water pump drivebelt defective or out of adjustment (Chapter 1).
4   Thermostat sticking (Chapter 3).

Automatic transaxle

Note: *Due to the complexity of the automatic transaxle, it's difficult for the home mechanic to properly diagnose and service this component. For problems other than the following, the vehicle should be taken to a dealer service department or a transmission shop.*

30   Fluid leakage

1   Automatic transmission fluid is a deep red color. Fluid leaks should not be confused with engine oil, which can easily be blown by airflow to the transaxle.
2   To pinpoint a leak, first remove all built-

up dirt and grime from the transaxle housing with degreasing agents and/or steam cleaning. Drive the vehicle at low speeds so air flow will not blow the leak far from its source. Raise the vehicle and determine where the leak is coming from. Common areas of leakage are:

a) *Fluid pan (Chapter 1)*
b) *Filler pipe (Chapter 7)*
c) *Fluid cooler lines (Chapter 7)*
d) *Vehicle Speed Sensor (Chapter 6)*

31 Transaxle fluid brown or has a burned smell

Transaxle overheated. Change fluid (Chapter 1).

32 General shift mechanism problems

1 Chapter 7 deals with checking and adjusting the shift linkage on automatic transaxles. Common problems which may be attributed to a poorly adjusted linkage are:

a) *Engine starting in gears other than Park or Neutral.*
b) *Indicator on shifter pointing to a gear other than the one actually being used.*
c) *Vehicle moves when in Park.*

2 Refer to Chapter 7 for the shift linkage adjustment procedure.

33 Transaxle will not downshift with accelerator pedal pressed to the floor

Shift solenoid or control circuit problem. Consult a transmission repair specialist.

34 Engine will start in gears other than Park or Neutral

Park/Neutral Position switch malfunctioning (Chapter 7).

35 Transaxle slips, shifts roughly, is noisy or has no drive in forward or reverse gears

There are many probable causes for the above problems, but the home mechanic should be concerned with only one possibility - fluid level. Before taking the vehicle to a repair shop, check the level and condition of the fluid as described in Chapter 1.

Correct the fluid level as necessary or change the fluid and filter if needed. If the problem persists, have a professional diagnose the probable cause.

Driveaxles

36 Clicking noise in turns

Worn or damaged outer CV joint. Check for cut or damaged boots (Chapter 1). Repair as necessary (Chapter 8).

37 Knock or clunk when accelerating after coasting

Worn or damaged CV joint. Check for cut or damaged boots (Chapter 1). Repair as necessary (Chapter 8).

38 Shudder or vibration during acceleration

1 Worn or damaged CV joints. Repair or replace as necessary (Chapter 8).
2 Sticking inner joint assembly. Correct or replace as necessary (Chapter 8).

Brakes

Note: *Before assuming that a brake problem exists, make sure . . .*

a) *The tires are in good condition and properly inflated (Chapter 1).*
b) *The front end alignment is correct (Chapter 10).*
c) *The vehicle isn't loaded with weight in an unequal manner.*

39 Vehicle pulls to one side during braking

1 Incorrect tire pressures (Chapter 1).
2 Front end out of alignment (have the front end aligned).
3 Unmatched tires on same axle.
4 Restricted brake lines or hoses (Chapter 9).
5 Sticking caliper piston (Chapter 9).
6 Loose suspension parts (Chapter 10).
7 Contaminated brake pad material (Chapter 9).

40 Noise (high-pitched squeal when the brakes are applied)

Disc brake pads worn out. The noise comes from the wear sensor rubbing against the disc. Replace pads with new ones immediately (Chapter 9).

41 Brake roughness or chatter (pedal pulsates)

1 Excessive brake disc lateral runout (Chapter 9).

2 Parallelism of disc not within specifications (Chapter 9).
3 Uneven pad wear caused by caliper not sliding due to improper clearance or dirt (Chapter 9).
4 Defective brake disc (Chapter 9).

42 Excessive pedal effort required to stop vehicle

1 Malfunctioning power brake booster (Chapter 9).
2 Partial system failure (Chapter 9).
3 Excessively worn pads (Chapter 9).
4 One or more caliper pistons seized or sticking (Chapter 9).
5 Brake pads contaminated with oil or grease (Chapter 9).
6 New pads installed and not yet seated. It may take a while for the new material to seat.

43 Excessive brake pedal travel

1 Partial brake system failure (Chapter 9).
2 Insufficient fluid in master cylinder (Chapters 1 and 9).
3 Air trapped in system (Chapter 9).
4 Faulty master cylinder (Chapter 9).

44 Dragging brakes

1 Master cylinder pistons not returning correctly (Chapter 9).
2 Restricted brakes lines or hoses (Chapters 1 and 9).
3 Incorrect parking brake adjustment (Chapter 9).

45 Grabbing or uneven braking action

1 Malfunction of proportioning valve (Chapter 9).
2 Malfunction of power brake booster unit (Chapter 9).
3 Binding brake pedal mechanism (Chapter 9).
4 Contaminated brake linings (Chapter 9).

46 Brake pedal feels spongy when depressed

1 Air in hydraulic lines (Chapter 9).
2 Master cylinder mounting bolts loose (Chapter 9).
3 Master cylinder defective (Chapter 9).

47 Brake pedal travels to the floor with little resistance

Little or no fluid in the master cylinder

reservoir caused by leaking caliper, or loose, damaged or disconnected brake lines (Chapter 9).

48 Parking brake does not hold

Parking brake linkage improperly adjusted (Chapter 9).

Suspension and steering systems

Note: *Before attempting to diagnose the suspension and steering systems, perform the following preliminary checks:*

a) *Check the tire pressures and look for uneven wear.*
b) *Check the steering universal joints or coupling from the column to the steering gear for loose fasteners and wear.*
c) *Check the front and rear suspension and the steering gear assembly for loose and damaged parts.*
d) *Look for out-of-round or out-of-balance tires, bent rims and loose and/or rough wheel bearings.*

49 Vehicle pulls to one side

1   Mismatched or uneven tires (Chapter 10).
2   Broken or sagging springs (Chapter 10).
3   Wheel alignment incorrect (Chapter 10).
4   Front brakes dragging (Chapter 9).

50 Abnormal or excessive tire wear

1   Front wheel alignment incorrect (Chapter 10).
2   Sagging or broken springs (Chapter 10).
3   Tire out-of-balance (Chapter 10).
4   Worn strut or shock absorber (Chapter 10).
5   Overloaded vehicle.
6   Tires not rotated regularly.

51 Wheel makes a "thumping" noise

1   Blister or bump on tire (Chapter 1).
2   Improper strut or shock absorber action (Chapter 10).

52 Shimmy, shake or vibration

1   Tire or wheel out-of-balance or out-of-round (Chapter 10).
2   Loose or worn wheel bearings (Chapter 10).
3   Worn tie-rod ends (Chapter 10).
4   Worn balljoints (Chapter 10).
5   Excessive wheel runout (Chapter 10).
6   Blister or bump on tire (Chapter 1).

53 Hard steering

1   Lack of lubrication at balljoints, tie-rod ends and steering gear assembly (Chapter 10).
2   Front wheel alignment incorrect (Chapter 10).
3   Low tire pressure (Chapter 1).

54 Steering wheel does not return to center position correctly

1   Lack of lubrication at balljoints and tie-rod ends (Chapters 1 and 10).
2   Binding in steering column (Chapter 10).
3   Defective rack-and-pinion assembly (Chapter 10).
4   Front wheel alignment problem (Chapter 10).

55 Abnormal noise at the front end

1   Lack of lubrication at balljoints and tie-rod ends (Chapter 1).
2   Loose upper strut mount (Chapter 10).
3   Worn tie-rod ends (Chapter 10).
4   Loose stabilizer bar (Chapter 10).
5   Loose wheel lug nuts (Chapter 1).
6   Loose suspension bolts (Chapter 10).

56 Wander or poor steering stability

1   Mismatched or uneven tires (Chapter 10).
2   Lack of lubrication at balljoints or tie-rod ends (Chapters 1 and 10).
3   Worn shock absorbers (Chapter 10).
4   Loose stabilizer bar (Chapter 10).
5   Broken or sagging springs (Chapter 10).
6   Front wheel alignment incorrect.
7   Worn steering gear clamp bushings (Chapter 10).

57 Erratic steering when braking

1   Wheel bearings worn (Chapter 10).
2   Broken or sagging springs (Chapter 10).
3   Leaking caliper (Chapter 9).
4   Warped rotors (Chapter 9).
5   Worn steering gear clamp bushings (Chapter 10).
6   Wheel alignment incorrect.

58 Excessive pitching and/or rolling around corners or during braking

1   Loose stabilizer bar (Chapter 10).
2   Worn shock absorbers or mounts (Chapter 10).
3   Broken or sagging springs (Chapter 10).
4   Overloaded vehicle.

59 Suspension bottoms

1   Overloaded vehicle.
2   Worn struts or shock absorbers (Chapter 10).
3   Incorrect, broken or sagging springs (Chapter 10).

60 Cupped tires

1   Front wheel alignment incorrect (Chapter 10).
2   Worn struts or shock absorbers (Chapter 10).
3   Wheel bearings worn (Chapter 10).
4   Excessive tire or wheel runout (Chapter 10).
5   Worn balljoints (Chapter 10).

61 Excessive tire wear on outside edge

1   Inflation pressures incorrect (Chapter 1).
2   Excessive speed in turns.
3   Wheel alignment incorrect (excessive toe-in or positive camber). Have professionally aligned.
4   Suspension arm bent or twisted (Chapter 10).

62 Excessive tire wear on inside edge

1   Inflation pressures incorrect (Chapter 1).
2   Wheel alignment incorrect (toe-out or excessive negative camber). Have professionally aligned.
3   Loose or damaged steering components (Chapter 10).

63 Tire tread worn in one place

1   Tires out-of-balance.
2   Damaged or buckled wheel. Inspect and replace if necessary.
3   Defective tire (Chapter 1).

64 Excessive play or looseness in steering system

1   Wheel bearings worn (Chapter 10).
2   Tie-rod end loose or worn (Chapter 10).
3   Steering gear loose (Chapter 10).

65 Rattling or clicking noise in rack and pinion

Steering gear clamps loose (Chapter 10).

Chapter 1
Tune-up and routine maintenance

Contents

Specifications

Recommended lubricants and fluids

Note: *Listed here are manufacturer recommendations at the time this manual was written. Manufacturers occasionally upgrade their fluid and lubricant specifications, so check with you local auto parts store for current recommendations.*

Engine oil
Type... API "Certified for gasoline engines"
Viscosity .... See accompanying chart

Engine oil viscosity chart - 1992 and 1993 models

Engine oil viscosity chart - 1994 through 1999 models

Engine oil viscosity chart - 2000 and later models

LOOK FOR
ONE OF
THESE LABELS

Automatic transaxle fluid .... DEXRON IIE or DEXRON III ATF
Engine coolant
   1995 and earlier models.. 50/50 mixture of water and ethylene glycol-based antifreeze
         (and cooling system sealant)
   1996 and later models.. 50/50 mixture of water and GM or Havoline DEX-COOL coolant
         (and cooling system sealant)
Brake fluid... DOT 3
Power steering fluid .... GM Power Steering Fluid or equivalent
Chassis lubrication .... Multi-purpose, lithium-base chassis grease

Capacities*

Engine oil
   4.6L engine.. 7.5 quarts
   4.9L engine.. 5.5 quarts
Cooling system
   Seville
      1992 models .... 12.1 quarts
      1993 and 1994 models .... 12.3 quarts
      1995 and later models .... 12.5 quarts
   DeVille
      1994 models .... 12.3 quarts
      1995 through 1997 models .... 12.5 quarts
      1998 and 1999 models .... 10.7 quarts
      2000 and later models .... 12.5 quarts
Automatic transaxle (when draining pan and replacing filter only)
   4T60-E .... 6.0 quarts
   4T80-E
      1996 and earlier models .... 8.0 quarts
      1997 and later models .... 11.0 quarts

Note: *The best way to determine the amount of fluid to add during a routine fluid change is to measure the amount drained. It is important not to overfill the transaxle. After draining the transaxle, begin the refilling procedure by initially adding four quarts, then adding 1/2-pint at a time until the level is correct on the dipstick.*

* All capacities approximate. Add as necessary to bring to the appropriate level.

Ignition system

Spark plug type and gap
   4.6L engine
      1994 and earlier models .... AC 41-900 or equivalent @ 0.050 inch
      1995 and 1996 models .... AC 41-929 or equivalent @ 0.050 inch
      1997 through 1999 models... AC 41-950 or equivalent @ 0.050 inch
      2000 and later models .... AC 41-937 or equivalent @ 0.050 inch
   4.9L engine.. AC 41-902 or equivalent @ 0.060 inch
Ignition timing
   4.6L engine.. N/A
   4.9L engine.. 10-degrees BDTC @ any speed less
         than 800 rpm (with terminals A and B
         of the ALDL connector jumpered)

Firing order
   4.6L engine.. 1-2-7-3-4-5-6-8
   4.9L engine.. 1-8-4-3-6-5-7-2

Brakes

Brake pad minimum thickness .... 1/8 inch

Torque specifications

                                                  Ft-lbs (unless otherwise indicated)
Accessory drivebelt tensioner bolt 37
Automatic transaxle oil pan bolts
   4T60-E .... 120 to 156 in-lbs
   4T80-E
      Step 1... 27 in-lbs
      Step 2... 53 in-lbs
      Step 3... 106 in-lbs
Engine oil drain plug
   4.6L models.. 15
   4.9L models.. 22
Spark plugs
   4.6L models.. 132 in-lbs
   4.9L models.. 15
Water pump drivebelt tensioner bolts (4.6L engine)..................... 89 in-lbs
Wheel lug nuts 100

Cylinder location and distributor rotation diagram - 4.9L engine
(The blackened terminal shown on the distributor cap indicates the Number One spark plug wire position)

Cylinder and coil terminal locations (only 1999 and earlier models are equipped with an ignition coil pack like the one shown here; later models have an ignition coil assembly mounted in the top of each valve cover

Engine compartment component layout (1998 Seville)

1	Windshield washer fluid reservoir	6	Power steering fluid reservoir	11	Brake fluid reservoir
2	Fuse/relay panel	7	Spark plug wires	12	Cooling system pressure cap
3	Drivebelt	8	Engine oil dipstick	13	Automatic transaxle fluid dipstick
4	Power steering fluid return hose	9	Radiator hose	14	Ignition coil pack
5	Engine oil filler cap	10	Air filter housing	15	Water pump drivebelt (under cover)

Engine compartment component layout (2000 DeVille)

1	Brake fluid reservoir	6	Water pump drivebelt (under cover)	11	Remote positive terminal (for jump starting)
2	Air filter housing	7	Ignition coil assembly - front bank (spark plugs underneath)	12	Power steering fluid reservoir
3	Automatic transaxle fluid filler cap/dipstick	8	Engine oil filler cap	13	Drivebelt
4	Radiator hose	9	Windshield washer fluid reservoir	14	Cooling system pressure cap
5	Engine oil dipstick	10	Fuse/relay panel		

1

Typical engine compartment underside components (2000 DeVille shown)

1   Radiator drain valve
2   Engine oil filter
3   Brake caliper
4   Automatic transaxle fluid pan
5   Engine oil drain plug
6   Steering gear boot
7   Driveaxle boot
8   Balljoint

Typical rear underside components

1   Muffler
2   Shock absorber
3   Coil spring
4   Fuel tank
5   Stabilizer bar
6   Stabilizer bar bushing
7   Charcoal canister
8   Fuel filter

1 Maintenance schedule

The following maintenance intervals are based on the assumption that the vehicle owner will be doing the maintenance or service work, as opposed to having a dealer service department do the work. Although the time/mileage intervals are loosely based on factory recommendations, most have been shortened to ensure, for example, that such items as lubricants and fluids are checked/changed at intervals that promote maximum engine/driveline service life. Also, subject to the preference of the individual owner interested in keeping his or her vehicle in peak condition at all times, and with the vehicle's ultimate resale in mind, many of the maintenance procedures may be performed more often than recommended in the following schedule. We encourage such owner initiative.

When the vehicle is new it should be serviced initially by a factory authorized dealer service department to protect the factory warranty. In many cases the initial maintenance check is done at no cost to the owner (check with your dealer service department for more information).

Every 250 miles or weekly, whichever comes first

Check the engine oil level (Section 4)
Check the engine coolant level (Section 4)
Check the windshield washer fluid level (Section 4)
Check the brake fluid level (Section 4)
Check the tires and tire pressures (Section 5)

Every 3000 miles or 3 months, whichever comes first

All items listed above plus:
Check the power steering fluid level (Section 6)*
Check the automatic transaxle fluid level (Section 7)*
Change the engine oil and filter (Section 8)*
Check the seat belts (Section 9)
Inspect and replace, if necessary, the windshield wiper blades (Section 10)

Every 6000 miles or 6 months, whichever comes first

All items listed above plus:
Check and service the battery (Section 11)
Check the engine drivebelts (Section 12)
Inspect and replace, if necessary, all underhood hoses (Section 13)
Check the cooling system (Section 14)
Check the park/neutral switch (Section 15)
Rotate the tires (Section 16)
Lubricate the chassis components (Section 17)
Inspect the suspension, steering and driveaxle boots (Section 18)*
Inspect the exhaust system (Section 19)*
Check the brakes (Section 20)*

Every 15,000 miles or 12 months, whichever comes first

Replace the interior ventilation filter (2000 and later models) (Section 21)

Every 30,000 miles or 24 months, whichever comes first

All items listed above plus:
Inspect the fuel system (Section 22)
Change the automatic transaxle fluid and filter (Section 23)**
Replace the air filter (Section 24)*
Service the cooling system (drain, flush and refill) (green-colored ethylene glycol antifreeze) (Section 25)
Inspect and replace, if necessary, the PCV valve (Section 26)
Check the EGR system (4.9L engine only) (Section 27)
Replace the spark plugs (conventional-type plugs) (Section 28)
Inspect the spark plug wires (1999 and earlier models only) (Section 29)
Inspect and replace, if necessary, the distributor cap and rotor (4.9L engines only) (Section 30)
Check and adjust, if necessary, the ignition timing (4.9L engines only) (Section 31)

Every 60,000 miles or 48 months, whichever comes first

Replace the fuel filter (Section 32)
Replace the brake fluid (Section 33)

Every 100,000 miles or 60 months, whichever comes first

Service the cooling system (drain, flush and refill) (orange-colored DEX-COOL antifreeze) (Section 25)
Replace the spark plugs (platinum or iridium type) (Section 28)

This item is affected by "severe" operating conditions as described below. If the vehicle is operated under severe conditions, perform all maintenance indicated with an asterisk (*) at 3000 mile/3 month intervals. Severe conditions are indicated if the vehicle is operated mainly . . .

in dusty areas
while towing a trailer
when allowed to idle for extended periods and/or at low speeds when outside temperatures remain below freezing and most trips are less than four miles long

** *If operated under one or more of the following conditions, change the automatic transaxle fluid every 15,000 miles.*

In heavy city traffic where the outside temperature regularly reaches 90-degrees F or higher
In hilly or mountainous terrain
Frequent trailer pulling

1

2　Introduction

This Chapter is designed to help the home mechanic maintain the Cadillac Seville and DeVille with the goals of maximum performance, economy, safety and reliability in mind.

Included is a master maintenance schedule, followed by procedures dealing specifically with each item on the schedule. Visual checks, adjustments, component replacement and other helpful items are included. Refer to the **accompanying illustrations** of the engine compartment and the underside of the vehicle for the locations of various components.

Servicing your vehicle in accordance with the mileage/time maintenance schedule and the step-by-step procedures will result in a planned maintenance program that should produce a long and reliable service life. Keep in mind that it's a comprehensive plan, so maintaining some items but not others at the specified intervals will not produce the same results.

As you service your vehicle, you'll discover that many of the procedures can - and should - be grouped together because of the nature of the particular procedure you're performing or because of the close proximity of two otherwise unrelated components to one another.

For example, if the vehicle is raised, you should inspect the exhaust, suspension, steering and fuel systems while you're under the vehicle. When you're rotating the tires, it makes good sense to check the brakes since the wheels are already removed. Finally, let's suppose you have to borrow or rent a torque wrench. Even if you only need it to tighten the spark plugs, you might as well check the torque of as many critical fasteners as time allows.

The first step in this maintenance program is to prepare yourself before the actual work begins. Read through all the procedures you're planning to do, then gather up all the parts and tools needed. If it looks like you might run into problems during a particular job, seek advice from a mechanic or an experienced do-it-yourselfer.

Owner's Manual and VECI label information

Your vehicle Owner's Manual was written for your year and model and contains very specific information on component locations, specifications, fuse ratings, part numbers, etc. The Owner's Manual is an important resource for the do-it-yourselfer to have; if one was not supplied with your vehicle, it can generally be ordered from a dealer parts department.

Among other important information, the Vehicle Emissions Control Information (VECI) label contains specifications and procedures for tune-up adjustments (if applicable) and, in some instances, spark plugs (see Chapter 6

for more information on the VECI label). The information on this label is the *exact* maintenance data recommended by the manufacturer. This data often varies by intended operating altitude, local emissions regulations, month of manufacture, etc.

This Chapter contains procedural details, safety information and more ambitious maintenance intervals than you might find in the manufacturer's literature. However, you may also find procedures or specifications in your Owner's Manual or VECI label that differ with what's printed here. In these cases, the Owner's Manual or VECI label can be considered correct, since it is specific to your particular vehicle.

3　Tune-up general information

The term tune-up is used in this manual to represent a combination of individual operations rather than one specific procedure.

If, from the time the vehicle is new, the routine maintenance schedule is followed closely and frequent checks are made of fluid levels and high wear items, as suggested throughout this manual, the engine will be kept in relatively good running condition and the need for additional work will be minimized.

More likely than not, however, there will be times when the engine is running poorly due to lack of regular maintenance. This is even more likely if a used vehicle, which has not received regular and frequent maintenance checks, is purchased. In such cases, an engine tune-up will be needed outside of the regular routine maintenance intervals.

The first step in any tune-up or diagnostic procedure to help correct a poor running engine is a cylinder compression check. A compression check (see Chapter 2C) will help determine the condition of internal engine components and should be used as a guide for tune-up and repair procedures. If, for instance, a compression check indicates serious internal engine wear, a conventional tune-up won't improve the performance of the engine and would be a waste of time and money. Because of its importance, the compression check should be done by someone with the right equipment and the knowledge to use it properly.

The following procedures are those most often needed to bring a generally poor running engine back into a proper state of tune.

Minor tune-up

Check all engine related fluids (Section 4)
Clean, inspect and test the battery
　(Section 11)
Check the drivebelts (Section 12)
Check all underhood hoses (Section 13)
Check the cooling system (Section 14)
Check the air filter (Section 24)
Check the PCV valve (Section 26)
Replace the spark plugs (Section 28)

Inspect the spark plug wires (1999 and
　earlier models only) (Section 29)
Inspect the distributor cap and rotor
　(4.9L engine only) (Section 30)
Check and adjust, if necessary, the
　ignition timing (4.9L engine only)
　(Section 31)

Major tune-up

All items listed under Minor tune-up plus . . .

Check the fuel system (Section 22)
Replace the air filter (Section 24)
Check the EGR system (Section 27)
Check the charging system (Chapter 5)
Replace the spark plug wires (1999 and
　earlier models only) (Section 29)
Replace the distributor cap and rotor
　(4.9L engine only) (Section 30)

4　Fluid level checks (every 250 miles or weekly)

Note: *The following are fluid level checks to be done on a 250 mile or weekly basis. Additional fluid level checks can be found in specific maintenance procedures which follow. Regardless of intervals, be alert to fluid leaks under the vehicle which would indicate a problem to be corrected immediately.*

1　Fluids are an essential part of the lubrication, cooling, brake and windshield washer systems. Because the fluids gradually become depleted and/or contaminated during normal operation of the vehicle, they must be periodically replenished. See *Recommended lubricants and fluids* at the beginning of this Chapter before adding fluid to any of the following components. **Note:** *The vehicle must be on level ground when fluid levels are checked.*

Engine oil

Refer to illustrations 4.2, 4.4 and 4.6

2　The engine oil level is checked with a dipstick **(see illustration)**. The dipstick

4.2　The dipstick is located at the left end of the engine on some models; on others it's located between the front cylinder bank and the radiator

4.4 The oil level should be in the cross-hatched area on the dipstick - if it's below the ADD line, add enough oil to bring the level into the cross-hatched area

4.6 Unscrew the oil filler cap from the valve cover to add oil

extends through a metal tube down into the oil pan.

3   The oil level should be checked before the vehicle has been driven, or about five minutes after the engine has been shut off. If the oil is checked immediately after driving the vehicle, some of the oil will remain in the upper part of the engine, resulting in an inaccurate reading on the dipstick.

4   Pull the dipstick from the tube and wipe all the oil from the end with a clean rag or paper towel. Insert the clean dipstick all the way back into the tube and pull it out again. Note the oil at the end of the dipstick. Add oil as necessary to keep the level above the ADD mark in the cross-hatched area of the dipstick **(see illustration)**.

5   Do not overfill the engine by adding too much oil since this may result in oil fouled spark plugs, oil leaks or oil seal failures.

6   Oil is added to the engine after removing a twist off cap located on the valve cover **(see illustration)**. It's a good idea to use a funnel to prevent spills.

7   Checking the oil level is an important preventive maintenance step. A consistently low oil level indicates oil leakage through damaged seals, defective gaskets or past worn rings or valve guides. If the oil looks milky in color or has water droplets in it, the cylinder head gasket may be blown or the head or block may be cracked. The engine should be checked immediately. The condition of the oil should also be checked. Whenever you check the oil level, slide your thumb and index finger up the dipstick before wiping off the oil. If you see small dirt or metal particles clinging to the dipstick, the oil should be changed (see Section 8).

Engine coolant

Refer to illustration 4.9

Warning 1: *Do not allow antifreeze to come in contact with your skin or painted surfaces of the vehicle. Flush contaminated areas immediately with plenty of water. Do not store new coolant or leave old coolant lying around where it's accessible to children or pets - they're attracted by its sweet smell. Ingestion*

of even a small amount of coolant can be fatal! Wipe up garage floor and drip pan coolant spills immediately. Keep antifreeze containers covered and repair leaks in the cooling system immediately.

Warning 2: *If you have to remove the radiator cap or expansion tank cap, wait until the engine has cooled completely, then wrap a thick cloth around the cap and turn it to the first stop. If coolant or steam escapes, let the engine cool down longer, then remove the cap.*

8   All vehicles covered by this manual are equipped with a pressurized coolant system. Some models use a plastic coolant reservoir that is connected by a hose to the radiator filler neck; if the engine overheats, coolant escapes through a valve in the radiator cap and travels through the hose into the reservoir. As the engine cools, the coolant is automatically drawn back into the cooling system to maintain the correct level. Other models use a pressurized expansion tank; the level in the tank will vary with the temperature of the coolant. This type of system does not have a cap on the radiator. Instead, the pressure cap is mounted on the expansion tank.

9   The coolant level in the reservoir or expansion tank should be checked regularly. **Warning:** *Do not remove the radiator cap or expansion tank cap to check the coolant level when the engine is warm.* When the engine is cold, the coolant level should be at or slightly above the FULL COLD mark on the reservoir or expansion tank **(see illustration)**. If it isn't, remove the cap from the reservoir or expansion tank and add a 50/50 mixture of the recommended antifreeze and water (see this Chapter's Specifications). **Warning:** *On models with an expansion tank, unscrew the cap slowly. If you hear a hissing sound as the cap is unscrewed, STOP and allow the system to cool down for awhile.* On some models the coolant and windshield washer reservoirs are similar-looking, so be sure to add the correct fluids; the caps are clearly marked.

10   Drive the vehicle and recheck the coolant level. If only a small amount of coolant is required to bring the system up to

4.9 When the engine is cold, the coolant level must be maintained at the FULL COLD mark on the expansion tank or coolant reservoir

the proper level, water can be used. However, repeated additions of water will dilute the antifreeze and water solution. In order to maintain the proper ratio of antifreeze and water, always top up the coolant level with the correct mixture. An empty plastic milk jug or bleach bottle makes an excellent container for mixing coolant. Do not use rust inhibitors or additives.

11   If the coolant level drops consistently, there may be a leak in the system. Inspect the radiator, hoses, filler cap, drain plugs and water pump (see Section 14).

12   If no leaks are noted, have the pressure cap tested by a service station.

13   Check the condition of the coolant as well. It should be relatively clear. If it is brown or rust colored, the system should be drained, flushed and refilled. Even if the coolant appears to be normal, the corrosion inhibitors wear out, so it must be replaced at the specified intervals.

Windshield washer fluid

Refer to illustration 4.14

14   Fluid for the windshield washer system

4.14 Regardless of where the windshield washer reservoir is mounted, the cap is clearly marked

4.18 The fluid level inside the brake fluid reservoir can be checked by observing the level from the outside

5.2 Use a tire tread depth indicator to monitor tire wear - they are available at auto parts stores and service stations and cost very little

is located in a plastic reservoir on the side of the engine compartment **(see illustration)**. **Note:** *Depending on model and year, the reservoir may be located on the left or the right side of the engine compartment, but the cap is clearly marked.* In milder climates, plain water can be used in the reservoir, but it should be kept no more than two-thirds full to allow for expansion if the water freezes. In colder climates, use windshield washer system antifreeze, available at any auto parts store, to lower the freezing point of the fluid. Mix the antifreeze with water in accordance with the manufacturer's directions on the container. **Caution:** *Do not use cooling system antifreeze - it will damage the vehicle's paint.*

15   To help prevent icing in cold weather, warm the windshield with the defroster before using the washer.

Battery electrolyte

16   All vehicles covered by this manual are equipped with a battery which is permanently sealed (except for vent holes) and has no filler caps. Water does not have to be added to these batteries at any time.

Brake fluid

Refer to illustration 4.18

17   The brake master cylinder is mounted on the front of the power booster unit in the engine compartment.

18   The fluid level is readily visible through the translucent reservoir - the level should be at the MAX mark on the reservoir **(see illustration)**. If a low level is indicated, be sure to clean the reservoir cap, to prevent contamination of the brake system, before removing it.

19   When adding fluid, pour it carefully into the reservoir to avoid spilling it on surrounding painted surfaces. Be sure the specified fluid is used, since mixing different types of brake fluid can cause damage to the system. See *Recommended lubricants and fluids* at the front of this Chapter or your owner's manual. **Warning:** *Brake fluid can harm your eyes and damage painted surfaces, so use extreme caution when handling or pouring it.*

Do not use brake fluid that has been standing open or is more than one year old. Brake fluid absorbs moisture from the air. Excess moisture can cause a dangerous loss of braking effectiveness.

20   At this time the fluid and master cylinder can be inspected for contamination. The system should be drained and refilled if deposits, dirt particles or contamination are seen in the fluid.

21   After filling the reservoir to the proper level, make sure the cap is on tight to prevent fluid leakage.

22   The brake fluid level in the master cylinder will drop slightly as the pads at each wheel wear down during normal operation. If the master cylinder requires repeated replenishing to keep it at the proper level, this is an indication of leakage in the brake system, which should be corrected immediately. Check all brake lines and connections (see Section 20 for more information).

23   If, when checking the master cylinder fluid level, you discover one or both reservoirs empty or nearly empty, the brake system should be bled (see Chapter 9) and the cause of the fluid loss found.

---

5   Tire and tire pressure checks (every 250 miles or weekly)

Refer to illustrations 5.2, 5.3, 5.4a, 5.4b and 5.8

1   Periodic inspection of the tires may spare you the inconvenience of being stranded with a flat tire. It can also provide you with vital information regarding possible problems in the steering and suspension systems before major damage occurs.

2   The original tires on this vehicle are equipped with 1/2-inch wide bands that appear when tread depth reaches 1/16-inch, at which point the tires can be considered worn out. Tread wear can be monitored with a simple, inexpensive device known as a tread depth indicator **(see illustration)**.

3   Note any abnormal tread wear **(see illustration)**. Tread pattern irregularities such

as cupping, flat spots and more wear on one side than the other are indications of front end alignment and/or balance problems. If any of these conditions are noted, take the vehicle to a tire shop or service station to correct the problem.

4   Look closely for cuts, punctures and embedded nails or tacks. Sometimes a tire will hold air pressure for a short time or leak down very slowly after a nail has embedded itself in the tread. If a slow leak persists, check the valve stem core to make sure it's tight **(see illustration)**. Examine the tread for an object that may have embedded itself in the tire or for a "plug" that may have begun to leak (radial tire punctures are repaired with a plug that's installed in the hole). If a puncture is suspected, it can be easily verified by spraying a solution of soapy water onto the suspected area **(see illustration)**. The soapy solution will bubble if there's a leak. Unless the puncture is unusually large, a tire shop or service station can usually repair the tire.

5   Carefully inspect the inner sidewall of each tire for evidence of brake fluid. If you see any, inspect the brakes immediately.

6   Correct air pressure adds miles to the lifespan of the tires, improves mileage and enhances overall ride quality. Tire pressure cannot be accurately estimated by looking at a tire, especially if it's a radial. A tire pressure gauge is essential. Keep an accurate gauge in the vehicle. The pressure gauges attached to the nozzles of air hoses at gas stations are often inaccurate.

7   Always check tire pressure when the tires are cold. Cold, in this case, means the vehicle has not been driven over a mile in the three hours preceding a tire pressure check. A pressure rise of four to eight pounds is not uncommon once the tires are warm.

8   Unscrew the valve cap protruding from the wheel or hubcap and push the gauge firmly onto the valve stem **(see illustration)**. Note the reading on the gauge and compare the figure to the recommended tire pressure shown on the label attached to the rear edge of the driver's door. Be sure to reinstall the

UNDERINFLATION

CUPPING

Cupping may be caused by:
- Underinflation and/or mechanical irregularities such as out-of-balance condition of wheel and/or tire, and bent or damaged wheel.
- Loose or worn steering tie-rod or steering idler arm.
- Loose, damaged or worn front suspension parts.

OVERINFLATION

5.3 This chart will help you determine the condition of the tires, the probable cause(s) of abnormal wear and the corrective action necessary

INCORRECT TOE-IN OR EXTREME CAMBER

FEATHERING DUE TO MISALIGNMENT

1

5.4a If a tire loses air on a steady basis, check the valve core first to make sure it's snug (special inexpensive wrenches are commonly available at auto parts stores)

5.4b If the valve core is tight, raise the corner of the vehicle with the low tire and spray a soapy water solution onto the tread as the tire is turned slowly - leaks will cause small bubbles to appear

5.8 To extend the life of the tires, check the air pressure at least once a week with an accurate gauge (don't forget the spare!)

valve cap to keep dirt and moisture out of the valve stem mechanism. Check all four tires and, if necessary, add enough air to bring them up to the recommended pressure.

9   Don't forget to keep the spare tire inflated to the specified pressure (refer to your owner's manual or the tire sidewall).

6   Power steering fluid level check (every 3000 miles or 3 months)

Refer to illustrations 6.2 and 6.6

1   The power steering system relies on fluid which may, over a period of time, require replenishing.

2   The fluid reservoir for the power steering pump is located at the front (drivebelt end) of the engine **(see illustration)**.

3   For the check, the front wheels should be pointed straight ahead and the engine should be off.

4   Use a clean rag to wipe off the reservoir cap and the area around the cap. This will help prevent any foreign matter from entering the reservoir during the check.

5   Twist off the cap and check the temperature of the fluid at the end of the dipstick with your finger.

6   Wipe off the fluid with a clean rag, reinsert it, then withdraw it and read the fluid level. The level should be at the HOT mark or

6.2 The power steering fluid reservoir is located near the front (accessory drivebelt end) of the engine

6.6 The marks on the power steering fluid dipstick indicate the safe fluid level range

7.3 The automatic transaxle fluid dipstick on later models is part of the filler cap and is located on the top of the transaxle case

7.6a The automatic transaxle fluid level must be maintained within the cross-hatched area of the dipstick when the fluid is hot. This is an early model dipstick . . .

7.6b . . . and this is a later model dipstick

near the upper part of the cross-hatched area if the fluid was hot to the touch **(see illustration)**. It should be down near the COLD mark or the lower area of the cross-hatched area if the fluid was cool to the touch. Note that on some models the marks (FULL HOT and COLD) are on opposite sides of the dipstick. At no time should the fluid level drop below the ADD mark.

7   If additional fluid is required, pour the specified type directly into the reservoir, using a funnel to prevent spills.

8   If the reservoir requires frequent fluid additions, all power steering hoses, hose connections, the power steering pump and the steering gear should be carefully checked for leaks.

---

7   Automatic transaxle fluid level check (every 3000 miles or 6 months)

Refer to illustrations 7.3, 7.6a and 7.6b

1   The automatic transaxle fluid level should be carefully maintained. Low fluid level can lead to slipping or loss of drive, while overfilling can cause foaming (which can lead to burned clutch discs in the transaxle) and loss of fluid.

2   With the parking brake set, start the engine, then move the shift lever through all the gear ranges, ending in Park. The fluid level must be checked with the vehicle level

and the engine running at idle. **Note:** *Incorrect fluid level readings will result if the vehicle has just been driven at high speeds for an extended period, in hot weather in city traffic, or if it has been pulling a trailer. If any of these conditions apply, wait until the fluid has cooled (about 30 minutes).*

3   With the transaxle at normal operating temperature, remove the dipstick. On some models the dipstick is located at the rear of the engine compartment; on others, its part of the cap on top of the transaxle case **(see illustration)**.

4   Carefully touch the fluid at the end of the dipstick to determine if the fluid is cool, warm or hot. Wipe the fluid from the dipstick with a clean rag and reinstall it until the cap seats.

5   Remove the dipstick again and note the fluid level.

6   If the fluid felt cool, the level should be about 1/8-to-3/8 inch below the "ADD 1 PT" mark on early models or in the COLD range on later models **(see illustrations)**. If it felt warm, the level should be close to the "ADD 1 PT" mark on early models, or between the COLD and HOT ranges on later models. If the fluid was hot, the level should be within the cross-hatched area. If additional fluid is required, pour it directly into the tube using a funnel. Add no more than 1/2-pint at a time between checking the level, because overfilling the transaxle can damage it.

7   The condition of the fluid should also be checked along with the level. If the fluid at the end of the dipstick is a dark reddish-brown color, or if the fluid has a burned smell, the fluid should be changed. If you're in doubt about the condition of the fluid, purchase some new fluid and compare the two for color and smell.

---

8   Engine oil and filter change (every 3000 miles or 3 months)

Refer to illustrations 8.2, 8.7, 8.12 and 8.14
Note: *These vehicles are equipped with an oil*

8.2 These tools are required when changing the engine oil and filter

1   *Drain pan* - It should be fairly shallow in depth, but wide to prevent spills
2   *Rubber gloves* - When removing the drain plug and filter, you will get oil on your hands (the gloves will prevent burns)
3   *Breaker bar* - Sometimes the oil drain plug is tight, and a long breaker bar is needed to loosen it
4   *Socket* - To be used with the breaker bar or a ratchet (must be the correct size to fit the drain plug - six-point preferred)
5   *Filter wrench* - This is a metal band-type wrench, which requires clearance around the filter to be effective
6   *Filter wrench* - This type fits on the bottom of the filter and can be turned with a ratchet or breaker bar (different-size wrenches are available for different types of filters)

8.7 The engine oil drain plug is located at the bottom edge of the oil pan - it's usually very tight, so use a box-end wrench or socket to avoid rounding-off the hex

8.12 The oil filter is usually on very tight as well and will require a special wrench for removal - DO NOT use the wrench to tighten the new filter!

8.14 Lubricate the oil filter gasket with clean engine oil before installing the filter on the engine

life indicator system that illuminates a light or message on the instrument panel when the system deems it necessary to change the oil. A number of factors are taken into consideration to determine when the oil should be considered "worn out." Generally, this system will allow the vehicle to accumulate more miles between oil changes than the traditional 3000 mile interval, but we believe that frequent oil changes are "cheap insurance" and will prolong engine life. If you do decide not to change your oil every 3000 miles and rely on the oil life indicator instead, make sure you don't exceed 10,000 miles before the oil is changed, regardless of what the oil life indicator shows.

1   Frequent oil changes are the best preventive maintenance the home mechanic can give the engine, because aging oil becomes diluted and contaminated, which leads to premature engine wear.

2   Make sure you have all the necessary tools before you begin this procedure **(see illustration)**. You should also have plenty of rags or newspapers handy for mopping up any spills.

3   Access to the underside of the vehicle is greatly improved if the vehicle can be lifted on a hoist, driven onto ramps or supported by jackstands. **Warning:** *Do not work under a vehicle which is supported only by a hydraulic or scissors-type jack.*

4   If this is your first oil change, get under the vehicle and familiarize yourself with the locations of the oil drain plug and the oil filter. The engine and exhaust components will be warm during the actual work, so try to anticipate any potential problems before the engine and accessories are hot.

5   Park the vehicle on a level spot. Start the engine and allow it to reach its normal operating temperature. Warm oil and sludge will flow out more easily. Turn off the engine when it's warmed up. Remove the filler cap from the valve cover.

6   Raise the vehicle and support it securely on jackstands. **Warning:** *Never get beneath the vehicle when it is supported only by a jack. The jack provided with your vehicle is designed solely for raising the vehicle to remove and replace the wheels. Always use jackstands to support the vehicle when it becomes necessary to place your body underneath the vehicle.*

7   Being careful not to touch the hot exhaust components, place the drain pan under the drain plug in the bottom of the pan and remove the plug **(see illustration)**. It's a good idea to wear gloves while unscrewing the plug the final few turns to prevent contact with the hot, contaminated oil.

8   Allow the old oil to drain into the pan. It may be necessary to move the pan farther under the engine as the oil flow slows to a trickle. Inspect the old oil for the presence of metal shavings and chips.

9   After all the oil has drained, wipe off the drain plug with a clean rag. Even minute metal particles clinging to the plug would immediately contaminate the new oil.

10   Clean the area around the drain plug opening, reinstall the plug and tighten it to the torque listed in the Specifications at the beginning of this Chapter.

11   Move the drain pan into position under the oil filter.

12   Loosen the oil filter **(see illustration)** by turning it counterclockwise with the filter wrench. Use a quality filter wrench of the correct size and be careful not to collapse the canister as you apply pressure. Once the filter is loose, use your hands to unscrew it from the block. Just as the filter is detached from the block, immediately tilt the open end up to prevent the oil inside the filter from spilling out.

13   Use a clean rag to remove all oil, dirt and sludge from the area where the oil filter contacts the engine. Check the old filter to make sure the rubber gasket isn't stuck to the sealing surface on the engine.

14   Compare the old filter with the new one to make sure they are the same type. Smear some clean engine oil on the rubber gasket of the new filter and screw it into place **(see illustration)**. Attach the new filter to the engine, following the tightening directions on the filter canister or packing box. Most filter manufacturers recommend against using a filter wrench due to the possibility of over-tightening and damaging the seal.

15   Remove all tools, rags, etc. from under the vehicle, being careful not to spill the oil in the drain pan, then lower the vehicle.

16   Add new oil to the engine through the oil filler cap in the valve cover. Use a funnel, if necessary, to prevent oil from spilling. Pour five quarts (4.9L engine) or seven quarts (4.6L engine) of fresh oil into the engine. Wait a few minutes to allow the oil to drain into the pan, then check the level on the oil dipstick (see Section 4 if necessary). If the oil level is at or near the upper mark on the dipstick, install the filler cap hand tight, start the engine and allow the new oil to circulate.

17   Allow the engine to run for about a minute then turn it off. Wait about five minutes to allow the oil to trickle down into the pan, then recheck the level on the dipstick and, if necessary, add enough oil to bring the level to the upper mark.

18   Reset the oil life indicator (see Section 34).

19   During the first few trips after an oil change, make it a point to check frequently for leaks and proper oil level.

20   The old oil drained from the engine cannot be re-used in its present state and should be discarded. Check with your local refuse disposal company, disposal facility or environmental agency to see if they will accept the oil for recycling. Don't pour used oil into drains or onto the ground. After the oil has cooled, it can be drained into a suitable container (capped plastic jugs, topped bottles, milk cartons, etc.) for transport to one of these disposal sites.

1

10.5a Using a small screwdriver, gently lift the release lever . . .

10.5b . . . or pry on the spring at the center of the windshield wiper blade . . .

10.5c . . . while pulling the blade assembly away from the arm

10.7a If the rubber element is retained in the blade by small clips, the metal backing of the rubber element can be compressed at one end with pliers, allowing the element to slide out of the clips

10.7b If the element is retained by a clip at the end, use needle nose pliers to compress it and pull it out

9   Seat belt check (every 6000 miles or 6 months)

Warning: *Some of the models covered by this manual are equipped with side-impact airbags located in the seat backs. Some are also equipped with seat belt pre-tensioners, which are pyrotechnic (explosive) devices which tighten the seat belts during an impact of sufficient force. Be sure to disarm the airbag system when working in the vicinity of any of the airbag system or seat belt pre-tensioner components (see Chapter 12).*

1   Check the seat belts, buckles, latch plates and guide loops for obvious damage and signs of wear.
2   See if the seat belt reminder light comes on when the key is turned to the Run or Start position. A chime should also sound.
3   The seat belts are designed to lock up during a sudden stop or impact, yet allow free movement during normal driving. Make sure the retractors return the belt against your chest while driving and rewind the belt fully when the buckle is unlatched.
4   If any of the above checks reveal problems with the seat belt system, replace parts as necessary.

10   Wiper blade inspection and replacement (every 6000 miles or 6 months)

1   The windshield wiper and blade assembly should be inspected periodically for damage, loose components and cracked or worn blade elements.
2   Road film can build up on the wiper blades and affect their efficiency, so they should be washed regularly with a mild detergent solution.
3   The action of the wiping mechanism can loosen the bolts, nuts and fasteners, so they should be checked and tightened, as necessary, at the same time the wiper blades are checked.
4   If the wiper blade elements are cracked, worn or warped, they should be replaced with new ones.

Early models

Refer to illustrations 10.5a, 10.5b, 10.5c 10.7a and 10.7b

5   Remove the wiper blade assembly from

the wiper arm by inserting a small screwdriver into the spring under the release lever while pulling on the blade to release it **(see illustrations)**.
6   With the blade removed, you can remove the rubber element from the blade.
7   Using pliers, pinch the metal backing or pull out the retaining clip of the element **(see illustrations)**, then slide the element out of the blade assembly.
8   Compare the new element with the old for length, design, etc.
9   Slide the new element into place. It will automatically lock at the correct location.
10   Reinstall the blade onto the arm, wet the windshield glass and test for proper operation.

Later models

Refer to illustrations 10.12a and 10.12b

11   Lift the wiper blade away from the windshield.
12   Press the release lever and slide the blade assembly out of the hook in the end of the wiper arm **(see illustrations)**. Carefully rest the wiper arm on the windshield.
13   The rubber wiper element is secured to the blade assembly at one end of the blade element channel. Compress the locking fea-

10.12a Depress the release lever . . .

10.12b . . . then slide the wiper blade
down and out of the hook in the end
of the arm

11.1 Tools and materials required for
battery maintenance

ture on the element so it clears the tangs on the blade assembly channel claw and then slide the element out of the frame. **Note:** *On some models the rubber element may not be available separately, which will require replacement of the entire blade.*
14   Installation is the reverse of removal. Make sure the rubber element and blade assembly is securely attached. Wet the windshield glass and test for proper operation.

11   Battery check, maintenance and charging (every 6000 miles or 6 months)

Refer to illustrations 11.1, 11.2, 11.7a, 11.7b and 11.7c
Warning: *Certain precautions must be followed when checking and servicing the battery. Hydrogen gas, which is highly flammable, is always present in the battery cells, so keep lighted tobacco and all other open flames and sparks away from the battery. The electrolyte inside the battery is actually dilute sulfuric acid, which will cause injury if splashed on your skin or in your eyes. It will also ruin clothes and painted surfaces. When removing the battery cables, always detach*

the negative cable first and hook it up last!
Note: *The battery is located in the engine compartment on 1997 and earlier models. On 1998 and 1999 DeVille models, the battery is located in the engine compartment. On 1998 and 1999 Seville models and all 2000 and later models, the battery is located under the rear seat cushion. If you need help removing the rear seat cushion, refer to Chapter 11.*
1   A routine preventive maintenance program for the battery in your vehicle is the only way to ensure quick and reliable starts. But before performing any battery maintenance, make sure that you have the proper equipment necessary to work safely around the battery **(see illustration).**
2   There are also several precautions that should be taken whenever battery maintenance is performed. Before servicing the battery, always turn the engine and all accessories off and disconnect the cable from the negative terminal of the battery **(see illustration).**
3   The battery produces hydrogen gas, which is both flammable and explosive. Never create a spark, smoke or light a match around the battery. Always charge the battery

1   *Face shield/safety goggles* - When removing corrosion with a brush, the acidic particles can easily fly up into your eyes
2   *Baking soda* - A solution of baking soda and water can be used to neutralize corrosion
3   *Petroleum jelly* - A layer of this on the battery terminals will help prevent corrosion
4   *Battery post/cable cleaner* - This wire brush cleaning tool will remove all traces of corrosion from the battery and cable terminals
5   *Treated felt washers* - Placing one of these on each terminal will help prevent corrosion
6   *Rubber gloves* - Another safety item to consider when servicing the battery. Remember, that's acid inside the battery!

in a ventilated area.
4   Electrolyte contains poisonous and corrosive sulfuric acid. Do not allow it to get in your eyes, on your skin on your clothes. Never ingest it. Wear protective safety glasses when working near the battery. Keep children away from the battery.
5   Note the external condition of the battery. Look for any corroded or loose connections, cracks in the case or cover or loose hold-down clamps. Also check the entire length of each cable for cracks and frayed conductors.
6   If corrosion, which looks like white, fluffy deposits is evident, particularly around the terminals, the battery should be removed for cleaning. Loosen the cable clamp bolts with a wrench, being careful to remove the ground cable first, and detach the cables from the battery. Then disconnect the hold-down clamp bolt, remove the clamp and lift the battery from the engine compartment.
7   Clean the cable terminals thoroughly with a battery terminal tool and brush or a ter-

11.2 On 1998 and 1999 Seville models and all 2000 and later models, the battery is located under the rear seat cushion

11.7a A tool like this one (available at auto parts stores) is used to clean the side terminal type battery contact area

11.7b Use the brush to finish the cleaning job

11.7c The result should be a clean, shiny terminal area

ACCEPTABLE

Cracks Running Across "V" Portions of Belt

1/2"

Missing Two or More Adjacent Ribs 1/2" or longer

UNACCEPTABLE

12.2 Small cracks in the underside of a serpentine belt are acceptable - lengthwise cracks or missing pieces are cause for replacement

Cracks Running Parallel to "V" Portions of Belt

minal cleaner and a solution of warm water and baking soda. Wash the terminals and the top of the battery case with the same solution but make sure that the solution doesn't get into the battery. When cleaning the cables, terminals and battery top, wear safety goggles and rubber gloves to prevent any solution from coming in contact with your eyes or hands. Wear old clothes too - even diluted, sulfuric acid splashed onto clothes will burn holes in them. If the terminals have been extensively corroded, clean them up with a terminal cleaner tool **(see illustrations)**. Thoroughly wash all cleaned areas with plain water.

8   Make sure that the battery tray is in good condition and the clamp bolts are tight. If the battery is removed from the tray, make sure no parts remain in the bottom of the tray when the battery is reinstalled. When reinstalling the hold-down clamp bolts, do not overtighten them.

9   Information on removing and installing the battery can be found in Chapter 5. Information on jump starting can be found at the front of this manual. For more detailed battery checking procedures, refer to the *Haynes Automotive Electrical Manual.*

Cleaning

10   Corrosion on the hold-down compo-

nents, battery case and surrounding areas can be removed with a solution of water and baking soda. Thoroughly rinse all cleaned areas with plain water.

11   Any metal parts of the vehicle damaged by corrosion should be covered with a zinc-based primer, then painted.

Charging

Warning: *When batteries are being charged, hydrogen gas, which is very explosive and flammable, is produced. Do not smoke or allow open flames near a charging or a recently charged battery. Wear eye protection when near the battery during charging. Also, make sure the charger is unplugged before connecting or disconnecting the battery from the charger.*

12   Slow-rate charging is the best way to restore a battery that's discharged to the point where it will not start the engine. It's also a good way to maintain the battery charge in a vehicle that's only driven a few miles between starts. Maintaining the battery charge is particularly important in the winter when the battery must work harder to start the engine and electrical accessories that drain the battery are in greater use.

13   It's best to use a one or two-amp battery charger (sometimes called a "trickle" charger). They are the safest and put the least strain on the battery. They are also the least expensive. For a faster charge, you can use a higher amperage charger, but don't use one rated more than 1/10th the amp/hour rating of the battery. Rapid boost charges that claim to restore the power of the battery in one to two hours are hardest on the battery and can damage batteries not in good condition. This type of charging should only be used in emergency situations.

14   The average time necessary to charge a battery should be listed in the instructions

that come with the charger. As a general rule, a trickle charger will charge a battery in 12 to 16 hours.

---

12   Drivebelt check and replacement (every 6000 miles or 6 months)

Accessory drivebelt

Refer to illustrations 12.2, 12.5a and 12.5b

1   A single serpentine drivebelt is located at the front of the engine and plays an important role in the overall operation of the engine and its components. Due to its function and material make up, the belt is prone to wear and should be periodically inspected. The serpentine belt drives the alternator, power steering pump, water pump and air conditioning compressor.

2   With the engine off, open the hood and use your fingers (and a flashlight, if necessary), to move along the belt checking for cracks and separation of the belt plies. Also check for fraying and glazing, which gives the belt a shiny appearance **(see illustration)**. Both sides of the belt should be inspected, which means you will have to twist the belt to check the underside.

3   Check the ribs on the underside of the belt. They should all be the same depth, with none of the surface uneven.

4   The tension of the belt is maintained by the tensioner assembly and isn't adjustable. The belt should be checked at the specified mileage interval; if the belt shows noticeable damage or wear during these checks it should be replaced.

5   Rotate the tensioner clockwise to release belt tension **(see illustration)**. **Note:** *These models have a drivebelt routing decal to help during drivebelt installation* **(see illustration)**. *If the decal is missing, make a sketch.*

12.5a Insert a 1/2-inch drive breaker bar (A) into the square hole in the tensioner (B), then pull back on the breaker bar (rotating the tensioner clockwise)

12.5b Most models have a drivebelt routing decal on the upper radiator panel

12.8 The water pump drivebelt (A) is located at the left end of the engine. The cover is retained by two nuts and a bolt (B)

12.9 Rotate the tensioner clockwise and slip the belt off the pulleys

6   Remove the belt from the pulleys and slowly release the tensioner.

7   Route the new belt over the various pulleys, again rotating the tensioner to allow the belt to be installed, then release the belt tensioner. Make sure the belt is positioned properly on all of the pulleys.

Water pump drivebelt (4.6L engine)

Refer to illustrations 12.8 and 12.9

8   The water pump drivebelt is located at the left end of the engine and is driven by a pulley attached to the end of the front cylinder bank intake camshaft. The belt and pulley are protected by a cover, but part of the belt can be view without removing the cover **(see illustration)**.

9   To replace the belt, remove the cover **(see illustration 12.8)**, place a wrench on the bolt in the center of the tensioner pulley, then rotate the tensioner clockwise and remove the belt **(see illustration)**. Slowly release the tensioner.

10   Route the new belt over the pulleys, again rotating the tensioner to allow the belt to be installed, then release the belt ten-

sioner. Make sure the belt is positioned properly on the pulleys. Reinstall the cover and tighten the fasteners securely.

Tensioner replacement

11   Remove the drivebelt as described previously.

12.14 The water pump drivebelt tensioner is retained by two bolts

Accessory drivebelt tensioner

12   Remove the bolt in the center of the tensioner, then detach the tensioner from the engine.

13   Installation is the reverse of removal. Be sure to tighten the tensioner bolt to the torque listed in this Chapter's Specifications.

Water pump drivebelt tensioner (4.6L engine)

Refer to illustration 12.14

14   Unscrew the two stud bolts securing the tensioner to the water pump housing, then remove the tensioner **(see illustration)**.

15   Installation is the reverse of removal. Be sure to tighten the tensioner bolts to the torque listed in this Chapter's Specifications.

13   Underhood hose check and replacement (every 6000 miles or 6 months)

General

1   **Caution:** *Replacement of air conditioning hoses must be left to a dealer service*

department or air conditioning shop that has the equipment to depressurize the system safely. Never remove air conditioning components or hoses until the system has been depressurized.

2   High temperatures under the hood can cause the deterioration of the rubber and plastic hoses used for engine, accessory and emission systems operation. Periodic inspection should be made for cracks, loose clamps, material hardening and leaks. Information specific to the cooling system hoses can be found in Section 14.

3   Some, but not all, hoses are secured to the fittings with clamps. Where clamps are used, check to be sure they haven't lost their tension, allowing the hose to leak. If clamps aren't used, make sure the hose hasn't expanded and/or hardened where it slips over the fitting, allowing it to leak.

Vacuum hoses

4   It's quite common for vacuum hoses, especially those in the emissions system, to be color coded or identified by colored stripes molded into each hose. Various systems require hoses with different wall thicknesses, collapse resistance and temperature resistance. When replacing hoses, be sure the new ones are made of the same material.

5   Often the only effective way to check a hose is to remove it completely from the vehicle. If more than one hose is removed, be sure to label the hoses and fittings to ensure correct installation.

6   When checking vacuum hoses, be sure to include any plastic T-fittings in the check. Inspect the fittings for cracks and the hose where it fits over the fitting for distortion, which could cause leakage.

7   A small piece of vacuum hose (1/4-inch inside diameter) can be used as a stethoscope to detect vacuum leaks. Hold one end of the hose to your ear and probe around vacuum hoses and fittings, listening for the "hissing" sound characteristic of a vacuum leak. **Warning:** *When probing with the vacuum hose stethoscope, be careful not to allow your body or the hose to come into contact with moving engine components such as the drivebelt, cooling fan, etc.*

Fuel hose

Warning: *Gasoline is extremely flammable, so take extra precautions when you work on any part of the fuel system. Don't smoke or allow open flames or bare light bulbs near the work area, and don't work in a garage where a gas-type appliance (such as a water heater or a clothes dryer) is present. Since gasoline is carcinogenic, wear fuel-resistant gloves when there's a possibility of being exposed to fuel, and, if you spill any fuel on your skin, rinse it off immediately with soap and water. Mop up any spills immediately and do not store fuel-soaked rags where they could ignite. The fuel system is under constant pressure, so, if any fuel lines are to be disconnected, the fuel pressure in the system must*

be relieved first (see Chapter 4). When you perform any kind of work on the fuel system, wear safety glasses and have a Class B type fire extinguisher on hand.

8   Check all rubber fuel lines for deterioration and chafing. Check especially for cracks in areas where the hose bends and just before fittings, such as where a hose attaches to the fuel filter or fuel injection fuel rail.

9   High quality fuel line meeting original equipment specifications must be used for fuel line replacement. Never, under any circumstances, use unreinforced vacuum line, clear plastic tubing or water hose for fuel lines.

10   Spring-type clamps are commonly used on fuel lines. These clamps often lose their tension over a period of time, and can be "sprung" during the removal process. Therefore, spring-type clamps should be replaced with screw-type clamps whenever a hose is replaced.

Metal lines

11   Sections of steel tubing are often used for fuel line between the fuel pump and engine compartment. Check carefully for cracks, kinks and flat spots in the line.

12   If a section of metal fuel line must be replaced, only seamless steel tubing should be used, since copper and aluminum tubing do not have the strength necessary to withstand normal engine vibration.

13   Check the metal brake lines where they enter the master cylinder and the ABS hydraulic unit (see Chapter 9) for cracks in the lines and loose fittings. Any sign of brake fluid leakage calls for an immediate thorough inspection of the brake system.

---

14   Cooling system check (every 6000 miles or 6 months)

Refer to illustration 14.4
Warning: *The engine must be completely cool before beginning this procedure.*

1   Many major engine failures can be attributed to a faulty cooling system. The cooling system also cools the transaxle fluid and plays an important role in prolonging transaxle life.

2   The cooling system should be checked with the engine cold. Do this before the vehicle is driven for the day or after the engine has been shut off for at least three hours.

3   Remove the radiator cap or expansion tank cap by turning it to the left until it reaches a stop. If you hear any hissing sounds (indicating there is still pressure in the system), wait until it stops. Now press down on the cap with the palm of your hand and continue turning to the left until the cap can be removed. Thoroughly clean the cap, inside and out, with clean water. Also clean the filler neck on the radiator or expansion tank. All traces of corrosion should be removed. The coolant inside the radiator should be rela-

Check for a chafed area that could fail prematurely.

Check for a soft area indicating the hose has deteriorated inside.

Overtightening the clamp on a hardened hose will damage the hose and cause a leak.

Check each hose for swelling and oil-soaked ends. Cracks and breaks can be located by squeezing the hose.

14.4 Hoses, like drivebelts, have a habit of failing at the worst possible time - to prevent the inconvenience of a blown radiator or heater hose, inspect them carefully as shown here

---

tively transparent. If it is rust colored, the system should be drained and refilled (Section 25). If the coolant level is not up to the top, add additional antifreeze/coolant mixture of the proper type (Section 4).

4   Carefully check the large upper and lower radiator hoses along with any smaller diameter heater hoses which run from the engine to the firewall. Inspect each hose along its entire length, replacing any hose that is cracked, swollen or shows signs of deterioration. Cracks may become more apparent if the hose is squeezed **(see illustration)**.

5   Make sure all hose connections are tight. A leak in the cooling system will usually show up as white or rust colored deposits on the areas adjoining the leak. If wire-type clamps are used at the ends of the hoses, it may be wise to replace them with more secure screw-type clamps.

16.2a Tire rotation diagram for *non-directional* radial tires

16.2b Tire rotation diagram for *directional* radial tires

17.1 Materials required for chassis and body lubrication

1 *Engine oil - Light engine oil in a can like this can be used for door and hood hinges*
2 *Graphite spray - Used to lubricate lock cylinders*
3 *Grease - Grease, in a variety of types and weights, is available for use in a grease gun. Check the Specifications for your requirements*
4 *Grease gun - A common grease gun, shown here with a detachable hose and nozzle, is needed for chassis lubrication if grease fittings are provided. After use, clean it thoroughly*

6 Use compressed air or a soft brush to remove bugs, leaves, etc. from the front of the radiator or air conditioning condenser. Be careful not to damage the delicate cooling fins or cut yourself on them.

7 Every other inspection, or at the first indication of cooling system problems, have the cap and system pressure tested. If you don't have a pressure tester, most gas stations and repair shops will do this for a minimal charge.

15 Park/Neutral Position (PNP) switch check (every 6000 miles or 6 months)

Warning: *During the following checks there's a chance the vehicle could lunge forward, possibly causing damage or injuries. Allow plenty of room around the vehicle, apply the parking brake and hold down the regular brake pedal during the checks.*

1 Try to start the engine in each gear. The engine should crank only in Park or Neutral. If it starts in any other position, adjust or replace the switch, as necessary (see Chapter 7).

2 Also make sure the steering column lock allows the key to go into the Lock position only when the shift lever is in Park.

3 The ignition key should come out only in the Lock position.

16 Tire rotation (every 6000 miles or 6 months)

Refer to illustrations 16.2a and 16.2b

1 The tires should be rotated at the specified intervals and whenever uneven wear is noticed.

2 Refer to the **accompanying illustrations** for the preferred tire rotation pattern.

3 Refer to the information in *Jacking and towing* at the front of this manual for the proper procedures to follow when raising the

vehicle and changing a tire. If the brakes are to be checked, don't apply the parking brake as stated. Make sure the tires are blocked to prevent the vehicle from rolling as it's raised. **Note:** *Loosen the wheel lug nuts 1/2-turn before raising the vehicle.*

4 Preferably, the entire vehicle should be raised at the same time. This can be done on a hoist or by jacking up each corner and then lowering the vehicle onto jackstands placed under the frame rails. Always use four jackstands and make sure the vehicle is safely supported.

5 After rotation, check and adjust the tire pressures as necessary and be sure to tighten the lug nuts to the torque listed in this Chapter's Specifications.

17 Chassis lubrication (every 6000 miles or 6 months)

Refer to illustrations 17.1 and 17.6

1 Refer to *Recommended lubricants and fluids* at the front of this Chapter to obtain the necessary lubricants. You'll also need a grease gun **(see illustration)**. Occasionally plugs will be installed rather than grease fittings. If so, grease fittings will have to be purchased and installed.

2 Look under the vehicle and see if grease fittings or plugs are installed in the balljoints and tie-rod ends. If there are plugs, remove them and buy grease fittings, which will thread into the component. An auto parts store will be able to supply the correct fittings. Straight, as well as angled, fittings are available. **Note:** *Not all balljoints or tie-rod ends have grease fittings or plugs (some are lubricated for life).*

3 For easier access under the vehicle, raise it with a jack and place jackstands under the frame. Make sure it's securely supported by the stands. If the wheels are being removed at this interval for rotation or brake inspection, loosen the lug nuts slightly while the vehicle is still on the ground.

4 Before beginning, force a little grease out of the nozzle to remove any dirt from the end of the gun. Wipe the nozzle clean with a rag.

5 With the grease gun and plenty of clean rags, crawl under the vehicle and begin lubricating the components.

6 Wipe off the grease fitting and push the nozzle firmly over it **(see illustration)**. Squeeze the trigger on the grease gun to

17.6 After cleaning the grease fitting, push the gun nozzle firmly into place and pump the grease into the component (usually about two pumps will be sufficient)

18.9a Inspect the control arm bushings and balljoint . . .

18.9b . . . the stabilizer bar links and bushings . . .

force grease into the component. The balljoints and tie-rod ends should be lubricated until each rubber seal is firm to the touch. Do not pump too much grease into the fitting or it could rupture the seal. If the grease escapes around the grease gun nozzle, the fitting is clogged or the nozzle isn't completely seated on the fitting. Resecure the gun nozzle to the fitting and try again. If necessary, replace the fitting with a new one.

7   Wipe the excess grease off the components and the grease fitting. Repeat the procedure for the remaining fittings.

8   Open the hood and smear a little chassis grease on the hood latch mechanism. Have an assistant pull the hood release lever from inside the vehicle as you lubricate the cable at the latch.

9   Lubricate all the hinges (door, hood, etc.) with engine oil.

10   The key lock cylinders can be lubricated with spray graphite or silicone lubricant, which is available at auto parts stores. **Caution:** *The manufacturer doesn't recommend using oil in black plastic lock cylinders - it could damage them by washing out the factory-applied lubricant.*

11   Lubricate the door weatherstripping with silicone spray. This will reduce chafing and retard wear.

---

18   Steering, suspension and driveaxle boot check (every 6000 miles or 6 months)

Note: *The steering linkage and suspension components should be checked periodically. Worn or damaged suspension and steering linkage components can result in excessive and abnormal tire wear, poor ride quality and vehicle handling, and reduced fuel economy. For detailed illustrations of the steering and suspension components, refer to Chapter 10.*

Shock absorber/strut check

1   Park the vehicle on level ground, turn the engine off and set the parking brake.

18.9c . . . and the tie-rod ends and balljoint boots

Check the tire pressures.

2   Push down at one corner of the vehicle, then release it while noting the movement of the body. It should stop moving and come to rest in a level position within one or two bounces.

3   If the vehicle continues to move up-and-down or if it fails to return to its original position, a worn or weak shock absorber or strut is probably the reason.

4   Repeat the above check at each of the three remaining corners of the vehicle.

5   Raise the vehicle and support it securely on jackstands.

6   Check the front struts and rear struts or shock absorbers for evidence of fluid leakage. A light film of fluid is no cause for concern. Make sure that any fluid noted is from the shocks or struts and not from some other source. If leakage is noted, replace the shocks or struts as a set.

7   Check the shocks and/or struts to be sure that they are securely mounted and undamaged. Check the upper mounts for damage and wear. If damage or wear is noted, replace the shocks or struts as a set (front or rear).

8   If the shocks or struts must be replaced, refer to Chapter 10 for the procedure.

18.9d Check the steering gear boots for cracks and leaking steering fluid (if fluid is present, the rack seals are leaking)

Steering and suspension check

Refer to illustrations 18.9a, 18.9b, 18.9c, 18.9d and 18.11

9   Visually inspect the steering and suspension components for damage and distortion. Look for damaged seals, boots and bushings and leaks of any kind **(see illustrations)**.

10   Clean the lower end of the steering knuckle. Have an assistant grasp the lower edge of the tire and move the wheel in-and-out while you look for movement at the steering knuckle-to-control arm balljoint. If there is any movement the suspension balljoint(s) must be replaced.

11   Grasp each front tire at the front and rear edges, push in at the front, pull out at the rear and feel for play in the steering system components. If any freeplay is noted, check the steering gear mounts and the tie-rod ends for looseness **(see illustration)**.

12   Additional steering and suspension system information and illustrations can be found in Chapter 10.

22.3 Check the fuel line connections at the fuel rail for leakage

22.9a Inspect the charcoal canister and hoses for damage and leaks; this one's on an early model, mounted in the engine compartment . . .

22.9b . . . on later models, it's mounted under the vehicle, forward of the fuel tank

sure it slides in evenly and all the way, until the retaining tab holds it in place.

5   Reinstall the cover, engaging the side nearest the windshield first, then swing it down until the two tabs click into place.

22   Fuel system check (every 30,000 miles or 24 months)

Refer to illustrations 22.3, 22.9a and 22.9b
Warning: *Gasoline is extremely flammable, so take extra precautions when you work on any part of the fuel system. Don't smoke or allow open flames or bare light bulbs near the work area, and don't work in a garage where a gas-type appliance (such as a water heater or clothes dryer) is present. Since gasoline is carcinogenic, wear fuel-resistant gloves when there's a possibility of being exposed to fuel, and, if you spill any fuel on your skin, rinse it off immediately with soap and water. Mop up any spills immediately and do not store fuel-soaked rags where they could ignite. When you perform any kind of work on the fuel system, wear safety glasses and have a Class B type fire extinguisher on hand. The fuel system is under constant pressure, so, before any lines are disconnected, the fuel system pressure must be relieved (see Chapter 4).*

1   If you smell gasoline while driving or after the vehicle has been sitting in the sun, inspect the fuel system immediately.

2   Remove the fuel filler cap and inspect it for damage and corrosion. The rubber gasket should have an unbroken sealing imprint. If the gasket is damaged or corroded, install a new cap.

3   Inspect the fuel feed and return lines for cracks. Make sure that the connections between the fuel lines and the fuel injection system and between the fuel lines and the in-line fuel filter are secure **(see illustration)**.
Warning: *Your vehicle is fuel injected, so you must relieve the fuel system pressure before servicing fuel system components. The fuel system pressure-relief procedure is outlined in Chapter 4.*

4   If the fuel injectors are visible, look for signs of fuel leakage (wet spots) around any of the injectors, they may need new O-rings (see Chapter 4).

5   Since some components of the fuel system - the fuel tank and part of the fuel feed and return lines, for example - are underneath the vehicle, they can be inspected more easily with the vehicle raised on a hoist. If that's not possible, raise the vehicle and support it on jackstands.

6   With the vehicle raised and safely supported, inspect the fuel tank and filler neck for punctures, cracks and other damage. The connection between the filler neck and the tank is particularly critical. Sometimes a rubber filler neck will leak because of loose clamps or deteriorated rubber. Inspect all fuel tank mounting brackets and straps to be sure that the tank is securely attached to the vehicle. **Warning:** *Do not, under any circumstances, try to repair a fuel tank (except rubber components). A welding torch or any open flame can easily cause fuel vapors inside the tank to explode.*

7   Carefully check all rubber hoses and metal lines leading away from the fuel tank. Check for loose connections, deteriorated hoses, crimped lines and other damage. Repair or replace damaged sections as necessary (see Chapter 4).

8   The evaporative emissions control system can also be a source of fuel odors. The function of the system is to store fuel vapors from the fuel tank in a charcoal canister until they can be routed to the intake manifold where they mix with incoming air before being burned in the combustion chambers.

9   The most common symptom of a faulty evaporative emissions system is a strong odor of fuel coming from the engine compartment or from under the rear of the vehicle, depending on model (on early models the canister is located in the engine compartment; on later models it's located under the vehicle, near the fuel filter). If a fuel odor has been detected, and you have already

checked the areas described above, check the charcoal canister and the hoses connected to it **(see illustrations)**.

23   Automatic transaxle fluid and filter change (every 30,000 miles or 24 months)

Refer to illustrations 23.7, 23.10a, 23.10b and 23.13
Note: *These vehicles are equipped with an transaxle fluid life indicator system that illuminates a light or message on the instrument panel when the system deems it necessary to change the fluid. A number of factors are taken into consideration to determine when the fluid should be considered "worn out." Generally, this system will allow the vehicle to accumulate more miles between oil changes than the traditional 30,000 mile interval, but we believe that frequent fluid changes are "cheap insurance" and will prolong transaxle life. If you do decide not to change the fluid at least every 30,000 miles and rely on the fluid life indicator instead, make sure you don't exceed 100,000 miles before the fluid and filter are changed, regardless of what the fluid life indicator shows.*

1   At the specified intervals, the transaxle fluid should be drained and replaced. Since the fluid will remain hot long after driving, perform this procedure only after everything has cooled down completely.

2   Before beginning work, purchase the specified transaxle fluid (see *Recommended lubricants and fluids* at the front of this Chapter) and a new filter.

3   Other tools necessary for this job include jackstands to support the vehicle in a raised position, a drain pan capable of holding several quarts, newspapers and clean rags.

4   Raise and support the vehicle on jackstands.

5   With a drain pan in place, remove the front and side transaxle pan mounting bolts.

6   Loosen the rear pan bolts one turn.

23.7 After removing the front and side pan bolts, loosen the rear bolts and allow the fluid to drain, then remove the bolts and detach the pan from the transaxle

23.10a Pull the filter straight down to remove it

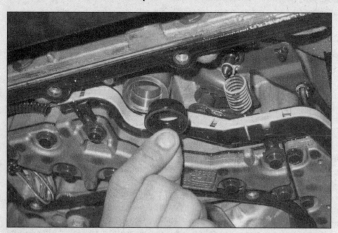

23.10b If the old seal isn't on the filter, remove it from the bore

23.13 After cleaning the pan, place the magnet (if equipped) in position and install the gasket

7   Carefully pry the transaxle pan loose with a screwdriver, allowing the fluid to drain **(see illustration)**.

8   Remove the remaining bolts, pan and gasket. Carefully clean the gasket surface of the transaxle to remove all traces of the old gasket and sealant.

9   Drain the fluid from the transaxle pan, clean the pan with solvent and dry it. Be careful not to lose the magnet, if equipped.

10   Remove the filter. Check the filter for the presence of a rubber seal on the filter tube - if it isn't on the filter, reach up into the filter bore and retrieve it **(see illustrations)**.

11   If you're working on a 4T80-E transaxle (some 1992 and 1993 models and all 1994 and later models), remove the plug from the bottom of the transaxle case; this will drain the fluid from the side cover. Once all the fluid has drained, reinstall the plug and tighten it securely.

12   Install a new filter seal onto the filter tube or push a new filter seal fully into its bore, as applicable, then install the new filter.

13   Make sure the gasket surface on the transaxle pan is clean, then install the magnet and a new gasket **(see illustration)**. Put the pan in place against the transaxle and install

the bolts. Working around the pan, tighten each bolt a little at a time until the final torque figure is reached.

14   Lower the vehicle and add the specified type and amount of automatic transmission fluid to the transaxle (see Section 7 and this Chapter's Specifications).

15   With the shift lever in Park and the parking brake set, run the engine at a fast idle, but don't race it.

16   Move the shift lever through each gear and back to Park. Check the fluid level, adding as necessary to bring it to the appropriate level.

17   Check under the vehicle for leaks during the first few trips.

24   Air filter replacement (every 30,000 miles or 24 months)

Refer to illustrations 24.2a, 24.2b and 24.2c

1   At the specified intervals, the air filter should be replaced with a new one. A thorough preventive maintenance schedule would also require the filter to be inspected between filter changes.

2   Unscrew the wing nuts and lift up the air

filter cover **(see illustrations)**. Withdraw the air filter.

3   While the filter housing cover is off, be careful not to drop anything into the air duct or air filter housing.

24.2a On early models, unscrew the four air filter cover wing nuts and detach the cover, then remove the filter element

24.2b On later models, unscrew the two wing nuts . . .

25.4 The under-vehicle splash shield is retained by numerous fasteners - pull the center post of the plastic fastener out, then pry out the fastener

24.2c . . . then lift the cover up and remove the filter element

4   Wipe out the inside of the air filter housing with a clean rag.

5   Place a new air filter in the air filter housing. Make sure it seats properly in the bottom of the housing.

6   Install the cover and retaining nuts and connect the clips securely. **Note:** *On later models, make sure the tabs on the filter cover engage with the slots in the filter housing.*

25   Cooling system servicing (draining, flushing and refilling) (see the *Maintenance schedule* for service interval)

Warning: *Do not allow antifreeze to come in contact with your skin or painted surfaces of the vehicle. Rinse off spills immediately with plenty of water. Antifreeze is highly toxic if ingested. Never leave antifreeze lying around in an open container or in puddles on the floor; children and pets are attracted by it's sweet smell and may drink it. Check with local authorities about disposing of used antifreeze. Many communities have collection centers which will see that antifreeze is disposed of safely.*

1   Periodically, the cooling system should be drained, flushed and refilled to replenish the antifreeze mixture and prevent formation of rust and corrosion, which can impair the

performance of the cooling system and cause engine damage.

2   At the same time the cooling system is serviced, all hoses and the radiator cap/expansion tank cap should be inspected and replaced if defective (see Section 14).

3   Since antifreeze is poisonous, be careful not to spill any of the coolant mixture on your skin. Also, antifreeze will damage paint. If antifreeze contacts your skin or the vehicle's paint, rinse it off immediately with plenty of clean water. Consult local authorities about the dumping of antifreeze before draining the cooling system. In many areas, reclamation centers have been set up to collect automobile oil and drained antifreeze/water mixtures, rather than allowing them to be added to the sewage system.

Draining

Refer to illustrations 25.4 and 25.6

Warning: *Wait until the engine is completely cool before beginning this procedure.*

4   Apply the parking brake and block the rear wheels. If the vehicle has just been driven, wait several hours to allow the engine to cool down before beginning this procedure. Remove the under-vehicle splash shield **(see illustration)**. If necessary for access, raise the front of the vehicle and support it securely on jackstands.

5   Once the engine is completely cool, remove the radiator cap or expansion tank cap.

6   Drain the radiator by opening the drain valve at the bottom of the radiator **(see illustration)**. If the valve is corroded and can't be turned easily, or if the radiator isn't equipped with a drain valve, disconnect the lower radiator hose to allow the coolant to drain. Be careful not to get antifreeze on your skin or in your eyes.

7   Disconnect the hose from the coolant reservoir or expansion tank and remove the

25.6 The radiator drain is located at the lower corner of the radiator

reservoir or tank (see Chapter 3 if necessary).

Note: *If the pressure cap is present on the radiator, your system uses a coolant reservoir instead of an expansion tank. Flush the reservoir/tank out with water until it's clean, and if necessary, wash the inside with soapy water and a brush to make reading the fluid level easier.*

8   While the coolant is draining, check the condition of the radiator hoses, heater hoses and clamps (refer to Section 14 if necessary). Replace any damaged clamps or hoses.

Flushing

Refer to illustration 25.11

9   Once the system is completely drained, remove the thermostat from the engine (see Chapter 3). Then reinstall the thermostat housing without the thermostat. This will allow the system to be flushed. On models with an expansion tank, reinstall it now.

10   Tighten the radiator drain valve. Reinstall any disconnected hoses.

25.11 With the thermostat removed, disconnect the upper radiator hose and flush the radiator and engine block with a garden hose

11   Disconnect the upper radiator hose from the radiator, then place a garden hose in the upper radiator inlet and flush the system until the water runs clear out of the upper radiator hose **(see illustration)**.
12   In severe cases of contamination or clogging of the radiator, remove the radiator (see Chapter 3) and have a radiator repair facility clean and repair it if necessary.
13   Many deposits can be removed by the chemical action of a cleaner available at auto parts stores. Follow the procedure outlined in the manufacturer's instructions. **Note:** *When the coolant is regularly drained and the system refilled with the correct antifreeze/water mixture, there should be no need to use chemical cleaners or descalers.*

Refilling

Note: *Special cooling system sealant pellets must be added to these engines. Check with your local auto parts store or dealer parts department for the proper sealant to use.*
14   To refill the system, install the thermostat, reconnect any radiator hoses and, on models with a coolant reservoir, install the reservoir and the overflow hose. On models equipped with an expansion tank, detach the lower radiator hose and install three cooling system sealant pellets, the reconnect the hose and tighten the clamp.
15   Place the heater temperature control in the maximum heat position.
16   Fill the cooling system with the proper type and mixture of antifreeze and water through the radiator filler neck (see this Chapter's Specifications).
17   Slowly fill the radiator or expansion tank to the base of the filler neck. On models with a coolant reservoir, add coolant to the reservoir until it reaches the FULL COLD mark. Wait five minutes and recheck the coolant level in the radiator, adding if necessary.
18   Leave the radiator cap or expansion tank cap off and run the engine in a well-ventilated area until the thermostat opens (coolant will begin flowing through the radiator and the upper hose will become hot).
19   Turn the engine off and let it cool completely. Add more coolant mixture to bring

the level up to the base of the filler neck. On models with a coolant reservoir add three sealant pellets to the radiator.
20   Squeeze the upper radiator hose to expel air, then add more coolant mixture if necessary. Reinstall the radiator cap or expansion tank cap.
21   Start the engine and allow it to reach normal operating temperature and check for leaks.

26   Positive Crankcase Ventilation (PCV) valve check and replacement (every 30,000 miles or 24 months)

Refer to illustrations 26.1a, 26.1b and 26.2
1   If you're working on a model with a 4.6L engine, remove the engine cover. With the engine idling at normal operating temperature, pull the valve (with hose attached) out of the rubber grommet in the valve cover **(see illustrations)**.
2   Place your finger over the end of the valve. If there is no vacuum at the valve, check for a plugged hose, manifold port, or the valve itself. Replace any plugged or deteriorated hoses **(see illustration)**.
3   Turn off the engine and shake the PCV valve, listening for a rattle. If the valve doesn't rattle, replace it with a new one.
4   To replace the valve, pull it out of the end of the hose, noting its installed position and direction.
5   When purchasing a replacement PCV valve, make sure it's for your particular vehicle, model year and engine size. Compare the old valve with the new one to make sure they are the same.
6   Push the valve into the end of the hose until it's seated.
7   Inspect the rubber grommet for damage and replace it with a new one if necessary.
8   Push the PCV valve and hose securely into position in the valve cover. If you're working on a 4.6L engine, reinstall the engine cover.

26.1a The PCV valve plugs into the front valve cover on 4.9L engines

26.1b On 4.6L engines the PCV valve plugs into the rear valve cover

26.2 With the engine running, remove the PCV valve, then feel for suction at the end of the valve; with the engine off, shake the valve, listening for a rattling sound

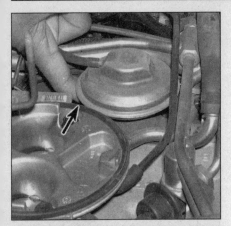

27.2 The diaphragm, reached from under the EGR valve, should move with finger pressure

27 Exhaust Gas Recirculation (EGR) system check (4.9L engine only) (every 30,000 miles or 24 months)

Refer to illustration 27.2

1   The EGR valve is located on the intake manifold. Most of the time, when a problem develops in the emissions system, it's due to a stuck or corroded EGR valve.

2   With the engine cold to prevent burns, reach under the valve and push on the diaphragm **(see illustration)**. Using moderate pressure, you should be able to move the diaphragm.

3   If the diaphragm doesn't move or moves only with much effort, replace the EGR valve with a new one. If in doubt about the condition of the valve, compare the free movement with a new valve.

4   Refer to Chapter 6 for more information on the EGR system.

28 Spark plug replacement (see the *Maintenance schedule* for service interval)

Refer to illustrations 28.2, 28.5a, 28.5b, 28.6a, 28.6b, 28.8, 28.9 and 28.10

1   All vehicles covered by this manual are equipped with transversely mounted engines which locate the spark plugs at the front and the rear of the engine compartment.

2   In most cases, the tools necessary for spark plug replacement include a spark plug socket which fits onto a ratchet (spark plug sockets are padded inside to prevent damage to the porcelain insulators on the new plugs), various extensions and a gap gauge to check and adjust the gaps on the new plugs **(see illustration)**. A special plug wire removal tool is available for separating the wire boots from the spark plugs, and is a good idea on models which use spark plug wires because the boots fit very tightly. A torque wrench should be used to tighten the new plugs. It is a good idea to allow the

28.2 Tools required for changing spark plugs

1   **Spark plug socket** - *This will have special padding inside to protect the spark plug's porcelain insulator*

2   **Torque wrench** - *Although not mandatory, using this tool is the best way to ensure the plugs are tightened properly*

3   **Ratchet** - *Standard hand tool to fit the spark plug socket*

4   **Extension** - *Depending on model and accessories, you may need special extensions and universal joints to reach one or more of the plugs*

5   **Spark plug gap gauge** - *This gauge for checking the gap comes in a variety of styles. Make sure the gap for your engine is included*

engine to cool before removing or installing the spark plugs.

3   The best approach when replacing the spark plugs is to purchase the new ones in advance, adjust them to the proper gap and replace the plugs one at a time. When buying the new spark plugs, be sure to obtain the correct plug type for your particular engine. The plug type can be found in the Specifications at the front of this Chapter and, on some models, on the *Emission Control Information* label located under the hood. If these two sources list different plug types, consider the emission control label correct.

4   Allow the engine to cool completely before attempting to remove any of the plugs. While you are waiting for the engine to cool, check the new plugs for defects and adjust the gaps. **Caution:** *Platinum and iridium spark plugs generally come pre-gapped. If you check the gap, treat them very gently and do not scratch the coating on the electrodes. Also, don't attempt to adjust the gap on used platinum or iridium spark plugs.*

5   Check the gap by inserting the proper thickness gauge between the electrodes at the tip of the plug **(see illustration)**. The gap between the electrodes should be the same as the one specified on the *Emissions Control Information* label or as listed in this Chapter's Specifications. The wire should slide between the electrodes with a slight amount of drag. If the gap is incorrect, use the adjuster on the gauge body to bend the curved side electrode slightly until the proper gap is obtained

28.5a Spark plug manufacturers recommend using a wire type gauge when checking the gap - if the wire does not slide between the electrodes with a slight drag, adjustment is required

28.5b To change the gap, bend the side electrode only, as indicated by the arrows, and be very careful not to crack or chip the porcelain insulator surrounding the center electrode

(see illustration). If the side electrode is not exactly over the center electrode, bend it with the adjuster until it is. Check for cracks in the porcelain insulator (if any are found, the plug should not be used).

6   If you're working on a 1999 or earlier model, remove the spark plug wire from one spark plug. Pull only on the boot at the end of the wire - do not pull on the wire. A plug wire removal tool should be used if available **(see**

TWIST AND PULL

28.6a When removing the spark plug wires, pull only on the boot and twist it back-and-forth

1

28.6b After removing the ignition coil assemblies, remove the spark plug boots (2000 and later models)

28.8 Removing a spark plug from a 4.6L engine

28.9 Apply a thin coat of anti-seize compound to the spark plug threads

illustration). Additionally, remove the ignition coil assembly from the rear cylinder bank for access to the rear spark plugs (see Chapter 5). If you're working on a 2000 or later model, remove both ignition coil assemblies from the valve covers, then remove the spark plug boots from the spark plug recesses **(see illustration)**

7   If compressed air is available, use it to blow any dirt or foreign material away from the spark plug hole. The idea here is to eliminate the possibility of debris falling into the cylinder as the spark plug is removed.

8   The spark plugs on these models are, for the most part, difficult to reach, so a spark plug socket and an extension will be necessary. If you're working on a 4.9L engine, a socket incorporating a universal joint may be necessary. Place the spark plug socket over the plug and remove it from the engine by turning it in a counterclockwise direction **(see illustration)**.

9   Compare the spark plug with the chart shown on the inside back cover of this manual to get an indication of the general running condition of the engine. Before installing the new plugs, it's a good idea to apply a thin coat of anti-seize compound to the threads **(see illustration)**.

10   Thread one of the new plugs into the hole until you can no longer turn it with your fingers, then tighten it with a torque wrench (which is highly recommended) or the ratchet. It's a good idea to slip a short length of rubber hose over the end of the plug to use as a tool to thread it into place **(see illustration)**. The hose will grip the plug well enough to turn it, but will start to slip if the plug begins to cross-thread in the hole - this will prevent damaged threads and the accompanying repair costs.

11   On 1999 and earlier models, inspect the spark plug wire following the procedures outlined in Section 29.

12   On 1999 and earlier models, attach the plug wire to the new spark plug, again using a twisting motion on the boot until it's seated on the spark plug. On 2000 and later models,

install the spark plug boot.

13   Repeat the procedure for the remaining spark plugs, replacing them one at a time to prevent mixing up the spark plug wires.

14   Install the ignition coil assemblies (see Chapter 5).

29   Spark plug wire check and replacement (every 30,000 miles or 24 months)

Note: *This procedure applies to 1999 and earlier models only.*

1   The spark plug wires should be checked at the recommended intervals and whenever new spark plugs are installed in the engine.

2   The wires should be inspected one at a time to prevent mixing up the order, which is essential for proper engine operation.

3   Disconnect the plug wire from the spark plug. To do this, grab the rubber boot, twist slightly and pull the wire off. Do not pull on the wire itself, only on the rubber boot. A special tool is available to make this easier **(see illustration 28.6a)**.

4   Check inside the boot for corrosion, which will look like a white crusty powder. Push the wire and boot back onto the end of the spark plug. It should be a tight fit on the plug. If it isn't, remove the wire and use pliers to carefully crimp the metal connector inside the boot until it fits securely on the end of the spark plug.

5   Using a clean rag, wipe the entire length of the wire to remove any built-up dirt and grease. Once the wire is clean, check for burns, cracks and other damage. Do not bend the wire excessively or pull the wire lengthwise - the conductor inside might break.

6   Disconnect the wire from the distributor. Again, pull only on the rubber boot. Check for corrosion and a tight fit in the same manner as the spark plug end. Reconnect the wire at the distributor.

7   Check the remaining spark plug wires one at a time, making sure they are securely fastened at the ignition coil or distributor and

28.10 A length of snug-fitting rubber hose will save time and prevent damaged threads when installing the spark plugs

the spark plug when the check is complete.

8   If new spark plug wires are required, purchase a set for your specific engine model. Wire sets are available pre-cut, with the rubber boots already installed. Remove and replace the wires one at a time to avoid mix-ups in the firing order.

30   Distributor cap and rotor check and replacement (4.9L engines only) (every 30,000 miles or 24 months)

Refer to illustrations 30.2 and 30.3

1   At the distributor cap, disconnect the electrical connectors.

2   Remove the distributor cap. On some models it is secured by four screws **(see illustration)**. On other models it may be secured by four spring-loaded latches which are disengaged by placing a screwdriver on the slotted head of each latch, press down and turn each latch 90-degrees to release the hooks. When all the screws are removed or the latches are disengaged, separate the cap from the distributor with the spark plug wires still attached.

3   Inspect the cap for cracks and other damage. Closely examine the terminals on

30.2 Distributor cap retaining
screw locations

30.3 Inspect the distributor cap for cracks and carbon tracks and the terminals for
corrosion and damage

the inside of the cap for excessive corrosion
(see illustration). Slight pitting is normal.
Deposits on the terminals may be removed
with a small file.
4   The rotor is visible, with the cap
removed, at the top of the distributor shaft.
Remove the two retaining screws and
remove the rotor.
5   Inspect the rotor for cracks and other
damage. Carefully check the condition of the
rotor tip and the metal contact at the top of
the rotor for excessive burning or pitting.
Check the top of the rotor for carbon tracks,
replace the rotor if carbon tracks are visible.
6   Install the rotor (either new or original).
Note that the rotor will fit only one way.
Tighten the screws securely.
7   If a new cap is being installed, release
the locking tabs to the spark plug wire retaining ring and remove the ring with the wires
attached (this will prevent mixing the wires). If
the ring is missing, or the wires have been
previously replaced with a type that does not
attach to the ring, make sure you label the
wires and mark the cap before removing so
they can be reinstalled in their original locations. Transfer the ignition coil to the new cap
(see Chapter 5).
8   Install the cap to the distributor. Note
that the tab on the cap engages the slot in
the distributor housing when the cap is properly seated. Tighten the screws securely or
engage the latches by pushing down and
rotating 90 degrees. Connect the electrical
connectors to the coil.

31 Ignition timing check and
adjustment (4.9L engines only)
(every 30,000 miles or 24 months)

Refer to illustrations 31.1, 31.2 and 31.4
Note: It is imperative that the procedures
included on the Vehicle Emission Control
Information label be followed when adjusting
the ignition timing. The label will include all
information concerning preliminary steps to
be performed before adjusting the timing as
well as the timing specifications.

31.1 Tools needed to check and adjust
the ignition timing

1   Vacuum plugs - Vacuum plugs may
     have to be disconnected and plugged.
     Molded plugs in various shapes and
     sizes are available for this
2   Inductive pick-up timing light -
     flashes a bright, concentrated beam of
     light when the number one spark plug
     fires. Connect the leads according to
     the instructions supplied with the light
3   Distributor wrench - On some
     models, the hold-down bolt for the
     distributor is difficult to reach and turn
     with conventional wrenches or
     sockets. A special wrench like this
     must be used

1   Locate the VECI label under the hood
and read through and perform the preliminary
instructions, if any. Some special tools will be
needed for this procedure (see illustration).
2   Locate the timing scale, near the
crankshaft pulley, and the notch on the
crankshaft pulley. Clean the timing scale and
mark the notch with a dab of white paint (see
illustration).
3   Connect the pick-up lead of the timing
light to the number one spark plug wire and
the power leads to the battery, according to

31.2 The ignition timing scale is located at
the front of the engine

31.4 When checking ignition timing on the
4.9L engine, terminals A and B of the
ALDL connector must be jumped with a
wire or paper clip (the ALDL connector is
located under the instrument panel, to the
left of the steering column

the manufacturer's instructions.
4   Connect terminals A and B of the ALDL
connector with a jumper wire while NOT in
the diagnostic mode (see illustration).
5   Start the engine and allow it to reach
normal operating temperature. Aim the timing
light at the timing scale and note at what
point on the scale the notch is lined up with.
The numbers on the scale represent degrees
of advance (BTDC) or retard (ATDC), with the
zero representing TDC.
6   If the notch is not lined up at the correct
point, loosen the distributor hold-down bolt
slightly, and while watching the scale rotate

the distributor until the notch lines up with the correct mark. Refer to the VECI label under the hood or the Specifications at the beginning of this Chapter for the proper timing setting.

7   Tighten the distributor hold-down bolt and recheck the timing.

8   Turn off the engine and remove the timing light. Be sure to remove the jumper wire from the ALDL connector.

32   Fuel filter replacement (every 60,000 miles or 48 months)

Refer to illustration 32.3

Warning: *Gasoline is extremely flammable, so extra precautions must be taken when working on any part of the fuel system. See the* **Warning** *in Section 22.*

1   Relieve the fuel system pressure (see Chapter 4), then disconnect the cable from the negative terminal of the battery (see Chapter 5).

2   Raise the rear of the vehicle and support it securely on jackstands.

3   Detach the fuel line fittings from the filter. On some models a threaded fitting is used on one end and a quick-connect fitting is used on the other end. If equipped with a threaded fitting, unscrew the fuel line-to-fuel filter fitting **(see illustration)**. Use an open-end wrench on the filter to prevent twisting the line as the fitting is loosened.

4   If equipped with a quick-connect fitting(s), twist the fitting 1/4-turn in each direction to loosen any debris within the connector, then blow out any dirt or debris from the connector. Squeeze the plastic tabs on the male end of the connector and pull the connector apart **(see illustration 32.3)**.

5   Remove the filter from the clip or bracket. **Note:** *Later models do not use a mount; the filter is supported by the line with the threaded fitting.*

6   Install the new filter securely into the clip or bracket, if equipped. If there's an arrow on the filter, make sure it points in the direction of fuel flow (toward the engine).

7   Wipe off the male end of the connector on the filter, then apply a drop of clean engine oil onto the connector where it is inserted into the female connector. Position the new filter so the arrow on the filter points toward the engine. Reattach the fuel lines to the filter, using new O-ring seals where present. When connecting quick-connect fittings, push the female connector(s) onto the

32.3 To disconnect a threaded fitting, loosen the fitting nut (A) with a flare-nut wrench while holding the hex on the filter (B) with an open-end wrench. To disconnect a quick-connect fitting, squeeze the plastic tabs (C) and pull the line off the filter

fuel filter's male connector(s) and push until the plastic tabs snap and lock into place.

8   Pull on the female end of each quick-connect fitting to make sure it is securely locked into place.

9   Reconnect the battery cable. Pressurize the fuel system by turning the ignition key to the On position, then check for fuel leaks.

33   Brake fluid change (every 60,000 miles or 48 months)

Warning: *Brake fluid can harm your eyes and damage painted surfaces, so use extreme caution when handling or pouring it. Do not use brake fluid that has been standing open or is more than one year old. Brake fluid absorbs moisture from the air. Excess moisture can cause a dangerous loss of braking effectiveness.*

1   At the specified intervals, the brake fluid should be drained and replaced. Since the brake fluid may drip or splash when pouring it, place plenty of rags around the master cylinder to protect any surrounding painted surfaces.

2   Before beginning work, purchase the specified brake fluid (see *Recommended lubricants and fluids* at the beginning of this Chapter).

3   Remove the cap from the master cylinder reservoir.

4   Using a hand-held suction pump or similar device, withdraw the fluid from the master cylinder reservoir.

5   Add new fluid to the master cylinder until it rises to the base of the filler neck.

6   Bleed the brake system as described in Chapter 9 at all four brakes until new and uncontaminated fluid is expelled from the

bleeder screw. Be sure to maintain the fluid level in the master cylinder as you perform the bleeding process. If you allow the master cylinder to run dry, air will enter the system.

7   Refill the master cylinder with fluid and check the operation of the brakes. The pedal should feel solid when depressed, with no sponginess. **Warning:** *Do not operate the vehicle if you are in doubt about the effectiveness of the brake system.*

34   Oil life indicator - general information and resetting

1   These models have an oil life indicator on the instrument panel that automatically lights when an engine oil change or transaxle fluid change is required.

Engine oil life indicator

2   After changing the engine oil, push the INFORMATION or INFO button on the instrument panel until *Engine Oil Life* appears on the driver's information display.

3   To reset the indicator, push the INFO RESET button and hold it the display changes to *100-percent Engine Oil Life*.

Transaxle fluid life indicator

4   To reset the transaxle fluid life indicator on early models, press the OFF and REAR DEFOG buttons simultaneously until the *Trans Fluid Reset* message is displayed on the information center.

5   On later models, press the INFORMATION or INFO button on the instrument panel until *Trans Fluid Life* appears on the driver's information display. Then push and hold the INFO RESET button until the display changes to *100-percent Trans Oil Life*.

Chapter 2 Part A
4.9L V8 engine

Contents

Specifications

General

Engine designation	VIN Code B
Displacement	4.9 liters (300 cubic inches)
Cylinder numbers (timing chain end-to-transaxle end)	
Front (left) side	1-3-5-7
Rear (right) side	2-4-6-8
Firing order	1-8-4-3-6-5-7-2

Torque specifications

Ft-lbs (unless otherwise indicated)

Intake manifold bolts (in sequence - **see illustration 6.15**)	
Step 1 (all bolts, in sequence)	96 in-lbs
Step 2 (all bolts, in sequence)	144 in-lbs
Step 3 (all bolts, in sequence)	144 in-lbs
Exhaust manifold-to-cylinder head bolts	16
Power steering bracket at front exhaust	19
Camshaft sprocket bolt	36
Damper-to-crankshaft	
1992 through 1994 models	70
1995 models	118

Cylinder location and distributor rotation

The blackened terminal shown on the distributor cap indicates the Number One spark plug wire position

Torque specifications (continued)

Ft-lbs (unless otherwise indicated)

Cylinder head bolts (in sequence - **see illustrations 8.7a and 8.7b**)

1992 through 1994 models

Step 1	38
Step 2	68
Step 3 (bolts 1, 3 and 4)	90

1995 models

Step 1	29
Step 2	50
Step 3	82
Step 4 (bolts 1, 3, 4, 7 and 8)	90
Step 5 (bolts 1, 3 and 4)	95

Driveplate-to-crankshaft bolts	70
Oil pan bolts	168 in-lbs
Valve cover bolts	96 in-lbs
Rocker arm pivot-to-support bolts	22
Rocker arm support-to-head bolt nuts	36

Front cover bolts

Lower 4 bolts	17
Upper 4 bolts	30
Subframe to chassis bolts	74

1 General information and engine identification

General information

This Part of Chapter 2 is devoted to in-vehicle repair procedures for the Cadillac 4.9L V8 engines. All information concerning engine removal and installation can be found in Part C of this Chapter.

Since the repair procedures included in this Part are based on the assumption that the engine is still installed in the vehicle, if they are being used during a complete engine overhaul (with the engine already out of the vehicle and on a stand) many of the steps included here will not apply.

The specifications included in this Part of Chapter 2 apply only to the procedures found here. Additional specifications can be found in Part C.

The Cadillac 4.9L V8 engine in these models is constructed of an aluminum block with cast iron cylinder heads. Because the engine is largely aluminum, particular care must be taken to accommodate the characteristics of this metal. Bolts that thread into aluminum must not be over-tightened or the threads may be damaged. The cylinder head tightening procedure must be strictly followed to insure proper sealing of the head gasket. When cleaning the gasket surfaces of the aluminum, use soft wire brushes or dull scrapers. Blow out all debris from the bolt holes to avoid inaccurate torque readings.

There are some differences between the various years of this Cadillac engine, but overall, repair and maintenance procedures are nearly identical. Where differences occur, they will be noted.

2 Repair operations possible with the engine in the vehicle

Many major repair operations can be accomplished without removing the engine from the vehicle.

Clean the engine compartment and the exterior of the engine with some type of degreaser before any work is done. A clean engine will make the job easier and will help keep dirt out of the internal areas of the engine.

Depending on the components involved, it may be a good idea to remove the hood to improve access to the engine as repairs are performed (refer to Chapter 11 if necessary).

If oil or coolant leaks develop, indicating a need for gasket or seal replacement, the repairs can generally be made with the engine in the vehicle. The oil pan gasket, the cylinder head gaskets, intake and exhaust manifold gaskets, timing cover gaskets and the crankshaft oil seals are accessible with the engine in place.

Exterior engine components, such as the water pump, the starter motor, the alternator, the distributor and the fuel system components, as well as the intake and exhaust manifolds, can be removed for repair with the engine in place.

Since the cylinder heads can be removed without pulling the engine, valve component servicing can also be accomplished with the engine in the vehicle.

Replacement of, repairs to, or inspection of the timing chain and sprockets, and the oil pump are all possible with the engine in place. Camshaft replacement, however, requires the engine to be removed (see Chapter 2, Part C).

In extreme cases, caused by a lack of necessary equipment, repair or replacement of piston rings, pistons, connecting rods and rod bearings is possible with the engine in the vehicle. However, this practice is not recommended because of the cleaning and preparation work that must be performed on the components involved.

3 Top Dead Center (TDC) for number one piston - locating

Refer to illustrations 3.4 and 3.6

1   Top Dead Center (TDC) is the highest point in the cylinder that each piston reaches as it travels up and down when the crankshaft turns. Each piston reaches TDC on the compression stroke and again on the exhaust stroke, but TDC generally refers to piston position on the compression stroke. The timing marks on the vibration damper installed on the front of the crankshaft are referenced to the number one piston at TDC on the compression stroke.

2   Positioning the piston(s) at TDC is an essential part of many procedures such as valve seal replacement, timing chain and sprocket replacement and distributor removal.

3   In order to bring any piston to TDC, the crankshaft must be turned using one of the methods outlined below. When looking at the front of the engine, normal crankshaft rotation is clockwise. **Warning:** *Before beginning this procedure, be sure to place the transaxle in Neutral and unplug the wire connector at the distributor to disable the ignition system.*

a)   *The preferred method is to turn the crankshaft with a large socket and breaker bar attached to the vibration damper bolt threaded into the front of the crankshaft.*

4.5 Detach the spark plug wires and cover from the valve cover

3.4 Make a mark on the distributor body, directly below the number one plug wire terminal of the cap - align the rotor to this mark when finding TDC

3.6 Timing marks on the 4.9L V8 engine

b) *A remote starter switch, which may save some time, can also be used. Attach the switch leads to the S (switch) and B (battery) terminals on the starter motor. Once the piston is close to TDC, use a socket and breaker bar as described in the previous paragraph.*

c) *If an assistant is available to turn the ignition switch to the Start position in short bursts, you can get the piston close to TDC without a remote starter switch. Use a socket and breaker bar as described in paragraph a) to complete the procedure.*

4   Make a mark on the distributor housing directly below the number one spark plug wire terminal on the distributor cap **(see illustration)**. **Note:** *The terminal numbers may be marked on the spark plug wires near the distributor.*

5   Remove the distributor cap as described in Chapter 1.

6   Turn the crankshaft (see Step 3) until the line on the vibration damper is aligned with the zero mark on the timing indicator **(see illustration)**.

7   The rotor should now be pointing directly at the mark on the distributor housing **(see illustration 3.4)**. If it isn't, the piston may be at TDC on the exhaust stroke. To get the piston to TDC on the compression stroke, turn the crankshaft one complete turn (360-degrees) clockwise. The rotor should now be pointing at the mark.

8   When the rotor is pointing at the number one spark plug wire terminal in the distributor cap (which is indicated by the mark on the housing) and the ignition timing marks are aligned, the number one piston is at TDC on the compression stroke. **Warning:** *After setting TDC, remove the socket and breaker bar. If left in place on the crankshaft bolt when the engine is turned or started, it could cause injury to you or damage to the vehicle.*

9   After the number one piston has been positioned at TDC on the compression stroke, TDC for any of the remaining cylinders can be located by turning the crankshaft 90-degrees at a time and following the firing order (refer to the Specifications).

4   Valve covers - removal and installation

Refer to illustrations 4.5, 4.7, 4.8 and 4.11

1   If you are removing a rear valve cover and the fuel lines are in the way, refer to Chapter 4 and relieve the fuel system pressure. Disconnect the negative cable from the battery (see Chapter 5).

2   Remove the air cleaner assembly (see Chapter 4 if necessary).

3   Label and disconnect any emissions or vacuum lines and wires which are routed over the valve cover(s).

4   Refer to Chapter 10 and move the power steering pump reservoir when accessing the front valve cover.

5   Label and disconnect the spark plug wires and detach the spark plug wires and cover from the valve cover **(see illustration)**.

6   Detach any remaining accessories as necessary.

7   The rear cover is encumbered by several items. Refer to Chapter 6 and remove the MAP sensor, then refer to Chapter 4 and disconnect the fuel lines **(see illustration)**.

8   Remove the valve cover bolts **(see illus-**

4.7 Access to the rear valve cover is by removing the heater hose (A), the MAP sensor (B), and the fuel lines (C)

4.8 Valve cover bolt locations (front cover shown)

2A

4.11 Coat the new triangular rubber seals with RTV before installing the valve cover

5.2a All of the rocker arms are bolted to a support, held to the head by four bolts (A) and five nuts (B) - remove the nuts/bolts and take the rockers/support out as an assembly

5.2b Keep the components in their original locations - if you must remove a rocker arm and fulcrum/bridge from the support, number the components so they can be returned to their original location

5.6 Inspect the pivots and wear surfaces of the rocker arms - apply moly-based lubricant to these points before reassembly

tration). **Note:** *Keep track of the location of nuts/studs used as valve cover fasteners, as well as wiring tabs, hose clamps or other brackets retained by the valve cover fasteners.*

9   Remove the valve cover. **Caution:** *Do not pry on the sealing flange. To do so may damage the mating surface, causing oil leaks. Tap on the sides of the cover with a rubber mallet until it pops loose.*

10   Thoroughly clean the mating surfaces, removing all traces of old gasket material. Use acetone or lacquer thinner and a clean rag to remove any traces of oil.

11   Remove the two triangular rubber plugs and clean their mounting points thoroughly. Apply RTV sealant to the mounting points and install new rubber triangles **(see illustration)**.

12   Install a new gasket in the cover and install it with cleaned bolts, tightening them to the torque listed in this Chapter's Specifications. Do not overtighten them, as the covers may be deformed.

13   Reinstall the remaining parts in the reverse order of removal.

14   Run the engine and check for leaks.

5   Rocker arms and pushrods - removal, inspection and installation

Removal

Refer to illustrations 5.2a and 5.2b

1   Refer to Section 4 and detach the valve cover(s) from the cylinder head(s).

2   Remove each of the rocker arm support bolts and nuts, then remove the rocker arm assembly as a unit, loosening them evenly **(see illustration)**. Place them in order **(see illustration)**. **Note:** *The rocker arms can be unbolted and removed from the support for individual replacement if necessary. Be sure to mark each rocker arm pivot Left or Right to insure proper installation.*

3   Remove the pushrods and store them in order to make sure they don't get mixed up during installation **(see illustration 5.2b)**.

Inspection

Refer to illustration 5.6

4   Check each rocker arm for wear, cracks and other damage, especially where the

pushrods and valve stems contact the rocker arm faces.

5   Make sure the hole at the pushrod end of each rocker arm is open.

6   Check each rocker arm pivot area for wear, cracks and galling. If the rocker arms are worn or damaged, replace them with new ones and use new pivots as well **(see illustration)**.

7   Inspect the pushrods for cracks and excessive wear at the ends. Roll each pushrod across a piece of plate glass to see if it's bent (if it wobbles, it's bent).

Installation

8   Lubricate the lower end of each pushrod with clean engine oil or moly-base grease and install them in their original locations. Make sure each pushrod seats completely in the lifter.

9   Apply moly-base grease to the ends of the valve stems and the upper ends of the pushrods before positioning the rocker arm assembly over the studs on the head.

10   Bolt the rocker arm supports to the head, tightening the nuts first, then the bolts. Leave the rocker arm bolts loose until each pushrod is seated under its rocker arm, then

6.8 Remove the bolts (A) and the brace between the strut towers - (B) is the cruise control actuator

6.15 Intake manifold mounting bolts - (A) indicates the two dowel pins that locate the manifold

6.18a At the four corners (arrows indicate two) where the heads and block come together, apply a dab of RTV sealant

6.18b The side gaskets usually come fitted with small plastic rivets that locate the gasket precisely on the cylinder head

tighten the rocker arm bolts to the torque in this Chapter's Specifications.
11 The remainder of assembly is the reverse of the disassembly process. Start the engine and check for leaks and valvetrain noise.

6 Intake manifold - removal and installation

Warning: *Wait until the engine is completely cool before beginning this procedure.*

Removal

Refer to illustrations 6.8 and 6.15

1 Relieve the fuel system pressure (see Chapter 4), then disconnect the cable from the negative terminal of the battery (see Chapter 5).
2 Drain the cooling system (see Chapter 1).
3 Remove the air filter housing (see Chapter 4).
4 Detach all coolant hoses from the intake manifold.
5 Label and disconnect any wiring and vacuum, emission and/or fuel lines which attach to the intake manifold. Detach the injector wires and remove the injectors and fuel rail (see Chapter 4).
6 Refer to Chapter 5 and remove the distributor, with the engine set to TDC (see Sec-

tion 3). Mark the orientation of the distributor body and where the rotor is pointing.
7 Refer to Chapter 1 and remove the drivebelt.
8 Remove the brace between the strut towers **(see illustration)**.
9 Remove the coolant reservoir (see Chapter 3).
10 Refer to Chapter 5 and unbolt the alternator and set it aside.
11 Refer to Chapter 10 and unbolt the power steering pump and set it aside.
12 Disconnect the cruise control actuator and remove it **(see illustration 6.8)**.
13 Remove the EGR solenoid and its bracket (see Chapter 6), if equipped.
14 Remove the valve covers (see Section 4), then remove the rocker arms and rocker arm supports as an assembly (see Section 5).
15 Remove the intake manifold bolts, keeping track of the location of each bolt **(see illustration)**. There are three lengths of intake manifold bolts. Identify and mark each of the 16 intake manifold bolts as to their exact location upon removal, to aid in later assembly.
16 When all of the bolts are removed, pry up the intake manifold at the ends. **Note:** *The intake manifold fits over a large dowel pin at each end of the block. When prying the manifold off, pry at both ends at the same time to pry the manifold straight up off the dowels* **(see illustration 6.15)**.

Installation

Refer to illustrations 6.18a, 6.18b and 6.18c

17 Clean the gasket surfaces of the intake manifold with a scraper followed by lacquer thinner or brake system cleaner. If the manifold was equipped with an EGR valve, clean any carbon buildup from the EGR passages with carburetor spray cleaner, using a screwdriver, drill bit or lengths of coat-hanger wire to chip out hard carbon. Make sure the whole passage is clear.
18 Position new side gaskets and ridge seals, using RTV sealant in the corners to

6.18c Glue the rubber end gaskets to the block with RTV sealant, then install the side gaskets and apply RTV in the corners where the side and end gaskets meet

7.7 Remove the two bolts at the power steering reservoir (A), and the two nuts (B) to remove this bracket

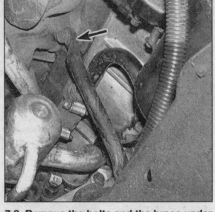

7.8 Remove the bolts and the brace under the front manifold

7.9 Remove the front manifold fasteners (arrows indicate five of the seven)

7.12 Remove the nuts at the rear pipe-to-manifold joint

7.13a Support the rear of the subframe with a floor jack, loosen the front subframe bolts (A), remove the rear subframe bolts (B), and lower the engine transaxle assembly just enough to withdraw the manifold - do not crawl underneath when the engine is supported only by the jack!

hold them in place **(see illustrations)**. Use plastic gasket retainer pins, if provided. Follow the gasket manufacturer's instructions and markings such as "UP", "TOP" or "FRONT". The end gaskets should be glued to the block, with the ends tucking into the pockets at the ends of the cylinder heads. Where the end gaskets and the side gaskets meet, apply a small dab of RTV sealant and a thin coat along the top surfaces that face the manifold.

19   Set the manifold into position until it starts onto the two dowels. Be sure all the bolt holes are lined up and start all the bolts by hand before tightening any of them (lightly oil the threads of the bolts before installation). **Note:** *Locate each bolt/stud in its original location. Putting the wrong-length bolt in a hole could cause a leak or stripped threads.*

20   Tighten the bolts in stages, following the appropriate sequence **(see illustration 6.15)** until the specified torque is reached.

21   The remainder of installation is the reverse of removal. Be sure to refill the cooling system and change the engine oil and filter (see Chapter 1), as coolant often gets into the oil during manifold removal.

22   Run the engine and check for fluid and vacuum leaks. Adjust the ignition timing, if the distributor was disturbed (see Chapter 1). Road test the vehicle, checking for proper operation of engine and accessories.

7   Exhaust manifolds - removal and installation

Removal

1   Allow the engine to cool completely.

2   Place protective covers on the fenders.

3   Disconnect the cable from the negative terminal of the battery (see Chapter 5).

4   Raise the vehicle and support it securely on jackstands.

5   Spray penetrating oil on the threads of fasteners holding the exhaust pipe(s) to the manifold(s) you wish to remove. Go on to the next steps, allowing the penetrating oil to soak in.

6   Remove the air cleaner and duct.

Front manifold

Refer to illustrations 7.7, 7.8 and 7.9

7   On front exhaust manifolds, remove the fasteners and take off the power steering reservoir bracket **(see illustration)**.

8   Under the front manifold, disconnect the

nuts holding the crossunder pipe to the manifold and remove the brace from the exhaust stud to the motor mount **(see illustration)**. **Note:** *If more working room is needed, refer to Chapter 3 and remove the engine cooling fan.*

9   Detach the heat shield from the front manifold, then remove the fasteners **(see illustration)**. Keep track of the locations of any stud/nut fasteners.

10   Remove the manifold(s) from the engine compartment.

Rear manifold

Refer to illustrations 7.12, 7.13a and 7.13b

11   Raise the vehicle and support it securely on jackstands.

12   Remove the nuts (after soaking with penetrating oil) securing the rear exhaust pipe to the rear manifold **(see illustration)**. Disconnect the oxygen sensor wire, if applicable.

13   Support the engine/transaxle assembly subframe with a heavy-duty floor jack. Loosen the front subframe bolts and remove the rear subframe bolts **(see illustration)**. Lower the subframe far enough so that the manifold can be withdrawn, then support the rear of the subframe with a jackstand. **Warning:** *Never place any part of your body under the vehicle or the engine/transaxle assembly*

7.13b Remove the nuts (arrows indicate four of the seven) on the rear manifold - the lower right nut in this photo shows the top of a brace that connects to the right-rear powertrain mount; remove the lower bolt from the brace at the mount

8.5 Remove the bolt attaching the dipstick tube to the front cylinder head

8.7a Cylinder head bolt TIGHTENING sequence on 1992 through 1994 models; loosen in the opposite sequence

8.7b Cylinder head bolt TIGHTENING sequence on 1995 models; loosen in the opposite sequence

2A

while it is supported only by a jack! Remove the manifold retaining nuts and lower the manifold out and to the left of the vehicle **(see illustration)**.

Installation

14   Thoroughly clean and inspect the sealing surfaces, removing all traces of old gasket material. Look for cracks and damaged threads. If the gasket was leaking, take the manifold to an automotive machine shop to inspect/correct for warpage.

15   If replacing the manifold, transfer all parts to the new unit. Using new gaskets (where applicable), install the manifold and start the bolts by hand. **Note:** *Apply graphite dry film lubricant to the exhaust manifold and cylinder head mating surfaces to prevent the exhaust manifold from cracking.*

16   Working from the center outward, tighten the bolts to the torque listed in this Chapter's Specifications.

17   Reinstall the remaining components in the reverse order of removal.

18   Run the engine and check for exhaust leaks.

8   Cylinder heads - removal and installation

Caution: *The engine must be completely cool when the heads are removed. Failure to allow the engine to cool off could result in head warpage.*

Removal

Refer to illustrations 8.5, 8.7a, 8.7b, 8.7c, 8.8, 8.9 and 8.10

1   Remove the intake manifold (see Section 6).

2   Remove the valve cover(s) as described in Section 4.

3   Remove the exhaust manifolds (see Section 7).

4   Unbolt the engine accessories and brackets as necessary and set them aside. See Chapter 5 for alternator removal. When removing the power steering pump and the drivebelt idler (see Chapter 10), leave the hoses attached and secure the unit in an upright position. The refrigerant lines should remain attached to the air conditioning com-

pressor (see Chapter 3). **Warning:** *The air conditioning system is under high pressure. Do not loosen any hose or fitting until the refrigerant has been discharged by an automotive air conditioning technician.*

5   Recheck to be sure nothing is still connected to the head(s) you intend to remove, including ground wires bolted to the heads, temperature senders or engine lifting brackets (one on each cylinder head). If you're removing the front cylinder head, unbolt the oil dipstick tube from the head **(see illustration)**.

6   Using a new gasket, outline the cylinders and bolt pattern on a piece of cardboard. Be sure to indicate the front of the engine for reference. Punch holes at the bolt locations.

7   Loosen the head bolts in 1/4-turn increments until they can be removed by hand. Work from bolt to bolt in a pattern that's the reverse of the tightening sequence **(see illustrations)**. Store the bolts in the cardboard holder as they are removed; this will insure the bolts are reinstalled in their original holes. **Note:** *The top (inner) row of head bolts are*

8.7c Use a deep socket to remove the inner row of studs

8.8 To dislodge the head, pry only at a casting protrusion, not between the block and head

8.9 When the heads are off, keep a cylinder liner holding tool in place to keep the liners from moving and losing their bottom O-ring seal

8.10 Scrape the block surface, vacuum up any debris, then clean the surface with lacquer thinner and a clean rag

studs, which will require a deep socket for removal **(see illustration)**.

8   Lift the head(s) off the engine. If excessive resistance is felt, do not pry between the head and block as damage to the mating surfaces may result. To dislodge the head, place a block of wood against the end of it and strike the wood with a hammer, or pry on a casting protrusion **(see illustration)**.

9   Store the head(s) on their sides to prevent damage to the gasket surface. **Note:** Install a cylinder liner holder, available at some auto parts stores and automotive tool suppliers, to the engine block to prevent the liners from shifting in the event the engine is turned over or disturbed **(see illustration)**.

Caution: If the crankshaft is turned while the cylinder heads are removed, the iron cylinder bore liners may lose their sealing at the O-rings in the block, causing water leaks later.

10   Use a gasket scraper to remove all traces of carbon and old gasket material, then clean the mating surfaces with lacquer thinner or acetone or brake system cleaner **(see illustration)**. If there's oil on the mating surfaces when the heads are installed, the gaskets may not seal properly and leaks may develop. When working on the block, cover the lifter valley with shop rags to keep out debris. Use a vacuum cleaner to remove any debris that falls into the cylinders. **Caution:** The block is aluminum - use care not to

gouge the surface when cleaning it, and do not disturb the liner-to-block sealing.

11   Check the block and head mating surfaces for nicks, deep scratches and other damage. If damage is slight, it can be removed with a file. If the gasket seemed to be leaking, have the head(s) checked for cracks and warpage by an automotive machine shop. Surface damage or warpage can usually be corrected by machining. Cracks normally require replacement of the head.

Installation

Refer to illustration 8.13

12   Use a tap of the correct size to chase the threads in the head bolt holes. Mount each bolt in a vise and run a die down the threads to remove any corrosion and restore the threads. Dirt, corrosion, sealant and damaged threads will affect torque readings. This kind of fastener and thread cleaning is especially important on the aluminum block in the vehicles covered by this manual.

13   Most gaskets have "THIS SIDE UP" stamped into them, but follow the gasket manufacturer's instructions for sealant to use, if any. Most composition gaskets are installed without sealant. Position a new gasket over the dowel pins in the block **(see illustration)**.

8.13 Install the new head gasket, locating it over the dowel pins on the block

9.5 Remove the bolt in the center of the crankshaft damper while using a chain or strap wrench to keep the damper from turning - if using a chain wrench, protect the damper's grooves with a leather strap or a piece of old drivebelt wrapped around the pulley

9.6 Use a three-jaw puller to remove the damper from the crankshaft on 1991 and later models (the jaws must grasp the hub - not the outer circumference of the damper)

9.7 Use a screwdriver or seal removal tool (shown) to pull out the front seal, being careful not to nick the crankshaft surface

14   Be sure the head bolt holes are clean. Apply a light coating of engine assembly lube on the threads and under the bolt heads. Head bolts that enter water jacket areas should be coated with a non-hardening sealant such as Permatex No. 2.

15   Install the bolts in their original locations and tighten them finger tight. Follow the recommended sequence **(see illustrations 8.7a and 8.7b)** and tighten the bolts to the torque values listed in this Chapter's Specifications.

16   The remaining installation steps are the reverse of removal.

17   Add coolant, change the engine oil and filter (see Chapter 1), then start the engine and check carefully for leaks.

9   Crankshaft front oil seal - replacement

Timing cover in place

Refer to illustrations 9.5, 9.6 and 9.7

1   Remove the drivebelt (see Chapter 1).

2   Loosen the bolts on the right front wheel, raise the vehicle and support it securely on jackstands. Remove the right front wheel.

3   On some models, there isn't enough room between the engine and the right fenderwell for the damper to be removed. When this is the case, raise the vehicle and support it securely on jackstands, support the engine/transaxle subframe with a heavy-duty floor jack and loosen the rear subframe bolts. Remove the front subframe bolts (see Chapter 2C). Using a floor jack, lower the engine/transaxle subframe several inches, until the crankshaft damper is clear of the fenderwell. **Warning:** *Do not place your body under the engine at any time that it is supported only by a jack!*

4   Use a strap wrench or chain wrench

over the damper to hold it while the bolts are removed. If a chain wrench is used, place a rubber strap, a length of old leather belt or a length of old drivebelt between the damper grooves and the chain to prevent damage.

5   Use the chain wrench as described above to hold the damper while you use a long breaker bar to remove the center bolt of the damper **(see illustration)**. **Caution:** *It will take lots of leverage and force to remove this bolt unless you have an air-powered impact wrench. Be certain that the engine is securely locked from turning (an assistant is helpful) while you use both hands and a long breaker bar to loosen the bolt. Make sure your hands are not going to hit anything when the bolt does break loose.*

6   Attach a puller to the damper and draw it off the crankshaft. Be careful not to drop it as it comes free. A gear puller that grabs the hub must be used **(see illustration)**.

7   Carefully pull the seal out of the cover with a seal removal tool or pry it out with a large screwdriver **(see illustration)**. Be careful not to distort the cover or scratch the wall of

the seal bore (cover the screwdriver tip with electrical tape to avoid nicking the crankshaft). It's a good idea to apply penetrating oil to the seal-to-cover joint and allow it to soak in before attempting to pull the seal out.

8   Clean the bore to remove any old seal material and corrosion. Position the new seal in the bore with the open end of the seal facing IN. A small amount of oil applied to the outer edge of the new seal will make installation easier.

9   Drive the seal squarely into the bore with a large socket and hammer until it's completely seated **(see illustration)**. Select a socket that's the same outside diameter as the seal (a section of pipe can be used if a socket isn't available). **Caution:** *If the crankshaft has a Woodruff key in place, the socket used must be big enough in diameter to clear the key while driving on the seal*. Proceed to Step 13.

Timing cover removed

Refer to illustrations 9.10 and 9.12

10   Use a punch or screwdriver and hammer to drive the seal out of the cover from the

9.9 Use an appropriate-size socket to drive the new seal squarely into the front cover, to the same depth as the original seal

9.10 Support the front cover on wood blocks and drive the seal out from the backside with a hammer and punch - don't distort the seal bore

9.12 Use a block of wood to squarely drive in the new seal

10.6a Remove the front cover lower bolts and pull off the cover - the front pan bolts must be loosened (arrows also indicate the two pan bolts that must be removed)

10.6b Remove the upper front cover bolts

back side. Support the cover as close to the seal bore as possible **(see illustration)**. Be careful not to distort the cover or scratch the wall of the seal bore. If the engine has accumulated a lot of miles, apply penetrating oil to the seal-to-cover joint on each side and allow it to soak in before attempting to drive the seal out.

11   Clean the bore to remove any old seal material and corrosion. Support the cover on blocks of wood and position the new seal in the bore with the open end of the seal facing IN. A small amount of oil applied to the outer edge of the new seal will make installation easier.

12   Drive the seal into the bore with a wood block and hammer until it's completely seated **(see illustration)**. Proceed to the next Step.

Damper installation

13   Apply anti-seize compound to the snout of the crankshaft and multi-purpose grease or clean engine oil to the lips of the seal in the front cover, then install the damper, making sure the keyway in the hub is aligned with the key on the crankshaft.

14   The damper retaining bolt can be used

to pull the damper onto the crankshaft. When tightening the damper bolt, use the chain wrench and long breaker bar as described in Step 5.

10   Timing chain - removal, inspection and installation

Warning: *Wait until the engine is completely cool before beginning this procedure.*

Removal

Refer to illustrations 10.6a, 10.6b, 10.8, 10.9 and 10.10

1   Disconnect the cable from the negative terminal of the battery (see Chapter 5). Remove the battery.

2   Refer to Chapter 3 and remove the coolant reservoir.

3   Drain the cooling system and disconnect the radiator hoses, heater hose (where applicable) and the small by-pass hose (where applicable).

4   Loosen the bolts on the water pump

pulley, then remove the drivebelt (see Chapter 1). Remove the pulley.

5   Remove the crankshaft damper (see Section 9).

6   Remove the nuts and bolts that attach the cover to the engine, then pull the cover free **(see illustrations)**. If it's stuck, knock it loose with a hammer and a wood block. Don't pry between the mating surfaces, or oil leaks may result. Keep track of the location of the studs. **Note:** *The water pump and the water pump inlet (on the back of the front cover) can remain bolted to the front cover during removal.*

7   Thoroughly clean all gasket mating surfaces (do not allow the old gasket material to fall into the oil pan), then wipe them with a cloth soaked in lacquer thinner. Clean sealant and gasket material from the exposed front edges of the oil pan.

8   Slide the oil slinger off of the end of the crankshaft **(see illustration)**.

9   Turn the crankshaft until the marks on the camshaft and crankshaft sprockets are perfectly aligned **(see illustration)**. DO NOT attempt to remove either sprocket or the chain until this is done. Also, do not turn the camshaft or the crankshaft after the sprockets are removed.

10.8 Slide the oil slinger from the crankshaft, noting which way it was installed

10.9 Timing gear marks aligned at TDC for number 1 cylinder

10.10 Remove the camshaft thrust bearing - it snaps out of the camshaft gear

10.14 If a new timing chain set is installed, the new crankshaft sprocket may have to be tapped on with a large socket and hammer - make sure the keyway is aligned and that the socket doesn't hit the Woodruff key

11.3a Remove the driveplate cover **bolts** from below . . .

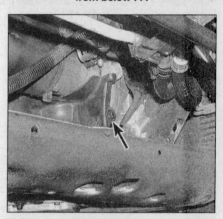

11.3b . . . and the one bolt near the **starter motor from the front**

10   Remove the camshaft thrust bearing and the bolt securing the sprocket to the end of the camshaft **(see illustration)**.

11   Generally speaking, the camshaft sprocket and the timing chain can be slipped off the crankshaft sprocket together. If resistance is encountered, it may be necessary to use two screwdrivers to carefully pry the sprocket off of the camshaft. If resistance is encountered on a crankshaft sprocket, a gear puller will be required.

12   If the crankshaft and the camshaft are not disturbed while the timing chain and sprockets are out of place, then installation can begin with Step 13. If the engine is completely dismantled, or if the crankshaft or camshaft are disturbed while the timing chain is off, then the engine must be positioned at TDC before the timing chain and sprockets are installed (see Section 3).

Installation

Refer to illustration 10.14

13   Align the hole in the camshaft sprocket with the dowel pin in the end of the camshaft, then slip the sprocket onto the end of the camshaft to align the timing marks **(see illustration 10.9)**. Note: *When the camshaft and crankshaft timing marks are aligned, the engine is positioned at TDC compression for cylinder number 1.*

14   Slip the crankshaft sprocket onto the end of the crankshaft (make sure the key and

keyway are properly aligned), then turn the crankshaft until the timing mark on the sprocket is pointed straight up **(see illustration)**.

15   Now remove the camshaft sprocket and lay the timing chain over the sprocket. Slip the other end of the chain under the crankshaft sprocket (keep the timing marks aligned as this is done) and reinstall the camshaft sprocket.

16   Install the camshaft sprocket bolt, then recheck the alignment of the timing marks.

17   Tighten the camshaft sprocket bolt to the torque listed in this Chapter's Specifications, then install the camshaft thrust bearing. If the original bearing looks at all worn, install a new one.

18   Be sure to clean the mating surfaces of the front cover and cylinder block, and install a new gasket, using RTV sealant around the water passage holes. **Note:** *Be sure to reinstall the oil slinger on the crankshaft before installing the front cover.*

19   Apply a bead of RTV sealant to the front of the oil pan, especially where the oil pan meets the block.

20   Install the water pump and water pump inlet to the cover with new gaskets (if removed from cover).

21   Install the cover, aligning it over the two

dowels in the block, and install all the bolts finger-tight.

22   Tighten all bolts to the torque values listed in this Chapter's Specifications and install all components in the reverse order of removal. Apply lubricant to the front hub seal before installing the crankshaft damper (see Section 9).

11   Oil pan - removal and installation

Warning: *Do not place any part of your body below the engine when it is supported solely by a jack or hoist.*

Removal

Refer to illustrations 11.3a, 11.3b and 11.5

1   Disconnect the cable from the negative terminal of the battery (see Chapter 5) and drain the engine oil (see Chapter 1). Allow the engine to cool before removing the oil pan.

2   Raise the vehicle and support it securely on jackstands.

3   Remove the driveplate cover bolts and the cover **(see illustrations)**.

4   Remove the exhaust crossunder pipe (see Chapter 4).

5   Remove the oil pan bolts **(see illustration)**. Note the different sizes and their locations.

11.5 Remove the oil pan bolts (not all bolts are visible in this photo)

2A

11.8a   Apply a bead of RTV sealant to the joints between the block and the front cover . . .

11.8b   . . . and where the rear main cap meets the block

6   Remove the oil pan by tilting it down at the rear and then working the front clear of the subframe. It may be necessary to use a rubber mallet to break the seal - don't pry between the pan and the block!

Installation

Refer to illustrations 11.8a and 11.8b

7   Before installing, thoroughly clean the gasket sealing surfaces on the engine block and on the oil pan. All sealant and gasket material must be removed.

8   Apply a bead of RTV sealant to the corners where the block meets the rear main cap and the front cover **(see illustrations)**.

9   Apply a continuous bead of RTV sealant to the pan, making sure the bead travels around the inside of the bolt holes. Install the pan while the sealant is still wet.

10   Lift the pan into position and install all bolts finger-tight. There is no specific order for tightening the bolts; however, it is a good policy to tighten the end bolts first, and all of the bolts should be started before any are tightened to Specifications.

11   The remainder of installation is the reverse of the removal procedure. Allow at least an hour after installing the pan for the sealant to cure, then fill the engine with the correct grade and quantity of oil (see Chapter 1), start the engine and check for leaks.

12   Oil pump - removal, inspection and installation

Removal

Refer to illustration 12.2

1   Remove the oil pan as described in Section 11.

2   Remove the bolts securing the oil pump assembly to the main bearing cap **(see illustration)**. Remove the oil pump with its pickup tube and screen as an assembly from the engine block. Once the pump is removed, the oil pump driveshaft can be withdrawn from the block.

Inspection

3   Remove the pump cover and fill the cavity with engine oil. If it slowly leaks out, this is an indication that the pressure relief valve is not closing properly.

4   Inspect the pump housing and cover for signs of wear or debris. Check the cover with a straightedge for flatness.

5   Because of the critical importance of the oil pump and the risk of engine damage if an overhauled pump doesn't perform like new, we do not recommend overhauling the oil pump on these models. Always replace the pump with a new unit.

Installation

Refer to illustration 12.6

6   To install, slip the driveshaft extension into the oil pump driveshaft, with the hex into the pump **(see illustration)**. **Note:** *Pour clean engine oil into the pickup and turn the driveshaft to prime the pump.*

7   Install new O-rings at each end of the oil pump's supply tube (at the pump and the block).

8   Move the pump assembly into position and align the extension with the lower end of the distributor. The distributor drives the oil pump, so it is essential that these two components mate properly. The driveshaft extension fits into the slot in the distributor drive gear.

12.2 The oil pump is bolted to the rear main bearing cap - remove the mounting bolts and nut

12.6 Lube the gears in the pump, install a new gasket on the pump body and install the hex end of the driveshaft into the drive gear in the pump

13.3 Mark the driveplate with reference to the end of the crankshaft before removal - hold the driveplate by jamming a large screwdriver through one of the holes and against the block, while removing the driveplate mounting bolts

14.2 Use a seal removal tool or a screwdriver to pry out the old seal - tape the screwdriver tip to protect the crankshaft (typical application shown)

2A

9   Install the bolts and tighten them securely. Make sure the oil pump screen is parallel with the oil pan rails of the block. The screen must be in this position to fit into the oil pan properly.

10   Install the oil pan (see Section 11). Refill the crankcase with oil (see Chapter 1), run the engine and check for leaks.

13   Driveplate - removal and installation

Refer to illustration 13.3

Removal

1   Refer to Chapter 7 and remove the transaxle.

2   Use a scribe or a marking pen to draw a line from the driveplate to the end of the crankshaft for correct alignment during reinstallation.

3   Remove the bolts that secure the driveplate to the crankshaft rear flange. If difficulty is experienced in removing the bolts due to movement of the crankshaft, wedge a screwdriver to keep the driveplate from turning **(see illustration)**.

4   Remove the driveplate from the crankshaft flange, noting the location and installed direction of any spacer rings. **Caution:** *Wear gloves or protect your hands with rags; the ring gear teeth can be sharp.*

5   Clean any grease or oil from the driveplate. Check for cracked or broken starter ring gear teeth. Lay the driveplate on a flat surface and use a straightedge to check for warpage.

6   Clean the mating surfaces of the driveplate and the crankshaft.

Installation

7   Position the driveplate against the crankshaft, matching the alignment marks made during removal. Before installing the bolts, apply a non-hardening thread-locking compound to the threads.

8   Wedge a screwdriver through the driveplate or into the ring gear teeth to keep the crankshaft from turning. Tighten the bolts to the torque listed in this Chapter's Specifications in two or three steps, working in a crisscross pattern.

9   The remainder of installation is the reverse of the removal procedure.

14   Rear main oil seal - replacement

Refer to illustration 14.2

1   Refer to Section 13 and remove the driveplate.

2   Using a thin screwdriver or a seal removal tool, carefully remove the oil seal from the engine block **(see illustration)**. Be very careful not to damage the crankshaft surface while prying the seal out.

3   Clean the bore in the block and the seal contact surface on the crankshaft. Check the seal contact surface on the crankshaft for scratches and nicks that could damage the new seal and cause oil leaks - if the crankshaft is damaged, the only alternative is a new or different crankshaft. Inspect the seal bore for nicks or scratches. Carefully smooth it with a fine file if necessary, but don't nick the crankshaft in the process.

4   A special tool, available at most auto parts stores, is recommended to install the new seal. Lubricate the lips of the seal with clean engine oil. Slide the seal onto the mandrel until the dust lip bottoms squarely against the collar of the tool. **Note:** *If the tool isn't available, carefully work the seal over the crankshaft and tap it into place squarely and evenly with a hammer and large-diameter socket or length of pipe.*

5   Align the dowel pin on the tool with the dowel pin hole in the crankshaft and attach the tool to the crankshaft by hand-tightening the bolts.

6   Turn the tool handle until the collar bottoms against the case, seating the seal.

7   Loosen the tool handle, then remove the

bolts and the tool.

8   Check that the seal is installed evenly, and to the same depth as the original.

9   The remainder of installation is the reverse of removal.

15   Engine mounts - check and replacement

Warning: *A special engine support fixture should be used to support the engine during repair operations. These fixtures are available from equipment rental yards. Improper lifting methods or devices are hazardous and could result in severe injury or death. DO NOT place any part of your body under the engine/transaxle assembly when it's supported only by a jack. Failure of the lifting device could result in serious injury or death.*

1   Engine mounts seldom require attention, but broken or deteriorated mounts should be replaced immediately or the added strain placed on the driveline components may cause damage or wear. The 4.9L V8 engine has four main engine mounts, plus a torque strut.

Check

2   During the check, the engine must be raised slightly to remove the weight from the mounts.

3   Raise the vehicle and support it securely on jackstands, then position a jack under the engine oil pan. Place a large block of wood between the jack head and the oil pan, then carefully raise the engine just enough to take the weight off the mounts. **Warning:** *DO NOT place any part of your body under the engine when it's supported only by a jack!*

4   Check the mounts to see if the rubber is cracked, hardened or separated from the metal plates. Sometimes the rubber will split right down the center.

5   Check for relative movement between the mount plates and the engine or frame (use a large screwdriver or prybar to attempt

15.8a Right-front mount - remove the two nuts at the engine bracket and two nuts below the subframe

15.8b The right-rear mount is attached at the top with nuts (nuts are hidden here, but arrow shows where) . . .

15.8c . . . and below at the subframe

15.14a On some models, the transaxle end of the powertrain is supported by two mounts, arrow indicates the left-front

15.14b The left-rear is mounted to the engine bracket and the subframe

15.14c Instead of two left-side mounts, some models have an aluminum "cradle" attached to the transaxle, which is isolated from the chassis by a single mount - remove the upper nuts (A) at the cradle, then the lower nuts (B) at the subframe

to move the mounts). If movement is noted, lower the engine and tighten the mount fasteners.

6   Rubber preservative may be applied to the mounts to slow deterioration.

Replacement

7   Disconnect the cable from the negative terminal of the battery (see Chapter 5), then raise the vehicle and support it securely on jackstands.

Front, rear and right-side mounts

Refer to illustrations 15.8a, 15.8b and 15.8c

8   Raise the engine slightly with a jack or hoist. Install an engine support fixture as described in the **Warning** above. Remove the fasteners and detach the mount from the frame bracket **(see illustrations)**.

9   Remove the mount-to-block bracket bolts/nuts and detach the mount.

10   Installation is the reverse of the removal procedure.

Left-side mounts

Refer to illustrations 15.14a, 15.14b and 15.14c

11   The 1995 Seville and all DeVille models are equipped with two left-side mounts, a front and a rear, while 1992 through 1994 Seville models have a "cradle" attached to the left end of the transaxle and a single mount between this cradle and the subframe.

12   The left front mount on 1995 Seville and all DeVille models is attached to the transaxle near the engine/transaxle juncture, with the left-rear mount between the rear of the transaxle and the subframe.

13   Support the engine with an engine support fixture.

14   Remove the lower mounting nuts at the subframe and the nuts at the bracket to remove the mounts **(see illustrations)**.

15   Installation is the reverse of the removal procedure.

Engine torque strut

16   The engine torque strut mounts between the engine and the upper radiator support on the body. It can be replaced without jacking up the engine, by removing the through-bolts and the bolts attaching the strut to the mounts on the radiator support. **Note:** *When reinstalling this mount, you may have to use a prybar to rotate the engine toward or away from the radiator to align the through-bolts.*

17   Installation is the reverse of removal. Use thread-locking compound on the threads and be sure to tighten everything securely.

Chapter 2 Part B
4.6L V8 engine

Contents

2B

Specifications

General

Engine designation	VIN Code 9 or Y
Displacement	4.6 liters (279 cubic inches)
Cylinder numbers (timing chain end-to-transaxle end)	
Front (left) side	2-4-6-8
Rear (right) side	1-3-5-7
Firing order	1-2-7-3-4-5-6-8

Warpage limits

Intake manifold	0.005 inch
Exhaust manifolds	0.020 inch

Torque specifications

Ft-lbs (unless otherwise indicated)

Camshaft seal retainer bolts	
1993 through 1998 models	10 in-lbs
1999 and later models	27 in-lbs
Intake manifold bolts	
1993 and 1994 models **(see illustration 4.24)**	
Intake manifold bolts	
Step 1	71 in-lbs
Step 2	Tighten an additional 120-degrees
1995 and later models	89 in-lbs
Exhaust manifold bolts	18 to 25

Cylinder and coil terminal locations (only 1999 and earlier models are equipped with an ignition coil pack like the one shown here; later models have an ignition coil assembly mounted in the top of each valve cover

Torque specifications (continued)

Ft-lbs (unless otherwise indicated)

Crankshaft damper bolt
  1993 models
    Step 1... 105
    Step 2... Tighten an additional 120-degrees
  1994 through 1996 models
    Step 1... 44
    Step 2... Tighten an additional 120-degrees
  1997 and later models
    Step 1... 37
    Step 2... Tighten an additional 120-degrees
Driveplate bolts*
  Step 1 .... 132 in-lbs
  Step 2 .... Tighten an additional 50-degrees
Front cover bolts... 89 in-lbs
Drivebelt Idler pulley bolt 37
Drivebelt tensioner bolt... 37
Valve cover bolts .... 89 in-lbs
Oil pump mounting bolts
  1993 models
    Step 1 .... 84 in-lbs
    Step 2... Tighten an additional 35-degrees
  1994 and later models
    Step 1 .... 89 in-lbs
    Step 2... 20
Oil pan bolts.. 89 in-lbs
Oil strainer mounting nut/bolt
  Bolt .... 89 in-lbs
  Nut.. 18
Engine/transaxle subframe mounting bolts
  1993 through 1999 models 74
  2000 and later models... 141

* Apply thread locking compound to the threads prior to installation

---

1   General information

This Part of Chapter 2 is devoted to in-vehicle repair procedures for the 4.6L V8 Northstar engine. The 4.6L V8 engine is designed with a Double-OverHead-Cam (DOHC) arrangement with four valves per cylinder (32 in all).

All information concerning engine removal and installation and engine block and cylinder head overhaul can be found in Part C of this Chapter.

The following repair procedures are based on the assumption that the engine is installed in the vehicle. If the engine has been removed from the vehicle and mounted on a stand, many of the steps outlined in this Part of Chapter 2 will not apply.

The Cadillac 4.6L V8 Northstar engine is an all-aluminum engine with a die-cast aluminum alloy engine block. The block is a two piece design with the lower section split at the crankshaft center line. The upper section is equipped with cast iron cylinder liners. The cylinder heads are cast aluminum with two intake valves and two exhaust valves for each cylinder. Because the engine is mostly aluminum, particular care must be taken to accommodate the characteristics of this metal. Bolts that thread into aluminum must not be over-tightened or the threads may be damaged. When cleaning the gasket surfaces of the aluminum, use soft wire brushes or dull scrapers. Blow out all debris from the bolt holes to avoid inaccurate torque readings.

The Specifications included in this Part of Chapter 2 apply only to the procedures contained in this Part. Additional specifications can be found in Chapter 2, Part C.

2   Repair operations possible with the engine in the vehicle

1   Many major repair operations can be accomplished without removing the engine from the vehicle. Clean the engine compartment and the exterior of the engine with some type of degreaser before any work is done. It will make the job easier and help keep dirt out of the internal areas of the engine.

2   Depending on the components involved, it may be helpful to remove the hood to improve access to the engine as repairs are performed (refer to Chapter 11 if necessary). Cover the fenders to prevent damage to the paint. Special pads are available, but an old bedspread or blanket will also work.

3   If vacuum, exhaust, oil or coolant leaks develop, indicating a need for gasket or seal replacement, the repairs can generally be made with the engine in the vehicle. The intake and exhaust manifold gaskets, crankshaft oil seals and valve cover gaskets are all accessible with the engine in place.

4   Exterior engine components, such as the intake and exhaust manifolds, the water pump, the starter motor, the alternator and the fuel system components can be removed for repair with the engine in place.

5   There are no repair procedures for timing chains and sprockets, camshafts and cylinder heads in this Chapter. These repair procedures are not included in this Chapter because of the special tools required and the level of difficulty. Have the vehicle repaired by a dealer service department or other qualified automotive repair facility.

3   Valve covers - removal and installation

Removal

Refer to illustration 3.2

1   Disconnect the cable from the negative terminal of the battery (see Chapter 5).

3.2 Remove the two nuts and lift the intake manifold service cover from the engine - there are two rubber alignment grommets under the rear section of the cover

2   On 1995 and later models, remove the intake manifold service cover **(see illustration)**. **Caution:** *On 1993 and 1994 models, do not loosen the four intake manifold bolts. If the four bolts for the intake manifold are loosened, the intake manifold may leak vacuum.*

3   Remove the spark plug wires (1993 through 1999 models) or the coil/ignition modules (2000 and later models) from the valve covers (see Chapter 5). Remove the spark plug boots from the valve cover(s).

4   Disconnect any vacuum lines or wires that may interfere with the removal process. Mark them carefully to insure proper reassembly.

Front (left) valve cover

Refer to illustrations 3.13, 3.16 and 3.17

5   Drain the coolant from the radiator and the engine (see Chapter 1).

6   Remove the upper radiator hose (see Chapter 3).

7   Disconnect the PCV tube from the valve cover (see Chapter 6).

8   On early models, remove the EGR pipe (see Chapter 6).

3.13 Remove the two bolts/studs from the coolant crossover housing and separate the drivebelt tensioner from the housing

9   On early models, disconnect the wiring harness connector at the alternator. Remove the alternator harness from the valve cover and position it off to the side.

10   Remove the cooling fans (see Chapter 3).

11   Remove the left and right torque struts from the engine compartment, if equipped (see Section 15).

12   Remove the water pump drivebelt (see Chapter 1).

13   Remove the water pump drivebelt tensioner **(see illustration)**.

14   Remove the water pump pulley using a special tool (see Section 8).

15   Remove the camshaft seal retainer screws (see Section 8).

16   Remove the valve cover retaining bolts **(see illustration)**, then detach the cover. If the cover is stuck to the head, bump the end with a wood block and a hammer to jar it loose. If that doesn't work, try to slip a flexible putty knife between the head and cover to break the seal. **Caution:** *Don't pry at the cover-to-head joint or damage to the sealing surfaces may occur, leading to oil leaks after the cover is reinstalled.*

17   Lift the front (timing chain end) of the valve cover up and pivot the entire valve cover over the water pump drive shaft **(see illustration)**.

18   Remove the valve cover from the engine compartment.

Rear (right) valve cover

19   Disconnect the exhaust system Y pipe at the catalytic converter (see Chapter 4).

20   Raise the vehicle and support it securely on jackstands.

1993 through 1999 models

21   Remove the brace from the engine compartment strut towers, if equipped.

22   Remove the left and right torque struts from the engine compartment, if equipped (see Section 15).

23   Remove the purge control solenoid from the rear of the valve cover (see Chapter 6).

24   Support the front of the engine using a floor jack and remove the front subframe mounting bolts.

25   Lower the engine/transaxle assembly to provide room at the rear of the engine compartment for the valve cover removal. Secure the front of the engine/transaxle assembly with floor jacks while the valve cover procedure is performed. Proceed to Step 27.

2000 and later models

26   Remove the secondary AIR vent solenoid connector and the AIR assembly (see Chapter 6) from the valve cover. Proceed to Step 27.

All models

27   Remove the valve cover retaining bolts, then detach the cover. If the cover is stuck to the head, bump the end with a wood block and a hammer to jar it loose. If that doesn't work, try to slip a flexible putty knife between the head and cover to break the seal. **Caution:** *Don't pry at the cover-to-head joint or damage to the sealing surfaces may occur, leading to oil leaks after the cover is reinstalled.*

28   Remove the valve cover from the engine compartment.

2B

3.16 Valve cover bolt locations on the front (left) bank valve cover

3.17 Angle the valve cover over the water pump drive shaft

3.29 Use a screwdriver to pry the locking tabs on the valve cover gasket

1 *Circular rubber seals*
2 *Locking tangs*

3.31 Be sure the locking tang snap fits over the valve cover edge

Installation

Refer to illustrations 3.29 and 3.31

29   Remove the valve cover gasket and the valve cover circular seals **(see illustration)**.
30   The mating surfaces of the cylinder head and cover must be clean when the cover is installed. Use a gasket scraper to remove all traces of sealant and old gasket material, then clean the mating surfaces with lacquer thinner or acetone. If there's residue or oil on the mating surfaces when the cover is installed, oil leaks may develop.
31   Position new rubber circular seals into the valve cover(s) and install the new valve cover gasket **(see illustration)**.

Front (left) valve cover

32   Insert the intake camshaft end through the hole in the valve cover.
33   Position the valve cover by pivoting the valve cover down and to the left allowing it to clear the drive chain. Align the valve cover bolt holes with the holes in the cylinder head.
34   Install the valve cover bolts and tighten them to the torque listed in this Chapter's Specifications.
35   Install the camshaft seal retainer and tighten the bolts to the torque listed in this Chapter's Specifications.
36   Install the water pump pulley using a special tool (see Section 8).
37   Reinstall the remaining parts, run the engine and check for oil leaks.

Rear (right) valve cover

38   Guide the valve cover into place and align the bolt holes with the holes in the cylinder head.
39   Install the valve cover bolts and tighten them to the torque listed in this Chapter's Specifications.
40   Raise the engine/transaxle subframe and install the mounting bolts (1999 and earlier models).
41   Install the torque struts, if equipped (see Section 15).
42   Reinstall the remaining parts, run the engine and check for oil leaks.

4   Intake manifold - removal and installation

Warning: *The engine must be completely cool before beginning this procedure.*
Note: *1993 and 1994 models are equipped with an EGR distribution assembly that includes the multi-function spacer, the insulator, the vacuum collector and the EGR distribution plate. The assembly is sealed top and bottom by a formed silicone gasket that can be reused.*

Removal

1   Disconnect the cable from the negative terminal of the battery (see Chapter 5).
2   On 1995 and later models, remove the intake manifold service cover. **Caution:** *On 1993 and 1994 models, do not loosen the intake manifold service cover bolts. The intake manifold will be removed with the service cover attached. If the fuel injectors must be serviced, refer to Chapter 4 for the intake manifold service cover removal, installation and torque sequence.*
3   Disconnect the accelerator cable and the cruise control cable from the throttle body actuator (see Chapter 4).
4   Relieve the fuel pressure (see Chapter 4).
5   Disconnect the fuel inlet and return hoses at the intake manifold (see Chapter 4).
6   Remove the air intake duct from the throttle body (see Chapter 4).
7   Remove the air filter housing, throttle body (1995 through 1999 models) and fuel injectors (see Chapter 4). **Note:** *On 1995 through 1999 models, the throttle body and spacer must be removed to access the fuel rail. Refer to Chapter 4 for the throttle body, spacer and fuel rail removal procedures.*
8   Remove the transaxle vent hose and the transaxle shift cable at the bracket (see Chapter 7).
9   Disconnect the throttle position sensor (TPS) and the IAC valve connectors (see Chapter 6).
10   Drain the coolant into a clean container (see Chapter 1).

1993 through 1999 models

11   Remove the engine compartment brace from the strut towers, if equipped.
12   Disconnect the EGR pipe and the PCV hose from the intake manifold (see Chapter 6).

4.16 Intake manifold details on a 2000 model

1   *Intake boot clamp*
2   *Fuel rail*
3   *Coolant tube*
4   *Intake manifold front mounting bolts (rear bolts not visible)*

4.18 Lift the intake manifold from the engine as a single unit

4.24 Intake manifold bolt tightening sequence -
1993 and 1994 models

13   Label and remove the ignition wires from the coil packs (see Chapter 5).

2000 and later models
Refer to illustration 4.16

14   Disconnect the coil module connectors from each coil/module assembly (see Chapter 5).
15   Disconnect the vacuum tubes from the AIR solenoid (see Chapter 6).
16   Loosen the intake manifold duct clamp **(see illustration)**.

All models
Refer to illustration 4.18

17   Clearly label, then detach all remaining wires, hoses and brackets still attached to the intake manifold.
18   Remove the mounting nuts and bolts, then detach the intake manifold from the cylinder heads **(see accompanying illustration and illustration 4.24)**.
19   If it's stuck, don't pry between the gasket mating surfaces or damage may result. Make several passes to insure that the intake manifold is separated from the cylinder heads evenly to avoid damage to the manifold surfaces.

Installation
Refer to illustration 4.24

20   Inspect the intake manifold gaskets:
a) On 1993 and 1994 models, the intake manifold gaskets include an EGR distribution assembly that includes the multi-function spacer (the insulator, the vacuum collector and the EGR distribution plate). The assembly is sealed top and bottom by formed silicone gaskets that can be reused if they aren't damaged. The upper gasket is mounted to the top of the spacer, tightly sealing the intake ports. The lower gasket mounts over the intake ports on the cylinder heads.
b) On 1995 through 1999 models, the intake manifold carrier gaskets are attached to the intake manifold by a snap-lock mechanism. The gasket will

remain on the intake manifold when it is lifted from the cylinder heads. This type of gasket is reusable. The gasket should be replaced only when the rubber seals or the plastic housing is damaged.
c) On 2000 and later models, the intake manifold gaskets must be replaced when the intake manifold has been removed for service.
21   Use a scraper to remove all traces of old gasket material and sealant from the intake manifold and cylinder heads, then clean the mating surfaces with lacquer thinner or acetone. Install new gaskets.
22   Position the intake manifold on the engine:
a) On 1993 and 1994 models, make sure the multi-function spacer and the upper and lower gaskets are mounted properly to the cylinder heads with the corresponding stud/holes in the cylinder heads.
a) On 1994 through 1999 models, lower the intake manifold assembly evenly onto the cylinder heads. Align the mounting studs and the bolt holes with the corresponding stud/holes in the cylinder heads.
b) On 2000 and later models, lower the intake manifold into the intake duct boot first, make sure that it mates with the intake manifold and then lower the front of the intake manifold onto the cylinder heads. Align the mounting studs and the bolt holes with the corresponding stud/holes in the cylinder heads.
23   Make sure the gaskets haven't shifted and install the nuts and the bolts. Start with the inner bolts first and work your way to the outer bolts on the manifold. Make several passes to insure that the intake manifold is mated to the cylinder heads evenly to avoid damage to the cylinder head and manifold surfaces.
24   Tighten the nuts and bolts to the torque listed in this Chapter's Specifications:
a) On 1993 and 1994 models, a special torque sequence for tightening the

intake manifold is required **(see illustration)**. *Follow the correct sequence and the correct torque values.*
b) On 1995 and later models, tighten the intake manifold bolts by working from the center out towards the ends to avoid warping the manifold.
25   On 2000 and later models, tighten the duct clamp securely.
26   Install the remaining parts in the reverse order of removal.
27   Refill the cooling system and change the engine oil and filter (see Chapter 1). Run the engine and check for fuel, vacuum and coolant leaks.

5   Exhaust manifolds - removal and installation

Warning: *The engine must be completely cool before beginning this procedure.*

Removal

1   Disconnect the cable from the negative terminal of the battery (see Chapter 5).

Front (left) exhaust manifold

2   Raise the vehicle and support it securely on jackstands.
3   Remove the lower splash pan from below the front of the engine compartment (see Chapter 3).
4   Remove the engine cooling fans (see Chapter 3).
5   Remove the radiator (see Chapter 3).

1993 through 1999 models
Refer to illustration 5.9

6   Remove the air filter housing (see Chapter 4).
7   Remove the left and right torque struts from the engine compartment (see Section 15).
8   Remove the front engine mount nuts (see Section 15). Support the engine/transaxle subframe with floor jacks.

5.9 Remove the bolts from the brace and separate it from the cylinder head

9   Remove the front engine mount brace from the engine compartment **(see illustration)**. The front engine mount brace must be removed by carefully lifting the engine/transaxle assembly (see Section 15).
10   Spray penetrating oil on the exhaust manifold and exhaust flange fasteners and allow it to soak in.
11   Remove the exhaust Y-pipe from the catalytic converter and position the catalytic converter to the side.
12   Disconnect the front oxygen sensor (see Chapter 6).
13   Remove the rear alternator bracket (see Chapter 5).
14   Remove the exhaust flange nuts from the exhaust manifold. Remove the exhaust crossover pipe (see Chapter 4).
15   Unbolt the front exhaust manifold from the cylinder head.
16   Replace the oxygen sensor, if necessary (see Chapter 6).

2000 and later models
17   Remove the front oxygen sensor (see Chapter 6).
18   Remove the EGR pipe from the coolant crossover housing and the exhaust crossover pipe, if equipped (see Chapter 6). **Note:** *The EGR pipe incorporates a crush seal that cannot be reused. Replace the EGR pipe with a new part once it has been removed.* **Note:** *Some models are equipped with an AIR tube that connects to the exhaust manifold. Remove the AIR tube, the AIR valve and bracket (see Chapter 6).*
19   Remove the exhaust crossover pipe from the exhaust manifold (see Chapter 4).
20   Remove the left side coolant heater assembly, if equipped, from the engine block.
21   Remove the oil dipstick tube.
22   Spray penetrating oil on the exhaust manifold and exhaust flange fasteners and allow it to soak in.
23   Unbolt the front exhaust manifold from the cylinder head.

Rear (right) exhaust manifold
24   Disconnect the rear oxygen sensor(s) harness connector (see Chapter 6).
25   Raise the vehicle and support it securely on jackstands.

1993 through 1999 models
26   Remove the exhaust Y-pipe from the catalytic converter (see Chapter 4).
27   Disconnect the suspension position sensors located on each lower control arm (see Chapter 10).
28   Disconnect the intermediate shaft from the power steering gear (see Chapter 10).
29   Remove the rear transaxle mount (see Section 15).
30   Remove the transaxle/engine brace, if equipped.
31   Remove the EGR pipe from the exhaust manifold, if equipped (see Chapter 6).
32   Support the rear section of the engine/transaxle assembly subframe with a floor jack and remove the four subframe bolts from the rear section of the subframe. Carefully lower the engine/transaxle assembly to access the rear exhaust manifold.
33   Support the engine/transaxle assembly using jackstands.
34   Remove the exhaust Y-pipe from the exhaust manifold.
35   Unbolt the exhaust manifold from the cylinder head.

2000 and later models
36   Remove the exhaust Y-pipe from the catalytic converter (see Chapter 4).
37   Remove the exhaust crossover pipe (see Chapter 4).
38   Remove the right side coolant heater assembly, if equipped, from the engine block.
39   Unbolt the exhaust manifolds from the cylinder heads.

Installation
40   Carefully inspect the manifolds and fasteners for cracks and damage.
41   Use a scraper to remove all traces of old gasket material and carbon deposits from the manifolds and cylinder head mating surfaces. If the gasket was leaking, have the manifolds checked for warpage at an automotive machine shop and resurfaced if necessary.
42   Position new gaskets over the cylinder head studs.
43   Install the manifolds and thread the mounting nuts into place.
44   Working from the center out, tighten the nuts to the torque listed in this Chapter's Specifications.

Front (left) exhaust manifold
45   Install the front engine mount and bracket (see Section 15).
46   Install the radiator and the engine cooling fans (see Chapter 3). Refill the cooling system (see Chapter 1).
47   Reinstall the remaining parts in the reverse order of removal. Use new gaskets when connecting the exhaust pipes.
48   Run the engine and check for exhaust leaks.

Rear (right) exhaust manifold
49   Install the exhaust Y-pipe to the catalytic converter (see Chapter 4).
50   Install the intermediate shaft to the steering gear (see Chapter 10).
51   Reinstall the remaining parts in the reverse order of removal. Use new gaskets when connecting the exhaust pipes.
52   Refill the cooling system (see Chapter 1). Run the engine and check for exhaust leaks.

---

6   Timing chain and sprockets - removal, inspection and installation

This repair procedure requires several expensive special tools. Because of the difficulty of this repair procedure and the necessary special tools, it is recommended to have the timing chain and sprockets replaced by a dealer service department or other qualified automotive repair facility.

---

7   Crankshaft front oil seal - replacement

Timing cover in place
1   Remove the drivebelt (see Chapter 1).
2   Loosen the bolts on the right front wheel, raise the vehicle and support it securely on jackstands. Remove the right front wheel.
3   Remove the splash shields from below the engine compartment and the right fenderwell (see Chapter 3).
4   Remove the engine-to-transaxle brace (see Section 15). Remove the torque converter cover (see Chapter 7) and lock the flywheel to the transaxle using a special tool.
5   On some models, there isn't enough room between the engine and the right fenderwell for the damper to be removed. When this is the case, raise the vehicle and support it securely on jackstands, support the engine/transaxle subframe with a heavy-duty floor jack and loosen the rear subframe bolts. Remove the front subframe bolts (see Chapter 2C). Using a floor jack, lower the engine/transaxle subframe several inches, until the crankshaft damper is clear of the fenderwell. **Warning:** *Do not place your body*

8.2 Remove the plastic dust cap from the center of the
water pump pulley

8.4 Use a special puller to remove the water pump drivebelt
from the driveshaft

*under the engine at any time that it is sup-
ported only by a jack!*

6   Use a strap wrench or chain wrench
over the damper to hold it while the bolts are
removed. If a chain wrench is used, place a
rubber strap, a length of old leather belt or a
length of old drivebelt between the damper
grooves and the chain to prevent damage.

7   Use the chain wrench as described
above to hold the damper while you use a
long breaker bar to remove the center bolt of
the damper (see Chapter 2A). **Caution:** *It will
take lots of leverage and force to remove this
bolt unless you have an air-powered impact
wrench. Be certain that the engine is securely
locked from turning (an assistant is helpful)
while you use both hands and a long breaker
bar to loosen the bolt. Make sure your hands
are not going to hit anything when the bolt
does break loose.*

8   Attach a puller to the damper and draw
it off the crankshaft. Be careful not to drop it
as it comes free. A puller that grabs the hub
must be used.

9   Carefully pull the seal out of the cover
with a seal removal tool. Be careful not to distort the cover or scratch the wall of the seal
bore. It's a good idea to apply penetrating oil
to the seal-to-cover joint and allow it to soak
in before attempting to pull the seal out.

10   Clean the bore to remove any old seal
material and corrosion. Position the new seal
in the bore with the open end of the seal facing IN. A small amount of oil applied to the
outer edge of the new seal will make installation easier.

11   Drive the seal squarely into the bore with
a large socket and hammer until it's completely seated. Select a socket that's the
same outside diameter as the seal (a section
of pipe can be used if a socket isn't available). **Caution:** *If the crankshaft has a
Woodruff key in place, the socket used must
be big enough in diameter to clear the key
while driving on the seal.* Proceed to Step 25.

Timing cover removed

12   Remove the drivebelt (see Chapter 1).
13   Remove the power steering hose
bracket bolt and position the power steering
hose to the side.
14   Remove the drivebelt tensioner bolt and
separate the tensioner from the front of the
engine.
15   Remove the drivebelt idler pulley bolt
and separate the idler pulley from the lower
section of the front of the engine.
16   Remove the crankshaft damper (see
Steps 6 through 8).
17   Remove the right engine mount and
bracket (see Section 15).
18   Remove the engine front cover and gasket. If it's stuck, pry it loose very carefully
with a small screwdriver or putty knife. Don't
damage the mating surfaces of the front
cover or oil leaks could develop.
19   Use a punch or screwdriver and a hammer to drive the seal out of the cover from the
back side. Support the cover as close to the
seal bore as possible. Be careful not to distort the cover or scratch the wall of the seal
bore. If the engine has accumulated a lot of
miles, apply penetrating oil to the seal-to-
cover joint on each side and allow it to soak
in before attempting to drive the seal out.
20   Clean the bore to remove any old seal
material and corrosion. Support the cover on
blocks of wood and position the new seal in
the bore with the open end of the seal facing
IN. A small amount of oil applied to the outer
edge of the new seal will make installation
easier.
21   Drive the seal into the bore with a wood
block and hammer until it's completely
seated. Proceed to the next Step.
22   Use a scraper to remove all traces of old
sealant from the front cover and the engine
block. Clean the mating surfaces with lacquer
thinner or acetone.
23   Make sure the threaded bolt holes in the

engine block and the front cover are clean.
24   Apply a small amount of RTV sealant to
the split line (upper section and lower section) mating surface of the engine block. Also,
apply a small bead of RTV sealant to the
cover gasket.
25   Install the front cover and torque the
bolts to the torque listed in this Chapter's
Specifications. Start with the inner bolts first
and work your way to the outer bolts. Tighten
the bolts in two or three equal steps.

Damper installation

26   Apply anti-seize compound to the snout
of the crankshaft and multi-purpose grease
or clean engine oil to the lips of the seal in the
front cover, then install the damper, making
sure the keyway in the hub is aligned with the
key on the crankshaft.
27   The damper retaining bolt can be used to
pull the damper onto the crankshaft. When
tightening the damper bolt, use the method
described in Step 5.

---

8   Camshaft oil seal - replacement

Refer to illustrations 8.2, 8.4, 8.5 and 8.8
Note: *The 4.6L engine is equipped with a
camshaft seal behind the water pump pulley
on the front (left) cylinder bank. The seal is
part of a retainer that is bolted to the cylinder
head.*

1   Remove the water pump drivebelt from
the water pump pulley (see Chapter 1).
2   Remove the plastic dust cap from the
center of the water pump pulley **(see illustration)**.
3   Remove the water pump drivebelt tensioner (see Section 3).
4   Remove the water pump pulley from the
camshaft using a special puller **(see illustration)**.
5   Remove the bolts and detach the

8.5 Remove the bolts from the camshaft seal retainer

8.8 Use a special tool to install the water pump pulley onto the driveshaft

camshaft seal retainer from the cylinder head **(see illustration)**.

6   Thoroughly clean the area around the seal bore to remove any oil, debris or gasket material.

7   Reinstall the camshaft seal and retainer and tighten the bolts to the torque listed in this Chapter's Specifications.

8   Reinstall the water pump pulley using a special installation tool, available at most auto parts stores **(see illustration)**.

9   The remaining installation is the reverse of removal.

10   Run the engine and check for oil leaks at the camshaft seal.

9   Camshafts and lifters - removal, inspection and installation

This repair procedure requires several expensive special tools. Because of the difficulty of this repair procedure and the necessary special tools, it is recommended to have the camshafts and lifters replaced by a dealer service department or other qualified automotive repair facility.

10   Cylinder heads - removal and installation

This repair procedure requires several expensive special tools. Because of the difficulty of this repair procedure and the necessary special tools, it is recommended to have the cylinder heads and gaskets replaced by a dealer service department or other qualified automotive repair facility.

11   Oil pan - removal and installation

Warning: *On 1993 through 1999 models, the oil pan can only be removed after the engine and transaxle assembly had been removed*

(see Chapter 2C). If all the necessary equipment is not available, have the oil pan removed by a professional automotive repair facility.

Removal

Refer to illustration 11.5

1   Drain the engine oil and remove the oil filter.

2   Access the oil pan:

 a) *On 1993 through 1999 models, remove the engine/transaxle assembly from the vehicle (see Chapter 2C).*

 b) *On 2000 and later models, remove the crossover pipe from the front (right) exhaust manifold (see Chapter 4).*

3   Access the oil pan mounting bolts:

 a) *On 1993 through 1999 models, place the engine on a heavy duty engine stand and lock the stand in position.*

 b) *On 2000 and later models, the oil pan bolts are accessed under the engine/transaxle assembly with the vehicle secured on jackstands.*

4   On 2000 and later models, raise the vehicle and secure it on jackstands.

5   Disconnect the oil level sensor **(see illustration)**.

6   Remove the bolts securing the oil pan to the lower section of the engine block. If it's stuck, pry it loose very carefully with a small screwdriver or putty knife. Don't damage the mating surfaces of the pan or oil leaks could develop.

7   Remove the oil pump strainer.

Installation

8   Use a scraper to remove all traces of old sealant from the block and the oil pan. Clean the mating surfaces with lacquer thinner or acetone.

9   Make sure the threaded bolt holes in the engine block and the oil pan are clean.

10   Check the flange of the oil pan for distortion, particularly around the bolt holes. If necessary, place the pan on a wood block

and use a hammer to flatten and restore the gasket surface.

11   Inspect the oil pump pick-up/strainer assembly for cracks and a blocked strainer. If the pick-up was removed, clean it with solvent or thinner and install it now, using a new gasket. Tighten the fasteners to the torque listed in this Chapter's Specifications.

12   Install a new oil pan gasket, working the seal into the groove of the oil pan. Work the seal into the pan from both directions. Be sure the groove and oil pan surface is free of oil and debris. Once the gasket becomes contaminated with oil, it will become soft and difficult to work with.

13   Carefully position the oil pan on the engine block and install the bolts. Start with the inner bolts first and work your way to the outer bolts on the oil pan. Tighten them in two or three steps to the torque listed in this Chapter's Specifications.

14   The remainder of installation is the reverse of removal. Be sure to add oil and install a new oil filter (see Chapter 1).

15   Run the engine and check for oil pressure and leaks.

11.5 Release the locking tab and disconnect the electrical connector from the oil level sensor

15.10 Details of the front engine mount

1 Engine mount-to-subframe nut
2 Engine mount-to-engine block nuts
3 Engine brace

15.15 Details of the right side engine mount

1 Engine mount-to-bracket nut
2 Engine mount-to-engine block bolts
3 Engine mount-to-frame bolts

12 Oil pump - removal and installation

Note: *The internal parts of the oil pump are not serviced separately. The entire oil pump must be replaced as a complete unit.*

Removal

1   Remove the front cover (see Section 7).
2   Remove the three mounting bolts.
3   Slide the oil pump assembly over the nose of the crankshaft.
4   Remove the drive spacer from the pump housing.

Installation

5   Install the drive spacer into the oil pump assembly.
6   Install the oil pump assembly onto the engine.
7   Install the oil pump mounting bolts in their original locations and tighten them to the torque listed in this Chapter's Specifications. Follow the correct torque sequence. Start with bolt number 1 located in the lower left corner, then bolt number 2 in the right corner and finally bolt number 3 in the upper left side of the oil pump assembly.
8   Reinstall the remaining parts in the reverse order of removal.
9   Add oil and install a new filter (see Chapter 1), start the engine and check for oil leaks.
10   Recheck the engine oil level.

13 Driveplate - removal and installation

Refer to Chapter 2, Part A for this procedure, but be sure to use the torque specifications in this Part of Chapter 2 for the 4.6L V8 engine.

14 Rear main oil seal - replacement

Refer to Chapter 2, Part A for this proce-

dure, but be sure to use the torque specifications in this Part of Chapter 2 for the 4.6L V8 engine.

15 Engine mounts - check, replacement and torque strut adjustment

Warning: *A special engine support fixture should be used to support the engine during repair operations. These fixtures are available from equipment rental yards. Improper lifting methods or devices are hazardous and could result in severe injury or death. DO NOT place any part of your body under the engine/transaxle subframe when it's supported only by a jack. Failure of the lifting device could result in serious injury or death.*
1   Engine mounts seldom require attention, but broken or deteriorated mounts should be replaced immediately or the added strain placed on the driveline components may cause damage or wear. The 4.6L V8 engine has four main engine/transaxle mounts, plus a torque strut (1993 through 1999 models) or a front and a passenger side engine mount plus two transaxle/subframe mounts, one in the rear and the other on the left side (2000 and later models).

Check

2   During the check, the engine must be raised slightly to remove the weight from the mounts.
3   Raise the vehicle and support it securely on jackstands, then position a jack under the engine oil pan. Place a large block of wood between the jack head and the oil pan, then carefully raise the engine just enough to take the weight off the mounts. **Warning:** *DO NOT place any part of your body under the engine when it's supported only by a jack!*
4   Check the mounts to see if the rubber is cracked, hardened or separated from the metal plates. Sometimes the rubber will split right down the center.
5   Check for relative movement between

the mount plates and the engine or frame (use a large screwdriver or prybar to attempt to move the mounts). If movement is noted, lower the engine and tighten the mount fasteners.
6   Rubber preservative may be applied to the mounts to slow deterioration.

Replacement

7   Disconnect the cable from the negative terminal of the battery (see Chapter 5), then raise the vehicle and support it securely on jackstands.

Front mount

Refer to illustration 15.10
8   Remove the cooling fans (see Chapter 3).
9   Remove the right and the left torque struts, if equipped (see Steps 24 through 26).
10   Install an engine support fixture as described in the **Warning** above. Remove the fasteners and detach the front mount from the subframe and the engine **(see illustration)**.
11   Remove the front brace bolts from the cylinder head **(see illustration 5.9)**.
12   Raise the engine, if necessary, and remove the front engine mount.
13   Installation is the reverse of the removal procedure. Use thread-locking compound on the threads and be sure to tighten everything securely.

Right side mount

Refer to illustration 15.15
14   Remove the right and the left torque struts, if equipped (see Steps 24 through 26).
15   Install an engine support fixture as described in the **Warning** above. Remove the fasteners and detach the mount from the engine and the bracket **(see illustration)**.
16   Raise the engine, if necessary, and remove the engine mount.
17   Installation is the reverse of the removal procedure. Use thread-locking compound on the threads and be sure to tighten everything securely.

2B

15.21a Location of the rear subframe/transaxle mount

15.21b Location of the left side transaxle mount

Subframe/transaxle mounts

Refer to illustrations 15.21a and 15.21b

18   The design and location of the subframe/transaxle mounts change slightly depending on the year and the model.

19   The left front mount is attached to the transaxle near the frame, with the rear mount between the rear of the transaxle and the subframe.

20   Remove the right and the left torque struts, if equipped (see Steps 24 through 26).

21   Install an engine support fixture as described in the **Warning** above. Remove the fasteners and detach the mount from the transaxle and the subframe/bracket **(see illustrations)**.

22   Raise the engine, if necessary, and remove the front subframe/transaxle mount(s).

23   Installation is the reverse of the removal procedure. Use thread-locking compound on the threads and be sure to tighten everything securely.

Engine torque strut

24   The engine torque strut mounts between the engine and the upper radiator support on the body. It can be replaced without jacking up the engine, by removing the through-bolts and the bolts attaching the strut to the mounts on the radiator support.

Note: *When reinstalling this mount, you may have to use a prybar to rotate the engine toward or away from the radiator to align the through-bolts.*

Torque strut adjustment

25   After installing the torque strut, do not preload the strut by tightening the bolts in the installed position. Be sure the engine/transaxle assembly is positioned properly (no lifting devices attached) and all the torque struts are installed.

26   Use thread-locking compound on the threads and be sure to tighten everything securely.

Chapter 2 Part C
General engine overhaul procedures

Contents

2C

Specifications

General

Displacement	
4.6L models	279 cubic inches
4.9L models	300 cubic inches
Bore and stroke	
4.6L models	3.660 x 3.310 inches
4.9L models	3.622 x 3.622 inches
Cylinder compression pressure	Lowest cylinder must be no less than 75 percent of highest cylinder
Oil pressure (minimum)	
4.6L engines	
At curb idle	5 psi
At 2000 rpm	35 psi
4.9L engines	
At curb idle	11 psi
At 2000 rpm	53 psi

Torque specifications

Driveplate-to-torque converter bolts	See Chapter 7
Connecting rod bearing cap bolts (4.9L engines)	22
Main bearing cap bolts (4.9L engines)	85
Engine/transaxle subframe mounting bolts	
1998 and earlier DeVille, 1997 and earlier Seville	76
1999 and later DeVille, 1998 and later Seville	141

1   General information - engine overhaul

Refer to illustrations 1.1, 1.2, 1.3, 1.4, 1.5 and 1.6

Note: *The 4.6L Northstar engine requires expensive special tools and parts for the rebuilding procedures. It is recommended that the home mechanic purchase a Northstår long block from the dealer or other reliable engine builder when considering engine overhaul. The following information refers only to the 4.9L engine.*

Included in this portion of Chapter 2 are general information and diagnostic testing procedures for determining the overall mechanical condition of your engine.

The information ranges from advice concerning preparation for an overhaul and the purchase of replacement parts and/or components to detailed, step-by-step procedures covering removal and installation.

The following Sections have been written to help you determine whether your engine needs to be overhauled and how to remove and install it once you've determined it needs to be rebuilt. For information concerning in-vehicle engine repair, see Chapter 2A or 2B.

The Specifications included in this Part are general in nature and include only those necessary for testing the oil pressure and checking the engine compression. Refer to Chapter 2A or 2B for additional engine Specifications.

It's not always easy to determine when, or if, an engine should be completely overhauled, because a number of factors must be considered.

High mileage is not necessarily an indication that an overhaul is needed, while low mileage doesn't preclude the need for an overhaul. Frequency of servicing is probably the most important consideration. An engine that's had regular and frequent oil and filter changes, as well as other required maintenance, will most likely give many thousands of miles of reliable service. Conversely, a neglected engine may require an overhaul very early in its service life.

Excessive oil consumption is an indication that piston rings, valve seals and/or valve guides are in need of attention. Make sure that oil leaks aren't responsible before deciding that the rings and/or guides are bad. Perform a cylinder compression check to determine the extent of the work required (see Section 3). Also check the vacuum readings under various conditions (see Section 4).

Check the oil pressure with a gauge installed in place of the oil pressure sending unit and compare it to this Chapter's Specifications. If it's extremely low, the bearings and/or oil pump are probably worn out.

Loss of power, rough running, knocking or metallic engine noises, excessive valve train noise and high fuel consumption rates may also point to the need for an overhaul,

1.1 An engine block being bored. An engine rebuilder will use special machinery to recondition the cylinder bores

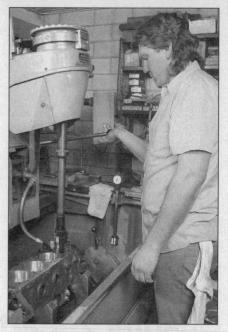

1.2 If the cylinders are bored, the machine shop will normally hone the engine on a machine like this

especially if they're all present at the same time. If a complete tune-up doesn't remedy the situation, major mechanical work is the only solution.

An engine overhaul involves restoring the internal parts to the specifications of a new engine. During an overhaul, the piston rings are replaced and the cylinder walls are reconditioned (rebored and/or honed) **(see illustrations 1.1 and 1.2)**. If a rebore is done by an automotive machine shop, new oversize pistons will also be installed. The main bearings, connecting rod bearings and camshaft bearings are generally replaced with new ones and, if necessary, the crankshaft may be reground to restore the journals **(see illustration 1.3)**. Generally, the valves are serviced as well, since they're usu-

ally in less-than-perfect condition at this point. While the engine is being overhauled, other components, such as the distributor, starter and alternator, can be rebuilt as well. The end result should be similar to a new engine that will give many trouble free miles. **Note:** *Critical cooling system components such as the hoses, drivebelts, thermostat and water pump should be replaced with new parts when an engine is overhauled. The radiator should be checked carefully to ensure that it isn't clogged or leaking (see Chapter 3). If you purchase a rebuilt engine or short block, some rebuilders will not warranty their engines unless the radiator has been professionally flushed. Also, we don't recommend overhauling the oil pump - always install a new one when an engine is rebuilt.*

1.3 A crankshaft having a main bearing journal ground

1.4 A machinist checks for a bent connecting rod, using specialized equipment

1.5 A bore gauge being used to check the main bearing bore

1.6 Uneven piston wear like this indicates a bent connecting rod

2.2a The oil pressure sending unit on 4.9L engines is located on the rear of the engine block, above the oil filter

Overhauling the internal components on today's engines is a difficult and time-consuming task which requires a significant amount of specialty tools and is best left to a professional engine rebuilder (see illustrations 1.4, 1.5 and 1.6). A competent engine rebuilder will handle the inspection of your old parts and offer advice concerning the reconditioning or replacement of the original engine, never purchase parts or have machine work done on other components until the block has been thoroughly inspected by a professional machine shop. As a general rule, time is the primary cost of an overhaul, especially since the vehicle may be tied up for a minimum of two weeks or more. Be aware that some engine builders only have the capability to rebuild the engine you bring them while other rebuilders have a large inventory of rebuilt exchange engines in stock. Also be aware that many machine shops could take as much as two weeks time to completely rebuild your engine depending on shop workload. Sometimes it makes more sense to simply exchange your engine for another engine that's already rebuilt to save time.

2 Oil pressure check

Refer to illustrations 2.2a, 2.2b, 2.3 and 2.4

1   Low engine oil pressure can be a sign of an engine in need of rebuilding. A "low oil pressure" indicator (often called an "idiot light") is not a test of the oiling system. Such indicators only come on when the oil pressure is dangerously low. Even a factory oil pressure gauge in the instrument panel is only a relative indication, although much better for driver information than a warning light. A better test is with a mechanical (not electrical) oil pressure gauge.

2   Locate the oil pressure sending unit on the engine block (see illustrations).

3   Unscrew and remove the oil pressure sending unit and then screw in the hose for your oil pressure gauge. If necessary, install an adapter fitting. Use Teflon tape or thread sealant on the threads of the adapter and/or the fitting on the end of your gauge's hose (see illustration).

4   Connect an accurate tachometer to the engine, according to the tachometer manufacturer's instructions.

5   Check the oil pressure with the engine

2.2b The oil pressure sending unit on 4.6L engines is located on the oil filter adapter, above the oil filter

running (normal operating temperature) at the specified engine speed, and compare it to this Chapter's Specifications (see illustration). If it's extremely low, the bearings and/or oil pump are probably worn out.

2C

2.3 Remove the oil pressure sending unit and install an adapter

2.4 Install the oil pressure gauge into the adapter

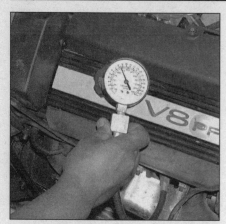

3.6 Use a compression gauge with a threaded fitting for the spark plug hole, not the type that requires hand pressure to maintain the seal

3   Cylinder compression check

Refer to illustration 3.6

1   A compression check will tell you what mechanical condition the upper end of your engine (pistons, rings, valves, head gaskets) is in. Specifically, it can tell you if the compression is down due to leakage caused by worn piston rings, defective valves and seats or a blown head gasket. **Note:** *The engine must be at normal operating temperature and the battery must be fully charged for this check.*

2   Begin by cleaning the area around the spark plugs before you remove them (compressed air should be used, if available). The idea is to prevent dirt from getting into the cylinders as the compression check is being done.

3   Remove all of the spark plugs from the engine (see Chapter 1).

4   Block the throttle wide open.

5   Disable the ignition system and the fuel pump system:

a)   *To disable the ignition system on 4.9L engines, disconnect the primary ignition wire at the distributor* (see Chapter 5). *On 4.6L engines, disconnect the primary ignition harness connector at the coil packs (1993 through 1999 models) or at each coil/module assembly (2000 and later models)* (see Chapter 5).

b)   *To disable the fuel system, remove the fuel pump fuse and the fuel pump relay* (see Chapter 4). *The relays are located in the power distribution center in the engine compartment* (see Chapter 12).

6   Install a compression gauge in the spark plug hole **(see illustration)**.

7   Crank the engine over at least seven compression strokes and watch the gauge. The compression should build up quickly in a healthy engine. Low compression on the first stroke, followed by gradually increasing pressure on successive strokes, indicates worn piston rings. A low compression reading on the first stroke, which doesn't build up during successive strokes, indicates leaking valves

or a blown head gasket (a cracked head could also be the cause). Deposits on the undersides of the valve heads can also cause low compression. Record the highest gauge reading obtained.

8   Repeat the procedure for the remaining cylinders and compare the results to this Chapter's Specifications.

9   Add some engine oil (about three squirts from a plunger-type oil can) to each cylinder, through the spark plug hole, and repeat the test.

10   If the compression increases after the oil is added, the piston rings are definitely worn. If the compression doesn't increase significantly, the leakage is occurring at the valves or head gasket. Leakage past the valves may be caused by burned valve seats and/or faces or warped, cracked or bent valves.

11   If two adjacent cylinders have equally low compression, there's a strong possibility that the head gasket between them is blown. The appearance of coolant in the combustion chambers or the crankcase would verify this condition.

12   If one cylinder is slightly lower than the others, and the engine has a slightly rough idle, a worn lobe on the camshaft could be the cause.

13   If the compression is unusually high, the combustion chambers are probably coated with carbon deposits. If that's the case, the cylinder head(s) should be removed and decarbonized.

14   If compression is way down or varies greatly between cylinders, it would be a good idea to have a leak-down test performed by an automotive repair shop. This test will pinpoint exactly where the leakage is occurring and how severe it is.

4   Vacuum gauge diagnostic checks

Refer to illustrations 4.4 and 4.6

A vacuum gauge provides inexpensive but valuable information about what is going on in the engine. You can check for worn rings or cylinder walls, leaking head or intake manifold gaskets, incorrect carburetor adjustments, restricted exhaust, stuck or burned valves, weak valve springs, improper ignition or valve timing and ignition problems.

Unfortunately, vacuum gauge readings are easy to misinterpret, so they should be used in conjunction with other tests to confirm the diagnosis.

Both the absolute readings and the rate of needle movement are important for accurate interpretation. Most gauges measure vacuum in inches of mercury (in-Hg). The following references to vacuum assume the diagnosis is being performed at sea level. As elevation increases (or atmospheric pressure decreases), the reading will decrease. For every 1,000 foot increase in elevation above approximately 2000 feet, the gauge readings will decrease about one inch of mercury.

4.4 A simple vacuum gauge can be handy in diagnosing engine condition and performance

Connect the vacuum gauge directly to the intake manifold vacuum, not to ported (throttle body) vacuum **(see illustration)**. Be sure no hoses are left disconnected during the test or false readings will result.

Before you begin the test, allow the engine to warm up completely. Block the wheels and set the parking brake. With the transaxle in Park, start the engine and allow it to run at normal idle speed. **Warning:** *Keep your hands and the vacuum gauge clear of the fans.*

Read the vacuum gauge; an average, healthy engine should normally produce about 17 to 22 in-Hg with a fairly steady needle **(see illustration)**. Refer to the following vacuum gauge readings and what they indicate about the engine's condition:

1   A low steady reading usually indicates a leaking gasket between the intake manifold and cylinder head(s) or throttle body, a leaky vacuum hose, late ignition timing or incorrect camshaft timing. Check ignition timing with a timing light and eliminate all other possible causes, utilizing the tests provided in this Chapter before you remove the timing chain cover to check the timing marks.

2   If the reading is three to eight inches below normal and it fluctuates at that low reading, suspect an intake manifold gasket leak at an intake port or a faulty fuel injector.

3   If the needle has regular drops of about two-to-four inches at a steady rate, the valves are probably leaking. Perform a compression check or leak-down test to confirm this.

4   An irregular drop or down-flick of the needle can be caused by a sticking valve or an ignition misfire. Perform a compression check or leak-down test and read the spark plugs.

5   A rapid vibration of about four in-Hg vibration at idle combined with exhaust smoke indicates worn valve guides. Perform a leak-down test to confirm this. If the rapid vibration occurs with an increase in engine speed, check for a leaking intake manifold gasket or head gasket, weak valve springs, burned valves or ignition misfire.

Low, steady reading   Low, fluctuating needle   Regular drops

Irregular drops   Rapid vibration

Large fluctuation   Slow fluctuation

STD-O-OBR HAYNES

4.6 Typical vacuum gauge readings

6   A slight fluctuation, say one inch up and down, may mean ignition problems. Check all the usual tune-up items and, if necessary, run the engine on an ignition analyzer.

7   If there is a large fluctuation, perform a compression or leak-down test to look for a weak or dead cylinder or a blown head gasket.

8   If the needle moves slowly through a wide range, check for a clogged PCV system, incorrect idle fuel mixture, throttle body or intake manifold gasket leaks.

9   Check for a slow return after revving the engine by quickly snapping the throttle open until the engine reaches about 2,500 rpm and let it shut. Normally the reading should drop to near zero, rise above normal idle reading (about 5 in-Hg over) and then return to the previous idle reading. If the vacuum returns slowly and doesn't peak when the throttle is snapped shut, the rings may be worn. If there is a long delay, look for a restricted exhaust system (often the muffler or catalytic converter). An easy way to check this is to temporarily disconnect the exhaust ahead of the suspected part and redo the test.

5   Engine rebuilding alternatives

Note: *The 4.6L Northstar engine requires expensive special tools and parts for the rebuilding procedures. It is recommended that the home mechanic purchase a Northstar long block from the dealer or other reliable engine builder when considering engine over-*

haul. The following information refers only to the 4.9L engine.

The do-it-yourselfer is faced with a number of options when purchasing a rebuilt engine. The major considerations are cost, warranty, parts availability and the time required for the rebuilder to complete the project. The decision to replace the engine block, piston/connecting rod assemblies and crankshaft depends on the final inspection results of your engine. Only then can you make a cost effective decision whether to have your engine overhauled or simply purchase an exchange engine for your vehicle.

Some of the rebuilding alternatives include:

Individual parts - If the inspection procedures reveal that the engine block and most engine components are in reusable

condition, purchasing individual parts and having a rebuilder rebuild your engine may be the most economical alternative. The block, crankshaft and piston/connecting rod assemblies should all be inspected carefully by a machine shop first.

Short block - A short block consists of an engine block with a crankshaft and piston/connecting rod assemblies already installed. All new bearings are incorporated and all clearances will be correct. The existing camshaft, valve train components, cylinder heads and external parts can be bolted to the short block with little or no machine shop work necessary.

Long block - A long block consists of a short block plus an oil pump, oil pan, cylinder head, valve cover, camshaft and valve train components, timing sprockets and chain or gears and timing cover. All components are installed with new bearings, seals and gaskets incorporated throughout. The installation of manifolds and external parts is all that's necessary.

Low mileage used engines – Some companies now offer low mileage used engines which is a very cost effective way to get your vehicle up and running again. These engines often come from vehicles which have been in totaled in accidents or come from other countries which have a higher vehicle turn over rate. A low mileage used engine also usually has a similar warranty like the newly remanufactured engines.

Give careful thought to which alternative is best for you and discuss the situation with local automotive machine shops, auto parts dealers and experienced rebuilders before ordering or purchasing replacement parts.

6   Engine removal - methods and precautions

Refer to illustrations 6.1, 6.2, 6.3, 6.4 and 6.5

These engines are removed using heavy duty jackstands, a heavy duty engine hoist and a vehicle hoist. Once the vehicle is raised on the hoist, it is then slowly lowered so the engine/transaxle assembly can be supported using four jackstands under the subframe **(see illustration 6.7)**. After all the engine,

2C

6.2 After tightly wrapping water-vulnerable components, use a spray cleaner on everything, with particular concentration on the greasiest areas, usually around the valve cover and lower edges of the block. If one section dries out, apply more cleaner

6.3 Depending on how dirty the engine is, let the cleaner soak in according to the directions, then hose off the grime and cleaner. Get the rinse water down into every area you can get at; then dry important components with a hair dryer or paper towels

6.4 Get an engine stand sturdy enough to firmly support the engine while you're working on it. Stay away from three-wheeled models: they have a tendency to tip over more easily, so get a four-wheeled unit.

transaxle and driveline components are disconnected, the vehicle is raised using the vehicle hoist and the engine/transaxle assembly remains on the shop floor. The engine/transaxle assembly can then be moved using a heavy duty engine hoist.

Engine removal is not recommended unless your shop is equipped with a vehicle hoist, jackstands and floor jacks.

Cleaning the engine compartment and engine before having the engine removed will help keep tools clean and organized **(see illustrations 6.2 and 6.3)**.

Arrange for or obtain all of the tools and equipment you'll need prior to be-ginning the job **(see illustrations 6.4 and 6.5)**.

Plan for the vehicle to be out of use for quite a while. A machine shop can do the work that is beyond the scope of the home mechanic. Machine shops often have a busy schedule, so before removing the engine, consult the shop for an estimate of how long it will take to rebuild or repair the components that may need work.

7   Engine - removal and installation

Warning 1: *Engine removal can only be performed using a heavy duty vehicle hoist, jack-*

6.5 A heavy duty engine hoist can be used to safely move the engine/transaxle assembly after it has been removed

stands and a heavy duty engine hoist. If all the necessary equipment is not available, have the engine/transaxle assembly removed by a professional automotive repair facility.
Warning 2: *The models covered by this manual are equipped with Supplemental Restraint systems (SRS), more commonly known as airbags. Always disable the airbag system before working in the vicinity of the impact sensors, steering column or instrument panel to avoid the possibility of accidental deployment of the airbag, which could cause personal injury (see Chapter 12).*
Warning 3: *Gasoline is extremely flammable, so take extra precautions when you work on any part of the fuel system. Don't smoke or allow open flames or bare light bulbs near the*

work area, and don't work in a garage where a gas-type appliance (such as a water heater or a clothes dryer) is present. Since gasoline is carcinogenic, wear latex gloves when there's a possibility of being exposed to fuel, and, if you spill any fuel on your skin, rinse it off immediately with soap and water. Mop up any spills immediately and do not store fuel-soaked rags where they could ignite. The fuel system is under constant pressure, so, if any fuel lines are to be disconnected, the fuel pressure in the system must be relieved first (see Chapter 4 for more information). When you perform any kind of work on the fuel system, wear safety glasses and have a Class B type fire extinguisher on hand.
Warning 4: *The air conditioning system is under high pressure, and refrigerant is expensive. Have a dealer service department or an automotive air conditioning shop discharge the system before beginning this procedure.*

Removal

Refer to illustrations 7.6, 7.7, 7.16, 7.34 and 7.36

1   Have the air conditioning system discharged by an automotive air conditioning technician.
2   Loosen the front wheel lug nuts. Position the vehicle on the vehicle hoist and raise it until it just contacts the vehicle, at the front and rear jacking points along the rocker panel flanges. **Warning:** *Make sure the vehicle is safely positioned on the vehicle hoist and the lifting points are secured to insure proper weight distribution of the vehicle when the weight of the engine/transaxle assembly is removed.*
3   Relieve the fuel system pressure (see Chapter 4), then disconnect the negative cable from the battery (see Chapter 5).
4   Cover the fenders and cowl. Special pads are available to protect the fenders, but an old bedspread or blanket will also work.
5   Remove the air filter housing (see Chapter 4).
6   On models with a brace between the two front strut towers, remove the nuts/bolts and the brace **(see illustration)**.
7   Label the vacuum lines, emissions system hoses, electrical connectors, ground straps and fuel lines, to ensure correct reinstallation, then detach them. Pieces of masking tape with numbers or letters written on

7.6 Remove the strut tower brace from the engine compartment

7.7 Label both ends of each wire and hose before disconnecting them

7.16 Location of the mounting fasteners for the engine splash pan

them work well (see illustration). If there's any possibility of confusion, make a sketch of the engine compartment and clearly label the lines, hoses and wires.

8   Label and detach all coolant hoses from the engine. Disconnect the coolant reservoir hoses and the heater hoses.

9   Remove the transaxle oil cooler lines (see Chapter 7).

10   Disconnect the fuel lines from the fuel rail (see Chapter 4). Plug or cap all open fittings and lines.

11   Disconnect the accelerator cable, cruise control cables and throttle valve, if equipped, from the engine (see Chapter 4 and Chapter 7).

12   Detach the shift cable from the transaxle (see Chapter 7).

13   Remove the drivebelt (see Chapter 1).

14   Unbolt the power steering pump (see Chapter 10). Leave the lines/hoses attached and make sure the pump is kept in an upright position in the engine compartment. Use wire or rope to restrain it out of the way.

15   Raise the vehicle on the hoist.

16   Remove the splash pan from below the front of the engine compartment (see illustration).

17   Drain the engine oil (see Chapter 1) and remove the filter.

18   Drain the cooling system (see Chapter 1). Warning: *The engine must be com-*

pletely cool before draining the coolant.

19   If the engine is to be separated from the transaxle, mark the relationship of the torque converter to the driveplate, then remove the torque converter-to-driveplate bolts.

20   Remove the cooling fans, shroud and radiator (see Chapter 3).

21   Disconnect the air conditioning pressure sensor, if equipped (see Chapter 3).

22   Remove the air conditioning compressor (see Chapter 3).

23   Disconnect the brake lines from the brake pressure modulator valve (BPMV) for the ABS system. Remove the bolts and separate the BPMV from the engine compartment.

24   Place the steering wheel in the straight-ahead position with the front tires pointing forward. Run the seat belt through the steering wheel and clip it into place to prevent the steering column from turning.

25   Disconnect the intermediate shaft from the steering gear (see Chapter 10). Caution: *Failure to disconnect the intermediate shaft from the steering gear can cause damage to the steering gear and/or the intermediate shaft.* Also disconnect the power steering fluid lines from the steering gear.

26   Remove the driveaxles following the procedure described in Chapter 8. However, instead of separating the strut from the steering knuckle, separate the control arm balljoint from the steering knuckle (see Chapter 10).

27   On models equipped with road sensing suspension, disconnect the sensor links from the control arms.

28   Disconnect any wiring harnesses from the subframe.

29   Disconnect the secondary AIR pump hoses and electrical connectors, if equipped (see Chapter 6).

30   Remove the left transaxle and the right engine mount nut from the engine brace.

31   Remove the left and the right torque struts, if equipped (see Chapters 2A or 2B). Remove the torque strut braces.

32   Remove the exhaust crossover pipe (see Chapter 4).

33   Remove the exhaust flange bolts and separate the exhaust pipes from the exhaust manifolds (see Chapter 4). Note: *It's possible to remove the engine/transaxle assembly with both exhaust manifolds in place.*

34   Position four jackstands, one on each corner of the engine subframe (see illustration) to support the engine/transaxle assembly. Be sure the jackstands will only contact the subframe, not the engine or transaxle. Do not place the jackstands where they could interfere with subframe bolt removal.

35   Slowly lower the vehicle hoist until the subframe just contacts the jackstands.

36   Remove the subframe-to-chassis mounting bolts (see illustration). Warning: *DO NOT place any part of your body under*

2C

7.34 Position four jackstands under the corners of the subframe

7.36 Location of the subframe mounting bolts on a 2000 DeVille

the engine/transaxle assembly.

37   Raise the vehicle hoist slowly. Check to make sure all electrical connectors, vacuum lines, hoses, ground straps, etc. are disconnected and labeled properly.

38   After the vehicle is clear of the engine/transaxle assembly, attach a lifting chain to the engine/transaxle, connect a heavy duty engine hoist and roll the assembly out from under the vehicle.

39   Raise the assembly and place the jackstands under the subframe once again, then lower the assembly and detach the remaining mounts from the subframe. The engine/transaxle assembly can now be raised up and separated from the subframe.

40   To separate the transaxle from the engine, support the engine with the hoist, or on blocks on the floor, then support the transaxle with a floor jack, remove the bolts and pull the transaxle away from the engine. Have at least one other person help you do this.

Installation

41   Installation is the reverse of removal, noting the following points:

a) *Check the engine and transaxle mounts. If they're worn or damaged, replace them.*

b) *Don't install the torque converter-to-driveplate bolts until after the assembly has been installed in the vehicle. Be sure to tighten these bolts to the torque listed in the Chapter 7 Specifications.*

c) *Tighten the subframe mounting bolts to the torque listed in this Chapter's Specifications.*

d) *Bleed the brake system (see Chapter 9).*

e) *Add coolant, engine oil, power steering and transaxle fluid as needed.*

f) *Run the engine and check for leaks and proper operation of all accessories, then test drive the vehicle.*

g) *Have the air conditioning system recharged and leak tested by the shop that discharged it.*

8   Engine overhaul - disassembly sequence

Note: *The 4.6L Northstar engine requires expensive special tools and parts for the rebuilding procedures. It is recommended that the home mechanic purchase a Northstar long block from the dealer or other reliable engine builder when considering engine overhaul. The following information refers only to the 4.9L engine.*

1   It's much easier to remove the external components if it's mounted on a portable engine stand. A stand can often be rented quite cheaply from an equipment rental yard. Before the engine is mounted on a stand, the flywheel/driveplate should be removed from the engine.

2   If a stand isn't available, it's possible to remove the external engine components with it blocked up on the floor. Be extra careful not to tip or drop the engine when working without a stand.

3   If you're going to obtain a rebuilt engine, all external components must come off first, to be transferred to the replacement engine. These components include:

> *Driveplate*
> *Ignition system components*
> *Emissions-related components*
> *Engine mounts and mount brackets*
> *Engine rear cover (spacer plate between driveplate and engine block)*
> *Intake/exhaust manifolds*
> *Fuel injection components*
> *Oil filter*
> *Spark plug wires and spark plugs*
> *Thermostat and housing assembly*
> *Water pump*

Note: *When removing the external components from the engine, pay close attention to details that may be helpful or important during installation. Note the installed position of gaskets, seals, spacers, pins, brackets, washers, bolts and other small items.*

4   If you're going to obtain a short block (assembled engine block, crankshaft, pistons and connecting rods), then remove the cylinder heads, oil pan, oil pump strainer, oil pump and water pump from your engine so that you can turn in your old short block to the rebuilder as a core. See *Engine rebuilding alternatives* for additional information regarding the different possibilities to be considered.

9   Pistons and connecting rods - removal and installation

Caution: *On 4.9L engines, it is necessary to remove the cylinder liners in order to properly clean the block. Carefully mark the alignment of each liner to the cylinder block if they are to be reused. However, this particular engine is a difficult one for the home mechanic to rebuild, because of the cylinder liners and other rebuilding problems. It is suggested that when rebuilding this engine, have the short-block cleaned and rebuilt at a professional engine shop. They will install new pistons with new, matching liners, carefully fit new O-rings to the bottom of the liners and* set the correct liner height in the block.

Note: *The 4.6L Northstar engine requires expensive special tools and parts for the rebuilding procedures. It is recommended that the home mechanic purchase a Northstar long block from the dealer or other reliable engine builder when considering engine overhaul. The following information refers only to the 4.9L engine.*

Removal

Refer to illustrations 9.1, 9.3, 9.4a, 9.4b and 9.6

Note: *Prior to removing the piston/connecting rod assemblies, remove the cylinder heads and oil pan (see Chapter 2A).*

1   Use your fingernail to feel if a ridge has formed at the upper limit of ring travel (about 1/4-inch down from the top of each cylinder). If carbon deposits or cylinder wear have produced ridges, they must be completely removed with a special tool **(see illustration)**. Follow the manufacturer's instructions provided with the tool. Failure to remove the ridges before attempting to remove the piston/connecting rod assemblies may result in piston breakage.

2   After the cylinder ridges have been removed, turn the engine so the crankshaft is facing up.

3   Before the main bearing cap assembly and connecting rods are removed, check the connecting rod endplay with feeler gauges. Slide them between the first connecting rod and the crankshaft throw until the play is removed **(see illustration)**. Repeat this procedure for each connecting rod. The endplay is equal to the thickness of the feeler gauge(s). Check with an automotive machine shop for the endplay service limit. If the play exceeds the service limit, new connecting rods will be required. If new rods (or a new crankshaft) are installed, the endplay may fall under the minimum allowable clearance. If it does, the rods will have to be machined to restore it. If necessary, consult an automotive machine shop for advice.

4   Check the connecting rods and caps for identification marks **(see illustration)**. If they aren't plainly marked, use a small center-punch to make the appropriate number of indentations on each rod and cap (1, 2, 3,

9.1 Before you try to remove the pistons, use a ridge reamer to remove the raised material (ridge) from the top of the cylinders

9.3 Checking the connecting rod endplay (side clearance)

9.4a If the connecting rods and caps are not marked, use a center punch or numbered impression stamps to mark the caps to the rods by cylinder number (for example, this would be the No. 4 connecting rod)

9.4b A liner holding tool must be used on 4.9L engines to keep the liners from moving and losing their bottom seal

9.6 Push a short section of plastic or rubber hose over the connecting rod bolts to prevent damage to the crankshaft journals during piston/rod removal

etc., depending on the cylinder they're associated with). **Note:** *On 4.9L engines, if the original cylinder liners are to be reused, install a cylinder liner holder, available at special tool distributors, to the engine block to prevent the liners from shifting when the pistons are withdrawn* (**see illustration**). *Also, mark the position of the liners relative to the block with indelible ink to ensure they do not shift.*

5   Loosen each of the connecting rod cap nuts or bolts 1/2-turn at a time until they can be removed by hand. Remove the number one connecting rod cap and bearing insert. Don't drop the bearing insert out of the cap.

6   Slip a short length of plastic or rubber hose over each connecting rod bolt to protect the crankshaft journal and cylinder wall as the rod is removed (**see illustration**).

7   Remove the bearing insert and push the connecting rod/piston assembly out through the top of the engine. Use a wooden or plastic hammer handle to push on the upper bearing surface in the connecting rod. If resistance is felt, double-check to make sure that all of the ridge was removed from the cylinder.

8   Repeat the procedure for the remaining cylinders. **Note:** *If the connecting rod caps*

are secured by bolts (instead of nuts), discard the old rod cap bolts. Use new bolts when reassembling the engine.

9   After removal, reassemble the connecting rod caps and bearing inserts in their respective connecting rods and install the cap bolts finger tight. Leaving the old bearing inserts in place until reassembly will help prevent the connecting rod bearing surfaces from being accidentally nicked or gouged.

10   The pistons and connecting rods are now ready for inspection and overhaul at an automotive machine shop.

Piston ring installation

Refer to illustrations 9.13, 9.14, 9.15, 9.17, 9.19a, 9.19b and 9.22

11   Before installing the new piston rings, the ring end gaps must be checked. It's assumed that the piston ring side clearance has been checked and verified correct.

12   Lay out the piston/connecting rod assemblies and the new ring sets so the ring sets will be matched with the same piston and cylinder during the end gap measurement and engine assembly.

13   Insert the top (number one) ring into the first cylinder and square it up with the cylin-

der walls by pushing it in with the top of the piston (**see illustration**). The ring should be near the bottom of the cylinder, at the lower limit of ring travel.

14   To measure the end gap, slip feeler

9.13 Install the piston ring into the cylinder then push it down into position using a piston so the ring will be square in the cylinder

ENGINE BEARING ANALYSIS

Debris

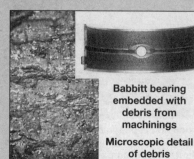

Babbitt bearing embedded with debris from machinings

Microscopic detail of debris

Microscopic detail of gouges

Overplated copper alloy bearing gouged by cast iron debris

Aluminum bearing embedded with glass beads

Microscopic detail of glass beads

Damaged lining caused by dirt left on the bearing back

Misassembly

Result of a lower half assembled as an upper - blocking the oil flow

Excessive oil clearance is indicated by a short contact arc

Polished and oil-stained backs are a result of a poor fit in the housing bore

Result of a wrong, reversed, or shifted cap

Overloading

Damage from excessive idling which resulted in an oil film unable to support the load imposed

Damaged upper connecting rod bearings caused by engine lugging; the lower main bearings (not shown) were similarly affected

The damage shown in these upper and lower connecting rod bearings was caused by engine operation at a higher-than-rated speed under load

Misalignment

A warped crankshaft caused this pattern of severe wear in the center, diminishing toward the ends

A poorly finished crankshaft caused the equally spaced scoring shown

A tapered housing bore caused the damage along one edge of this pair

A bent connecting rod led to the damage in the "V" pattern

Lubrication

Result of dry start: The bearings on the left, farthest from the oil pump, show more damage

Result of a low oil supply or oil starvation

Severe wear as a result of inadequate oil clearance

Corrosion

Microscopic detail of corrosion

Corrosion is an acid attack on the bearing lining generally caused by inadequate maintenance, extremely hot or cold operation, or interior oils or fuels

Microscopic detail of cavitation

Example of cavitation - a surface erosion caused by pressure changes in the oil film

Damage from excessive thrust or insufficient axial clearance

Bearing affected by oil dilution caused by excessive blow-by or a rich mixture

9.14 With the ring square in the cylinder, measure the ring end gap with a feeler gauge

9.15 If the ring end gap is too small, clamp a file in a vise as shown and file the piston ring ends - be sure to remove all raised material

gauges between the ends of the ring until a gauge equal to the gap width is found **(see illustration)**. The feeler gauge should slide between the ring ends with a slight amount of drag. A typical ring end gap should fall between 0.010 and 0.020-inch for compression rings, and up to 0.030 for the oil ring steel rails. Check with an automotive machine shop for the correct ring end gap for your engine. If the gap is larger or smaller than specified, double-check to make sure you have the correct rings before proceeding.

15   If the gap is too small, it must be enlarged or the ring ends may come in contact with each other during engine operation, which can cause serious damage to the engine. The end gap can be increased by filing the ring ends very carefully with a fine file. Mount the file in a vise equipped with soft jaws, slip the ring over the file with the ends contacting the file face and slowly move the ring to remove material from the ends. When performing this operation, file only by pushing the ring from the outside end of the file towards the vise **(see illustration)**.

16   Excess end gap isn't critical unless it exceeds approximately 0.040-inch.

17   Check the piston ring side clearances by laying each new piston ring in its respective groove in the piston and slipping a feeler gauge in beside it **(see illustration)**. Check the clearance at three or four locations around each groove. Be sure to use the correct ring for each groove (they are different). Check with an automotive machine shop for the correct side clearance for your engine. If the clearance is excessive, new pistons will have to be used.

18   Repeat the procedure for each ring that will be installed in the first cylinder and for each ring in the remaining cylinders. Remember to keep rings, pistons and cylinders matched up. Once the ring end gaps and side clearances have been checked/corrected, the rings can be installed on the pistons.

19   The oil control ring (lowest one on the piston) is usually installed first. It's composed of three separate components. Slip the spacer/expander into the groove **(see illustration)**. If an anti-rotation tang is used, make sure it's inserted into the drilled hole in the ring groove. Next, install the upper side rail in the same manner **(see illustration)**. Don't use a piston ring installation tool on the oil ring side rails, as they may be damaged. Instead, place one end of the side rail into the groove between the spacer/expander and the ring land, hold it firmly in place and slide a finger around the piston while pushing the rail into the groove. Finally, install the lower side rail.

20   After the three oil ring components have been installed, check to make sure that both the upper and lower side rails can be rotated smoothly inside the ring grooves.

21   The number two (middle) ring is installed next. It's usually stamped with a mark which must face up, toward the top of the piston. Do not mix up the top and middle rings, as they have different cross-sections. **Note:** *Always follow the instructions printed on the ring package or box - different manufacturers may require different approaches.*

22   Use a piston ring installation tool and make sure the identification mark is facing the top of the piston, then slip the ring into the middle groove on the piston **(see illustration)**. Don't expand the ring any more than necessary to slide it over the piston.

23   Install the number one (top) ring in the same manner. Make sure the mark is facing up. Be careful not to confuse the number one and number two rings.

24   Repeat the procedure for the remaining pistons and rings.

Installation

25   Before installing the piston/connecting rod assemblies, the cylinder walls must be perfectly clean, the top edge of each cylinder bore must be chamfered, and the crankshaft must be in place.

26   Remove the cap from the end of the number one connecting rod (refer to the marks made during removal). Remove the original bearing inserts and wipe the bearing surfaces of the connecting rod and cap with a clean, lint-free cloth. They must be kept spotlessly clean.

9.19a Installing the spacer/expander in the oil ring groove

9.19b DO NOT use a piston ring installation tool when installing the oil control side rails

9.22 Use a piston ring installation tool to install the number 2 and the number 1 (top) rings - be sure the directional mark on the piston ring(s) is facing toward the top of the piston

9.30 Position the piston ring end gaps as shown

2C

Connecting rod bearing oil clearance check

Refer to illustrations 9.30, 9.35, 9.37 and 9.41

27   Clean the back side of the new upper bearing insert, then lay it in place in the connecting rod. Make sure the tab on the bearing fits into the recess in the rod. Don't hammer the bearing insert into place and be very careful not to nick or gouge the bearing face. Don't lubricate the bearing at this time.

28   Clean the back side of the other bearing insert and install it in the rod cap. Again, make sure the tab on the bearing fits into the recess in the cap, and don't apply any lubricant. It's critically important that the mating surfaces of the bearing and connecting rod are perfectly clean and oil free when they're assembled.

29   Install a short section of plastic or rubber hose over the connecting rod bolts to avoid damaging the cylinder wall or crankshaft journal **(see illustration 9.6)**.

30   Position the piston ring gaps at 90-degree intervals around the piston as shown **(see illustration)**.

31   Lubricate the piston and rings with clean engine oil and attach a piston ring compressor to the piston. Leave the skirt protruding about 1/4-inch to guide the piston into the cylinder. The rings must be compressed until they're flush with the piston.

32   Rotate the crankshaft until the number one connecting rod journal is at BDC (bottom dead center) and apply a liberal coat of engine oil to the cylinder walls.

33   With the mark or arrow on top of the piston facing the front (timing chain end) of the engine, gently insert the piston/connecting rod assembly into the number one cylinder bore and rest the bottom edge of the ring compressor on the engine block.

34   Tap the top edge of the ring compressor to make sure it's contacting the block around its entire circumference.

35   Gently tap on the top of the piston with the end of a wooden or plastic hammer handle **(see illustration)** while guiding the end of the connecting rod into place on the crankshaft journal. The piston rings may try to pop out of the ring compressor just before entering the cylinder bore, so keep some downward pressure on the ring compressor. Work slowly, and if any resistance is felt as the piston enters the cylinder, stop immediately. Find out what's hanging up and fix it before proceeding. Do not, for any reason, force the piston into the cylinder - you might break a ring and/or the piston.

36   Once the piston/connecting rod assembly is installed, the connecting rod bearing oil clearance must be checked before the rod cap is permanently installed.

37   Cut a piece of the appropriate size Plastigage slightly shorter than the width of the connecting rod bearing and lay it in place on the number one connecting rod journal, parallel with the journal axis **(see illustration)**.

38   Clean the connecting rod cap bearing face and install the rod cap. Make sure the mating mark on the cap is on the same side as the mark on the connecting rod **(see illustration 9.4a)**.

39   Install the old rod bolts or nuts, at this time, and tighten them to the torque listed in this Chapter's Specifications, working up to it in three steps. **Note:** *Use a thin-wall socket to avoid erroneous torque readings that can result if the socket is wedged between the rod cap and the bolt or nut. If the socket tends to wedge itself between the fastener*

9.35 Use a plastic or wooden hammer handle to push the piston into the cylinder

9.37 Place Plastigage on each connecting rod bearing journal parallel to the crankshaft centerline

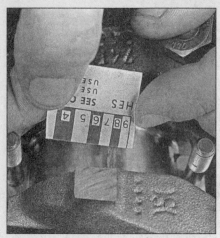

9.41 Use the scale on the Plastigage package to determine the bearing oil clearance - be sure to measure the widest part of the Plastigage and use the correct scale; it comes with both standard and metric scales

and the cap, lift up on it slightly until it no longer contacts the cap. DO NOT rotate the crankshaft at any time during this operation.

40   Remove the fasteners and detach the rod cap, being very careful not to disturb the Plastigage. Discard the cap bolts at this time as they cannot be reused. **Note:** *You MUST use new connecting rod bolts.*

41   Compare the width of the crushed Plastigage to the scale printed on the Plastigage envelope to obtain the oil clearance **(see illustration)**. The connecting rod oil clearance is usually about 0.001 to 0.002 inch. Consult an automotive machine shop for the clearance specified for the rod bearings on your engine.

42   If the clearance is not as specified, the bearing inserts may be the wrong size (which means different ones will be required). Before deciding that different inserts are needed, make sure that no dirt or oil was between the bearing inserts and the connecting rod or cap when the clearance was measured. Also, recheck the journal diameter. If the Plastigage was wider at one end than the other, the journal may be tapered. If the clearance still exceeds the limit specified, the bearing will have to be replaced with an undersize bearing. **Caution:** *When installing a new crankshaft always use a standard size bearing.*

Final installation

43   Carefully scrape all traces of the Plastigage material off the rod journal and/or bearing face. Be very careful not to scratch the bearing - use your fingernail or the edge of a plastic card.

44   Make sure the bearing faces are perfectly clean, then apply a uniform layer of clean moly-base grease or engine assembly lube to both of them. You'll have to push the piston into the cylinder to expose the face of the bearing insert in the connecting rod. **Caution:** *If the connecting rod caps are secured*

to the rods with bolts (instead of nuts), install new connecting rod cap bolts. Do NOT reuse old bolts - they have stretched and cannot be reused. Slide the connecting rod back into place on the journal, install the rod cap, install the nuts or new bolts and tighten them to the torque listed in this Chapter's Specifications. Again, work up to the torque in three steps.

45   Repeat the entire procedure for the remaining pistons/connecting rods.

46   The important points to remember are:

a) Keep the back sides of the bearing inserts and the insides of the connecting rods and caps perfectly clean when assembling them.

b) Make sure you have the correct piston/rod assembly for each cylinder.

c) The mark on the piston must face the front (timing belt end) of the engine.

d) Lubricate the cylinder walls liberally with clean oil.

e) Lubricate the bearing faces when installing the rod caps after the oil clearance has been checked.

47   After all the piston/connecting rod assemblies have been correctly installed, rotate the crankshaft a number of times by hand to check for any obvious binding.

48   As a final step, check the connecting rod endplay again (see Step 3). If it was correct before disassembly and the original crankshaft and rods were reinstalled, it should still be correct. If new rods or a new crankshaft were installed, the endplay may be inadequate. If so, the rods will have to be removed and taken to an automotive machine shop for resizing.

10   Crankshaft - removal and installation

Caution: *On 4.9L engines, it is necessary to remove the cylinder liners in order to properly clean the block. Carefully mark the alignment of each liner to the cylinder block if they are*

10.1 Checking crankshaft endplay with a dial indicator

to be reused. However, this particular engine is a difficult one for the home mechanic to rebuild, because of the cylinder liners and other rebuilding problems. It is suggested that when rebuilding this engine, have the short-block cleaned and rebuilt at a professional engine shop. They will install new pistons with new, matching liners, carefully fit new O-rings to the bottom of the liners and set the correct liner height in the block. **Note:** *The 4.6L Northstar engine requires expensive special tools and parts for the rebuilding procedures. It is recommended that the home mechanic purchase a Northstar long block from the dealer or other reliable engine builder when considering engine overhaul. The following information refers only to the 4.9L engine.*

Removal

Refer to illustrations 10.1 and 10.3

Note: *The crankshaft can be removed only after the engine has been removed from the vehicle. It's assumed that the driveplate, crankshaft pulley, timing chain, oil pan, oil pump and piston/connecting rod assemblies have already been removed.*

1   Before the crankshaft is removed, measure the endplay. Mount a dial indicator with the indicator in line with the crankshaft and just touching the end of the crankshaft as shown **(see illustration)**.

2   Pry the crankshaft all the way to the rear and zero the dial indicator. Next, pry the crankshaft to the front as far as possible and check the reading on the dial indicator. The distance traveled is the endplay. A typical crankshaft endplay should fall between 0.003 to 0.010-inch. If it's greater than that, check the crankshaft thrust surfaces for wear after its removed. If no wear is evident, new main bearings should correct the endplay.

3   If a dial indicator isn't available, feeler gauges can be used. Gently pry the crankshaft all the way to the front of the engine. Slip feeler gauges between the crankshaft and the front face of the thrust bearing or washer to determine the clearance **(see illustration)**.

4   Loosen the main bearing cap bolts 1/4-turn at a time each, until they can be removed by hand.

10.3 Checking crankshaft endplay with feeler gauges at the thrust bearing journal

10.17 Place the Plastigage onto the crankshaft bearing journal as shown

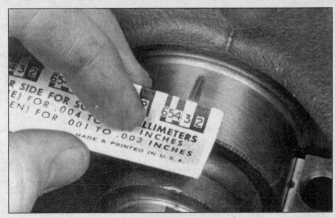

10.21 Use the scale on the Plastigage package to determine the bearing oil clearance - be sure to measure the widest part of the Plastigage and use the correct scale; it comes with both standard and metric scales

5   Gently tap the main bearing caps with a soft-face hammer to loosen them. Pull the main bearing caps straight up and off the cylinder block. Try not to drop the bearing inserts if they come out with the caps.

6   Carefully lift the crankshaft out of the engine. It may be a good idea to have an assistant available, since the crankshaft is quite heavy and awkward to handle. With the bearing inserts in place inside the engine block and main bearing caps, reinstall the main bearing caps onto the engine block and tighten the bolts finger tight. Make sure you install the main bearing caps with the arrows facing the front end of the engine.

Installation

7   Crankshaft installation is the first step in engine reassembly. It's assumed at this point that the engine block and crankshaft have been cleaned, inspected and repaired or reconditioned.

8   Position the engine block with the bottom facing up.

9   Remove the main bearing caps.

10   If they're still in place, remove the original bearing inserts from the block and from the main bearing caps. Wipe the bearing surfaces of the block and main bearing caps with a clean, lint-free cloth. They must be kept spotlessly clean. This is critical for determining the correct bearing oil clearance.

Main bearing oil clearance check

Refer to illustrations 10.17 and 10.21

11   Without mixing them up, clean the back sides of the new upper main bearing inserts (with grooves and oil holes) and lay one in each main bearing saddle in the block. Each upper bearing has an oil groove and oil hole in it. **Caution:** *The oil holes in the block must line up with the oil holes in the upper bearing inserts.* The thrust washer or thrust bearing insert must be installed in the number 3 crankshaft journal. Clean the back sides of the lower main bearing inserts and install

them in the main bearing caps. Make sure the tab on the bearing insert fits into the recess in the block or main bearing cap.

12   Clean the faces of the bearing inserts in the block and the crankshaft main bearing journals with a clean, lint-free cloth.

13   Check or clean the oil holes in the crankshaft, as any dirt here can go only one way - straight through the new bearings.

14   Once you're certain the crankshaft is clean, carefully lay it in position in the cylinder block.

15   Before the crankshaft can be permanently installed, the main bearing oil clearance must be checked.

16   Cut several strips of the appropriate size of Plastigage. They must be slightly shorter than the width of the main bearing journal.

17   Place one piece on each crankshaft main bearing journal, parallel with the journal axis as shown **(see illustration)**.

18   Clean the faces of the bearing inserts in the main bearing caps, then install the caps. DO NOT disturb the Plastigage. Make sure you install the main bearing caps with the arrows facing the front (timing chain end) of the engine.

19   Apply clean engine oil to all bolt threads prior to installation, then install all bolts finger-tight. Tighten main bearing cap bolts working from the center out, progressing in two steps, to the torque listed in this Chapter's Specifications. DO NOT rotate the crankshaft at any time during this operation.

20   Remove the bolts in the *reverse* order of the tightening sequence and carefully remove the main bearing caps, lifting them straight up and off the block. Do not disturb the Plastigage or rotate the crankshaft.

21   Compare the width of the crushed Plastigage on each journal to the scale printed on the Plastigage envelope to determine the main bearing oil clearance **(see illustration)**. A typical main bearing oil clearance should fall between 0.0015 to 0.0023-inch. Check with an automotive machine shop for the oil clearance for your engine.

22   If the clearance is not as specified, the

bearing inserts may be the wrong size (which means different ones will be required). Before deciding if different inserts are needed, make sure that no dirt or oil was between the bearing inserts and the cap assembly or block when the clearance was measured. If the Plastigage was wider at one end than the other, the crankshaft journal may be tapered. If the clearance still exceeds the limit specified, the bearing insert(s) will have to be replaced with an undersize bearing insert(s). **Caution:** *When installing a new crankshaft always install a standard bearing insert set.*

23   Carefully scrape all traces of the Plastigage material off the main bearing journals and/or the bearing insert faces. Be sure to remove all residue from the oil holes. Use your fingernail or the edge of a plastic card - don't nick or scratch the bearing faces.

Final installation

24   Carefully lift the crankshaft out of the cylinder block.

25   Clean the bearing insert faces in the cylinder block, then apply a thin, uniform layer of moly-base grease or engine assembly lube to each of the bearing surfaces. Be sure to coat the thrust faces as well as the journal face of the thrust bearing.

26   Make sure the crankshaft journals are clean, then lay the crankshaft back in place in the cylinder block.

27   Clean the bearing insert faces in the bearing caps and apply the same lubricant to them.

28   Install the main bearing caps onto the crankshaft and cylinder block.

29   Prior to installation, apply clean engine oil to all bolt threads wiping off any excess, then install all bolts finger-tight.

30   Tighten the bearing cap bolts to the specified torque, working from the center out, and approach the final torque in three steps.

31   Recheck crankshaft endplay with a feeler gauge or a dial indicator. The endplay should be correct if the crankshaft thrust faces aren't worn or damaged and if new

2C

bearings have been installed.

32   Rotate the crankshaft a number of times by hand to check for any obvious binding. It should rotate with a running torque of 50 in-lbs or less. If the running torque is too high, correct the problem at this time.

33   Install the new rear main oil seal (see Chapter 2A).

11   Engine overhaul - reassembly sequence

1   Before beginning engine reassembly, make sure you have all the necessary new parts, gaskets and seals as well as the following items on hand:

Common hand tools
A 1/2-inch drive torque wrench
New engine oil
Gasket sealant
Thread locking compound

2   If you obtained a short block it will be necessary to install the cylinder head, the oil pump and pick-up tube, the oil pan, the water pump, the timing belt and timing cover, and the valve cover (see Chapter 2A). In order to save time and avoid problems, the external components must be installed in the following general order:

Thermostat and housing cover
Water pump
Intake and exhaust manifolds
Fuel injection components
Emission control components
Spark plug wires and spark plugs
Ignition coils
Oil filter
Engine mounts and mount brackets
Driveplate

12   Initial start-up and break-in after overhaul

Warning: *Have a fire extinguisher handy when starting the engine for the first time.*

1   Once the engine has been installed in the vehicle, double-check the engine oil and coolant levels.

2   With the spark plugs out of the engine and the ignition system and fuel pump disabled, crank the engine until oil pressure registers on the gauge or the light goes out.

3   Install the spark plugs, hook up the plug wires and restore the ignition system and fuel pump functions.

4   Start the engine. It may take a few moments for the fuel system to build up pressure, but the engine should start without a great deal of effort.

5   After the engine starts, it should be allowed to warm up to normal operating temperature. While the engine is warming up, make a thorough check for fuel, oil and coolant leaks.

6   Shut the engine off and recheck the engine oil and coolant levels.

7   Drive the vehicle to an area with minimum traffic, accelerate from 30 to 50 mph, then allow the vehicle to slow to 30 mph with the throttle closed. Repeat the procedure 10 or 12 times. This will load the piston rings and cause them to seat properly against the cylinder walls. Check again for oil and coolant leaks.

8   Drive the vehicle gently for the first 500 miles (no sustained high speeds) and keep a constant check on the oil level. It is not unusual for an engine to use oil during the break-in period.

9   At approximately 500 to 600 miles, change the oil and filter.

10   For the next few hundred miles, drive the vehicle normally. Do not pamper it or abuse it.

11   After 2000 miles, change the oil and filter again and consider the engine broken in.

COMMON ENGINE OVERHAUL TERMS

B

Backlash - The amount of play between two parts. Usually refers to how much one gear can be moved back and forth without moving gear with which it's meshed.

Bearing Caps - The caps held in place by nuts or bolts which, in turn, hold the bearing surface. This space is for lubricating oil to enter.

Bearing clearance - The amount of space left between shaft and bearing surface. This space is for lubricating oil to enter.

Bearing crush - The additional height which is purposely manufactured into each bearing half to ensure complete contact of the bearing back with the housing bore when the engine is assembled.

Bearing knock - The noise created by movement of a part in a loose or worn bearing.

Blueprinting - Dismantling an engine and reassembling it to EXACT specifications.

Bore - An engine cylinder, or any cylindrical hole; also used to describe the process of enlarging or accurately refinishing a hole with a cutting tool, as to bore an engine cylinder. The bore size is the diameter of the hole.

Boring - Renewing the cylinders by cutting them out to a specified size. A boring bar is used to make the cut.

Bottom end - A term which refers collectively to the engine block, crankshaft, main bearings and the big ends of the connecting rods.

Break-in - The period of operation between installation of new or rebuilt parts and time in which parts are worn to the correct fit. Driving at reduced and varying speed for a specified mileage to permit parts to wear to the correct fit.

Bushing - A one-piece sleeve placed in a bore to serve as a bearing surface for shaft, piston pin, etc. Usually replaceable.

C

Camshaft - The shaft in the engine, on which a series of lobes are located for operating the valve mechanisms. The camshaft is driven by gears or sprockets and a timing chain. Usually referred to simply as the cam.

Carbon - Hard, or soft, black deposits found in combustion chamber, on plugs, under rings, on and under valve heads.

Cast iron - An alloy of iron and more than two percent carbon, used for engine blocks and heads because it's relatively inexpensive and easy to mold into complex shapes.

Chamfer - To bevel across (or a bevel on) the sharp edge of an object.

Chase - To repair damaged threads with a tap or die.

Combustion chamber - The space between the piston and the cylinder head, with the piston at top dead center, in which air-fuel mixture is burned.

Compression ratio - The relationship between cylinder volume (clearance volume) when the piston is at top dead center and cylinder volume when the piston is at bottom dead center.

Connecting rod - The rod that connects the crank on the crankshaft with the piston. Sometimes called a con rod.

Connecting rod cap - The part of the connecting rod assembly that attaches the rod to the crankpin.

Core plug - Soft metal plug used to plug the casting holes for the coolant passages in the block.

Crankcase - The lower part of the engine in which the crankshaft rotates; includes the lower section of the cylinder block and the oil pan.

Crank kit - A reground or reconditioned crankshaft and new main and connecting rod bearings.

Crankpin - The part of a crankshaft to which a connecting rod is attached.

Crankshaft - The main rotating member, or shaft, running the length of the crankcase, with offset throws to which the connecting rods are attached; changes the reciprocating motion of the pistons into rotating motion.

Cylinder sleeve - A replaceable sleeve, or liner, pressed into the cylinder block to form the cylinder bore.

D

Deburring - Removing the burrs (rough edges or areas) from a bearing.

Deglazer - A tool, rotated by an electric motor, used to remove glaze from cylinder walls so a new set of rings will seat.

E

Endplay - The amount of lengthwise movement between two parts. As applied to a crankshaft, the distance that the crankshaft can move forward and back in the cylinder block.

F

Face - A machinist's term that refers to removing metal from the end of a shaft or the face of a larger part, such as a flywheel.

Fatigue - A breakdown of material through a large number of loading and unloading cycles. The first signs are cracks followed shortly by breaks.

Feeler gauge - A thin strip of hardened steel, ground to an exact thickness, used to check clearances between parts.

Free height - The unloaded length or height of a spring.

Freeplay - The looseness in a linkage, or an assembly of parts, between the initial application of force and actual movement. Usually perceived as slop or slight delay.

Freeze plug - See Core plug.

G

Gallery - A large passage in the block that forms a reservoir for engine oil pressure.

Glaze - The very smooth, glassy finish that develops on cylinder walls while an engine is in service.

H

Heli-Coil - A rethreading device used when threads are worn or damaged. The device is installed in a retapped hole to reduce the thread size to the original size.

I

Installed height - The spring's measured length or height, as installed on the cylinder head. Installed height is measured from the spring seat to the underside of the spring retainer.

J

Journal - The surface of a rotating shaft which turns in a bearing.

K

Keeper - The split lock that holds the valve spring retainer in position on the valve stem.

Key - A small piece of metal inserted into matching grooves machined into two parts fitted together - such as a gear pressed onto a shaft - which prevents slippage between the two parts.

Knock - The heavy metallic engine sound, produced in the combustion chamber as a result of abnormal combustion - usually detonation. Knock is usually caused by a loose or worn bearing. Also referred to as detonation, pinging and spark knock. Connecting rod or main bearing knocks are created by too much oil clearance or insufficient lubrication.

L

Lands - The portions of metal between the piston ring grooves.

Lapping the valves - Grinding a valve face and its seat together with lapping compound.

Lash - The amount of free motion in a gear train, between gears, or in a mechanical assembly, that occurs before movement can begin. Usually refers to the lash in a valve train.

Lifter - The part that rides against the cam to transfer motion to the rest of the valve train.

M

Machining - The process of using a machine to remove metal from a metal part.

Main bearings - The plain, or babbit, bearings that support the crankshaft.

Main bearing caps - The cast iron caps, bolted to the bottom of the block, that support the main bearings.

O

O.D. - Outside diameter.

Oil gallery - A pipe or drilled passageway in the engine used to carry engine oil from one area to another.

Oil ring - The lower ring, or rings, of a piston; designed to prevent excessive amounts of oil from working up the cylinder walls and into the combustion chamber. Also called an oil-control ring.

Oil seal - A seal which keeps oil from leaking out of a compartment. Usually refers to a dynamic seal around a rotating shaft or other moving part.

O-ring - A type of sealing ring made of a special rubberlike material; in use, the O-ring is compressed into a groove to provide the sealing action.

Overhaul - To completely disassemble a unit, clean and inspect all parts, reassemble it with the original or new parts and make all adjustments necessary for proper operation.

P

Pilot bearing - A small bearing installed in the center of the flywheel (or the rear end of the crankshaft) to support the front end of the input shaft of the transmission.

Pip mark - A little dot or indentation which indicates the top side of a compression ring.

Piston - The cylindrical part, attached to the connecting rod, that moves up and down in the cylinder as the crankshaft rotates. When the fuel charge is fired, the piston transfers the force of the explosion to the connecting rod, then to the crankshaft.

Piston pin (or wrist pin) - The cylindrical and usually hollow steel pin that passes through the piston. The piston pin fastens the piston to the upper end of the connecting rod.

Piston ring - The split ring fitted to the groove in a piston. The ring contacts the sides of the ring groove and also rubs against the cylinder wall, thus sealing space between piston and wall. There are two types of rings: Compression rings seal the compression pressure in the combustion chamber; oil rings scrape excessive oil off the cylinder wall.

Piston ring groove - The slots or grooves cut in piston heads to hold piston rings in position.

Piston skirt - The portion of the piston below the rings and the piston pin hole.

Plastigage - A thin strip of plastic thread, available in different sizes, used for measuring clearances. For example, a strip of plastigage is laid across a bearing journal and mashed as parts are assembled. Then parts are disassembled and the width of the strip is measured to determine clearance between journal and bearing. Commonly used to measure crankshaft main-bearing and connecting rod bearing clearances.

Press-fit - A tight fit between two parts that requires pressure to force the parts together. Also referred to as drive, or force, fit.

Prussian blue - A blue pigment; in solution, useful in determining the area of contact between two surfaces. Prussian blue is commonly used to determine the width and location of the contact area between the valve face and the valve seat.

R

Race (bearing) - The inner or outer ring that provides a contact surface for balls or rollers in bearing.

Ream - To size, enlarge or smooth a hole by using a round cutting tool with fluted edges.

Ring job - The process of reconditioning the cylinders and installing new rings.

Runout - Wobble. The amount a shaft rotates out-of-true.

S

Saddle - The upper main bearing seat.

Scored - Scratched or grooved, as a cylinder wall may be scored by abrasive particles moved up and down by the piston rings.

Scuffing - A type of wear in which there's a transfer of material between parts moving against each other; shows up as pits or grooves in the mating surfaces.

Seat - The surface upon which another part rests or seats. For example, the valve seat is the matched surface upon which the valve face rests. Also used to refer to wearing into a good fit; for example, piston rings seat after a few miles of driving.

Short block - An engine block complete with crankshaft and piston and, usually, camshaft assemblies.

Static balance - The balance of an object while it's stationary.

Step - The wear on the lower portion of a ring land caused by excessive side and back-clearance. The height of the step indicates the ring's extra side clearance and the length of the step projecting from the back wall of the groove represents the ring's back clearance.

Stroke - The distance the piston moves when traveling from top dead center to bottom dead center, or from bottom dead center to top dead center.

Stud - A metal rod with threads on both ends.

T

Tang - A lip on the end of a plain bearing used to align the bearing during assembly.

Tap - To cut threads in a hole. Also refers to the fluted tool used to cut threads.

Taper - A gradual reduction in the width of a shaft or hole; in an engine cylinder, taper usually takes the form of uneven wear, more pronounced at the top than at the bottom.

Throws - The offset portions of the crankshaft to which the connecting rods are affixed.

Thrust bearing - The main bearing that has thrust faces to prevent excessive endplay, or forward and backward movement of the crankshaft.

Thrust washer - A bronze or hardened steel washer placed between two moving parts. The washer prevents longitudinal movement and provides a bearing surface for thrust surfaces of parts.

Tolerance - The amount of variation permitted from an exact size of measurement. Actual amount from smallest acceptable dimension to largest acceptable dimension.

U

Umbrella - An oil deflector placed near the valve tip to throw oil from the valve stem area.

Undercut - A machined groove below the normal surface.

Undersize bearings - Smaller diameter bearings used with re-ground crankshaft journals.

V

Valve grinding - Refacing a valve in a valve-refacing machine.

Valve train - The valve-operating mechanism of an engine; includes all components from the camshaft to the valve.

Vibration damper - A cylindrical weight attached to the front of the crankshaft to minimize torsional vibration (the twist-untwist actions of the crankshaft caused by the cylinder firing impulses). Also called a harmonic balancer.

W

Water jacket - The spaces around the cylinders, between the inner and outer shells of the cylinder block or head, through which coolant circulates.

Web - A supporting structure across a cavity.

Woodruff key - A key with a radiused backside (viewed from the side).

Chapter 3
Cooling, heating and air conditioning systems

Contents

Specifications

General

Pressure cap rating	
Radiator cap	12 to 15 psi
Expansion tank cap	15 to 18 psi
Thermostat rating (opening temperature)	
4.9L models	192 to 199 degrees F
4.6L models	185 to 192 degrees F
Cooling system capacity	See Chapter 1
Refrigerant type	
1992 and 1993 models	R-12
1994 and later models	R-134a
Refrigerant capacity	Refer to HVAC specification tag
Refrigerant oil	
R-12 systems	525 viscosity refrigerant oil
R-134a systems	Polyalkylene glycol (PAG) refrigerant oil

Torque specifications

	Ft-lbs (unless otherwise indicated)
Thermostat housing cover bolts	
4.9L engine	20
4.6L engine	89 in-lbs
Coolant crossover housing mounting bolts (4.6L models)	18
Condenser mounting bolts	115 in-lbs

Torque specifications (continued)

	Ft-lbs (unless otherwise indicated)
Cooling fan mounting bolts	
4.9L models...	97 in-lbs
4.6L models...	88 in-lbs
Radiator support mounting bolts	
4.9L models...	20
4.6L models...	18
Water pump pulley bolts 4.9L engine.................................	22
Water pump	
4.9L engine	
Torx-head bolts..	30
Lower hex-head screws	60 in-lbs
Upper hex-head screws	30
Stud nuts..	60 in-lbs
4.6L engine	
Water pump body	73
Water pump cover bolts	89 in-lbs

1   General information

Engine cooling system

Refer to illustrations 1.1 and 1.2

All vehicles covered by this manual employ a pressurized engine cooling system with thermostatically-controlled coolant circulation **(see illustration)**. An impeller-type water pump mounted on the engine block (4.9L) or in the coolant crossover housing (4.6L) pumps coolant through the engine. The coolant flows around each cylinder and toward the rear of the engine. Cast-in coolant passages direct coolant around the intake and exhaust ports, near the spark plug areas and in close proximity to the exhaust valve guides.

A wax-pellet type thermostat controls engine coolant temperature. During warm up, the closed thermostat prevents coolant from circulating through the radiator. As the engine nears normal operating temperature, the thermostat opens and allows hot coolant to travel through the radiator, where it's cooled before returning to the engine **(see illustration)**.

1.1 Cooling, heating and air conditioning components (2000 4.6L model shown)

1	Radiator support cover	4	Water pump (inside coolant crossover housing)	6	Air conditioning accumulator
2	Condenser			7	Coolant crossover housing
3	Cooling fans	5	Coolant expansion tank		

1.2 Typical thermostat

1	Flange	5	Valve seat
2	Piston	6	Valve
3	Jiggle valve	7	Frame
4	Main coil	8	Secondary
	spring		coil spring

The cooling system is sealed by a pressure cap, which raises the boiling point of the coolant and increases the cooling efficiency of the radiator. Some models use a plastic coolant reservoir that is connected by a hose to the radiator filler neck; if the engine overheats, coolant escapes through a valve in the radiator cap and travels through the hose into the reservoir. As the engine cools, the coolant is automatically drawn back into the cooling system to maintain the correct level. Other models use a pressurized expansion tank; the level in the tank will vary with the temperature of the coolant. This type of system does not have a cap on the radiator. Instead, the pressure cap is mounted on the expansion tank.

4.9L models are equipped with a coolant reservoir. As the vehicle is driven, the coolant expands with the heat and displaces into the coolant reservoir. As the vehicle cools, the displaced coolant contracts and is drawn back into the radiator by vacuum. The pressure (radiator) cap is mounted on the radiator on these systems, therefore the coolant reservoir is not pressurized.

4.6L models are equipped with an expansion tank. The tank is mounted at a point higher than the radiator to provide an air space for the coolant expansion and contraction. As coolant is circulated, air is allowed to bleed off. Coolant without air bubbles absorbs heat from the engine more efficiently. The pressure cap is mounted on the expansion tank on these models, therefore the expansion tank is pressurized.

1996 and later models use a special coolant called DEX-COOL (orange coolant) specifically designed for use in the cooling system. 1995 and earlier models use regular ethylene glycol (green coolant). When the cooling system (all models) is serviced, pel-lets must be added to the cooling system as a sealant supplement. Failure to use the specified coolant and the pellets (sealant supplement) could result in major engine damage.

The engine oil cooler is mounted in the side of the radiator. Depending on the year and model, one side of the radiator houses the transaxle oil cooler while the other side of the radiator houses the engine oil cooler.

The 4.9L engine is equipped with a conventional water pump mounted on the front of the engine. The 4.6L engine is equipped with a modular style water pump that is press fit into the coolant crossover housing. This type of water pump requires a special tool for water pump replacement.

The coolant temperature is monitored by the engine coolant temperature (ECT) sensor. The information is relayed to the computer and processed for the temperature gauge on the instrument panel. All ECT information is covered in Chapter 6.

Heating system

The heating system consists of a blower fan, a heater core located in the heater box, the hoses connecting the heater core to the engine cooling system and the heater/air conditioning control head on the dashboard. Hot engine coolant is circulated through the heater core. When the heater mode is activated, a flap door opens to expose the heater box to the passenger compartment. A fan switch on the control head activates the blower motor, which forces air through the core, heating the air.

The blower motor on 1992 through 1999 models (except 1998 and 1999 Sevilles) is located in the engine compartment, while on 2000 and later models (and 1998 and 1999 Sevilles) the blower motor is mounted behind the instrument panel in the passenger compartment.

Air conditioning system

The air conditioning system consists of a condenser mounted in front of the radiator, an evaporator mounted in the blower housing, a compressor mounted on the engine, an accumulator which filters moisture out of the refrigerant and the plumbing connecting all of the above components.

A blower fan forces the warmer air of the passenger compartment through the evaporator core (sort of a radiator-in-reverse), transferring the heat from the air to the refrigerant. The liquid refrigerant boils off into low pressure vapor, taking the heat with it when it leaves the evaporator.

---

2   Antifreeze - general information

Refer to illustration 2.4

Warning: *Do not allow antifreeze to come in contact with your skin or painted surfaces of the vehicle. Rinse off spills immediately with* plenty of water. Antifreeze is highly toxic if ingested. Never leave antifreeze lying around in an open container or in puddles on the floor; children and pets are attracted by its sweet smell and may drink it. Check with local authorities about disposing of used antifreeze. Many communities have collection centers that will see that antifreeze is disposed of safely. Never dump used anti-freeze on the ground or into drains.

Caution 1: *1996 and later models require DEX-COOL antifreeze in the cooling system. DEX-COOL is a long-lasting coolant designed for 100,000 miles or 5 years. Never mix green-colored ethylene glycol antifreeze and orange-colored DEX-COOL silicate-free coolant because doing so will destroy the efficiency of the DEX-COOL antifreeze.*

Caution 2: *All models require special pellets (sealant supplement) in the cooling system. The pellets must be added every time the coolant is changed. Failure to use the specified pellets (sealant supplement) in these cooling systems could result in engine damage. Consult with a dealer parts department or automotive parts store for the correct type of pellets that must be added to the cooling system.*

The cooling system on these models differ depending on the year of the vehicle. On 1995 and earlier models. the cooling system should be filled with a water/ethylene glycol based antifreeze solution (green coolant), which will prevent freezing down to at least -20-degrees F, or lower if local climate requires it. It also provides protection against corrosion and increases the antifreeze (coolant) boiling point. On 1996 and later models, the cooling system should be filled with DEX-COOL (orange-colored, silicate-free) coolant. Do not add any other type of coolant to these systems or the engine, radiator and heater core may be damaged. Also, any time the cooling system is serviced on all models, special pellets or sealant must be added to the cooling system. Failure to use the specified coolant and the pellets (sealant supplement) could result in major engine damage.

The cooling system should be drained, flushed and refilled at the specified intervals (see Chapter 1). Old or contaminated antifreeze solutions are likely to cause damage and encourage the formation of rust and scale in the system. Use distilled water with the antifreeze.

Before adding antifreeze, check all hose connections, because antifreeze tends to leak through very minute openings. Engines don't normally consume coolant, so if the level goes down, find the cause and correct it.

The exact mixture of antifreeze-to-water that you should use depends on the relative weather conditions. The mixture should contain at least 50-percent antifreeze, but should never contain more than 70-percent antifreeze. Consult the mixture ratio chart on the antifreeze container before adding coolant. Hydrometers are available at most

3

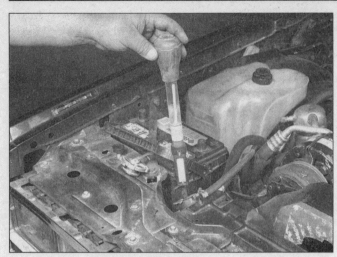

2.4 An inexpensive hydrometer can be used to test the condition of your coolant

3.8 Typical engine thermostat cover bolts (A) - if there is evidence of coolant stains below the thermostat housing (B), unbolt it and install a new gasket between the housing and the intake manifold

auto parts stores to test the coolant **(see illustration)**. Use antifreeze that meets the vehicle manufacturer's specifications.

3 Thermostat - check and replacement

Warning: *Do not remove the radiator cap or expansion tank cap, drain the coolant or replace the thermostat until the engine has cooled completely.*

Check

1   Before assuming the thermostat is to blame for a cooling system problem, check the coolant level, drivebelt tension (see Chapter 1) and temperature gauge operation.
2   If the engine seems to be taking a long time to warm up, based on heater output or temperature gauge operation, the thermostat is probably stuck open. Replace the thermo-

stat with a new one.
3   If the engine runs hot, use your hand to check the temperature of the upper radiator hose. If the hose isn't hot, but the engine is, the thermostat is probably stuck closed, preventing the coolant inside the engine from escaping to the radiator. Replace the thermostat. **Caution:** *Don't drive the vehicle without a thermostat. The computer may stay in open loop and emissions and fuel economy will suffer.*
4   If the upper radiator hose is hot, it means that the coolant is flowing and the thermostat is open. Consult the *Troubleshooting* section at the front of this manual for cooling system diagnosis.

Replacement

5   Disconnect the cable from the negative terminal of the battery (see Chapter 5).
6   Drain the cooling system (see Chapter 1). If the coolant is relatively new or in good condition (see Chapter 1), save it and

reuse it. Read the **Warning and Cautions** in Section 2.

4.9L models

Refer to illustration 3.8

7   Follow the upper radiator hose to the engine to locate the thermostat housing cover.
8   Loosen the hose clamp, then detach the hose from the fitting. If it's stuck, grasp it near the end with a pair of adjustable pliers and twist it to break the seal, then pull it off. If the hose is old or deteriorated, cut it off and install a new one **(see illustration)**.
9   If the outer surface of the large fitting that mates with the hose is deteriorated (corroded, pitted, etc.) it may be damaged further by hose removal. If it is, the thermostat housing cover will have to be replaced.
10   Remove the thermostat cover bolts and detach the housing cover. If the cover is stuck, tap it with a soft-face hammer to jar it loose. Be prepared for some coolant to spill as the gasket seal is broken.

3.14 Remove the two thermostat housing mounting bolts (4.6L model shown) - the thermostat housing on 4.6L models is located near the water pump drivebelt on the coolant crossover housing

3.15a Remove the thermostat from the housing (4.9L model shown)

3.15b Remove the thermostat from the housing (4.6L model shown)

3.17 Install a new rubber seal over the thermostat (4.9L model shown)

4.6L models

Refer to illustration 3.14

11 Remove the radiator support cover **(see illustrations 4.9a and 4.9b)**.
12 Remove the air filter housing (see Chapter 4).
13 Loosen the hose clamp, then detach the hose from the thermostat housing. If the clamp cannot be accessed, remove the thermostat housing cover with the radiator hose still attached.
14 Remove the thermostat cover mounting bolts **(see illustration)** and detach the housing cover. Be prepared for some coolant to spill as the seal is broken.

All models

Refer to illustrations 3.15a, 3.15b and 3.17

15 Note how it's installed, then remove the thermostat **(see illustrations)**.
16 Remove all traces of old gasket material

and/or sealant from the housing and cover.
17 Install a new rubber gasket over the thermostat **(see illustration)**.
18 Install the new thermostat in the housing without using sealant. Make sure the spring end is directed into the housing. Apply clean antifreeze to the O-rings for lubrication before installation.
19 Install the housing cover and bolts. Tighten the bolts to the torque listed in this Chapter's Specifications.
20 Reattach the hose and tighten the hose clamp securely. Install all components that were removed for access.
21 Refill the cooling system (see Chapter 1).
22 Start the engine and allow it to reach normal operating temperature, then check for leaks and proper thermostat operation (as described in Steps 2 through 4).

4   Engine cooling fans - check and replacement

Warning: *To avoid possible injury or damage, DO NOT operate the engine with a damaged fan. Do not attempt to repair fan blades - replace a damaged fan with a new one.*
Note: *All models have two fans. The following procedures apply to both.*

Check

Refer to illustrations 4.1a and 4.1b

1   If the engine is overheating and the cooling fan is not coming on when the engine temperature rises to an excessive level, unplug the fan motor electrical connector **(see illustrations)** and connect the motor directly to the battery with fused jumper wires. If the fan motor doesn't come on, replace the motor.

3

4.1a To test either fan motor, disconnect the electrical connector and use jumper wires to connect the fan directly to the battery and ground - if the fan still doesn't work, replace the motor (4.9L model shown)

4.1b Location of the fan electrical connector on a 4.6L model

4.8 Location of the mounting bolts for the engine splash shield

2   If the radiator fan motor is okay, but it isn't coming on when the engine gets hot, one of the fan relays might be defective, There are three cooling fan relays. A relay is used to control a circuit by turning it on and off in response to a control signal by the Powertrain Control Module (PCM). These control circuits are fairly complex, and checking them should be left to a dealer service department. Sometimes, the cooling fan system can be fixed by simply identifying and replacing a bad fuse and/or relay (see Chapter 12). **Note:** *1992 and 1993 models are equipped with a Power Module that assists the computer switching fan speeds and other climate control functions. These models do not use relays to switch cooling fan speeds. The Power Module is located in the blower/evaporator housing behind the instrument panel.*

3   Locate the fan relays in the engine compartment fuse/relay box (see Chapter 12).

4   Test each relay (see Chapter 12).

5   If the relays are okay, check all the wiring and connections to the fan motor. Refer to the wiring diagrams at the end of Chapter 12. If no obvious problems are found, the problem could be the engine coolant temperature (ECT) sensor or the Powertrain Control Module (PCM). Have the cooling fan system and circuit diagnosed by a dealer service department or repair shop with the proper diagnostic equipment.

6   All 1992 through 1994 models equipped with Electronic Climate Control can display trouble codes, which can be used to diagnose engine and body components. See Chapter 6 for entering the diagnostic mode, and how to access the Body Control Module (BCM) codes, which include those that cover heating, cooling and air conditioning. A problem with the engine cooling fan circuit will display a code. A problem with the ECT will display a code during the ECM diagnostics.

4.9a Location of the radiator support cover plastic retainers

4.9b Release the plastic retainers by pressing on the center lock

4.18 Remove the bolt and position the transaxle oil cooler line away from the cooling fans

Replacement

Refer to illustrations 4.8, 4.9a and 4.9b

Warning: *Wait until the engine is completely cool before beginning this procedure.*

7   Disconnect the cable from the negative terminal of the battery (see Chapter 5).

8   Set the parking brake and block the rear wheels to prevent the vehicle from rolling. Raise the front of the vehicle and support it securely with jackstands. Remove the lower splash pan, if equipped, from under the radiator **(see illustration)**.

9   Remove the radiator support cover, if equipped **(see illustrations)**.

4.9L models

10   Remove the right headlight bracket.

11   Remove the torque strut from the upper radiator support (see Chapter 2A).

12   Remove the transaxle oil cooler line bracket from the radiator (see Chapter 7).

4.6L models

Refer to illustrations 4.18 and 4.19

13   Remove the air filter housing (see

Chapter 4).

14   Remove the torque strut from the left side of the vehicle, if equipped (see Chapter 2B).

15   Drain the coolant from the engine (see Chapter 1).

16   Remove the upper radiator hose (see Section 6).

17   Remove the upper transaxle oil cooler line from the radiator (see Chapter 7).

18   On models with an oil cooler, remove the oil cooler pipe retaining bolt from the fan shroud **(see illustration)**.

19   Disconnect the oil cooler lines from the radiator **(see illustration)**.

All models

Refer to illustrations 4.21, 4.22a, 4.22b, 4.22c, 4.24a, 4.24b, 4.25a and 4.25b

20   Refer to Step 1 and disconnect the fan electrical connectors. Disconnect the cooling fan wiring harness from the cooling fan motor.

21   Remove the fan(s) lower mounting bolts **(see illustration)**. **Note:** *Some models are not equipped with lower mounting bolts for*

4.19 Remove the internal spring clip to detach the oil cooler line from the coupling

the cooling fans but instead secure the cooling fan assembly to the radiator using two locking tabs and mounts.

22   Unbolt the fan(s) from the radiator at the top **(see illustrations)**.

4.21 Remove the lower fan mounting bolts (arrows indicate the two main fan lower bolts and one of the two lower condenser fan bolts, seen from below) - later model shown, with two fans on engine side of radiator

4.22a Remove the upper fan mounting bolts (arrows indicate both of the main fan bolts and one of the two condenser fan bolts at right) (4.9L model shown)

4.22b Location of the left side cooling fan mounting bolt on a 4.6L model

4.22c Location of the right side cooling fan mounting bolt on a 4.6L model

4.24a To remove the fan, unscrew the left-hand-threaded nut in the center, then pull the fan blade from the motor shaft (4.9L model shown)

23   Carefully lift the fan out of the engine compartment. **Note:** *When removing the cooling fans from the engine compartment, move the fan assembly to the left and up then to the right and up. Remove the fan assembly cautiously without bending any components.*
24   To detach the fan from the motor, remove the motor shaft nut **(see illustrations)**. **Note:** *The nut has a **left-hand** thread. To unscrew it, turn it clockwise.*
25   To detach the fan motor from the shroud, remove the mounting bolts **(see illustrations)**.
26   Installation is the reverse of removal. Refill the cooling system, if drained (see Chapter 1), run the engine and check for leaks and proper operation.

5   Coolant reservoir/expansion tank - removal and installation

Refer to illustrations 5.2, 5.3, 5.7a and 5.7b
Warning: *Wait until the engine is completely cool before beginning this procedure.*
Caution: *There are two different types of coolant tanks on these models; coolant reservoirs or coolant expansion tanks. 4.9L models are equipped with a coolant reservoir. As the vehicle is driven, the coolant expands with*

the heat and displaces into the coolant reservoir. As the vehicle cools, the displaced coolant contracts and is drawn back into the radiator by vacuum. The pressure (radiator) cap is mounted on the radiator on these systems, therefore the coolant reservoir is not pressurized. 4.6L models are equipped with an expansion tank. The tank is mounted at a point higher than the radiator to provide an air space for the coolant expansion and contraction. As coolant is circulated, air is allowed to bleed off. Coolant without air bubbles absorbs heat from the engine more efficiently. The pressure cap is mounted on the expansion tank on these models; therefore the expansion tank is pressurized.
1   If you're working on a model with a 4.6L engine, drain the cooling system (see Chapter 1). On some models it will also be necessary to remove the radiator support cover for access to the expansion tank **(see illustrations 4.9a and 4.9b)**. **Note:** *The coolant reservoir/expansion tank is located in different locations depending on the year and the model. It may be necessary to remove a cover, a brace, etc. to access the coolant reservoir mounting bolts.*
2   On models with a 4.6L engine, detach the hose from the top of the expansion tank **(see illustration)**.

4.24b The 4.6L models are equipped with a left-hand-threaded nut also

3   Remove the radiator support brace from the strut tower, if equipped **(see illustration)**. On some models it may be necessary to remove the cross-vehicle brace.
4   Disconnect the coolant level sensor connector, if equipped.
5   Remove any relay mounting brackets or fuse/relay panels that may be in the way. On

4.25a Location of the fan motor mounting bolts on 4.9L models

4.25b Location of the fan motor mounting bolts on 4.6L models

5.2 Remove the hose from the top of the expansion tank (4.6L model shown)

5.3 On early models, remove the two bolts and the strut tower-to-radiator support brace

5.7a Remove the nuts and lift the coolant reservoir straight up, out of its bracket - location of the mounting nuts varies with year and model (4.9L model shown)

5.7b Location of the expansion tank mounting bolts on 4.6L models

some models it may be necessary to remove the battery (see Chapter 5).

6   On 4.6 L models, loosen the clamp from the lower hose at the bottom of the tank and remove the hose.

7   Remove the mounting bolts or nuts (see illustrations) and pull the coolant reservoir or expansion tank straight up and out of the vehicle.

8   Installation is the reverse of removal. For better viewing of the coolant level in the reservoir, clean the inside of the reservoir of any rust deposits or scale with hot, soapy water. Use a wad of cloth taped to the end of a bent coat hanger to scrub hard-to-reach areas inside the tank, then rinse with clean water.

9   Installation is the reverse of removal. Refill the cooling system, if drained (see Chapter 1).

6   Radiator - removal and installation

Refer to illustrations 6.8a, 6.8b, 6.10, 6.11a, 6.11b, 6.11c, 6.12, 6.13 and 6.14

Warning 1: These models are equipped with a Supplemental Inflatable Restraint (SIR) system (more commonly known as airbags). Always disable the airbag system before working in the vicinity of any airbag system component to avoid the possibility of acci-dental deployment of the airbag, which could cause personal injury (see Chapter 12).

Warning 2: Wait until the engine is completely cool before beginning this procedure.

1   Disconnect the cable from the negative terminal of the battery (see Chapter 5).

2   Remove the radiator support cover, if equipped (see illustrations 4.9a and 4.9b).

3   Drain the coolant (see Chapter 1). See the coolant Warning and Cautions in Section 2.

4   Remove the cooling fans (see Section 4).

5   Remove the air filter housing on models where it would interfere with removal (see Chapter 4).

6   On early models, remove the left and right torque struts (see Chapter 2A or 2B).

7   On early models, remove the airbag sensor from the front radiator brace (see Chapter 12).

8   Disconnect the transaxle oil cooler lines (and engine oil cooler lines, if equipped) from the radiator (see illustrations). To disconnect lines with quick-connect fittings, refer to illustration 4.19.

6.8a Disconnect the cooler lines from the radiator (arrow indicates lower of two fittings for the engine oil cooler, attached to the left tank) (4.9L model shown)

6.8b Location of the transaxle cooler lines on a 4.6L model

6.10 Loosen the hose clamps and disconnect the upper and lower radiator hoses

6.11a Remove the four bolts and lift the radiator top panel off to allow radiator removal (4.9L model)

9   Remove the auxiliary transaxle oil cooler, if equipped (see Chapter 7).

10   Disconnect the radiator upper and lower hoses (see illustration). Have a pan ready to catch any coolant that may spill onto the floor.

11   Remove the radiator support from the top of the radiator (see illustrations).

12   On models so equipped, disconnect the alternator cooling hose from the lower radiator side tank (see illustration).

13   On late models, remove the radiator to condenser mounting bolts (see illustration).

14   Lift the radiator straight up and out of the engine compartment. Lift the condenser slightly to release the bottom of the radiator from the rubber locking tabs (see illustration). Be careful not to drip coolant on any body paint; immediately wash it off with clear water as the antifreeze solution can damage the finish.

15   With the radiator removed, it can be inspected for leaks or damage. White stains on aluminum radiators indicate leakage. If in need of repairs, have a professional radiator shop perform the work, as special equipment and techniques are required.

16   Bugs and dirt can be cleaned from the radiator by using compressed air and a soft brush. Do not bend the cooling fins as this is done.

17   Inspect the rubber mounting pads and replace as necessary. Most models will have two rubber-lined insulators at the top and two at the bottom, in the radiator cradle.

18   Lift the radiator into position, making sure it is seated in the mounting pads.

6.11b On 4.6L models, first remove the radiator bracket mounting bolt and lift the bracket from the radiator post (one on each side of the radiator) . . .

6.11c . . . then, remove the radiator support bolts (two on each side of the radiator) and lift the support from the engine compartment

6.12 Disconnect the alternator coolant hose from the radiator, if equipped

6.13 Remove the condenser mounting bolts (right side shown)

6.14 Separate the radiator from the grommets and lift the radiator from the engine compartment

7.10 Remove the AIR check valve mounting bracket bolts and separate the bracket from the coolant crossover housing

7.23 Remove the coolant crossover housing mounting bolts (top bolts shown, others hidden from view)

19 Install the radiator support, the cooling fans, hoses and lines in the reverse order of removal.
20 Connect the negative battery cable and fill the radiator as described in Chapter 1.
21 Start the engine, allow the engine to reach normal operating temperature (upper radiator hose hot) and check for leaks.

7 Coolant crossover housing (4.6L models) - removal and installation

Refer to illustrations 7.10 and 7.23
Warning: *Wait until the engine is completely cool before beginning this procedure.*
1 Disconnect the cable from the negative terminal of the battery (see Chapter 5).
2 Drain the coolant (see Chapter 1). See the coolant **Warning and Cautions** in Section 2.
3 Remove the intake manifold service cover.
4 Remove the air filter housing (see Chapter 4).
5 Disconnect the brake booster vacuum hose from the coolant crossover housing.
6 Disconnect the fuel pressure regulator vacuum hose (see Chapter 4).
7 Remove the water pump drivebelt (see Chapter 1) and water pump belt tensioner (see Chapter 1).
8 If the vehicle is equipped with a secondary AIR system, disconnect the secondary AIR solenoid vacuum hose from the check valve (see Chapter 6).
9 Remove the secondary AIR check valve (see Chapter 6).
10 Remove the secondary AIR check valve bracket **(see illustration)** from the coolant crossover housing, if equipped.
11 Remove the throttle body (see Chapter 4).
12 Disconnect the fuel rail bracket mounting bolts and separate the bracket from the coolant crossover housing (see Chapter 4).

13 Remove the coolant expansion tank hose from the crossover housing.
14 Remove the engine lift bracket from the coolant crossover housing.
15 Remove the EGR valve (see Chapter 6).
16 Remove the EGR pipe from the coolant crossover housing (see Chapter 6).
17 Remove the EVAP canister purge valve (see Chapter 6).
18 Remove the MAP sensor (see Chapter 6).
19 Disconnect the shift cable from the transaxle and position the cable to the side (see Chapter 7).
20 Remove the upper and the lower radiator hoses from the coolant crossover housing.
21 Remove the water pump cover (see Section 8).
22 Label the vacuum lines, heater hoses, emissions system hoses, electrical connectors and ground straps, to ensure correct reinstallation, then detach them. Pieces of masking tape with numbers or letters written on them work well. If there's any possibility of confusion, make a sketch of the engine compartment and clearly label the lines, hoses and wires.
23 Remove the coolant crossover housing mounting bolts **(see illustration)**.
24 Separate the housing from the engine.
25 Clean the gasket surfaces of the housing with a scraper followed by lacquer thinner or brake system cleaner.
26 Position new gaskets and seals, using RTV sealant to hold them in place. Follow the gasket manufacturer's instructions and markings such as "UP", "TOP" or "FRONT".
27 Set the coolant crossover housing in position. Be sure all the bolt holes are lined up and start all the bolts by hand before tightening any of them (lightly oil the threads of the bolts before installation). **Note:** *Locate each bolt/stud in its original location. Putting the wrong-length bolt in a hole could cause a leak or stripped threads.*
28 Tighten the bolts to the torque listed in this Chapter's Specifications.

29 Install the remaining components in the reverse order of removal.
30 Refill the cooling system (see Chapter 1).

8 Water pump - check

Check

Refer to illustration 8.3
1 A failure in the water pump can cause serious engine damage due to overheating.
2 There are three ways to check the operation of the water pump while it's installed on the engine. If the pump is defective, it should be replaced with a new or rebuilt unit.
3 The water pump on 4.9L engines is equipped with a weep or vent hole **(see illustration)**. If a failure occurs in the pump seal, coolant will leak from the hole. In most cases you'll need a flashlight to find the hole on the water pump from underneath to check for leaks. **Note:** *Some small black staining around the weep hole is normal. If the stain is heavy brown or actual coolant is evident, replace the pump.* If the water pump seal fails on a 4.6L engine, coolant will leak out at the left front of the engine, between the cylinder

3

8.3 The weep hole is on the underside of the pump - you'll need a flashlight and small mirror to inspect it (4.9L engines)

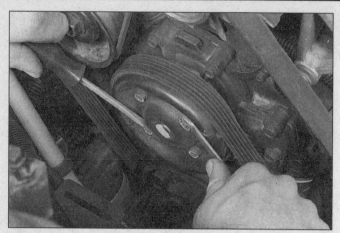

9.3 Loosen the water pump pulley bolts slightly with the drivebelt in place - the screwdriver helps keep the pulley from turning (4.9L models)

9.5a Water pump mounting bolts (arrows indicate most of the bolts) - 4.9L models

head and the coolant crossover housing.

4   If the water pump shaft bearings fail there may be a howling sound while the engine is running. With the engine off, shaft wear can be felt if the water pump pulley is rocked up-and-down. **Note:** *The 4.6L North-star models are equipped with a water pump that is mounted inside the water crossover housing. Because assess to the water pump pulley is restricted, this check will not apply.* Don't mistake drivebelt slippage, which causes a squealing sound, for water pump bearing failure.

5   A quick water pump performance check is to put the heater on. If the impeller in the pump is corroded, it won't be able to efficiently circulate hot coolant all the way to the heater core as it should.

9   Water pump - removal and installation

Refer to illustration 9.3
Warning: *Wait until the engine is completely cool before beginning this procedure.*

Caution: *The 4.6L models require a special tool to extract the water pump from the coolant crossover housing. This special tool is expensive and the removal procedure is difficult. Have the water pump replaced by a dealer service department or other qualified automotive repair facility if the tool is not available.*
Note: *It is not economical or practical to overhaul a water pump. If failure occurs, a new or rebuilt unit should be purchased to replace the faulty water pump.*

1   Disconnect the cable from the negative terminal of the battery (see Chapter 5).
2   Drain the coolant (see Chapter 1). See the coolant **Warning and Cautions** in Section 2.
3   Remove the water pump drivebelt (see Chapter 1).
  a) *On 4.9L models, loosen the bolts on the water pump pulley while the drivebelt is still tight, then refer to Chapter 1 and remove the drivebelt* **(see illustration)**.
  b) *On 4.6L models, the water pump drive-belt is mounted directly behind the coolant crossover assembly. The drive-*

belt shield must be removed to access the water pump drivebelt (see Chapter 1).

4.9L models
Refer to illustrations 9.5a, 9.5b, 9.6 and 9.7
4   Remove the coolant reservoir (see Section 5).
5   Remove the bolts that secure the water pump to the front cover of the engine. The bolts are different sizes, so be sure to note their locations and which ones are studs **(see illustrations)**. Pull the water pump away from the engine. If the pump is stuck to the engine, tap it gently with a soft-face hammer.
6   The water pump inlet is actually bolted to the backside of the timing chain cover. The water pump is bolted to the front side. Remove the hose from the inlet and examine the inlet pipe for corrosion **(see illustration)**. If there are leaks evident on the inlet-to-timing-cover gasket, refer to Chapter 2, Part A for timing cover removal, since the inlet can't be removed in-vehicle.
7   Clean the gasket surfaces of the front cover completely using a gasket scraper or

9.5b Do not pry on the water pump until all bolts are removed - new pump here illustrates all the bolt locations

9.6 The inlet is on the back of the timing cover; inspect the neck (A) (this one needs replacing) - (B) indicates two of the mounting bolts, but timing cover removal is necessary to replace the pump inlet

putty knife, then follow with lacquer thinner **(see illustration)**.

8   Use a thin coat of gasket sealant on the new gasket and install the new water pump. Place the pump into position on the front cover and secure it loosely with the bolts. **Note:** *If the engine front cover had been removed to replace the water pump inlet, assemble the inlet with a new gasket to the back of the front cover, then the water pump to the front of the cover. The bolts to the inlet can't be accessed once the front cover is installed on the engine.*

9   Tighten all water pump bolts to the torque listed in this Chapter's Specifications. Use sealant on those bolts immediately next to the water passages in the block.

4.6L models

Refer to illustrations 9.13, 9.14, 9.15a, 9.15b, 9.17 and 9.19

10   Remove the air filter housing (see Chapter 4).

11   Remove the secondary AIR check valve bracket **(see illustration 7.10)** from the coolant crossover housing, if equipped.

12   Remove the lower radiator hose from the thermostat housing.

9.7 Remove all traces of old gasket material with a scraper

13   Remove the water pump bypass hose from the coolant crossover assembly **(see illustration)**.

14   Remove the water pump cover **(see illustration)**.

15   Install the water pump removal tool into the slotted tangs on the water pump **(see illustration)** and rotate the tool clockwise to remove the water pump **(see illustration)**

9.13 Remove the clamp and separate the water bypass hose from the cover

from the housing.

16   Clean the coolant crossover housing mating surfaces at the rear of the housing and the cover to remove any material left from the old seals. Clean the surface with lacquer thinner.

17   Install a new O-ring in the groove in the coolant crossover housing **(see illustration)** and install the new water pump.

9.14 Remove the water pump cover bolts

9.15a Insert the water pump tool (A) into the slots on the perimeter of the water pump (B)

9.15b Rotate the water pump clockwise to remove it from the housing

9.17 Install a new water pump O-ring into the groove in the coolant crossover housing

3

9.19 Use a pick or small screwdriver to remove the O-ring seal on the water pump cover

10.10 The blower motor is located on the front of the firewall; (A) is the electrical connector, (B) the cooling hose, and (C) are the mounting screws

10.11 The fan can be removed after removing the nut from the blower motor shaft

10.13 Remove the trim panel mounting screws

18   Place the pump into position in the coolant crossover housing, align the slotted tangs with the housing, install the special tool and lock the water pump by turning it counterclockwise to the torque listed in this Chapter's Specifications. **Note:** *The notched locking ear on the water pump must be in the 7 o'clock position to match the tang in the housing.*

19   Install a new O-ring into the groove in the water pump cover **(see illustration)**.

20   Install the water pump cover and tighten the bolts to the torque listed in this Chapter's Specifications.

All models

21   Install the engine components in the reverse order of removal, tightening the fasteners securely.

22   Refill the cooling system (see Chapter 1). Run the engine and check for leaks.

10   Blower motor and auxiliary blower motor - removal and installation

Warning: *These models are equipped with a Supplemental Inflatable Restraint (SIR) system (more commonly known as airbags). Always disable the airbag system before working in the vicinity of any airbag system component to avoid the possibility of accidental deployment of the airbag, which could cause personal injury (see Chapter 12).*
Note: *The blower motor on 1992 through 1999 models (except 1998 and 1999 Sevilles) is located in the engine compartment, while on 2000 and later models (and 1998 and 1999 Sevilles) the blower motor is mounted behind the instrument panel in the passenger compartment.*

1   Disconnect the cable from the negative terminal of the battery (see Chapter 5).

Blower motor

1992 through 1999 models (except 1998 and 1999 Seville)

Refer to illustrations 10.10 and 10.11
2   Remove the strut tower cross brace, if equipped, from the engine compartment.
3   Remove the bracket from the relay center and position the relay center off to the side (see Chapter 12).
4   Remove the MAP sensor mounting bracket and position the MAP sensor off to the side (see Chapter 6).
5   On models with a 4.6L engine, remove the ignition coil assembly and position it off to the side (see Chapter 5).
6   Remove the solenoid purge valve, if equipped (see Chapter 6).
7   Use a sharp utility knife and cut the rubber insulator at the guide lines and remove the metal patch plate from the engine compartment.
8   Remove the inertial plate, if equipped, from the blower motor case.
9   Disconnect the wiring connector to the blower motor and remove the cooling hose.
10   Remove the mounting screws and pull the blower assembly out of the housing if there's enough room **(see illustration)**. On some models, rotate the blower motor until the flat edge is down, then remove the blower motor.
11   If there is not enough room to remove the blower and fan as an assembly (mostly on early models), angle the blower motor out enough to unscrew the nut on the fan, force the fan off the motor shaft, then remove the motor and fan separately **(see illustration)**. The fan can be used again on the new blower motor.
12   Installation is the reverse of removal. Check for proper operation. **Caution:** *Be sure that the ignition wires are not positioned close to the blower motor or damage may occur.*

10.16 Disconnect the dash integration module electrical connectors and push down on the release tab

10.17 Remove the bracket mounting bolts

1998 and 1999 Seville and all 2000 and later models

Refer to illustrations 10.13, 10.16, 10.17 and 10.19

13   Remove the trim panel from below the right side of the dash **(see illustration)**.
14   Pull back the carpet from the area surrounding the blower motor.
15   Remove the glove box (see Chapter 11).
16   Remove the dash integration module from the bracket **(see illustration)**.
17   Remove the dash integration module bracket **(see illustration)**.
18   Disconnect the blower motor electrical connector.
19   Remove the blower motor retaining screws **(see illustration)**.
20   Remove the blower motor from the housing.
21   Remove the circlip from the fan and separate the fan from the blower motor.
22   Installation is the reverse of removal.

Auxiliary blower motor

1992 through 1999 models (except 1998 and 1999 Seville)

23   Remove the center console (see Chapter 11).

24   Remove the center console rear cover.
25   Disconnect the auxiliary blower motor electrical connector.
26   Remove the mounting screws securing the blower to the console.
27   Remove the circlip from the fan and separate the fan from the blower motor.
28   Installation is the reverse of removal.

1998 and 1999 Seville and all 2000 and later models

Seville models

29   Remove the center console (see Chapter 11).
30   Disconnect the auxiliary blower motor electrical connector.
31   Disconnect the air ducts from the auxiliary blower motor.
32   Remove the retaining bracket from the auxiliary blower motor and the instrument panel.
33   Remove the insulator and push the blower motor down.
34   Separate the auxiliary blower motor from the rear air duct by pushing forward.
35   Remove the auxiliary blower motor from the right side of the passenger compartment.
36   Installation is the reverse of removal.

DeVille models

37   Remove the instrument panel (see Chapter 11).
38   Remove the left and right carpet retainers and pull back the carpet from the air ducts.
39   Remove the ducts from the center support assembly and the auxiliary blower motor.
40   Remove the center support assembly mounting bolts and separate the assembly from the auxiliary blower motor.
41   Installation is the reverse of removal.

11   Heater/air conditioner control assembly - removal and installation

Warning: *These models are equipped with a Supplemental Inflatable Restraint (SIR) system (more commonly known as airbags). Always disable the airbag system before working in the vicinity of any airbag system component to avoid the possibility of accidental deployment of the airbag, which could cause personal injury (see Chapter 12).*

1   Disconnect the cable from the negative terminal of the battery (see Chapter 5).

1992 through 1999 models (except 1998 and 1999 Seville)

2   The climate control panel is incorporated into the instrument cluster on these models. Refer to Chapter 12 for instrument cluster removal.

1998 and later Seville models

3   Remove the instrument panel center trim plate (see Chapter 11).
4   Remove the console trim plate screws and the trim plate.
5   Pull out the control assembly and radio partially and disconnect the electrical connectors from the radio and the control assembly.
6   Remove the control assembly bracket

10.19 Remove the blower motor mounting screws

3

11.9a The control assembly is retained to the dash by four locking tabs

11.9b Depress and hold the locking tabs to release the control assembly

11.10a Remove the control assembly from the dash

11.10b Disconnect the electrical connector from the control assembly

mounting screws and separate the radio from the control assembly.

7   Installation is the reverse of the removal procedure.

2000 and later DeVille models

Refer to illustrations 11.9a, 11.9b, 11.10a and 11.10b

8   Remove the instrument panel center trim plate (see Chapter 11).

9   Depress and hold each locking tab, located on the corners, to release the control assembly **(see illustrations)**.

10   Pull out the control assembly partially and disconnect the electrical connectors **(see illustrations)**.

11   Installation is the reverse of the removal procedure.

---

12 Heater core - replacement

Warning 1: *These models are equipped with a Supplemental Inflatable Restraint (SIR) system (more commonly known as airbags). Always disable the airbag system before working in the vicinity of any airbag system component to avoid the possibility of accidental deployment of the airbag, which could*

cause personal injury (see Chapter 12).
Warning 2: *Wait until the engine is completely cool before beginning this procedure.*

1   Disconnect the cable from the negative terminal of the battery (see Chapter 5).

2   Drain the cooling system (see Chapter 1).

1992 through 1999 models (except 1998 and 1999 Seville)

Refer to illustrations 12.4, 12.6, 12.7 and 12.9

3   The heater core is contained within the heater/air conditioning assembly. The assembly is divided by the firewall, with the blower motor and evaporator located in a housing in the engine compartment, and the heater core located in a housing in the passenger compartment, under the instrument panel. If only the heater core is being removed, there is no need to evacuate the refrigerant from the air conditioning system or remove the blower motor/evaporator housing.

4   Disconnect the heater hoses at the firewall **(see illustration)**.

5   Access the heater core cover:

a) *On 1992 through 1996 models, remove the glove box and the sound insulator panel below the right side of the dash (see Chapter 11).*

b) *On 1997 through 1999 models, remove the instrument panel (see Chapter 11).*

6   Disconnect the rod from the programmer to the blend-air door by squeezing the plastic connector and pulling it out of the arm **(see illustration)**.

7   Disconnect the vacuum and electrical connectors from the programmer, just to the right of the heater core housing **(see illustration)**.

12.4 Loosen the clamps and disconnect the heater hoses from the heater core inlet and outlet pipes at the firewall

12.6 Disconnect the blend-air door link rod (A) - (B) is the upper heater core cover mounting screw

12.7 Disconnect the electrical connector (A) and the vacuum connector (B) from the programmer - (C) is the lower heater core cover mounting screw

8   Remove the two heater core cover mounting screws (see illustrations 12.6 and 12.7) and pull the heater core cover (with programmer still attached) away from the heater housing.

9   Remove the two core mounting screws and carefully lower the heater/air conditioning assembly from under the dash (see illustration). Caution: *Have some rags or old towels on the floor to protect the carpet from any coolant that may spill.*

10   Installation is the reverse of removal. Note: *Make sure to transfer any weather-stripping/sealing material from the old core or cover to the new one.*

1998 and 1999 Seville and all 2000 and later models

11   The heater core is contained within the heater/ventilation/air conditioning (HVAC) assembly. The assembly includes the blower motor, the heater core and evaporator located in a housing in the passenger compartment, behind the instrument panel. If only the heater core is being removed, there is no need to evacuate the refrigerant from the air

conditioning system or remove the blower motor.

12   Disconnect the heater hoses at the firewall.

13   Remove the instrument panel (see Chapter 11).

14   Remove the heater core cover mounting screws and pull the heater core cover away from the HVAC assembly.

15   Remove the heater core retaining straps.

16   Remove the heater core mounting screws and remove the heater core from the HVAC assembly. Caution: *Have some rags or old towels on the floor to protect the carpet from any coolant that may spill.*

17   Installation is the reverse of removal. Note: *Install new heater core case seals into the HVAC assembly before installing the new heater core.*

13   Air conditioning and heating system - check and maintenance

Refer to illustrations 13.1a and 13.1b

Warning: *The air conditioning system is under high pressure. Do not loosen any hose*

fittings or remove any components until after the system has been discharged by a dealer service department or service station. Always wear eye protection when disconnecting air conditioning system fittings.

1   The following maintenance checks should be performed on a regular basis to ensure the air conditioner continues to operate at peak efficiency.

a) Check the compressor drivebelt. If it's worn or deteriorated, replace it (see Chapter 1).

b) Check the system hoses. Look for cracks, bubbles, hard spots and deterioration. Inspect the hoses and all fittings for oil bubbles and seepage. If there's any evidence of wear, damage or leaks, replace the hose(s).

c) Inspect the condenser fins for leaves, bugs and other debris. Use a "fin comb" or compressed air to clean the condenser.

d) Make sure the system has the correct refrigerant charge.

e) Check the evaporator housing drain tube (see illustrations) for blockage.

3

12.9 Remove the screws holding the heater core to the housing

13.1a Check that the evaporator housing drain tube at the firewall is clear of any blockage (4.9L model shown)

13.1b Location of the evaporator housing drain tube on a 2000 DeVille

13.8 Insert a thermometer in the center duct while operating the air conditioning system - the output air should be 35 to 40 degrees F less than the ambient temperature, depending on humidity (but no lower than 40-degrees F)

13.9 A basic charging kit is available at most auto parts stores - it must say R-134a and so must the cans of refrigerant you buy

2   It's a good idea to operate the system for about 10 minutes at least once a month, particularly during the winter. Long term non-use can cause hardening, and subsequent failure, of the seals.

3   Because of the complexity of the air conditioning system and the special equipment necessary to service it, in-depth troubleshooting and repairs are not included in this manual (refer to the *Haynes Automotive Heating and Air Conditioning Repair Manual*). However, simple checks and component replacement procedures are provided in this Chapter.

4   The most common cause of poor cooling is simply a low system refrigerant charge. If a noticeable drop in cool air output occurs, the following quick check will help you determine if the refrigerant level is low.

Checking the refrigerant charge

Refer to illustration 13.8

5   Warm the engine up to normal operating temperature.

6   Place the air conditioning temperature selector at the coldest setting and the blower at the highest setting. Open the doors (to make sure the air conditioning system doesn't cycle off as soon as it cools the passenger compartment).

7   With the compressor engaged - the clutch will make an audible click and the center of the clutch will rotate. If the compressor discharge line feels warm and the compressor inlet pipe feels cool, the system is properly charged.

8   Place a thermometer in the dashboard vent nearest the evaporator **(see illustration)** and operate the system until the indicated temperature is around 40 to 45 degrees F. If the ambient (outside) air temperature is very high, say 110 degrees F, the duct air temperature may be as high as 60 degrees F, but generally the air conditioning is 30-50 degrees F cooler than the ambient air. **Note:** *Humidity of the ambient air also affects the cooling capacity of the system. Higher ambient humidity lowers the effectiveness of the*

air conditioning system.

Adding refrigerant

Refer to illustrations 13.9 and 13.12

Caution: *There are two types of refrigerant used in automotive systems; R-12, which is used in 1992 and 1993 models, and the more environmentally-friendly R-134a used in later models covered by this manual. These two refrigerants, and their appropriate refrigerant oils, are not compatible and must never be mixed or components will be damaged. Make sure any refrigerant, refrigerant oil or replacement component you purchase is designated as compatible with the system (R-12 or R-134a) on your vehicle.*

9   Only R-134a systems can be recharged by the home mechanic. R-12 systems must be recharged by a qualified A/C technician using specialized equipment. If your system is R-134a compatible, then purchase an R-134a automotive charging kit at an auto parts store **(see illustration)**. A charging kit includes a 12-ounce can of refrigerant, a tap valve and a short section of hose that can be attached between the tap valve and the system low side service valve. Because one can of refrigerant may not be sufficient to bring the system charge up to the proper level, it's a good idea to buy an additional can. **Warning:** *Never add more than two cans of refrigerant to the system.* Make sure that one of the cans contains red refrigerant dye. If the system is leaking, the red dye will leak out with the refrigerant and help you pinpoint the location of the leak.

10   Hook up the charging kit by following the manufacturer's instructions. **Warning:** *DO NOT hook the charging kit hose to the system high side! The fittings on the charging kit are designed to fit **only** on the low side of the system.*

11   Back off the valve handle on the charging kit and screw the kit onto the refrigerant can, making sure first that the O-ring or rub-

ber seal inside the threaded portion of the kit is in place. **Warning:** *Wear protective eyewear when dealing with pressurized refrigerant cans.*

12   Remove the dust cap from the low-side charging connection and attach the quick-connect fitting on the kit hose **(see illustration)**.

13   Warm up the engine and turn on the air conditioner. Keep the charging kit hose away from the fan and other moving parts. **Note:** *The charging process requires the compressor to be running. Your compressor may cycle off if the pressure is low due to a low charge. If the clutch cycles off, you can pull the low-pressure cycling switch plug and attach a jumper wire. This will keep the compressor ON.*

14   Turn the valve handle on the kit until the stem pierces the can, then back the handle out to release the refrigerant. You should be able to hear the rush of gas. Add refrigerant to the low side of the system until both the receiver-drier surface and the evaporator inlet pipe feel about the same temperature. Allow stabilization time between each addition.

15   If you have an accurate thermometer, place it in the center air conditioning vent **(see illustration 13.8)** and note the temperature of the air coming out of the vent. A fully-charged system which is working correctly should cool down to about 40 degrees F. Generally, an air conditioning system will put out air that is 30 to 40 degrees F cooler than the ambient air. For example, if the ambient (outside) air temperature is very high (over 100 degrees F), the temperature of air coming out of the registers should be 60 to 70 degrees F.

16   When the can is empty, turn the valve handle to the closed position and release the connection from the low-side port. Replace the dust cap. **Warning:** *Never add more than two cans of refrigerant to the system.*

17   Remove the charging kit from the can and store the kit for future use with the pierc-

13.12 Add R-134a refrigerant to the low-side port only - the procedure will go faster if you wrap the can with a warm, wet towel to prevent icing (2000 DeVille shown)

13.24 To access the programmer, remove the insulator panel under the right side of the dash (see Chapter 11) - (A) is the programmer electrical connector, (B) is the vacuum connector

ing valve in the UP position, to prevent inadvertently piercing the can on the next use.

Heating systems

18   If the carpet under the heater core is damp, or if antifreeze vapor or steam is coming through the vents, the heater core is leaking. Remove it (see Section 12) and install a new unit. Most radiator shops will not repair a leaking heater core.

19   If the air coming out of the heater vents isn't hot, the problem could stem from any of the following causes:

a) *The thermostat is stuck open, preventing the engine coolant from warming up enough to carry heat to the heater core. Replace the thermostat (see Section 3).*

b) *There is a blockage in the system, preventing the flow of coolant through the heater core. Feel both heater hoses at the firewall. They should be hot. If one of them is cold, there is an obstruction in one of the hoses or in the heater core, or the heater control valve is shut. Detach the hoses and back flush the heater core with a water hose. If the heater core is clear but circulation is impeded, remove the two hoses and flush them out with a water hose.*

c) *If flushing fails to remove the blockage from the heater core, the core must be replaced (see Section 12).*

On-board diagnostics

20   A comprehensive system of self-diagnostics is used on these models. Early models are equipped with the LED portion of the climate control panel allowing display of trouble codes. Later models are equipped with the OBD-II self-diagnosis system that requires a scan tool to access the trouble codes.

21   Refer to Chapter 6 for the procedures to enter the self-diagnostics program, how to access the system that deals with heating

and air conditioning, and for a listing of trouble codes.

22   After any repair work, repeat the self-diagnostics procedure to check your work.

Programmer vacuum check (1992 through 1999 models - except 1998 and 1999 Seville)

Refer to illustration 13.24

23   Put the controls through all of their modes with the vehicle running. If necessary, have someone else operate the controls while you look under the dashboard to observe the action of the various vacuum motors controlling airflow and temperature modes. If there is any position of the controls that gives air from the heater ducts *and* the air conditioning ducts, this indicates a vacuum leak.

24   Vacuum is supplied to the heater/air conditioning control assembly by tubing attached to the intake manifold. Inspect the supply line, from the intake manifold to the programmer, for damage or leaks **(see illustration)**. The programmer is the black box mounted to the right side of the heater/air conditioning housing under the dashboard. To inspect it, remove the mounting screws and snap loose the rod connecting it to the blend-air door.

25   The vacuum lines run from the programmer to each of the mode actuators. Apply 8 inches of vacuum to each of the ports on the harness connector and observe the functions of that vacuum circuit.

26   If any of the circuits don't hold vacuum, follow the lines to their destination, isolate the source of the leak and repair it.

27   If there is vacuum in the line to the actuator when that function is selected, and there is no leak detected, check for binding of the door the actuator operates. If the door operates freely, independent of the actuator, then the actuator needs replacing.

Eliminating air conditioning odors

Refer to illustrations 13.31a and 13.31b

28   Unpleasant odors that often develop in air conditioning systems are caused by the growth of a fungus, usually on the surface of the evaporator core. The warm, humid environment is a perfect breeding ground for mildew to develop.

29   The evaporator core on most vehicles is difficult to access, and factory dealerships have a lengthy, expensive process for eliminating the fungus by opening up the evaporator case and using a powerful disinfectant and rinse on the core until the fungus is gone. You can service your own system at home, but it takes something much stronger than basic household germ-killers or deodorizers.

30   Aerosol disinfectants for automotive air-conditioning systems are available in most auto parts stores, but remember when shopping for them that the most effective treatments are also the most expensive. The basic procedure for using these sprays is to start by running the system in the RECIRC mode for ten minutes with the blower on its highest speed. Use the highest heat mode to dry out the system and keep the compressor from engaging by disconnecting the wiring connector at the compressor (see Section 14).

31   The disinfectant can usually comes with a long spray hose. There are two different methods depending on the year of the vehicle.

a) *On 1992 through 1999 models (except 1998 and 1999 Seville), remove the glovebox and lower dash panel (see Chapter 11), point the nozzle inside the hole and to the left towards the evaporator core, and spray according to the manufacturer's recommendations. Try to cover the whole surface of the evaporator core, by aiming the spray up, down and sideways. You can also spray through the cover of the heater core,*

3

aiming towards the back of the evaporator (see illustration). Follow the manufacturer's recommendations for the length of spray and waiting time between applications.

b) On 1998 and 1999 Seville and all 2000 and later models, drill a hole near the accelerator pedal into the HVAC assembly (see illustration). Drill a 1/8 inch diameter hole and do not allow the drill bit to penetrate the HVAC assembly more than 1 - 2 mm. With the blower motor on HIGH, point the nozzle inside the hole towards the evaporator core and spray according to the manufacturer's recommendations. Try to cover the whole surface of the evaporator core, by aiming the spray up, down and sideways. Follow the manufacturer's recommendations for the length of spray and waiting time between applications. Seal the hole using RTV sealant.

32   Once the evaporator has been cleaned, the best way to prevent the mildew from coming back again is to make sure your evaporator housing drain tube is clear.

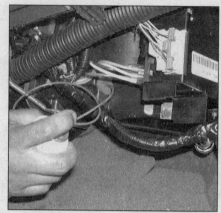

13.31a Using a can of automotive disinfectant and a long hose, spray through the heater core cover as shown to access the interior side of the evaporator core, and through the power module hole to spray the front side

13.31b Drill an 1/8 inch hole into the HVAC assembly but do not allow the drill bit to penetrate the housing more than 1 to 2 millimeters

---

14 Air conditioning compressor - removal and installation

Warning: *The air conditioning system is under high pressure. Do not loosen any hose fittings or remove any components until after the system has been discharged. Air conditioning refrigerant should be properly discharged into an EPA-approved recovery/recycling unit at a dealer service department or an automotive air conditioning repair facility. Always wear eye protection when disconnecting air conditioning system fittings.*
Caution: *When replacing entire components, additional refrigerant oil should be added equal to the amount that is removed with the component being replaced. Be sure to read the container before adding any oil to the system, to make sure it is compatible with the system in the vehicle, either R-12 or R-134a.*

Note: *If the compressor is being replaced due to damaged internal components, replace the accumulator and the orifice tube as well (refer to Sections 15 and 18).*

Removal

1   Have the air conditioning system refrigerant discharged and recovered by an air conditioning technician.
2   Disconnect the cable from the negative terminal of the battery (see Chapter 5).
3   Set the parking brake, block the rear wheels and raise the front of the vehicle, supporting it securely on jackstands.
4   Remove the drivebelt (see Chapter 1).

4.9L models

Refer to illustrations 14.7a, 14.7b, 14.7c and 14.7d
5   From below, remove the plastic splash shield just below the compressor. Remove the right-side fenderwell splash shield for access to the front of the compressor.
6   Disconnect the compressor clutch wiring harness **(see illustration 14.7a)**. Note:

On some models, there is a second electrical connector at the rear of the compressor that must be disconnected.
7   Disconnect the refrigerant lines from the compressor. Plug the open fittings to prevent entry of dirt and moisture **(see illustrations)**.
8   Unbolt the compressor from the mounting bracket and remove it from the vehicle.

4.6L models

Refer to illustration 14.14
9   Remove the right front wheel (see Chapter 1).
10   Remove the plastic splash shield just below the compressor. Remove the right-side fenderwell splash shield for access to the front of the compressor.
11   Remove the oil filter (see Chapter 1).
12   Remove the oil cooler lines at the oil filter adapter.
13   Remove the engine splash shield from below the engine compartment (see Chapter 2B).
14   Disconnect the refrigerant lines from the compressor **(see illustration)**. Plug the open fittings to prevent entry of dirt and moisture.

14.7a Remove the clutch connector (A), the bolt (B) retaining the refrigerant lines, and the top mounting bolt (C)

14.7b From below, remove the two lower compressor mounting bolts

14.7c Remove the refrigerant line bolt (A), the rear-facing front mounting bolt (B), and the two rear mounting bolts (C)

14.7d From the front, remove the two compressor mounting bolts

2000 and later models

15   Remove the secondary air pump from the right side (see Chapter 6).

16   Disconnect the brake line retaining clips from the frame and position them off to the side to allow compressor removal.

All models

Refer to illustrations 14.17a and 14.17b

17   Unbolt the compressor from the mounting bracket and remove it from the wheel housing **(see illustrations)**.

Installation

19   The clutch may have to be transferred from the old compressor to the new unit. This may require special tools and should be done by an air conditioning technician.

20   Add the proper amount of refrigerant oil to the new compressor using the following calculations:

a)   *Drain the refrigerant oil from the old compressor through the suction fitting and measure it in ounces.*

b)   *Drain the oil from the new compressor.*

c)   *If the amount drained from the old compressor was less than 1 ounce, add 1 ounce of new oil to the new compressor.*

d)   *If the amount drained from the old compressor was 1 ounce or more, add that exact amount of new oil to the new compressor.*

22   Installation is the reverse of removal, using new O-rings, lubricated with clean refrigerant oil, where the line fittings attach to the compressor.

23   Have the system evacuated, recharged and leak tested by an air conditioning technician.

15   Air conditioning accumulator - removal and installation

Refer to illustrations 15.4, 15.5a and 15.5b

Warning: *The air conditioning system is under high pressure. Do not loosen any hose fittings or remove any components until after the system has been discharged. Air conditioning refrigerant should be properly dis-*

14.14 Location of the compressor refrigerant line mounting bolt on a 4.6L model

charged into an EPA-approved recovery/recycling unit at a dealer service department or an automotive air conditioning repair facility. Always wear eye protection when disconnecting air conditioning system fittings.

14.17a Location of the air conditioning compressor right side mounting bolts on a 4.6L model

14.17b Location of the compressor front mounting bolts (top bolt hidden from view)

3

15.4   Location of the accumulator cover snap fittings on a late model 4.6L (two of the fittings are hidden from view by the wiring harness)

15.5a   Disconnect the pressure switch (A), then unscrew the refrigerant lines (B) - loosen the accumulator clamp bolt (C) to remove the accumulator (4.9L model shown)

Caution: *When replacing entire components, additional refrigerant oil should be added equal to the amount that is removed with the component being replaced. Be sure to read the container before adding any oil to the system, to make sure it is compatible with the system in the vehicle, either R-12 or R-134a.*

1   Disconnect the cable from the negative terminal of the battery (see Chapter 5).
2   Have the refrigerant discharged and recovered by an air-conditioning technician.
3   On 4.9L models, remove the air filter housing (see Chapter 4).
4   Remove the accumulator cover. Some models are equipped with an accumulator cover that unsnaps from the cover mounting studs **(see illustration)**.
5   Disconnect the refrigerant lines from the accumulator and cap the open fittings to prevent dirt and moisture entry **(see illustration)**. **Note:** *When disconnecting the lines on models with threaded fittings, hold the stationary fitting on the accumulator with one wrench and loosen the line fitting with another wrench. This will prevent twisting the*

line or breaking the stationary fitting off the accumulator. Disconnect the pressure switch connector.
6   Loosen the accumulator bracket clamping screw and lift the accumulator out of the vehicle.
7   Installation is the reverse of removal, using new O-rings, lubricated with refrigerant oil, where the lines connect to the accumulator. If the accumulator is being replaced, add 3.5 ounces of refrigerant oil to the new accumulator.
8   Have the system evacuated, charged and leak-tested by an air conditioning technician.

---

16   Air conditioning condenser - removal and installation

Warning: *The air conditioning system is under high pressure. Do not loosen any hose fittings or remove any components until after the system has been discharged. Air condi-*

tioning refrigerant should be properly discharged into an EPA-approved recovery/recycling unit at a dealer service department or an automotive air conditioning repair facility. Always wear eye protection when disconnecting air conditioning system fittings.
Caution: *When replacing entire components, additional refrigerant oil should be added equal to the amount that is removed with the component being replaced. Be sure to read the container before adding any oil to the system, to make sure it is compatible with the system in the vehicle, either R-12 or R-134a.*

Removal

Refer to illustrations 16.4a, 16.4b, 16.6a and 16.6b

1   Have the air conditioning system discharged by a dealer service department or air conditioning repair shop.
2   Disconnect the cable from the negative terminal of the battery. On models where the battery would interfere with removal, remove the battery (see Chapter 5).

15.5b   Location of the refrigerant lines at the accumulator on a 4.6L model

16.4a   Remove the battery for access to the condenser fittings on a 4.9L model

16.4b Location of the condenser fittings on a late model 4.6L

16.6a Remove the two condenser brackets (arrow indicates left bracket) from the radiator support (4.9L model shown)

3   Drain the cooling system (see Chapter 1).
4   Disconnect the refrigerant lines from the condenser and cap the open fittings to prevent dirt and moisture entry (see illustrations). Note: When disconnecting the lines on models with threaded fittings, hold the stationary fitting on the condenser with one wrench and loosen the line fitting with another wrench. This will prevent twisting the line or damaging the condenser.
5   Remove the radiator (see Section 6).
6   Remove the mounting bolts from the condenser brackets and lift the condenser out of the vehicle (see illustrations).
7   If the original condenser will be reinstalled, store it with the line fittings on top to prevent oil from draining out.

Installation

8   If a new condenser is being installed, pour one ounce of refrigerant oil into the new condenser prior to installation.
9   Reinstall the components in the reverse

order of removal. Be sure the rubber pads are in place under the condenser, on models so equipped. Also, be sure to use new O-rings on the refrigerant lines and lubricate them with a small amount of clean refrigerant oil. Caution: The condenser mounting bolts are designed with a special length to prevent damage to the radiator and the outside radiator tanks. Use only the correct length bolts for this application.
10   Have the system evacuated, recharged and leak tested by the shop that discharged it.

17   Orifice tube - replacement

Warning: The air conditioning system is under high pressure. DO NOT loosen any fittings or remove any components until after the system has been discharged. Air conditioning refrigerant should be properly discharged into an EPA-approved container at a dealership service department or an automo-

tive air conditioning repair facility. Always wear eye protection when disconnecting air conditioning system fittings.
Caution: When replacing entire components, additional refrigerant oil should be added equal to the amount that is removed with the component being replaced. Be sure to read the container before adding any oil to the system, to make sure it is compatible with the system in the vehicle, either R-12 or R-134a.
1   Have the air conditioning system discharged and the refrigerant recovered (see Warning and Caution above).

1992 through 1999 models (except 1998 and 1999 Seville)

Refer to illustration 17.2
2   Disconnect the refrigerant high-pressure line, using two wrenches to avoid twisting the lines. The orifice tube is located in the high-pressure line near the cowl, just ahead of the evaporator (see illustration). There is always a fitting junction next to the orifice location.

16.6b Location of the left side mounting bolt on the condenser (4.6L model shown)

17.2 The junction for the orifice tube is in the high-pressure line just before the evaporator

3

17.3 Hold the stationary fitting with one wrench while loosening
the tube nut with another wrench when separating
the air conditioning lines

17.5 The expansion tube (orifice) contains a precise orifice and
several screen filters - it should be replaced whenever a
compressor is replaced - install it the same direction
in the line as the original

1998 and 1999 Seville and all 2000 and later models

Refer to illustration 17.3

3   Working near the accumulator, disconnect the air conditioning lines using two wrenches **(see illustration)**.

4   Separate the flared tubing from the line.

All models

Refer to illustration 17.5

5   The expansion *(orifice)* tube is a tube with a fixed-diameter orifice and a mesh filter at each end **(see illustration)**. When you separate the pipe at the fitting you will see one end of the orifice tube inside the pipe leading to the evaporator. Use needle-nose pliers to remove the orifice tube.

6   The orifice tube acts to meter the refrigerant, changing it from a high-pressure liquid to a low-pressure liquid/vapor mixture. It is possible to reuse the orifice tube if:

a) *The screens aren't plugged with grit or foreign material.*

b) *Neither screen is torn.*

c) *The plastic housing over the screens is intact.*

d) *The brass orifice inside the plastic housing is unrestricted.*

7   Installation is the reverse of removal. Be sure to insert the expansion tube with the shorter end in first, toward the evaporator. **Caution:** *Always use a new O-ring when installing the expansion tube.*

8   Retighten the fitting and refrigerant line, then have the system evacuated, recharged and leak-tested by the shop that discharged it.

Chapter 4
Fuel and exhaust systems

Contents

4

Specifications

Fuel pressure
  4.9L engine .... 40 to 50 psi
  4.6L engine
    1995 and earlier .... 40 to 50 psi
    1996 and 1997 .... 48 to 55 psi
    1998
      DeVille .... 41 to 47 psi
      Seville .... 48 to 55 psi
    1999 .... 48 to 55 psi
    2000 on .... 41 to 47 psi
Fuel injector resistance
  4.9L models
    1992 and 1993 .... 15.8 to 16.6 ohms
    1994 and 1995 .... Not available
  4.6L models
    1993 .... 11.8 to 12.6 ohms
    1994 through 1996 .... Not available
    1997 .... 8 to 25 ohms
    1998 .... 11.8 to 12.6 ohms
    2000 .... 11.6 to 12.6 ohms
    2001 on .... 11.0 to 14.0 ohms

Torque specifications

4.9L engine

Fuel pressure regulator retaining screw	
1992 and 1993	108 in-lbs
1994 and 1995	84 in-lbs
Fuel rail retaining bolts..	18
Fuel tank strap retaining bolts	26
Throttle body mounting bolts	168 in-lbs

4.6L engine

Fuel rail end bracket bolt (all 1995 through 1997;	
1998 and 1999 DeVille)	71 in-lbs
Fuel rail end bracket bolt (1998 and 1999 Seville).................................	35 in-lbs
Fuel rail (2000 on)	
Fuel rail retaining studs	89 in-lbs
Fuel rail end bracket nut..	89 in-lbs
Fuel tank strap retaining bolts	26
Intake manifold cover bolts (1993 and 1994 models only)......................	106 in-lbs
Throttle body mounting bolts	106 in-lbs
Throttle body spacer mounting bolts (1995 through 1999 models only).	106 in-lbs

1.1a Typical Multi-Port Fuel Injection (MPFI) system (4.9L engine)

1	Quick connect fittings	4	Fuel pressure test port	7	Throttle body
2	Fuel delivery line	5	Fuel pressure regulator	8	Idle Speed Control (ISC) motor
3	Fuel return line	6	Fuel rail assembly	9	Distributor

1.1b Typical Multi-Port Fuel Injection (MPFI) system (4.6L engine)

1   Throttle body
2   Idle Air Control (IAC) valve
3   Throttle Position (TP) sensor
4   Fuel injector
5   Air intake manifold
6   Fuel pressure test port
7   Fuel rail
8   Fuel pressure regulator

2.2 To remove the intake manifold service cover on 4.6L models, remove these two nuts (does not apply to 1993 and 1994 models, which have a cover with eight bolts; also, 1995 and some other earlier models have four bolts instead of two)

1 General information

Multi-Port Fuel Injection (MPFI) system

Refer to illustrations 1.1a and 1.1b

The Multi-Port Fuel Injection (MPFI) system **(see illustrations)** includes the air cleaner assembly, the fuel tank, the in-tank electric fuel pump, the fuel pump relay, the fuel filter, the fuel pressure regulator, the fuel rail, the fuel injectors and the fuel supply and return lines.

Fuel pump and lines

Fuel is circulated from the fuel tank to the fuel injection system, and back to the fuel tank, through a pair of lines running along the underside of the vehicle. An electric fuel pump is attached to the fuel sending unit inside the fuel tank. A return system routes all vapors and excess fuel back to the fuel tank through separate return lines.

Exhaust system

The exhaust system includes an exhaust manifold fitted with an exhaust oxygen sensor, a catalytic converter, an exhaust pipe, and a muffler. The catalytic converter is an emission control device added to the exhaust system to reduce pollutants. A single-bed converter is used in combination with a three-way (reduction) catalyst. Refer to Chapter 6 for more information regarding the catalytic converter.

2 Fuel pressure relief procedure

Refer to illustrations 2.2, 2.3, 2.4a and 2.4b
Warning 1: *Before servicing any fuel system component, relieve the fuel pressure to minimize the risk of fire or personal injury. Failure to follow this procedure before servicing fuel lines or connections could result in serious injury.*
Warning 2: *Gasoline is extremely flammable, so take extra precautions when you work on any part of the fuel system. Don't smoke or allow open flames or bare light bulbs near the work area, and don't work in a garage where a gas-type appliance (such as a water heater or a clothes dryer) is present. Since gasoline is carcinogenic, wear latex gloves when* there's a possibility of being exposed to fuel, and, if you spill any fuel on your skin, rinse it off immediately with soap and water. Mop up any spills immediately and do not store fuel-soaked rags where they could ignite. The fuel system is under constant pressure, so, if any fuel lines are to be disconnected, the fuel pressure in the system must be relieved first. When you perform any kind of work on the fuel system, wear safety glasses and have a Class B type fire extinguisher on hand.

1   Remove the fuel filler cap - this will relieve any pressure built up in the tank.
2   On 4.6L models, remove the intake manifold service cover **(see illustration)**.
3   All vehicles covered by this manual are equipped with a fuel pressure test port, which is located on the fuel rail assembly **(see illustrations 1.1a and 1.1b)**. Obtain a fuel pressure gauge equipped with a bleeder valve **(see illustration)**. A setup like the one shown in the accompanying illustration is available at most automotive parts stores.

4

2.3 A typical setup for relieving fuel system pressure and for checking fuel pressure

1   *Schrader-valve test port quick-connect adapters (if you decide to hook up directly to the Schrader valve-type test port, an adapter isn't necessary)*
2   *Quick-connect fitting (for use with quick-connect adapter); not absolutely necessary, but quicker and not as messy*
3   *Fuel pressure/fuel pressure relief hose*
4   *Pressure gauge (not necessary for bleeding, but required for fuel pressure testing)*
5   *Bleeder valve (allows you to turn on and shut off fuel flowing from fuel rail)*
6   *Enough bleeder hose to reach a small container*

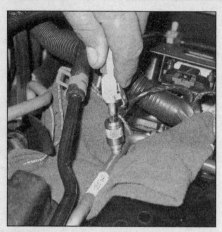

2.4a To hook up the pressure relief setup, screw on the appropriate adapter, insert the quick-connect fitting into the adapter and clamp it down securely (4.6L engine shown)

2.4b A typical fuel pressure relief setup installed (note the bottle to catch any residual pressurized fuel) (4.6L engine shown)

4   Hook up the pressure gauge hose onto the test port **(see illustration)** and relieve the pressure by bleeding the fuel through the bleed-off valve and into a container **(see illustration). Note:** *After the fuel pressure has been relieved, it's a good idea to lay a shop towel over any fuel connection to be disassembled, to absorb the residual fuel that may leak out when servicing the fuel system.*

5   If a setup like the one above is not available, the alternative is to cover the test port fitting with shop rags or towels, then carefully depress the Schrader valve with a small screwdriver or awl. Dispose of the rags in a covered, marked container.

6   Disconnect the cable from the negative terminal of the battery before working on any part of the fuel system (see Chapter 5).

3   Fuel pump/fuel pressure - check

Warning: *Gasoline is extremely flammable, so take extra precautions when you work on any part of the fuel system. Don't smoke or allow open flames or bare light bulbs near the work area, and don't work in a garage where a gas-type appliance (such as a water heater or a clothes dryer) is present. Since gasoline is carcinogenic, wear latex gloves when there's a possibility of being exposed to fuel, and, if you spill any fuel on your skin, rinse it off immediately with soap and water. Mop up any spills immediately and do not store fuel-soaked rags where they could ignite. The fuel system is under constant pressure, so, if any fuel lines are to be disconnected, the fuel pressure in the system must be relieved first (see Section 2). When you perform any kind of work on the fuel system, wear safety glasses and have a Class B type fire extinguisher on hand.*

Fuel pump output and pressure check

Refer to illustrations 3.2, 3.5 and 3.6
Note: *The following checks assume the fuel filter is in good condition. If you doubt its*

condition, *install a new one* (see Chapter 1).

1   Check that there is adequate fuel in the fuel tank. Relieve the fuel pressure (see Section 2).

2   Install a fuel pressure gauge onto the fuel lines or the fuel rail **(see illustration)**. All vehicles covered by this manual are equipped with a fuel pressure test port, which is located on the fuel rail assembly **(see illustrations 1.1a and 1.1b)**. Obtain a fuel pressure gauge equipped with a bleeder valve **(see illustration 2.3)**; a setup like the one shown in this illustration is available at most automotive parts stores. You will need a fuel pressure gauge capable of measuring high fuel pressure and equipped with the correct adapter fitting to thread onto the test port.

3   Turn the ignition switch ON (engine not running). The fuel pump should run for about two seconds - note the reading on the gauge. After the pump stops running the pressure should hold steady. It should be within the range listed in this Chapter's Specifications. If the pump does not turn on, check the fuel pump electrical circuits (see Step 9).

4   Start the engine and let it idle at normal operating temperature. The pressure should be lower by 3 to 10 psi. If all the pressure readings are within the limits listed in this Chapter's Specifications, the system is operating properly.

5   If the pressure did not drop by 3 to 10 psi after starting the engine, apply 12 to 14 inches of vacuum to the pressure regulator **(see illustration)**. If the pressure drops, repair the vacuum source to the regulator. If the pressure does not drop, replace the regulator.

6   If the fuel pressure is not within specifications, check the following:

a) *If the pressure is higher than specified, check for vacuum to the fuel pressure regulator* **(see illustration)**. *The vacuum signal to the pressure regulator must be higher at idle and should decrease when the throttle is opened rapidly. If the vacuum signal is satisfactory, check for a pinched or clogged fuel return hose or*

3.2 Attach the fuel pressure gauge to the test port and check the pressure with the ignition key turned to ON (engine not running) (4.9L model shown)

3.5 Connect a vacuum pump to the fuel pressure regulator, apply vacuum to the fuel pressure regulator and check the fuel pressure - the fuel pressure should decrease as the vacuum increases (4.9L model shown)

3.6 Checking vacuum to the fuel pressure regulator using a vacuum gauge (4.9L model shown)

line. If the return line is OK, replace the pressure regulator.
b) If the pressure is lower than specified, change the fuel filter to rule out the possibility of a clogged filter. If the pressure is still low, install a fuel line shut-off adapter between the pressure regulator and the return line. With the valve open, start the engine (if possible) and slowly close the valve. If the pressure rises above 50 psi, replace the regulator (see Section 14). **Warning:** Don't allow the fuel pressure to exceed 60 psi. And don't try to restrict the return line by pinching it. You probably won't be able to pinch it off completely, and even if you succeed in doing so, you will damage the (nylon or plastic) fuel line.
c) If the pressure is still low with the fuel return line restricted, the fuel pump is probably faulty.

7   After the testing is done, relieve the fuel pressure (see Section 2) and remove the fuel pressure gauge.

8   If there are no problems with any of the above-listed components, the fuel pump and circuit are functioning correctly.

Fuel pump electrical circuit check

9   Should the fuel system fail to deliver the correct amount of fuel, or any fuel at all, inspect it as follows. Remove the fuel filler cap. Have an assistant turn the ignition key to the ON position (engine not running) while you listen at the fuel filler neck opening. When the key is turned to ON, the Powertrain Control Module (PCM) energizes the fuel pump relay for a couple of seconds. The relay turns on the fuel pump circuit for two seconds to pressurize the fuel system so that it will be at the correct pressure when the engine is cranked over. During this two-second interval, you should hear a whirring sound; this is the sound of the pump pressurizing the fuel system.

10   If you don't hear anything, check the

fuel pump fuse.

On 1992 and 1993 Seville models, the fuel pump fuse is in the fuse and relay box located on the left side of the engine compartment.

On 1994 through 1997 DeVille and Seville models, and on 1998 through 2000 DeVille models, the fuel pump fuse is in the fuse and relay box located on the left side of the engine compartment.

On 1998 through 2002 Seville models, and on 2001 and 2002 DeVille models, the fuel pump fuse is in the fuse and relay box located under the passenger seat cushion (see Chapter 11 for the seat cushion removal procedure).

If the fuse is blown, replace it and see if it blows again. If it does, trace the fuel pump circuit for a short.

11   If the fuse is OK, remove the fuel pump relay. Depending on the year and model, the fuel pump relay is located in the fuse and relay box in the engine compartment or in the fuse and relay box under the rear seat:

On 1992 and 1993 Seville models, the fuel pump relay is in the fuse and relay box located on the left side of the engine compartment.

On 1994 through 1997 DeVille and Seville models, and on 1998 through 2000 DeVille models, the fuel pump relay is in the fuse and relay box located on the left side of the engine compartment.

On 1998 through 2002 Seville models, and on 2001 and 2002 DeVille models, the fuel pump relay is in the fuse and relay box located under the passenger seat cushion (see Chapter 11 for the seat cushion removal procedure).

12   Check for battery voltage to the fuel pump relay connector with the ignition key in the OFF position. Then turn the ignition key to the ON position and check for battery voltage from the PCM. The fuel pump relay has two circuits: The control circuit between the PCM and the relay, and the one between the fuel pump relay and the fuel pump. The circuit between the PCM and the fuel pump relay is controlled by the PCM and the circuit between the fuel pump relay and the fuel pump is controlled by the relay. This circuit provides battery voltage to the fuel pump only when the relay is energized by the PCM. With the ignition switch ON (engine not running), the PCM will ground the relay for several seconds. During cranking, the PCM grounds the fuel pump relay when it receives a signal from the Camshaft Position (CMP) sensor (see Chapter 6 for more information about the PCM and the CMP sensor). If there are no reference pulses from the CMP sensor, i.e. if the engine is not actually cranked, the CMP reference pulses cease after a few seconds and the fuel pump shuts off.

13   If there is no voltage present at the relay connector, check the fuel pump fuse and the wiring circuit between the PCM and the fuel pump relay (see Chapter 12). If voltage is pre-

sent at the relay connector, check the relay (see Chapter 12). If the relay is OK, check for battery voltage at the fuel pump connector (on some models, you should be able to access the fuel pump electrical connector without actually removing the fuel tank; on other models, you'll have to lower the tank slightly to get to the connector). If there is no voltage reaching the fuel pump connector, check for an open circuit between the fuel pump and the relay. If there is battery power at the fuel pump connector and the fuel pump still does not work, try bypassing the fuel pump circuit and, using fused jumper wires, try to power up the pump with battery voltage. If the pump still doesn't operate, replace it (see Section 8).

14   On some models, the oil pressure switch can also open the fuel pump circuit if oil pressure drops below the specified pressure level. Be sure to check the oil pressure and the oil pressure switch if the fuel pump fails to operate after you have verified that the circuits between the PCM and the fuel pump relay and between the relay and the fuel pump are both good (see Chapter 2C).

4   Fuel lines and fittings - repair and replacement

Warning: *Gasoline is extremely flammable, so take extra precautions when you work on any part of the fuel system. Don't smoke or allow open flames or bare light bulbs near the work area, and don't work in a garage where a gas-type appliance (such as a water heater or a clothes dryer) is present. Since gasoline is carcinogenic, wear latex gloves when there's a possibility of being exposed to fuel, and, if you spill any fuel on your skin, rinse it off immediately with soap and water. Mop up any spills immediately and do not store fuel-soaked rags where they could ignite. The fuel system is under constant pressure, so, if any fuel lines are to be disconnected, the fuel pressure in the system must be relieved first (see Section 2). When you perform any kind of work on the fuel system, wear safety glasses and have a Class B type fire extinguisher on hand.*

1   Always relieve the fuel pressure before servicing fuel lines or fittings (see Section 2).

2   The fuel feed, return and vapor lines extend from the fuel tank to the engine compartment. The lines are secured to the underbody with clip and screw assemblies. These lines must be occasionally inspected for leaks, kinks and dents.

3   If evidence of dirt is found in the system or fuel filter during disassembly, the line should be disconnected and blown out. Check the fuel strainer on the fuel pump (see Section 6) for damage and deterioration.

Steel and nylon tubing

4   Because fuel lines used on fuel-injected vehicles are under high pressure, they require special consideration.

4

4.10 Some 4.9L models are equipped with fuel lines that can be disconnected by pinching the tabs and separating each connector

A   Fuel return line   B   Fuel feed line

4.12a Typical aftermarket fuel line disconnect tools for quick-connect fittings (3/8 and 5/16-inch tools shown)

5   If replacement of a metal fuel line or emission line is called for, use welded steel tubing meeting original equipment manufacturers standards or its equivalent. Don't use copper or aluminum tubing to replace steel tubing. These materials cannot withstand normal vehicle vibration.

6   If it becomes necessary to replace a section of nylon fuel line, replace it only with the correct part number - don't use any substitutes.

7   Most fuel lines have threaded fittings with O-rings. Any time the fittings are loosened to service or replace components:

a) *Use a flare-nut wrench while loosening and tightening the fittings, and hold the stationary fitting with another wrench to prevent twisting the line or damaging the component.*

b) *Check all O-rings for cuts, cracks and deterioration. Replace any that appear worn or damaged.*

c) *If the lines are replaced, always use original equipment parts, or parts that meet the manufacturer's specifications.*

Rubber hose

Warning: *Use only original-equipment replacement hoses. Substandard hoses might burst when subjected to fuel system pressure.*

8   When replacing a rubber hose, use reinforced, fuel-resistant hose that meets original equipment manufacturer (OEM) standards. Non-OEM hoses are not appropriate for this application and might be dangerous. Make sure that the inside diameter of the replacement hose matches the outside diameter of the metal lines or the new hose will leak.

Warning: *Do NOT substitute rubber hose for metal line on high-pressure systems. Use only genuine factory replacement lines, or lines meeting factory specifications. And don't use rubber hose within four inches of any part of the exhaust system or within ten inches of the catalytic converter. Rubber hoses must never be allowed to chafe against the frame. A minimum of 1/4-inch clearance must be maintained around a hose to prevent contact with the frame.*

Removal and installation

4.9L models

Refer to illustrations 4.10, 4.12a, 4.12b and 4.13

9   Relieve the fuel system pressure (see Section 2). Disconnect the cable from the negative terminal of the battery (see Chapter 5).

10   Disconnect the fuel feed, return or vapor line at the fuel tank **(see illustration)**. Some fuel line connections may be threaded. Be sure to use a back-up wrench when separating the connections. On quick-disconnect (non-threaded) fittings, clean off the fittings before disconnection to prevent dirt from getting in the fittings.

11   Remove all fasteners attaching the lines to the vehicle body.

12   Detach the fitting(s) that attach the fuel hoses to the engine compartment metal lines **(see illustrations)**. Twisting them back and forth will allow them to separate more easily.

13   Installation is the reverse of removal. Be sure to clean the fittings and apply a few drops of oil before reconnecting them. And

4.12b On quick-connect fuel lines, use the special disconnect tools and push them into the connector to separate the fuel lines (4.9L models)

4.13 Always replace the fuel line O-rings (4.9L models)

4.15 If the metal-collar quick-connect fittings on 4.6L models are equipped with retainers like these, disengage the upper end of each retainer from the fitting

4.16 Grasp the female side of the fitting and twist it back and forth to loosen up any dirt inside the fitting (4.6L models)

4.18a Place the disconnect tool in position on the male side of the quick-connect fitting . . .

4.18b . . . insert it into the connector far enough to release the inner locking spring . . .

4.18c . . . and then pull off the connector (4.6L models)

4.20 Lubricate the male pipe end with a few drops of oil before reconnecting the quick-connect fitting

4.21 To reconnect the quick-connect fitting, push down until it snaps into place

4

be sure use new O-rings at all *threaded* fittings, if applicable **(see illustration)**.

4.6L models

Metal-collar quick-connect fittings

Refer to illustrations 4.15, 4.16, 4.18a, 4.18b, 4.18c, 4.20 and 4.21

Note: *The metal-collar quick-connect fittings shown here are at the fuel rail, but the following procedure applies to all metal-collar quick-connect fittings, regardless of their location on the vehicle.*

14   Relieve the fuel system pressure (see Section 2). Disconnect the cable from the negative terminal of the battery (see Chapter 5).

15   Release the retainer from the quick-connect fitting **(see illustration)**.

16   Grasp the female side of the fitting and twist it 1/4-turn in each direction to loosen any dirt inside the fitting **(see illustration)**.

17   Blow dirt out of the fitting with compressed air.

18   Using the correct tool, available at most auto parts stores **(see illustration 4.12a)**, insert the tool into the female side of the con-

nector and then push in to release the locking spring **(see illustrations)**. Pull the two metal lines apart **(see illustration)**.

19   Remove any rust or burrs from the fuel pipes with an emery cloth.

20   Apply a few drops of clean engine oil to the male pipe end **(see illustration)**.

21   Push the fitting together until the locking spring snaps into place **(see illustration)**.

22   Pull on both sides of the fitting to verify that the connection is fully connected.

23   Clip the retainer back into place.

Plastic-collar quick-connect fittings

Refer to illustrations 4.26, 4.27a, 4.27b, 4.28, 4.29a, 4.29b and 4.30

Note: *The plastic-collar quick-connect fittings shown here are at the fuel filter, but the following procedure applies to all plastic-collar quick-connect fittings, regardless of their location on the vehicle.*

24   Relieve the fuel system pressure (see Section 2). Disconnect the cable from the negative terminal of the battery (see Chapter 5).

25   Remove the retainer clips, if equipped,

4.26 Twist the female side of the quick-connect fitting back-and-forth to break loose any dirt inside the fitting

from the quick-connect fitting.

26   Twist the female connector 1/4-turn in each direction to loosen any dirt inside the fitting **(see illustration)**.

4.27a To disconnect a plastic-collar quick-connect fitting, release the locking tabs by squeezing them together with a pair of needle-nose pliers . . .

4.27b . . . then pull off the connector

4.28 Before reconnecting a plastic-collar quick-connect fitting, lubricate the male pipe with a few drops of oil

4.29a When reconnecting a plastic-collar quick-connect fitting, make sure that the inner locking tabs . . .

4.29b . . . snap firmly into the windows in the female side of the fitting

4.30 To verify that the locking tabs on a plastic-collar quick-connect fitting are correctly secured, try to pull the fitting apart

27   Squeeze the plastic tabs on the male end of the connector and pull apart the connection **(see illustrations)**.
28   Apply a few drops of clean engine oil to the male pipe end **(see illustration)**.
29   Push both sides of the fitting together until the locking tabs inside the connector snap into place **(see illustrations)**.
30   Pull on both sides of the fitting to verify that the connection is fully connected **(see illustration)**.
31   Install the retainer clips, if equipped, on the quick-connect fitting.

5   Fuel tank - removal and installation

Warning: *Gasoline is extremely flammable, so take extra precautions when you work on any part of the fuel system. Don't smoke or allow open flames or bare light bulbs near the work area, and don't work in a garage where a gas-type appliance (such as a water heater or a clothes dryer) is present. Since gasoline is carcinogenic, wear latex gloves when there's a possibility of being exposed to fuel, and, if you spill any fuel on your skin, rinse it*

off immediately with soap and water. Mop up any spills immediately and do not store fuel-soaked rags where they could ignite. The fuel system is under constant pressure, so, if any fuel lines are to be disconnected, the fuel pressure in the system must be relieved first (see Section 2). When you perform any kind of work on the fuel system, wear safety glasses and have a Class B type fire extinguisher on hand.
1   Relieve fuel system pressure (see Section 2).
2   Detach the cable from the negative terminal of the battery (see Chapter 5).
3   If the tank is full or nearly full, use a hand-operated pump to remove as much fuel through the filler tube as possible (if no pump is available, you can siphon the tank at the fuel feed line after raising the vehicle). **Warning:** *DO NOT start the siphoning action by mouth! Use a siphoning kit, available at most auto parts stores.*

4.9L models
Refer to illustrations 5.5a, 5.5b, 5.5c and 5.8
4   Raise the rear of the vehicle and place it securely on jackstands.
5   Disconnect the fuel lines, the vapor

return line and the fuel filler neck **(see illustrations)**. The fuel feed and return lines and the vapor return line are three different diameters, so reattachment is simplified. If you have any doubts, however, clearly label the three lines and their corresponding pipes. Be sure to plug the hoses to prevent leakage and

5.5a On some 4.9L models, the fuel feed and return lines are located on the side of the tank

5.5b On other models, the fuel feed and return lines are located at the front of the tank

5.5c Loosen the clamps and remove the fuel filler hose and vapor return hose (4.9L models)

5.8 Support the fuel tank with a jack and remove the fuel tank strap bolts (4.9L models)

5.14 If there's a cover over the opening for the fuel filler neck, pry it off (some 4.6L models)

5.15 To detach the fuel filler neck from the rubber fuel filler hose, loosen this hose clamp

4

contamination of the fuel system. Later model vehicles are equipped with quick-connect fittings at the fuel feed and return lines (see Section 4 for further information).

6   If fuel remains in the tank, siphon the fuel from the tank at the fuel feed line (not the return line). **Warning:** *DO NOT start the siphoning action by mouth! Use a siphoning kit, available at most auto parts stores.*

7   Support the fuel tank with a floor jack or other suitable means. Place a sturdy plank between the jack head and the fuel tank to protect the tank.

8   Disconnect both fuel tank retaining straps and pivot them down until they are hanging out of the way **(see illustration)**.

9   Lower the tank far enough to disconnect the electrical wires and ground strap (if equipped) from the fuel pump/fuel gauge sending unit. Remove the tank from the vehicle.

10   Installation is the reverse of removal.

4.6L models

Refer to illustrations 5.14, 5.15, 5.16a, 5.16b, 5.19a, 5.19b, 5.20a, 5.20b, 5.20c and 5.22

11   Remove the fuel filler cap and relieve the system fuel pressure (see Section 2). Disconnect the cable from the negative terminal of the battery (see Chapter 5).

5.16a Before removing the fuel tank, be sure to disconnect the EVAP hose from the EVAP canister . . .

12   Drain the fuel tank, if necessary, through the filler neck with a hand pump (there's no drain plug).

13   Loosen the wheel lug bolts for the left rear wheel. Raise the rear of the vehicle and place it securely on jackstands. Remove the left rear wheel.

14   Inside the left rear wheel well, remove the cover that covers the opening surround-

5.16b . . . and the fuel supply and return line connections (or disconnect the other ends of these lines at the fuel pump/fuel level sending unit module, on top of the fuel tank)

ing the fuel filler neck **(see illustration)**.

15   Loosen the hose clamp that secures the fuel tank filler neck to the rubber fuel inlet hose **(see illustration)**.

16   Disconnect the EVAP hose from the EVAP canister **(see illustration)**. Disconnect the quick-connect fittings for the fuel supply

5.19a To detach the spare tire cover, simply push down on this plastic handle (middle arrow) where indicated on the handle and lift out the cover; to detach the carpeted rear compartment floor trim, remove these four pop fasteners . . .

5.19b . . . and remove the remaining fasteners: two from each rear corner of the floor the two from each trim panel for the rear lights (right rear corner shown, left rear corner identical)

5.20a To gain access to the fuel pump/fuel level sending unit module, remove these screws and remove this access panel

5.20b Before lowering the fuel tank, be sure to disconnect the electrical connectors and fuel supply and return lines from the fuel pump/fuel level sending unit module

1　*Fuel tank pressure sensor electrical connector (already unplugged)*

2　*Lock for fuel pump/fuel level sending unit module connector (pull straight up to remove; push straight down to install*

3　*Fuel pump/fuel level sending unit electrical connector (do NOT disconnect until you have removed the lock)*

4　*Fuel supply line quick-connect fitting (plastic-collar type)*

5　*Fuel return line quick-connect fitting (plastic-collar type)*

and return lines **(see illustration)**. (The procedure for disconnecting plastic-collar type quick-connect fittings is in Section 4.)

17　Remove the exhaust system (see Section 16).

18　Unbolt the lower end of each rear shock absorber, then remove the rear suspension support assembly (see Chapter 10, Section 15).

19　Working inside the trunk, remove the spare tire cover, the jack and the spare tire, then remove the carpeted rear compartment floor trim **(see illustrations)**.

20　Remove the access plate from the floor of the trunk, disconnect the electrical connectors from the fuel tank pressure sensor and the fuel pump/fuel level sending unit, then disconnect the quick-connect fittings for

the fuel supply and return lines **(see illustrations)**.

21　Place a floor jack under the fuel tank to support it. Put a piece of plywood between the jack head and the tank to protect the tank.

22　Remove the bolts that secure the fuel tank straps **(see illustration)**.

23　Lower the tank just far enough to verify

5.20c Using a pair of needle-nose pliers, squeeze the locking tangs together as shown and pull off the quick-connect fittings for the fuel supply and return lines

5.22 Remove the exhaust system (A) and the rear suspension support mounting bolts (B indicates rear bolts), then remove the fuel tank strap bolts (C) to lower the tank

7.2 Check the resistance of the fuel tank sending unit as you move the float arm (4.9L model sending unit, later units similar)

7.8 Using a hammer and brass punch, tap the lock ring counterclockwise to loosen it (4.9L models)

that nothing is still connected. If it is, disconnect it now, before lowering the tank any further.

24   Remove the fuel tank.

25   Installation is the reverse of removal.

6   Fuel tank cleaning and repair - general information

1   Any repairs to the fuel tank or filler neck should be carried out by a professional who has experience in this critical and potentially dangerous work. Even after cleaning and flushing of the fuel system, explosive fumes can remain and ignite during repair of the tank.

2   If the fuel tank is removed from the vehicle, it should not be placed in an area where sparks or open flames could ignite the fumes coming out of the tank. Be especially careful inside garages where a gas-type appliance is located, because it could cause an explosion.

7   Fuel pump/fuel level sending unit module - check, removal and installation

Warning: *Gasoline is extremely flammable, so take extra precautions when you work on any part of the fuel system. Don't smoke or allow open flames or bare light bulbs near the work area, and don't work in a garage where a natural gas-type appliance (such as a water heater or a clothes dryer) with a pilot light is present. Since gasoline is carcinogenic, wear latex gloves when there's a possibility of being exposed to fuel, and, if you spill any fuel on your skin, rinse it off immediately with soap and water. Mop up any spills immediately and do not store fuel-soaked rags where they could ignite. The fuel system is under constant pressure, so, if any fuel lines are to be disconnected, the fuel pressure in the system must be relieved first (see Section 2). When you perform any kind of work on the* fuel system, wear safety glasses and have a Class B type fire extinguisher on hand.

Check

Refer to illustration 7.2

1   Remove the fuel level sending unit (see below).

2   Using an ohmmeter, connect the probes to the fuel level sending unit electrical connector terminals **(see illustration)**.

3   Check the resistance of the sending unit as you move the float from the empty position to the full position. Look for a change in resistance when the sending unit float travels from one position to the other. The resistance should change smoothly with the movement of the float arm.

4   If there is no resistance or there is very little change in resistance as the float travels from full to empty, replace the fuel level sending unit assembly.

Removal and installation

5   Relieve the fuel pressure (see Section 2), then disconnect the cable from the negative battery terminal (see Chapter 5).

6   Remove the fuel tank (see Section 5).

4.9L models

Refer to illustrations 7.8 and 7.9

7   The fuel pump/sending unit assembly is located inside the fuel tank. It is held in place by a cam lock ring mechanism consisting of an inner ring with three locking cams and an outer ring with three tangs. The outer ring is welded to the tank and can't be turned.

8   To unlock the fuel pump/sending unit assembly, turn the inner ring counterclockwise until the locking cams are free of the tangs **(see illustration)**. A special tool is available to loosen the lock ring, but if the tool is not available a hammer and brass punch can be used. **Warning:** *If you're going to use a punch to loosen the lock ring, make sure that you use a **brass** punch. Do NOT use a steel punch, which could cause sparks, which could cause an explosion!*

7.9 Carefully remove the fuel sending unit assembly through the opening (4.9L models)

9   Lift the fuel pump/sending unit assembly from the fuel tank **(see illustration)**. **Caution:** *The fuel level sending unit and float arm are delicate. Bumping them against the tank during removal can affect the accuracy of the sending unit.*

10   Inspect the condition of the rubber gasket around the opening of the tank. If it is dried, cracked or deteriorated, replace it.

11   If you're replacing the fuel level sending unit, separate the sending unit from the fuel pump assembly (see Section 8).

12   Installation is the reverse of removal.

4.6L models

Refer to illustrations 7.16, 7.17a, 7.17b and 7.18

13   Disconnect the cable from the negative battery terminal (see Chapter 5).

14   Working inside the trunk, remove the spare tire cover, the jack and the spare tire, then remove the carpeted rear compartment floor trim **(see illustrations 5.19a and 5.19b)**.

15   Remove the access plate, disconnect the electrical connectors for the fuel tank pressure sensor and the fuel pump/fuel level sending

4

7.16 To unlock the fuel pump/fuel level sending unit module from the fuel tank on a 4.6L model, tap the lock ring tabs in a counterclockwise direction with a brass punch, or use a pair of water pump pliers; to lock the module into place, tap the tangs in a clockwise direction or (as shown) until the slots in the lock ring tabs are fully engaged with the stationary stops (sticking up from the tank)

7.17a To remove the fuel pump/fuel level sending unit module from the tank on a 4.6L model, lift the unit straight up . . .

7.17b . . . angle it as shown to extricate the sending unit float arm from the tank and then carefully lift up the float arm (4.6L models)

7.18 If the big O-ring is damaged or deteriorated, replace it (4.6L models)

8.4 Use a small screwdriver or pliers to separate the strainer from the bottom of the fuel pump inlet; on some models it might be necessary to remove the strainer retaining clip first (4.9L models)

8.5 Disconnect the electrical connector(s) from the fuel pump (4.9L models)

unit, then disconnect the quick-connect fittings for the fuel supply and return lines (**see illustrations 5.20a, 5.20b and 5.20c**).

16   Using a brass punch and hammer, or a pair of water pump pliers (**see illustration**), turn the fuel pump/fuel level sending unit lock ring counterclockwise until the slots in the tabs are disengaged from the stationary stops on the tank.

17   Remove the fuel pump/fuel level sending unit module from the fuel tank (**see illustrations**).

18   Inspect the condition of the O-ring around the opening of the tank. If it is dried, cracked or deteriorated, replace it (**see illustration**).

19   If you're replacing the fuel level sending unit, separate the sending unit from the fuel pump assembly (see Section 8).

20   Installation is the reverse of removal.

8   Fuel pump/fuel level sending unit module - component replacement

Warning: *Gasoline is extremely flammable, so take extra precautions when you work on any part of the fuel system. Don't smoke or allow open flames or bare light bulbs near the work area, and don't work in a garage where a gas-type appliance (such as a water heater or a clothes dryer) is present. Since gasoline is carcinogenic, wear latex gloves when there's a possibility of being exposed to fuel, and, if you spill any fuel on your skin, rinse it off immediately with soap and water. Mop up any spills immediately and do not store fuel-soaked rags where they could ignite. The fuel system is under constant pressure, so, if any fuel lines are to be disconnected, the fuel pressure in the system must be relieved first (see Section 2). When you perform any kind of work on the fuel system, wear safety glasses and have a Class B type fire extinguisher on hand.*

4.9L models

Refer to illustrations 8.4, 8.5, 8.7a and 8.7b

1   Disconnect the cable from the negative terminal of the battery (see Chapter 5).

2   Remove the fuel tank (see Section 5).

3   Remove the fuel pump/sending unit module (see Section 7).

4   Remove and inspect the strainer on the lower end of the fuel pump (**see illustration**). If it's dirty, replace it.

5   Disconnect the electrical connector from the fuel pump (**see illustration**).

6   Loosen the fuel line retaining clamp or fuel pulsation dampener (if equipped).

7   Remove the pump from the sending unit (**see illustration**). On some models it will be necessary to push the fuel pump up into the rubber coupler and then slide the bottom of the pump away from the bottom support (**see illustration**). After the pump is clear of the bottom support, pull it out of the rubber coupler. Care should be taken to prevent damage to the rubber insulator during removal.

8   Inspect the sound insulator and all rubber components for cracks and or deterioration, replacing them if necessary. Reassem-

8.7a On some models the fuel pump is secured by a retaining clamp (4.9L models)

8.7b On other models it will be necessary to push the fuel pump towards the dampener to clear the retaining bracket at the bottom (4.9L models)

8.12 Disconnect the fuel pump/fuel level sending unit electrical connector from the fuel pump module (4.6L models)

8.13 Remove the sending unit from the retaining clip (4.6L models)

8.14 Pinch the tabs together and remove the fuel level sending unit from the fuel pump module (4.6L models)

ble the fuel pump onto the sending unit assembly. On vehicles equipped with a fuel pulsation dampener always install the rubber bumper onto the fuel pump first, then install the fuel pump into the pulsation dampener.
9   Install the fuel pump/fuel level sending unit module in the tank (see Section 7).
10   Install the fuel tank (see Section 5).

4.6L models

Refer to illustrations 8.12, 8.13 and 8.14
11   Remove the fuel pump/fuel level sending unit from the fuel tank (see Section 7).
12   Disconnect the fuel level sending unit electrical connector from the module cover **(see illustration)**.

13   Remove the sending unit retaining clip **(see illustration)**.
14   Pinch the tabs together and slide the fuel level sending unit off the module **(see illustration)**. Note the routing of the wiring for installation.
15   Reassembly is the reverse of disassembly.
16   Install the fuel pump/fuel level sending unit in the fuel tank (see Section 7).

9   Air filter housing - removal and installation

4.9L models

Refer to illustrations 9.1 and 9.3
1   Remove the air filter cover retaining nuts and the air duct-to-throttle body nut **(see illustration)**.
2   Lift the cover off and disconnect any vacuum hoses which would interfere with removal. Remove the cover and the air filter element from the engine compartment.
3   Remove the bolts securing the lower housing **(see illustration)**.

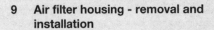

9.1 Typical air filter housing mounting details (4.9L models)

1   *Air duct-to-throttle body retaining nut*
2   *Air filter cover nuts*

9.3 To detach the lower half of the air filter housing, remove these bolts and plastic fasteners (4.9L models)

9.6 Disconnect the electrical connector from the Mass Air Flow (MAF) sensor (4.6L models)

9.7 Loosen the hose clamp that secures the air intake duct to the throttle body and pull the duct off the throttle body; if you are planning to replace the air intake duct itself, wait until you have removed the upper half of the air filter housing and then detach the duct from the upper housing half (4.6L models)

4   Remove the plastic fasteners and detach the fresh air intake duct, then remove the housing.

5   Installation is the reverse of removal.

4.6L models

Refer to illustrations 9.6, 9.7, 9.8, 9.9, 9.10, 9.11a and 9.11b

6   Disconnect the electrical connector from the Mass Air Flow (MAF)/Intake Air Temperature (IAT) sensor **(see illustration)**.

7   Loosen the hose clamp that secures the air intake duct to the throttle body **(see illustration)**, then pull the duct off the throttle body.

8   Unscrew (but don't try to remove) the two fasteners that attach the upper half of the air filter housing to the lower half **(see illustration)**.

9   Remove the upper half of the air filter housing and the air intake duct as a single assembly and remove the air filter element **(see illustration)**.

10   Remove the PCM housing cover screws **(see illustration)** and remove the cover.

11   Lift the PCM and the PCM harness **(see**

9.8 To detach the upper half of the air filter housing from the lower half, remove these two fasteners (4.6L models)

illustration) from the lower air filter housing. Remove the lower half of the air filter housing **(see illustration)**.

12   Installation is the reverse of removal.

9.9 Remove the upper half of the air filter housing and the air intake duct as a single assembly and remove the air filter element (4.6L models)

9.10 To remove the PCM cover, remove these screws

9.11a Before removing the lower half of the air filter housing, carefully lift out the PCM and the PCM harness and set them aside; to detach the lower half of the housing, remove these bolts . . .

9.11b ... and remove this bolt

10.2 Slide the accelerator cable through the slot in the pedal arm (4.9L models)

10.4 On 4.9L models rotate the throttle lever and pass the cable(s) through the slot in the lever

10.5a On some 4.9L models, it will be necessary to pry off the retaining clip to detach the cable from the cable bracket

10.5b On other 4.9L models, it will be necessary to squeeze the accelerator cable retaining tangs and pull the cable through the accelerator cable bracket

10 Accelerator cable - removal and installation

4.9L models

Refer to illustrations 10.2, 10.4, 10.5a and 10.5b

1 Detach the screws and the clip retaining the lower instrument panel trim and lower the

trim (if necessary) (see Chapter 11).
2 Detach the accelerator cable from the accelerator pedal (see illustration).
3 Squeeze the accelerator cable cover tangs and push the cable through the firewall into the engine compartment.
4 On 4.9L models, rotate the throttle lever

and pass the cable through the slot in the lever (see illustration).
5 Remove the cable from the accelerator cable bracket (see illustrations).
6 Remove any remaining cable retaining clips and remove the cable.
7 Installation is the reverse of removal. To prevent possible interference, flexible components (hoses, wires, etc.) must not be routed within two inches of moving parts, unless routing is controlled.
8 Operate the accelerator pedal and check for any binding condition by completely opening and closing the throttle.
9 Apply sealant around the accelerator cable at the engine compartment side of the firewall.

4.6L models

Refer to illustrations 10.10, 10.11, 10.12, 10.13, 10.14, 10.16a, 10.16b, 10.17a and 10.17b

10 Detach the transaxle breather hose, if equipped (see illustration).
11 Unlock the accelerator cable from the cable bracket then slide the cable out of the bracket (see illustration).
12 Rotate the throttle lever to the wide-open position and then disengage the accel-

10.10 If the transaxle breather hose is attached to the accelerator cable bracket, unclip it and set it aside (4.6L models)

10.11 To detach the accelerator cable from the cable bracket, pry up the locking tang on the bottom of the cable lock with a small screwdriver and then slide the cable to the right

4

10.12 Rotate the throttle cam in a counterclockwise direction to put some slack in the accelerator cable and then, holding the throttle cam in this position, disengage the small spherical plug end from the cam by prying it out of the cam, in the indicated direction, with a small screwdriver

10.13 To detach the accelerator cable (A) or the cruise control cable (B) from this clip, simply pull the cable out the slot from underneath the clip

10.14 The accelerator cable goes through the firewall at this plastic retainer, which is located just to the right of the power brake booster, but you'll have to release the cable retainer from inside the vehicle, under the dash, before you can pull it out

erator cable from the slot in the throttle lever cam **(see illustration)**.

13   Detach the accelerator cable from the cable clip near the brake fluid reservoir **(see illustration)**.

14   Trace the accelerator cable to the firewall area just to the right of the power brake booster and note the location of the retainer **(see illustration)** where the cable goes through the firewall.

15   Working inside the vehicle, under the dash, remove the knee bolster trim panel and the knee bolster (see Chapter 11).

16   Disengage the accelerator cable from the accelerator pedal **(see illustrations)**.

17   Locate the accelerator cable retainer again, this time from under the dash **(see illustration)**. Squeeze the accelerator cable retainer tangs together **(see illustration)** and then push the accelerator cable through the firewall.

18   Installation is the reverse of removal.

11   Fuel injection system - general information

1   All models are equipped with a Multi-Port Fuel Injection (MPFI) system **(see illustrations 1.1b and 1.1c)**. The MPFI system includes the fuel tank, the in-tank electric fuel pump/fuel level sending unit module, the fuel pump fuse and fuel pump relay, the fuel rail, the fuel pressure regulator, the fuel injectors and the fuel lines, hoses and connections between the fuel tank and the fuel rail. The air filter assembly, air intake duct, throttle body and air intake manifold are also part of the MPFI system.

2   Air is drawn through the air filter element inside the air filter housing, through the air intake duct and throttle body and then into the intake manifold. The air intake system is equipped with either a Manifold Absolute Pres-

10.16a The accelerator cable is connected to the top of the accelerator pedal

10.16b To disconnect the accelerator cable from the pedal, push the top of the pedal forward slightly (or pull the end of the cable back slightly) and then guide the cable out the slot in the top of the pedal

10.17a Locate the accelerator cable retainer, which protrudes through the firewall just ahead of the accelerator pedal

1   *Rubber washer (slide the washer toward the accelerator pedal to get it out of the way)*
2   *Accelerator cable retainer*

10.17b To release the accelerator cable retainer from its hole in the firewall, depress these two tangs (retainer removed for clarity; tangs are difficult to see when retainer is installed)

12.8 Use a stethoscope or screwdriver to determine if the injectors are working properly - they should make a steady clicking sound that rises and falls with engine speed changes

12.9 Checking the resistance of a fuel injector

sure (MAP) sensor or a Mass Air Flow (MAF) sensor to inform the PCM of volume and pressure variations (for more information on the MAP and MAF sensors, refer to Chapter 6).

3 While the engine is running, fuel is pumped from the fuel tank, through the fuel supply line and fuel filter, and then to the fuel rail, from which it's injected into the air intake passages by the fuel injectors. The fuel pressure regulator keeps the fuel pressure inside the fuel rail within its correct operating pressure. Unused fuel is routed through the pressure regulator and fuel return line back to the fuel tank.

4 The operation of the MPFI system is monitored and controlled by the Powertrain Control Module (PCM) to improve driveability and decrease emissions (for more information on the PCM, refer to Chapter 6).

12 Fuel injection system - check

Warning: *Gasoline is extremely flammable, so take extra precautions when you work on any part of the fuel system. Don't smoke or allow open flames or bare light bulbs near the work area, and don't work in a garage where a gas-type appliance (such as a water heater or a clothes dryer) is present. Since gasoline is carcinogenic, wear latex gloves when there's a possibility of being exposed to fuel, and, if you spill any fuel on your skin, rinse it off immediately with soap and water. Mop up any spills immediately and do not store fuel-soaked rags where they could ignite. The fuel system is under constant pressure, so, if any fuel lines are to be disconnected, the fuel pressure in the system must be relieved first (see Section 2). When you perform any kind of work on the fuel system, wear safety glasses and have a Class B type fire extinguisher on hand.*

General checks

Note: *The following procedure is based on the assumption that the fuel pump is working and the fuel pressure is adequate (see*

Section 3).

1 Verify that the battery is fully charged (see Chapter 1). The Powertrain Control Module (PCM) and information sensors depend on a stable and sufficient voltage supply to optimize fuel delivery and injection.

2 Inspect the air filter element (see Chapter 1). A dirty or partially blocked filter will impede performance and economy.

3 Inspect the fuel filter and replace it if necessary (see Chapter 1).

4 Make sure that all ground wire connections are tight. Inspect all electrical connectors that are related to the system. Loose connectors and poor grounds can cause many problems that resemble more serious malfunctions.

5 Check all pertinent fuses. If you find a blown fuse, replace it and see if it blows again. If it does, search for a grounded wire in the harness.

System checks

Refer to illustrations 12.8 and 12.9

6 Check the air intake duct to the throttle body for leaks, which will result in an excessively lean mixture. Also check the condition of all vacuum hoses connected to the intake manifold.

7 Remove the air intake duct or the air cleaner housing from the throttle body and check for dirt, carbon or other residue build-up. If it's dirty, clean it with aerosol carburetor cleaner and a rag.

8 On 4.6L models, remove the intake manifold service cover **(see illustration 2.2)**. With the engine running, place an automotive stethoscope against each injector, one at a time, and listen for a clicking sound, indicating operation **(see illustration)**. If you don't have a stethoscope, place the tip of a screwdriver against the injector and listen through the handle.

9 If you find an injector that doesn't make any noise, unplug the electrical connector and measure the resistance of the injector **(see illustration)**. Compare the indicated resistance to the injector resistance listed in

this Chapter's Specifications. **Note:** *There are no resistance specifications available for 1994 and 1995 4.9L models nor are there any resistance specifications for 1994 through 1996 4.6L models.*

10 If the resistance is out of specification, the injector is probably bad. If the resistance is OK, the circuit to the injector, or the PCM, may be faulty.

13 Throttle body - removal and installation

4.9L models

Refer to illustration 13.6

1 Remove the air intake duct (see Section 9).

2 Remove the ISC motor from the throttle body (see Chapter 6).

3 Unplug the electrical connector from the Throttle Position Sensor (TPS).

4 Disconnect the accelerator cable, throttle return spring(s), transmission detent cable (automatics) and, if equipped, cruise control cable.

5 Clearly label, then detach, all vacuum hoses.

6 Remove the throttle body mounting

13.6 Throttle body mounting bolts (4.9L models)

13.9 Disconnect the electrical connector from the Manifold Absolute Pressure (MAP) sensor, which is located on top of the throttle body (4.6L models)

13.10 Disconnect the Positive Crankcase Ventilation (PCV) fresh air hose from the throttle body (4.6L models)

13.11 To detach the cruise control cable from the accelerator cable bracket, pull out the locking pin on top and then slide the cable lock to the right (4.6L models)

13.15 Unplug the electrical connector from the Idle Air Control (IAC) valve (4.6L models)

13.16 Unplug the electrical connector from the Throttle Position (TP) sensor (4.6L models)

bolts **(see illustration)** and lift the throttle body from the intake manifold. Remove and discard the throttle body mounting gasket.

7   Installation is the reverse of removal. Be sure to clean the gasket mating surfaces, use a new gasket, and tighten the throttle body mounting bolts to the torque listed in this Chapter's Specifications.

4.6L models

Refer to illustrations 13.9, 13.10, 13.11, 13.13, 13.15, 13.16, 13.18, 13.19

8   Disconnect the Mass Air Flow (MAF)/ Intake Air Temperature (IAT) sensor electrical connector, loosen the air intake duct hose clamp and remove the intake duct and the upper part of the air cleaner housing as a single unit (see Section 9).

9   Disconnect the electrical connector from the Manifold Absolute Pressure (MAP) sensor **(see illustration)**.

10   Disconnect the PCV valve fresh air tube from the pipe on the throttle body **(see illustration)**.

11   Detach the cruise control cable from the accelerator cable bracket **(see illustration)**.

12   Detach the transaxle breather hose, if equipped, and detach the accelerator cable from the accelerator cable bracket (see Section 10).

13   Disconnect the cruise control cable from the throttle lever (see Section 10).

14   Disconnect the accelerator cable from the throttle lever (see Section 10).

15   On 1993 through 1995 models, disconnect the electrical connector from the Idle Speed Control (ISC) motor. On 1996 and later models, disconnect the electrical connector from the Idle Air Control (IAC) valve **(see illustration)**.

16   Disconnect the electrical connector from the Throttle Position (TP) sensor **(see illustration)**.

17   Detach the fuel feed and return lines from the retainer on top of the accelerator cable bracket. **Warning:** *On some models it may be necessary to detach the fuel lines from the fuel rail to allow you to move the fuel lines up far enough for throttle body removal. If this is the case on your model, be sure to first relieve the fuel system pressure (see Section 2), then refer to Section 4 for the fuel line disconnection procedure.*

18   Detach the transaxle shift cable clip **(see illustration)** from the accelerator cable bracket.

19   Remove the three bolts that secure the

throttle body to the coolant crossover housing **(see illustration)**.

20   Remove the throttle body from the coolant crossover. Remove and discard the old throttle body gasket.

21   Remove the accelerator cable bracket

13.18 To detach the transaxle shift cable clip from the accelerator cable bracket, squeeze the two locking tangs together (the tangs are on the underside of the bracket to which the clip is attached) and pull it straight up

13.19 To detach the throttle body from the coolant crossover housing, remove these three bolts (later 4.6L model shown; early 4.6L model throttle bodies use four bolts)

bolts and remove the cable bracket from the throttle body.
22   Installation is the reverse of removal. Be sure to use a new throttle body gasket and tighten the throttle body mounting bolts to the torque listed in this Chapter's Specifications.

14   Fuel pressure regulator - removal and installation

Warning: *Gasoline is extremely flammable, so take extra precautions when you work on any part of the fuel system. Don't smoke or allow open flames or bare light bulbs near the work area, and don't work in a garage where a gas-type appliance (such as a water heater or a clothes dryer) is present. Since gasoline is carcinogenic, wear latex gloves when there's a possibility of being exposed to fuel, and, if you spill any fuel on your skin, rinse it off immediately with soap and water. Mop up any spills immediately and do not store fuel-soaked rags where they could ignite. The fuel system is under constant pressure, so, if any fuel lines in the system are to be disconnected, the fuel pressure in the system must be relieved first (see Section 2). When you perform any kind of work on the fuel system, wear safety*

14.4 To remove the fuel pressure regulator on 4.9L models, detach the vacuum hose (A), unscrew the fuel return line (B) and then - after you have removed the fuel rail - remove the mounting bolt (C) and pull the regulator out of the crossover tube

glasses and have a Class B type fire extinguisher on hand.

4.9L models

Refer to illustration 14.4
1   Relieve the fuel system pressure (see Section 2).
2   Disconnect the negative battery cable (see Chapter 5).
3   Remove the air filter housing (see Section 9).
4   Disconnect the vacuum line from the fuel pressure regulator **(see illustration)**.
5   Unscrew the threaded fitting that connects the fuel return line to the fuel pressure regulator.
6   Remove the fuel rail (see Section 15).
7   Remove the pressure regulator retaining bolt and separate the pressure regulator from the fuel rail.
8   Remove and discard the old O-ring.
9   Be sure to replace the O-ring, even if you're installing the old regulator. Lightly oil the new O-ring before installing it.
10   Installation is otherwise the reverse of removal.

4.6L models

1993 and 1994 models

Refer to illustration 14.20
11   Relieve the fuel system pressure (see Section 2).
12   Disconnect the negative battery cable (see Chapter 5).
13   Reposition the spark plug wires. Remove the intake manifold cover bolts in the reverse order of the tightening sequence **(see illustration 14.20)**.
14   Disconnect the vacuum hose from the fuel pressure regulator.
15   Disconnect the fuel supply and return lines from the fuel rail and unbolt the fuel rail (see Section 15).
16   Raise up the fuel rail assembly high enough to disconnect the fuel return line from the fuel pressure regulator. Remove and discard the old O-ring in the fuel return line fitting.
17   Unbolt the fuel pressure regulator from the fuel rail, separate the regulator from the fuel rail and remove and discard the old O-ring.
18   Apply a light coat of oil to the new O-rings and install both O-rings on the fuel pressure regulator.
19   Install the regulator on the fuel rail and then install the fuel rail assembly (see Section 15).
20   Be sure to tighten the intake manifold cover bolts in the indicated sequence **(see illustration)** to the torque listed in this Chapter's Specifications. Installation is otherwise the reverse of removal.

1995 models

21   The fuel pressure regulator on these models is not removable from the fuel rail. If the fuel pressure regulator is defective, replace the fuel rail assembly (see Section 15).

1996 and later models

Refer to illustrations 14.24, 14.25, 14.26, 14.27 and 14.28
22   Relieve the fuel system pressure (see Section 2).
23   Disconnect the negative battery cable (see Chapter 5).
24   Disconnect the vacuum hose from the fuel pressure regulator **(see illustration)**.

4

14.20 Intake manifold cover bolt tightening sequence (1993 and 1994 4.6L models)

FRONT OF VEHICLE   36032-4-14.13 HAYNES

14.24 Disconnect the vacuum line from the fuel pressure regulator (4.6L models)

14.25 To remove the fuel pressure regulator, pull off this retaining clip . . .

14.26 . . . then, wiggle and twist it back-and-forth while pulling straight up (4.6L models)

14.27 Remove and discard the old fuel pressure regulator O-rings (4.6L models)

14.28 Remove the fuel pressure regulator filter, wash it in clean solvent and inspect it for damage

25   Remove the retainer clip from the fuel pressure regulator **(see illustration)**.
26   Pull out the fuel pressure regulator **(see illustration)**.
27   Remove and discard the old O-rings **(see illustration)**.
28   Remove the old filter **(see illustration)**.

Wash the filter in clean solvent and inspect it for damage. If the filter is damaged, replace it.
29   Installation is the reverse of removal.

---

15   Fuel rail and injectors - removal and installation

Warning: *Gasoline is extremely flammable, so take extra precautions when you work on any part of the fuel system. Don't smoke or allow open flames or bare light bulbs near the work area, and don't work in a garage where a gas-type appliance (such as a water heater or a clothes dryer) is present. Since gasoline is carcinogenic, wear latex gloves when there's a possibility of being exposed to fuel, and, if you spill any fuel on your skin, rinse it off immediately with soap and water. Mop up any spills immediately and do not store fuel-soaked rags where they could ignite. The fuel system is under constant pressure, so, if any fuel lines are to be disconnected, the fuel pressure in the system must be relieved first*

(see Section 2). When you perform any kind of work on the fuel system, wear safety glasses and have a Class B type fire extinguisher on hand.

4.9L models

Refer to illustrations 15.3, 15.5, 15.6, 15.7, 15.8 and 15.10
1   Relieve fuel system pressure (see Section 2), then disconnect the cable from the negative terminal of the battery (see Chapter 5).
2   Disconnect the vacuum line from the fuel pressure regulator, disconnect the Manifold Absolute Pressure (MAP) sensor vacuum line and disconnect the PCV valve to throttle body tube.
3   Detach the fuel feed and return lines from the fuel rail **(see illustration)**. **Note:** *Some models may require the use of special tools to separate the fuel feed and return lines from the fuel rail (see Section 4).*
4   Label and unplug the injector electrical connectors. **Note:** *On some 4.9L models it will be necessary to remove the power steering pump and the power steering pump mounting bracket.*

15.3 To allow removal of the fuel rail assembly on 4.9L models, detach the fuel feed and return lines (A), the MAP sensor vacuum line (B), the fuel pressure regulator vacuum line (C) and the PCV valve tube (D)

15.5 Fuel rail mounting bolts (4.9L models)

15.6 Pull upward on the fuel rail to separate the injectors from the intake manifold, then carefully maneuver the fuel rail assembly off the engine (4.9L model shown)

15.7 To remove an injector from the fuel rail, remove the retaining clip, then pull the injector from the fuel rail

15.8 Carefully pry the O-rings off the injectors

15.10 Install a new retaining clip onto the top of each injector, then push each injector into the injector cup until the retaining clip snaps into place around the cup lip

5   Remove the fuel rail retaining bolts **(see illustration)**.

6   Carefully remove the fuel rail with the injectors and the pressure regulator attached **(see illustration). Caution:** *Use care when handling the fuel rail assembly to avoid damaging the injectors.* **Note 1:** *On 4.9L models, an eight digit identification number is stamped on the side of the fuel rail assembly. Refer to this number if servicing or parts replacement is required.* **Note 2:** *On some models it may be necessary to remove the power steering pump to allow removal of the fuel rail.*

7   To remove the fuel injectors, remove the injector retaining clips and pull the injectors from the fuel rail **(see illustration)**. Discard the retaining clips; new ones should be used when installing the injectors.

8   Remove the injector O-ring seals **(see illustration)**.

9   Install the new O-ring seal(s), as required, on the injector(s) and lubricate them with a light film of engine oil.

10   Install a new retaining clip onto the top of each injector. Push each injector into the fuel rail cup until the retaining clip snaps into place around the fuel rail cup **(see illustration)**.

11   Installation is the reverse of the removal procedure.

4.6L models

Refer to illustrations 15.15, 15.17, 15.18, 15.19a, 15.19b, 15.20, 15.21, 15.22, 15.23 and 15.24

12   Relieve fuel system pressure (see Section 2), then disconnect the cable from the negative terminal of the battery.

13   On 1993 and 1994 models, remove the intake manifold cover (see *Intake manifold - removal and installation* in Chapter 2B). On 1995 and later models, remove the intake manifold service cover **(see illustration 2.2)**.

14   Remove the air intake duct between the air cleaner housing and the throttle body (see Section 9). On 1995 through 1999 models, remove the throttle body and throttle body gasket (see Section 13). On these same models, remove the throttle body spacer bolts, remove the spacer and remove the spacer gasket. Discard the old gaskets.

15   Disconnect the fuel supply and return lines from the fuel rail **(see illustration)**. For help disconnecting the metal-collar type quick-connect fittings, see Section 4).

16   Disconnect the vacuum hose from the fuel pressure regulator (see Section 14).

17   On 2000 and later models, disconnect the PCV fresh air tube from the throttle body and valve cover **(see illustration)**.

18   Remove the nut that attaches the fuel rail end-point bracket retainer **(see illustration)**.

4

15.15 Disconnect the fuel supply and return lines from the fuel rail (4.6L models)

15.17 Disconnect the PCV fresh air tube from the valve cover and from the throttle body (4.6L models)

15.18 To detach the front end of the fuel rail assembly from its mounting bracket, remove this nut (4.6L models)

15.19a Disconnect the electrical connectors from all eight fuel injectors (4.6L models)

15.19b To disconnect an electrical connector from a fuel injector, pull up on the lock on the side of the connector, then depress the lock with your thumb and pull off the connector (4.6L models)

15.20 To detach the coolant pipes from the front fuel rail mounting studs, remove these nuts (4.6L models)

15.21 To detach the fuel rail from the intake manifold, remove these four nuts (4.6L models)

15.22 Typical fuel rail/fuel injector assembly (4.6L models)

15.23 To remove an injector from the fuel rail, flip up the U-clip and pull the injector straight down

15.24 Remove the old O-rings from the injector and discard them; use new O-rings when installing the injector

19   Disconnect the electrical connectors from all eight fuel injectors **(see illustrations)** and set the fuel injector harness aside.

20   Remove the nuts that secure the coolant pipes to the front fuel rail mounting studs **(see illustration)** and set the coolant pipes aside.

21   Remove the fuel rail mounting bolts **(see illustration)**.

22   Remove the fuel rail and fuel injectors as a single assembly **(see illustration)**.

16.1a The exhaust crossover pipe connects the front exhaust manifold to the "front exhaust pipe" (the connector pipe between the *rear* exhaust manifold and the catalytic converter); to remove the crossover pipe, remove the protector bolts and the protector . . .

16.1b . . . then remove the flange bolts from each end of the crossover pipe (crossover-to-front exhaust manifold flange bolts shown)

16.1c The "front exhaust pipe" is actually the connector pipe between the rear exhaust manifold, the crossover pipe and the catalytic converter

16.1d To remove the front exhaust pipe, remove the two nuts from the forward flange (at the rear exhaust manifold) . . .

16.1e . . . and remove the four nuts from the rear flange (just in front of the catalytic converter)

4

23 To remove an injector from the fuel rail, flip up the U-clip retainer **(see illustration)**, then pull the injector from the fuel rail.

24 Remove the old O-rings from the injectors **(see illustration)** and discard them.

25 Be sure to use new O-rings when installing the injectors.

26 On 1995 through 1999 models, use a new gasket when installing the spacer. Tighten the spacer bolts to the torque listed in this Chapter's Specifications. On these same models, install a new throttle body gasket and the throttle body (see Section 13).

27 Installation is otherwise the reverse of removal.

28 When you're done, start the engine and check for fuel leaks.

16 Exhaust system servicing - general information

Refer to illustrations 16.1a through 16.1g, 16.3a and 16.3b

Warning: *If you have just driven the vehicle,*

make sure that you allow enough time for the exhaust system to cool off before you inspect or repair any exhaust component. Also, when working under the vehicle, make sure it is securely supported on jackstands.

1 The exhaust system consists of the following components:

Front and rear exhaust manifolds *(4.9L models, see Chapter 2A; 4.6L models, see Chapter 2B)*

Exhaust crossover pipe: The crossover pipe **(see illustrations)** *connects the front exhaust manifold and the "front exhaust pipe" (which is actually the connector pipe between the* rear *exhaust manifold and the catalytic converter).*

Front exhaust pipe: The front exhaust pipe **(see illustrations)** *connects the crossover pipe and the rear exhaust manifold to the catalytic converter)*

16.1f Exhaust system components:

1 Catalytic converter
2 Intermediate exhaust pipe
3 Post-converter oxygen sensor
4 Resonator

Catalytic converter (see Chapter 6)

Intermediate exhaust pipe: The intermediate exhaust pipe **(see illustration)** is located between the catalyst and the resonator; this is also the part of the exhaust system where the post-converter oxygen sensor is located.

Resonator: The resonator **(see illustration 16.1f)** is located between the intermediate exhaust pipe and the rear exhaust pipe.

Rear exhaust pipe: The rear exhaust pipe **(see illustration)** is located between the resonator and the mufflers.

Mufflers and Tail pipes **(see illustration 16.1g)**

Rubber exhaust hangers: There are two rubber exhaust hangers at the rear end of the intermediate pipe and at the suspension crossmember. There's also one rubber hanger at the rear of each muffler (see Step 3).

2   Conduct regular inspections of the exhaust system to keep it safe and quiet. Look for damaged or bent parts, open seams, holes, loose connections, excessive corrosion or other defects that could allow exhaust fumes to enter the vehicle. Deteriorated exhaust system components should not be repaired; they should be replaced with new parts.

3   One of the most common problems with modern exhaust systems is the rubber hangers, which deteriorate, crack, tear and then fail, allowing the exhaust system to drop. Anytime you're working under the vehicle, inspect all rubber exhaust hangers for wear

16.1g Exhaust system components (continued):

1   *Rear exhaust pipe*
2   *Mufflers*
3   *Tail pipes*

and damage and replace as necessary **(see illustrations).**

4   If the exhaust system components are extremely corroded or rusted together, welding equipment will probably be required to remove them. The convenient way to accomplish this is to have a muffler repair shop remove the corroded sections with a cutting torch. If, however, you want to save money by doing it yourself (and you don't have a welding outfit with a cutting torch), simply cut off the old components with a hacksaw. If you have compressed air, special pneumatic cutting chisels can also be used. If you do decide to tackle the job at home, be sure to wear safety goggles to protect your eyes from metal chips and work gloves to protect your hands.

5   Here are some simple guidelines to fol-

low when repairing the exhaust system:

a) Work from the back to the front when removing exhaust system components.

b) Apply penetrating oil to the exhaust system component fasteners to make them easier to remove.

c) Use new gaskets, hangers and clamps when installing exhaust system components.

d) Apply anti-seize compound to the threads of all exhaust system fasteners during reassembly.

e) Be sure to allow sufficient clearance between newly installed parts and all points on the underbody to avoid overheating the floor pan and possibly damaging the interior carpet and insulation. Pay particularly close attention to the catalytic converter and heat shield.

16.3a To replace a rubber exhaust hanger, disengage it from the metal bracket welded to the exhaust component . . .

16.3b . . . then remove the nut and pull off the hanger (some hangers are pushed onto another bracket, welded to the underside of the pan, instead of attached by a nut to a stud)

Chapter 5
Engine electrical systems

Contents

Specifications

General

HEI system (4.9L models)	
Ignition coil resistance	
Primary resistance	0.4 to 0.5 ohms
Secondary resistance	6000 to 30,000 ohms
Pick-up coil resistance	500 to 1500 ohms
DIS system ignition coil resistance (4.6L models)	Not available
Spark plug wire resistance	Less than 5000 ohms per foot
Cylinder numbers	See Chapter 2
Firing order	See Chapter 2

1 General information, precautions and battery disconnection

General information

The engine electrical systems include all ignition, charging and starting components. Because of their engine-related functions, these components are discussed separately from body electrical devices such as the lights, the instruments, etc. (which are included in Chapter 12).

Precautions

Always observe the following precautions when working on the electrical system:

a) Be extremely careful when servicing engine electrical components. They are easily damaged if checked, connected or handled improperly.
b) Never leave the ignition switched on for long periods of time when the engine is not running.
c) Never disconnect the battery cables while the engine is running.
d) Maintain correct polarity when connecting battery cables from another vehicle during jump starting - see the "Booster battery (jump) starting" section at the front of this manual.
e) Always disconnect the negative battery cable before working on the electrical system.

It's also a good idea to review the safety-related information regarding the engine electrical systems located in the "Safety first!" section at the front of this manual, before beginning any operation included in this Chapter.

Battery disconnection

Caution: On models equipped with a vehicle or audio security system, or both, make sure that you refer to the owner's manual for the proper procedure to follow for disabling the security system(s) on your vehicle before performing any procedure which requires disconnecting the battery.

Several systems on the vehicle require battery power to be available at all times, either to ensure their continued operation (such as the clock) or to maintain control unit memories (such as that in the engine management system's Powertrain Control Module [PCM]) which would be wiped out if the battery were to be disconnected. Therefore, whenever the battery is to be disconnected, first note the following to ensure that there are no unforeseen consequences of this action:

a) First, on any vehicle with power door locks, it is a wise precaution to remove the key from the ignition and to keep it with you, so that it does not get locked inside if the power door locks should engage accidentally when the battery is reconnected!
b) The engine management system's PCM will lose the information stored in its memory when the battery is disconnected. This includes idling and operating values, and any fault codes detected (see Chapter 6). Whenever the battery is disconnected, the information relating to idle speed control and other operating values will have to be re-programmed into the unit's memory. The PCM does this by itself, but until then, there may be surg-

3.3 To test the open circuit voltage of the battery, simply touch the black probe of the voltmeter to the negative terminal and the red probe to the positive terminal of the battery - a fully charged battery should read between 11.5 to 12.5 volts depending on the outside air temperature

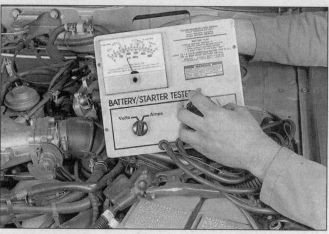

3.4 Some battery load testers are equipped with an ammeter which enables the battery load to be precisely dialed in, as shown - less expensive testers have a load switch and a voltmeter only

ing, hesitation, erratic idle and a generally inferior level of performance. To allow the PCM to relearn these values, start the engine and run it as close to idle speed as possible until it reaches its normal operating temperature, then run it for approximately two minutes at 1200 rpm. Next, drive the vehicle as far as necessary - approximately 5 miles of varied driving conditions is usually sufficient - to complete the relearning process.

Devices known as "memory-savers" can be used to avoid some of the above problems. Precise details vary according to the device used. Typically, it is plugged into the cigarette lighter, and is connected by its own wires to a spare battery; the vehicle's own battery is then disconnected from the electrical system, leaving the "memory-saver" to pass sufficient current to maintain audio unit security codes and PCM memory values, and also to run permanently live circuits such as the clock, all the while isolating the battery in the event of a short-circuit occurring while work is carried out. **Warning 1:** *Some of these devices allow a considerable amount of current to pass, which can mean that many of the vehicle's systems are still operational when the main battery is disconnected. If a "memory-saver" is used, ensure that the circuit concerned is actually "dead" before carrying out any work on it!* **Warning 2:** *If work is to be performed around any of the airbag system components, the battery must be disconnected and no "memory saver" can be used. If a memory saver device is used, power will be supplied to the airbag system and personal injury may result if the airbag is accidentally deployed.*

2 Battery - emergency jump starting

Refer to the Booster battery (jump) starting procedure at the front of this manual.

3 Battery - check and replacement

Warning: *Hydrogen gas is produced by the battery, so keep open flames and lighted cigarettes away from it at all times. Always wear eye protection when working around a battery. Rinse off spilled electrolyte immediately with large amounts of water.*
Caution: *Always disconnect the negative cable first and hook it up last or the battery may be shorted by the tool being used to loosen the cable clamps.*

Battery location

1   The battery is located in the engine compartment on 1992 through 1997 DeVille and Seville models. On 1998 and 1999 DeVille models, the battery is located in the engine compartment. On 1998 and 1999 Seville models, the battery is located under the rear seat. On all 2000 and later models, the battery is located under the rear seat. If you need help removing the rear seat cushion, refer to Chapter 11.

Check

Refer to illustrations 3.3 and 3.4
Note: *If you don't know where the battery is located, see Step 1.*
2   Detach the cables from the negative and positive terminals of the battery **(see illustration 3.5)**. **Warning:** *To prevent arcing, disconnect the negative (-) cable first, then remove the positive (+) cable.*
3   Check the battery state of charge. Visually inspect the indicator eye on the top of the battery; if the indicator eye is black in color charge the battery as described in Chapter 1. Next perform an open voltage circuit test using a digital voltmeter **(see illustration)**. **Note:** *The battery's surface charge must be removed before accurate voltage measurements can be made. Turn On the high beams for ten seconds, then turn them Off, let the vehicle stand for two minutes. With the engine and all accessories Off, touch the*

negative probe of the voltmeter to the negative terminal of the battery and the positive probe to the positive terminal of the battery. The battery voltage should be 11.5 to 12.5 volts or slightly above. If the battery is less than the specified voltage, charge the battery before proceeding to the next test. Do not proceed with the battery load test unless the battery charge is correct.
4   Perform a battery load test. An accurate check of the battery condition can only be performed with a load tester (available at most auto parts stores). This test evaluates the ability of the battery to operate the starter and other accessories during periods of heavy amperage draw (load). Install a special battery load testing tool onto the terminals **(see illustration)**. Load test the battery according to the manufacturer's instructions for the particular tool. This tool utilizes a carbon pile to increase the load demand (amperage draw) on the battery. Maintain the load on the battery for 15 seconds or less and observe that the battery voltage does not drop below 9.6 volts. If the battery condition is weak or defective, the tool will indicate this condition immediately. **Note:** *Cold temperatures will cause the minimum voltage requirements to drop slightly. Follow the chart given in the tool manufacturer's instructions to compensate for cold climates. Minimum load voltage for freezing temperatures (32 degrees F) should be approximately 9.1 volts.*

Replacement

Refer to illustrations 3.5, 3.6 and 3.7
Note: *If you don't know where the battery is located, see Step 1.*
5   Detach the cables from the negative and positive terminals of the battery **(see illustration)**. **Warning:** *To prevent arcing, disconnect the negative (-) cable first, then remove the positive (+) cable. If you're not sure which cable is positive and which one is negative, look at the color of the cable (positive cables are usually red, negative cables are always black) or look for the plus ("+") and minus ("-")*

3.5 When removing the cable bolts from the battery posts, always remove the ground cable first and hook it up last; note that the negative cable has been disconnected first

3.6 To disconnect the vent tube from the battery, simply pull it off (left vent shown, right vent identical)

3.7 To detach the battery from the floor, remove this bolt and the battery hold-down clamp which secures the base of the battery to the battery tray

signs on the top or side of the battery near the terminals.

6   Disconnect the vent tube, if equipped, from both ends of the battery **(see illustration)**.

7   Remove the hold-down clamp bolt **(see illustration)** and remove the hold-down clamp.

8   Carefully lift the battery out of the engine compartment or out from under the seat. **Note:** *The battery carrier (on vehicles with the battery in the engine compartment) and the hold-down clamp should be clean and free from corrosion before installing the battery. Make certain that there are no parts in the carrier before installing the battery.*

9   To install the battery, simply position it in the battery carrier (engine compartment installations) or on the floor (under-seat installations). Don't tilt it.

10   Install the hold-down clamp and bolt. The bolt should be snug, but overtightening it may damage the battery case.

11   Install both battery cables, positive first, then the negative. **Note:** *The battery terminals and cable ends should be cleaned prior to connection* (see Chapter 1).

12   If the battery is installed under the rear seat, install the rear seat cushion (see Chapter 11).

---

4   Battery cables - replacement

1   Periodically inspect the entire length of each battery cable for damage, cracked or burned insulation and corrosion. Poor battery cable connections can cause starting problems and decreased engine performance.

2   Check the cable-to-terminal connections at the ends of the cables for cracks, loose wire strands and corrosion. The presence of white, fluffy deposits under the insulation at the cable terminal connection is a sign that the cable is corroded and should be replaced. Check the terminals for distortion, missing mounting bolts and corrosion.

3   When replacing the cables, always dis-

connect the negative cable first and hook it up last or the battery may be shorted by the tool used to loosen the cable clamps. Even if only the lpositive cable is being replaced, be sure to disconnect the negative cable from the battery first.

Removal

Battery in the engine compartment

4   First, disconnect the battery cables from the battery (see Section 3).

5   The negative battery cable is bolted to the engine block and/or the body (on some models, there are *two* ground cables, one to the block and one to the body). Note the routing of each cable to ensure correct installation.

6   The positive battery cable is connected to the starter solenoid (see Section 17).

7   Installation is the reverse of removal.

Battery under the seat

Negative battery cable

Refer to illustration 4.10

8   Remove the rear seat cushion (see Chapter 11).

9   Disconnect the cable from the negative battery terminal (see Section 3).

10   Disconnect the body harness from the negative battery cable **(see illustration)**.

11   Disconnect the negative battery cable from the floorpan.

Positive battery cable

Refer to illustrations 4.14, 4.15a, 4.15b and 4.16

12   Remove the rear seat cushion (see Chapter 11).

13   Disconnect the cables from the positive and from the negative battery terminals (see Section 3).

14   To disconnect the shorter of the two positive battery cables, flip up the plastic protective cover from the terminal on the fuse and relay box to the left of the battery and remove the nut that secures the cable to the fuse block **(see illustration)**.

15   The longer positive cable is routed along

4.10 To remove the negative battery cable from a vehicle with the battery under the seat, disconnect the cable from the negative battery terminal, unplug the electrical connector to disconnect the body harness and remove the bolt that attaches the negative cable to the body

4.14 To disconnect the shorter positive battery cable from the rear fuse and relay panel (located to the left of the battery) on a vehicle with the battery under the rear seat, flip open the plastic cover and remove this nut

5

4.15a To remove the longer positive battery cable, pry off the rear right door sill plate . . .

4.15b . . . and the front right sill plate

4.16 To disconnect the forward end of the longer positive battery cable from the front fuse and relay compartment (located in the engine compartment), flip open the plastic cover and remove this nut

the right edge of the floor, underneath the carpet, between the passenger seat and the B-pillar. Remove the sill plates below each door **(see illustrations)** so that you can work the positive cable out from under the carpeting.

16 Disconnect the positive battery cable from the terminal on the front fuse and relay box, which is located on the right side of the engine compartment **(see illustration)**.

17 Disengage the battery cable grommet from the cowl panel.

18 Carefully remove the battery cable by pulling it out through the cowl panel.

Installation

19 If you are replacing either or both of the battery cables, take them with you when buying new cables. It is vitally important that you replace the cables with identical parts. Cables have characteristics that make them easy to identify: positive cables are usually red and larger in cross-section; ground cables are usually black and smaller in cross-section.

20 Clean the threads of the starter solenoid, the ground connection(s) and/or the terminals on the fuse and relay panels with a wire brush to remove rust and corrosion. Apply a light coat of battery terminal corrosion inhibitor or petroleum jelly to the threads to prevent future corrosion.

21 Attach the cable to the terminal and tighten the mounting nut/bolt securely.

22 Before connecting a new cable to the battery, make sure that it reaches the battery without having to be stretched.

23 Installation is otherwise the reverse of removal.

5   Ignition system - general information

Warning: *Because of the very high voltage generated by the ignition system, extreme care should be taken whenever an operation involving ignition components is performed. This not only includes the distributor, coil(s),*

module and spark plug wires, but related items that are connected to the systems as well, such as the plug connections, tachometer and other testing equipment.

The ignition system consists of the ignition switch, the battery, the ignition coils, the primary (battery voltage) and secondary (high-voltage) wiring circuits, the ignition control module(s), the distributor (4.9L models) and the spark plugs.

4.9L models

A High Energy Ignition (HEI) distributor with Electronic Spark Timing (EST) is used on all 4.9L models. The ignition coil is mounted in the distributor cap. The HEI distributor has an internal magnetic pick-up coil unit which contains a permanent magnet, a pole piece with internal teeth and a pick-up coil.

All spark timing changes in the HEI/EST distributor are carried out electronically by the Electronic Control Module (ECM), which monitors data from various engine sensors, computes the desired spark timing and signals the distributor to change the timing accordingly. A back-up spark advance system is incorporated to signal the ignition module in case of ECM failure. No vacuum or mechanical advance is used.

4.6L models

All 4.6L models are equipped with a distributorless electronic ignition system. There are two basic versions of this system. On 1993 through 1999 models, the ignition system consists of an ignition control module and four ignition coils in a single assembly mounted on the rear valve cover. This version uses a "waste spark" method of spark distribution, i.e. each ignition coil fires the spark plugs in two cylinders simultaneously. Each cylinder is paired with its opposing cylinder in the firing order (1-4, 2-5, 6-7 and 3-8) so that when one cylinder fires on its compression stroke, its opposing cylinder, where the piston is on the exhaust stroke, also fires at the same time. Since the compression pressure in the cylinder on the exhaust stroke is very low, it requires very little of the available volt-

age to fire its plug, so most of the voltage is used to fire the plug in the other cylinder, on the compression stroke.

On 2000 and later models, the ignition system consists of two ignition coil assemblies. Each coil assembly includes an integral ignition control module and four ignition coils. The ignition coil assemblies are mounted on top of the front and rear valves covers, directly above the spark plugs. The high-voltage end of each coil is inserted into the upper end of a short rubber boot, which is pushed onto the top of the spark plug. The ignition system also includes a single Camshaft Position (CMP) sensor and two Crankshaft Position (CKP) sensors and the Powertrain Control Module (PCM). For more information on the CMP sensor, CKP sensors and PCM, refer to Chapter 6.

Secondary (spark plug) wiring (4.9L models and 1999 and earlier 4.6L models)

The secondary (spark plug) wires are a carbon-impregnated cord conductor encased in an 8 mm (5/16-inch) diameter rubber jacket with an outer silicone covering. This type of wire will withstand very high temperatures and provides an excellent insulator for the high secondary ignition voltage. Silicone spark plug boots form a tight seal on the plug. The boot should be twisted 1/2-turn before removing (for more information on spark plug wiring refer to Chapter 1).

6   Ignition system - check

All models

Warning 1: *Because of the high voltage generated by the ignition system, be extreme careful when undertaking a test procedure involving ignition components. This includes not only the ignition coil itself, but related components and test equipment.*

6.2 To use a calibrated ignition tester (available at most auto parts stores), simply disconnect a spark plug wire, attach the wire to the tester, clip the tester to a convenient ground and operate the starter - if there's enough power to fire the plug, sparks will be visible between the electrode tip and the tester body

Warning 2: *During the following procedure, the engine must be cranked during testing, so make sure that you keep the meter leads, loose clothing, long hair, etc. away from moving parts (drivebelt, cooling fan, etc.) before cranking the engine.*
Note: *Special test equipment is required to perform the following procedure. Read through the procedure and obtain the necessary equipment before proceeding.*
1   Before checking the ignition system, check the following items:
  a) *Make sure the battery cable clamps, where they connect to the battery, are clean and tight.*
  b) *Test the condition of the battery (see Section 3). If it does not pass all the tests, replace it.*
  c) *Check the ignition coil and ignition control module wiring and connections.*
  d) *Check the related fuses inside the fuse and relay boxes in the engine compartment and inside the vehicle (either under the left end of the dash or under the rear seat) (see Chapter 12). If they're burned, determine the cause and repair the circuit.*

4.9L models and 1999 and earlier 4.6L models

Refer to illustrations 6.2 and 6.7
Warning: *Because of the very high voltage generated by the ignition system, extreme care should be taken whenever an operation is performed involving ignition components. This not only includes the coils, control module and spark plug wires, but related items connected to the system as well, such as the plug connections, tachometer and any test equipment.*
2   If the engine turns over, but won't start,

6.7 On 4.9L models, check for power at the BAT+ terminal on the HEI distributor with the ignition turned to ON

check for spark at the spark plug by installing a calibrated ignition system tester to one of the spark plug wires **(see illustration)**. **Note:** *The tool is available at most auto parts stores. Be sure to get the correct tool for your particular ignition system.*
3   Disable the fuel system by removing the fuel pump fuse or fuel pump relay from the fuse and relay panel.
4   Connect the clip on the tester to a ground such as a metal bracket or valve cover bolt, crank the engine and watch the end of the tester for bright blue, well defined sparks.
5   If sparks occur, sufficient voltage is reaching the plugs to fire the engine. However the plugs themselves may be fouled, so remove and check them as described in Chapter 1 or replace them with new ones.
6   If no sparks occur, the distributor cap or rotor (4.9L models) or the spark plug wires might be defective. On 4.9L models, remove the distributor cap and check the cap and rotor and (see Chapter 1). If moisture is present in the distributor cap, use WD-40 or something similar to dry out the cap and rotor, then reinstall the cap and repeat the spark test at the spark plug wire. On all models, inspect the spark plug wires (see Chapter 1). Replace defective parts as necessary.
7   If no sparks occur, check the primary wire connections at the coil to make sure they are clean and tight. Check for voltage to the ignition coil **(see illustration)**. Battery voltage should be available to the ignition coil with the ignition switch ON. **Note:** *If the reading is 7 volts or less, repair the primary circuit from the ignition switch to the ignition coil.*
8   If there's still no spark, check the ignition module and the ignition coil or other internal components that may be defective (4.9L models, see Section 8; 4.6L models, have the ignition system checked by a dealer service department).

2000 and later 4.6L models

9   There is no easy way to check the ignition system on these models. We strongly urge you to have the ignition system checked by a dealer service department.
10   The following method will tell you whether there is spark at each individual ignition coil, but it won't tell you whether the coil pack, the ignition control module or the Powertrain Control Module (PCM) is defective. There are two ignition coil packs on these models, one for the front cylinder and one for the rear cylinders. This method applies to either coil pack.
11   First, you'll need to obtain three or four spark plug wires with boots that will fit onto the high tension terminals of the ignition coils and onto the spark plugs. You'll also need a jumper wire, with alligator clips on either end, to ground the coil pack.
12   Disable the fuel system by removing the fuel pump fuse or fuel pump relay from the fuse and relay panel.
13   Remove the ignition coil assembly (see Section 9) but don't disconnect the electrical connector.
14   Remove the four spark plug boots from the valve cover (see Section 9).
15   Connect one end of each spark plug wire to each ignition coil high voltage terminal and connect the other end of three of the wires to the spark plugs fired by those three coils. Connect the other end of the fourth spark plug wire to a calibrated ignition system tester and ground the tester. If you only have three spark plug wires, you can use one of the spark plug boots for the coil that you're going to test: Install the upper end of the boot on the coil high tension terminal, install the calibrated ignition tester in the spark plug end of the boot and ground the tester. Finally, connect the jumper wire between the coil pack ground (the center terminal, with the coil spring, on the underside of the coil pack) and a good ground on the engine.
16   Now test each individual coil in the same manner as described in Steps 4 through 8. Just remember: As you swap the calibrated ignition tester from one plug wire to the next, the other three coils *must* be connected to their corresponding spark plugs and the coil pack *must* be grounded. Failure to do so could damage the ignition coil assembly, the ignition control module and/or the Powertrain Control Module (PCM).
17   If there's no spark at one or more of the coils, the ignition coil pack, the ignition control module or the Powertrain Control Module (PCM) is defective, but no further testing is possible at home. Have the ignition system checked by a dealer service department.

---

7   High Energy Ignition (HEI) system (4.9L models) - component check and replacement

Component checks
Ignition coil
Refer to illustrations 7.2 and 7.3
1   Remove the distributor cap.

5

7.2 To test the HEI type coil, attach the leads of an ohmmeter to the primary terminals and verify that the indicated resistance is zero or very near zero . . .

7.3 . . . then, using the high scale, attach one lead to the high tension terminal and the other to the GROUND terminal and then the TACH terminal. Verify that both of the readings are not infinite - if the indicated resistance is not as specified, replace the coil

7.6 Connect the ohmmeter to the pick-up coil terminal and the distributor body. If continuity is indicated, there is a short from the pick-up coil wiring to the distributor body

7.7 Measure the resistance of the pick-up coil. It should be between 500 and 1,500 ohms

2   Attach the leads of an ohmmeter across the two primary coil terminals as shown **(see illustration)**. The indicated resistance should be less than one ohm.

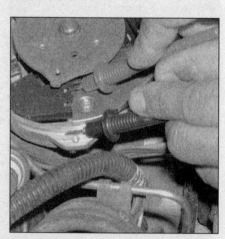

7.10 Check for battery voltage to the ignition module with the ignition key ON (engine not running)

3   Using the high scale, attach one lead of the ohmmeter to the SECONDARY terminal in the middle of the distributor and the other lead to the GROUND terminal and note the resistance **(see illustration)**. Next attach the ohmmeter leads across the SECONDARY and TACH terminals and note the resistance. If both readings indicate infinite resistance, replace the coil.

Distributor pick-up coil

Refer to illustrations 7.6 and 7.7

4   Disconnect the cable from the negative battery terminal. (see Section 1)

5   Unplug the electrical connectors, disengage the latches and remove the distributor cap and rotor.

6   To test the pick-up coil, remove the pick-up coil leads from the module. Connect the negative ohmmeter probe to the distributor body and the positive probe to the pick-up coil electrical connector **(see illustration)**. Resistance should be infinite. If continuity is indicated, there is a short to ground in the pick-up coil. Replace the pick-up coil.

7   Next, measure the pick-up coil resis-

tance across the two pick-up coil terminals. It should be 500 to 1,500 ohms **(see illustration)**. If the resistance is incorrect, replace the pick-up coil.

8   Flex the pick-up coil leads and pull on the connectors (with the ohmmeter connected to the pick-up coil leads). Any change in resistance would indicate a broken wire in the pick-up coil; replace the pick-up coil.

Ignition module

Refer to illustration 7.10

9   Remove the cap from the distributor (see Chapter 1). Verify that the ignition coil and the distributor pick-up coil are functioning properly as described above in Steps 1 through 8.

10   With the ignition coil leads connected to the distributor, check for battery voltage to the ignition module **(see illustration). Note:** *The ignition wiring to the distributor cap is short and will not allow much movement. Use a jumper wire from the BAT terminal on the distributor cap to the pink wire.*

11   If the module is receiving power and the pick-up coil, ignition coil and secondary cir-

7.14 To access the HEI ignition coil, remove the coil cover screws and the cover

7.16 To separate the coil from the distributor cap, clearly mark the wires, detach the coil ground wire and push the terminals from the underside of the cap

7.17 Before installing a new coil, make sure that the center electrode is in good condition (be sure to check the other end, which protrudes into the inside of the cap, as well)

7.23 To remove the ignition module, remove the two mounting screws, unplug the connectors and lift the module out

7.27 To remove the distributor shaft, drive the roll pin out of the shaft with a hammer and punch, remove the gear, shim and tanged washer from the shaft, inspect the shaft for any burrs that might prevent its removal, then pull it out (be careful not to lose the washer at the upper end of the shaft)

7.28 The pick-up coil and pole piece assembly can be removed after carefully prying out the C-clip

cuit are good, most likely the ignition module is defective. Have the module checked at a dealer service department.

Component replacement

Ignition coil

Refer to Illustrations 7.14, 7.16 and 7.17

12   Detach the cable from the negative terminal of the battery (see Section 1).
13   Disconnect the electrical connectors from the distributor cap.
14   Remove the coil cover screws and the cover **(see illustration)**.
15   Remove the screws securing the coil to the cap.
16   Note the position of each wire, marking them if necessary. Remove the coil ground wire, then push the terminals from the underside of the cap. Remove the coil from the distributor cap **(see illustration)**.
17   Installation is the reverse of the removal procedure. Be sure that the center electrode is in good condition **(see illustration)** and that the leads are connected to their original positions.

Ignition module

Refer to illustration 7.23

Note: *It's not necessary to remove the distributor from the engine to replace the ignition module.*

18   Disconnect the cable from the negative terminal of the battery (see Section 1).
19   Remove the air cleaner to provide room to work around the distributor.
20   Remove the distributor cap and wires as an assembly and position them out of the way (see Chapter 1).
21   Remove the rotor.
22   Carefully detach the electrical connectors from the module terminals.
23   Remove the screws and lift out the module **(see illustration)**.
24   Installation is the reverse of removal. Be sure to apply the silicone dielectric grease supplied with the new module to the distribu-

tor base - DO NOT use any other type of grease! If the grease isn't used, the module will overheat and destroy itself.

Distributor pick-up coil

Refer to illustrations 7.27 and 7.28

25   Remove the distributor (see Section 8).
26   Place the distributor in a vise, using blocks of wood to protect it.
27   Mark the relative positions of the gear and shaft. Drive the roll pin out **(see illustration)**. Remove the gear and pull the shaft from the distributor housing.
28   Remove the aluminum shield (if equipped) for access to the pick-up coil. Carefully pry the retaining clip from the distributor shaft and remove the pick-up coil and pole piece assembly **(see illustration)**.
29   Reassembly is the reverse of the disassembly procedure. After reassembly, spin the distributor shaft to make sure there is no contact between the pick-up coil and the pick-up teeth. Loosen and retighten the teeth to eliminate the contact, if necessary.

5

8.5 Make a mark on the distributor body to show the direction the rotor is pointing before removing the distributor

8.6 Mark the position of the distributor in relation to the engine before loosening the distributor hold-down clamp

8   Distributor (4.9L models) - removal and installation

Removal

Refer to illustrations 8.5 and 8.6

1   Position the number one cylinder at Top Dead Center (see Chapter 2). Disconnect the cable from the negative terminal of the battery.
2   Remove the air cleaner assembly (see Chapter 4).
3   Disconnect the electrical connectors from the distributor and the coil.
4   Remove the distributor cap (see Chapter 1).
5   Make a mark on the distributor body directly in-line with the tip of the rotor **(see illustration)**.
6   Mark the position of the distributor body in relation to the engine **(see illustration)**.
7   Remove the distributor hold-down bolt and clamp.
8   Remove the distributor from the engine. Do not rotate the engine with the distributor removed, or the mark you made in Step 5 will be useless.

Installation

Crankshaft not turned after distributor removal

9   Position the rotor in the exact location it was in when the distributor was removed.
10   Lower the distributor into the engine. To mesh the gears at the bottom of the distributor it may be necessary to turn the rotor slightly. It is possible that the distributor may not seat down fully against the block because the lower part of the distributor shaft has not properly engaged the oil pump shaft. Make sure the distributor and rotor are properly aligned with the marks made earlier, then use a large socket and breaker bar on the crankshaft bolt to turn the engine in the normal direction of rotation until the two shafts engage and the distributor drops down against the block.
11   With the base of the distributor seated against the engine block, turn the distributor

housing to align the marks made on the distributor base and the engine block. Make sure the rotor is pointing to its mark.
12   Place the hold-down clamp in position and loosely install the hold-down bolt.
13   Reconnect the distributor wiring harness connectors.
14   Install the distributor cap.
15   Reconnect the coil connector.
16   With the distributor in its original position, tighten the hold-down bolt.
17   Check the ignition timing (see Chapter 1).

Crankshaft turned after distributor removal

18   Remove the number one spark plug.
19   Place your finger over the spark plug hole while turning the crankshaft with a wrench on the pulley bolt at the front of the engine.
20   When you feel compression, continue turning the crankshaft slowly until the timing mark on the vibration damper is aligned with the "0" on the engine timing indicator.
21   Position the rotor between the number one and eight spark plug terminals on the cap.
22   Lower the distributor into the engine. To mesh the gears at the bottom of the distributor, it may be necessary to turn the rotor

9.2a Disconnect these electrical connectors from the right end of the coil . . .

slightly. If the distributor does not drop down flush against the block it is because the distributor shaft has not mated to the oil pump shaft. Place a large socket and breaker bar on the crankshaft bolt and turn the engine over slightly in the normal direction of rotation until the two shafts engage properly, allowing the distributor to seat flush against the block.
23   With the base of the distributor properly seated against the engine block, turn the distributor housing to align the marks made on the distributor base and the engine block.
24   Place the hold-down clamp in position and loosely install the hold-down bolt.
25   Reconnect the distributor wiring harness connectors.
26   Install the distributor cap. If the secondary wiring harness was removed from the cap, reinstall it.
27   Reconnect the coil connector.
28   With the distributor in its original position, tighten the hold-down bolt and check the ignition timing (see Chapter 1).

9   Ignition coil assembly (4.6L models) - removal and installation

1993 through 1999 models

Refer to illustrations 9.2a, 9.2b, 9.4a, 9.4b, 9.4c and 9.4d

1   Disconnect the negative battery cable (see Section 1).
2   If you're going to remove the complete ignition coil assembly, unplug the electrical connectors from the coil assembly **(see illustrations)**.
3   If the plug wires are not numbered, label them, then disconnect the plug wires from the coil assembly. If you're going to remove the complete coil assembly, label and disconnect all the spark plug wires. If you're replacing an individual coil, just disconnect the plug wires from that coil. **Note:** *If disconnecting some of the spark plug wires proves difficult with the coil assembly bolted into place, unbolt the coil assembly first (see next step), then disconnect the plug wires.*

9.2b . . . and unplug these connectors from the other end (1993 through 1999 models)

9.4a To detach the coil assembly, remove the coil assembly mounting bolts or nuts . . .

9.4b . . . and then remove the coil assembly (1993 through 1999 models)

9.4c To detach an individual coil from the coil assembly, remove the two screws that attach the coil to the mounting bracket . . .

9.4d . . . and remove the coil from the coil assembly (1993 through 1999 models)

9.8 Disconnect the electrical connector from the front ignition coil assembly and then loosen the bolts in the indicated sequence (2000 and later models)

4   If you're going to remove the complete ignition coil assembly, remove the coil assembly mounting bolts or nuts (see illustration) and lift the assembly from the vehicle (see illustration). Or, if you're replacing an individual coil, simply remove the two screws that attach that coil to the ignition coil mounting bracket and remove the coil (see illustrations).

5   Installation is the reverse of removal.

2000 and later models

Front ignition coil assembly

Refer to illustrations 9.8, 9.11, 9.12 and 9.13

6   Disconnect the negative battery cable (see Section1).

7   Remove the intake manifold service cover (see illustration 2.2 in Chapter 4).

8   Disconnect the electrical connector from the ignition control module (see illustration).

9   Remove the radiator support cover (see Section 4 in Chapter 3) and move the radiator hose out of the way.

10   Remove the ignition coil assembly bolts in the indicated sequence (see illustration 9.8).

11   Remove the ignition coil assembly from the valve cover (see illustration).

12   Pull out the spark plug boots (see illustration) and inspect them for carbon tracking

9.11 Removing the front ignition coil assembly (2000 and later models)

9.12 Pull out each spark plug boot and inspect it for carbon tracking, cracks and deterioration

5

9.13 Front ignition coil assembly mounting bolt tightening sequence (2000 and later models)

9.18 Disconnect the electrical connector from the rear ignition coil assembly (2000 and later models)

and deterioration.

13   When installing the ignition coil assembly, tighten the ignition coil assembly mounting bolts in the indicated sequence **(see illustration)**. Tighten the bolts gradually and evenly.

14   Installation is otherwise the reverse of removal.

Rear ignition coil assembly

Refer to illustration 9.18 and 9.20

15   Disconnect the negative battery cable (see Section 1).

16   Remove the intake manifold service cover **(see illustration 2.2 in Chapter 4)**.

17   Remove the Air Injection Reaction (AIR) vent solenoid (see Chapter 6).

18   Disconnect the electrical connector from the ignition control module **(see illustration)**.

19   Remove the ignition coil assembly bolts in the indicated sequence **(see illustration 9.8)**.

20   Remove the ignition coil assembly from the valve cover **(see illustration)**.

21   If you're replacing the ignition coil assembly or the ignition control module, see Section 10.

22   Tighten the ignition coil assembly mounting bolts in the indicated sequence **(see illustration 9.13)**. Tighten the bolts gradually and evenly.

23   Install the Air Injection Reaction (AIR) vent solenoid (see Chapter 6).

24   Installation is otherwise the reverse of removal.

---

10   Ignition control module (4.6L models) - replacement

1993 through 1999 models

1   Remove the ignition coil assembly (see Section 9).

2   Unscrew and remove the ignition control module from the ignition coil mounting bracket.

3   Installation is the reverse of removal.

2000 and later models

Refer to illustration 10.5

4   Remove the ignition coil assembly (see Section 9).

5   Remove the ignition control module mounting screws **(see illustration)** and remove the control module.

6   Installation is the reverse of removal.

---

11   Charging system - general information and precautions

The charging system consists of a belt-driven alternator with an integral voltage regulator and the battery. The voltage regulator limits the alternator's voltage to a preset value. This prevents power surges, circuit overloads, etc., during peak voltage output.

The charging indicator light on the dash lights up when the ignition switch is turned on and goes out when the engine starts. If the light stays on or comes on once the engine is running, a charging system problem has

9.20   Removing the rear ignition coil assembly (2000 and later models)

10.5   To detach the ignition control module from the ignition coil assembly, remove these two screws (2000 and later models)

12.2 To measure battery voltage, attach the voltmeter leads to the battery terminals (positive probe to positive terminal, negative probe to negative terminal) and note the indicated voltage; to measure charging voltage, start the engine and note the voltage reading again

13.4 Typical alternator mounting bolts (4.9L models)

13.5 On most 4.9L models, it will be necessary to remove the alternator mounting bolts first, then rotate the rear of the alternator upward to access the electrical connections

occurred. See Section 12 for the proper diagnosis procedure of the alternator.

The charging system does not ordinarily require periodic maintenance. The drivebelt, electrical wiring and connections should, however, be inspected at the intervals suggested in Chapter 1. Be very careful when making electrical circuit connections to a vehicle equipped with an alternator and note the following:

a) When reconnecting wires to the alternator from the battery, be sure to note the polarity.
b) Before using arc welding equipment to repair any part of the vehicle, disconnect the wires from the alternator and the battery terminals.
c) Never start the engine with a battery charger connected.
d) Always disconnect both battery leads before using a battery charger.
e) The alternator is driven by an engine drivebelt which could cause serious injury if your hand, hair or clothes become entangled in it with the engine running.
f) Because the alternator is connected directly to the battery, it could arc or cause a fire if overloaded or shorted out.

Few of the various alternators used on the vehicles covered in this manual can be rebuilt, and parts can be difficult to obtain for those that can. Therefore, no alternator overhaul information is included in this manual. Exchange a defective alternator for a rebuilt unit.

12 Charging system - check

Refer to illustration 12.2

1   If a malfunction occurs in the charging circuit, do not immediately assume that the alternator is causing the problem. First, check the following items:

a) Make sure the battery cable connections at the battery are clean and tight.

b) The battery electrolyte specific gravity (if possible). If it is low, charge the battery.
c) Check the external alternator wiring and connections. They must be in good condition.
d) Check the drivebelt condition and tension (see Chapter 1).
e) Make sure the alternator mounting bolts are tight.
f) Run the engine and check the alternator for abnormal noise (may be caused by a loose drive pulley, loose mounting bolts, worn or dirty bearings, defective diode or defective stator).
g) Check the charge light on the dash. It should illuminate when the ignition key is turned ON (engine not running). If it does not, check the circuit from the alternator to the charge light on the dash.
h) Check all the fuses that are in series with the charging system circuit. The location of these fuses may vary from year and model but the designations are generally the same. Refer to the wiring schematics at the end of Chapter 12 for additional information.

2   With the ignition key off, check the battery voltage **(see illustration)** with no accessories operating. It should be approximately 12.5 volts. It may be slightly higher if the engine has been operating within the last hour.

3   Start the engine and check the battery voltage again. It should now be greater than the voltage recorded in Step 2, but not more than 14.5 volts. Turn On all the vehicle accessories (air conditioning, rear window defogger, blower motor, etc.) and increase the engine speed to 2,000 rpm - the voltage should not drop below the voltage recorded in Step 2.

4   If the indicated voltage is greater than the specified charging voltage, replace the voltage regulator. **Note:** *The voltage regulator is an integral part of the alternator and cannot be replaced separately.*

5   If the indicated voltage reading is less than the specified charging voltage, the alter-

nator is probably defective. Have the charging system checked at a dealer service department or other properly equipped repair facility. **Note:** *Many auto parts stores will bench test an alternator off the vehicle. Refer to your local auto parts store regarding their policy, many will perform this service free of charge.*

13 Alternator - removal and installation

4.9L models

Refer to illustrations 13.4 and 13.5

1   Disconnect the cable from the negative terminal of the battery (see Section 1).
2   Remove the serpentine drivebelt (see Chapter 1).
3   Loosen the BAT+ terminal retaining nut.
4   Remove the alternator mounting bolts **(see illustration)**.
5   Clearly label, if necessary, then remove the electrical connectors from the rear of the alternator **(see illustration)**.
6   Remove the alternator from the engine.
7   Installation is the reverse of removal.

5

4.6L models

Refer to illustrations 13.14, 13.16 and 13.18
Warning: *Wait until the engine is completely cool before beginning this procedure.*

8   Disconnect the cable from the negative battery terminal (see Section 1).

9   Drain the engine coolant (see Chapter 1).

10   Remove the radiator and the engine cooling fan assembly (see Chapter 3).

11   Remove the serpentine drivebelt (see Chapter 1).

12   Raise the front of the vehicle and place it securely on jackstands.

13   Remove the engine splash shield **(see illustration 4.8 in Chapter 3)**.

14   Disconnect the coolant inlet and outlet hoses from the underside of the alternator, if equipped **(see illustration)**.

15   Remove the battery terminal nut **(see illustration 13.14)** and disconnect the battery cable from the terminal stud.

16   Remove the three upper alternator mounting bolts **(see illustration)**. Note the ground strap attached to the alternator by the right upper mounting bolt. Don't forget to reattach this ground strap when installing the alternator.

17   Remove the coolant outlet hose bracket bolt **(see illustration 13.14)**.

18   From underneath the vehicle, remove the lower alternator mounting bolt **(see illustration)**.

19   Remove the alternator.

20   Installation is the reverse of removal.

14   Starting system - general information and precautions

The starting system consists of the battery, the ignition switch, the starter relay, the starter motor, the starter solenoid and the electrical circuit connecting the components. The solenoid is mounted directly on the starter motor. The starting system includes a Park/Neutral Position (PNP) switch, which is located on the transaxle (see Chapter 7).

13.14 Alternator removal and installation details

1   *Coolant inlet hose*
2   *Coolant outlet hose*
3   *Battery terminal nut*
4   *Upper alternator mounting bolts*
5   *Ground strap*
6   *Coolant outlet hose bracket bolt*

The starter motor on 4.9L engines is located on the front side of the engine block, where the transaxle and engine bolt together. The starter motor on 4.6L models is installed on top of the engine block, at the left (driver's) end of the "valley" between the cylinder heads, near the transaxle bellhousing.

When the ignition key is turned to the START position, the starter solenoid is actuated through the starter control circuit. The starter solenoid then connects the battery to the starter. The battery supplies the electrical energy to the starter motor, which does the actual work of cranking the engine.

The starter motor on a vehicle equipped with a manual transaxle can be operated only when the clutch pedal is depressed; the starter on a vehicle equipped with an automatic transaxle can be operated only when the transaxle selector lever is in Park or Neutral.

Always observe the following precautions when working on the starting system:

a)   *Excessive cranking of the starter motor can overheat it and cause serious damage. Never operate the starter motor for more than 15 seconds at a time without pausing to allow it to cool for at least two minutes.*

b)   *The starter is connected directly to the battery and could arc or cause a fire if mishandled, overloaded or short circuited.*

c)   *Always detach the cable from the negative terminal of the battery before working on the starting system.*

15   Starter motor and circuit - check

Refer to illustrations 15.3 and 15.4

1   If a malfunction occurs in the starting circuit, do not immediately assume that the starter is causing the problem. First, check the following items:

a)   *Make sure the battery cable clamps, where they connect to the battery, are clean and tight.*

b)   *Check the condition of the battery cables (see Section 4). Replace any defective battery cables with new parts.*

c)   *Test the condition of the battery (see Section 3). If it does not pass all the tests, replace it with a new battery.*

d)   *Check the starter solenoid wiring and connections. Refer to the wiring diagrams at the end of Chapter 12.*

13.16 Alternator upper mounting bolts (note the ground strap on the middle bolt)

13.18 Lower alternator mounting bolt

15.3 Using an ammeter to measure battery current draw

15.4 Starter motor bench testing details

e) *Check the starter mounting bolts for tightness.*
f) *Check the ignition switch circuit for correct operation (see Chapter 12).*
g) *Check the operation of the Park/Neutral Position switch (automatic transaxle) or clutch-start switch (manual transaxle). Make sure the shift lever is in PARK or NEUTRAL (automatic transaxle) or the clutch pedal is depressed (manual transaxle). Refer to Chapter 7 for the Park/Neutral Position switch check and adjustment procedure. Refer to Chapter 12 wiring diagrams, if necessary, when performing circuit checks. These systems must operate correctly to provide battery voltage to the ignition solenoid.*
h) *Check the operation of the starter relay. The starter relay is located in the fuse/relay box inside the engine compartment. Refer to Chapter 12 for the testing procedure.*

2   If the starter does not actuate when the ignition switch is turned to the start position, check for battery voltage to the solenoid. This will determine if the solenoid is receiving the correct voltage signal from the ignition switch. Connect a test light or voltmeter to the starter solenoid positive terminal and while an assistant turns the ignition switch to the start position. If voltage is not available, refer to the wiring diagrams in Chapter 12 and check all the fuses and relays in series with the starting system. If voltage is available but the starter motor does not operate, remove the starter (see Section 16) and bench test it (see Step 4).
3   If the starter turns over slowly, check the starter cranking voltage and the current draw from the battery. This test must be performed with the starter assembly on the engine. Crank the engine over (for 10 seconds or less) and observe the battery voltage. It should not drop below 8.5 volts. Also, observe the current draw using an ammeter **(see illustration)**. It should not exceed 400 amps or drop below 250 amps. **Caution:** *The*

battery cables may be excessively heated because of the large amount of amperage being drawn from the battery. Discontinue the testing until the starting system has cooled down. If the starter motor cranking amp values are not within the correct range, replace it with a new unit. There are several conditions that may affect the starter cranking potential. The battery must be in good condition and the battery cold-cranking rating must not be under-rated for the particular application. Be sure to check the battery specifications carefully. The battery terminals and cables must be clean and not corroded. Also, in cases of extreme cold temperatures, make sure the battery and/or engine block is warmed before performing the tests.
4   If the starter is receiving voltage but does not activate, remove and check the starter/solenoid assembly on the bench. Most likely the solenoid is defective. In some rare cases, the engine may be seized so be sure to try and rotate the crankshaft pulley (see Chapter 2A or 2B) before proceeding. With the starter/solenoid assembly mounted in a vise on the bench, install one jumper cable from the negative battery terminal to the body of the starter **(see illustration)**. Install the other jumper cable from the positive battery terminal to the B+ terminal on the starter. Install a starter switch and apply battery voltage to the solenoid S terminal (for 10 seconds or less) and see if the solenoid plunger, shift lever and overrunning clutch extends and rotates the pinion drive. If the pinion drive extends but does not rotate, the solenoid is operating but the starter motor is defective. If there is no movement but the solenoid clicks, the solenoid and/or the starter motor is defective. If the solenoid plunger extends and rotates the pinion drive, the starter/solenoid assembly is working properly.

16   Starter motor - removal and installation

4.9L models
Removal and installation

Refer to illustrations 16.4, 16.5a and 16.5b
1   Disconnect the cable from the negative terminal of the battery (see Section 1).
2   Raise the front of the vehicle and support it securely on jackstands.
3   From under the vehicle, remove the flexplate inspection cover and the starter motor shield (if equipped). **Note:** *On some models it may be necessary to remove the crossover pipe from the exhaust system to allow removal of the starter (see Chapter 4).*
4   Disconnect the solenoid wire and battery cable from the terminals on the solenoid **(see illustration)**.

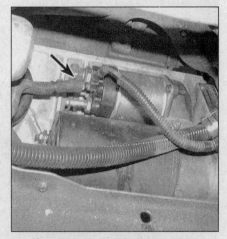

16.4 Remove the starter electrical connections on the solenoid (4.9L models)

16.5a Remove the starter mounting bolts (4.9L models)

16.5b Remove the starter support bracket retaining nut (4.9L models)

5   Remove the starter motor bolts **(see illustrations)**.

6   Remove the starter motor. Note the location of the spacer shim(s), if equipped.

7   Installation is the reverse of removal. Be sure to install the spacer shim(s) in exactly the same location, if equipped (see Steps 8 through 13 for the correct shim adjustment procedure).

Shim adjustment procedure

8   Remove the flywheel housing cover (see Chapter 7).

9   Inspect the flywheel or driveplate for signs of unusual wear such as chipped or missing gear teeth.

10   Using a wire type feeler gauge, measure the clearance between the top of the flywheel ring gear tooth and the bottom of the pinion tooth on the starter. Normal clearance should be 0.010 to 0.060 inch.

11   If the starter clearance is less than 0.020 inches and the starter whined after engagement, the starter is too close to the flywheel.

Add a 0.040 shim to gain clearance. Do not use more than two shims.

12   If the starter clearance is more than 0.060 inches and the starter whines during engagement, then the starter is too far from the flywheel. Remove a 0.040 shim to gain clearance. Do not remove more than two shims.

13   To install a shim, loosen the inside bolt, remove the outer bolt and slide the shim between the engine and the starter without removing the starter from the engine block.

4.6L models

Refer to illustrations 16.16

14   Disconnect the cable from the negative terminal of the battery (see Section 1).

15   Remove the intake manifold (see Chapter 2B).

16   Disconnect the starter cable from the starter solenoid terminal **(see illustration)**.

17   Remove the starter mounting bolts **(see illustration 16.16)**.

18   Installation is the reverse of removal.

17 Starter motor solenoid - replacement

Refer to illustration 17.3

1   Remove the starter unit (see Section 16).

2   Disconnect the connector strap from the starter motor terminal. Remove the two screws which secure the solenoid housing to the end-frame assembly.

3   Twist the solenoid in a clockwise direction to disengage the flange key and then withdraw the solenoid **(see illustration)**.

4   Install the solenoid to the starter motor by first checking that the return spring is in position on the plunger and then insert the solenoid body into the drive housing and turn the body counterclockwise to engage the flange key.

5   Install the two solenoid securing screws and connect the starter motor connector strap.

16.16 To remove the starter on a 4.6L engine, disconnect the starter cable and remove the starter mounting bolts

17.3 To disengage the solenoid from the starter, turn it in a clockwise direction

Chapter 6
Emissions and engine control systems

Contents

Specifications

Torque specifications

Ft-lbs (unless otherwise indicated)

4.9L engine

Engine Coolant Temperature (ECT) sensor	180 in-lbs
Exhaust Gas Recirculation (EGR) valve mounting bolts	168 in-lbs
Intake Air Temperature (IAT) sensor	
Brass shell	180 in-lbs
Steel shell	20
Oxygen sensor	30
Vehicle Speed Sensor (VSS)	20

4.6L engine

Camshaft Position (CMP) sensor (1996 on) retaining bolt	89 in-lbs
Crankshaft Position (CKP) sensor (1996 on) retaining bolt	89 in-lbs
Engine Coolant Temperature (ECT) sensor	
1994 and 1995	106 in-lbs
1996 through 1999	180 in-lbs
Exhaust Gas Recirculation (EGR) valve mounting bolts	18
Knock sensor	168 in-lbs
Oxygen sensors	30
Vehicle Speed Sensor (VSS)	89 in-lbs

1.1a Typical emission control component layout (4.9L models)

1   Intake Air Temperature (IAT) sensor
2   Throttle Position Sensor (TPS)
3   Manifold Absolute Pressure (MAP) sensor

4   Exhaust Gas Recirculation (EGR) valve
5   Engine Coolant Temperature (ECT) sensor
6   Evaporative emissions (EVAP) canister

7   Camshaft Position (CMP) sensor
8   Positive Crankcase Ventilation (PCV) valve
9   Idle Speed Control (ISC) motor

1.1b Typical emission control component layout (4.6L models)

1   Mass Air Flow (MAF) sensor
2   Idle Air Control (IAC) valve
3   Manifold Absolute Pressure (MAP) sensor
4   Throttle Position (TP) sensor
5   Positive Crankcase Ventilation (PCV) crankcase fresh air tube

6   Positive Crankcase Ventilation (PCV) valve
7   Secondary Air Injection (AIR) system check valve for rear exhaust manifold
8   Secondary Air Injection (AIR) system check valve for front exhaust manifold

1   General information

Refer to illustrations 1.1a, 1.1b, 1.6a and 1.6b

To prevent pollution of the atmosphere from incompletely burned and evaporating gases, and to maintain good driveability and fuel economy, a number of emission control systems **(see illustrations)** are incorporated. They include the:

On-Board Diagnostic (OBD) system (1993 through 1995 models)
On-Board Diagnostic II (OBD-II) system (1996 and later models)
Multi-Port Fuel Injection (MPFI) system
Electronic Spark Control (ESC) system
Electronic Spark Timing (EST) system (4.9L models)
Exhaust Gas Recirculation (EGR) system
Evaporative Emissions Control (EVAP) system
Positive Crankcase Ventilation (PCV) system
Secondary Air Injection (AIR) system
Catalytic converter

The Sections in this Chapter include general descriptions, checking procedures within the scope of the home mechanic and component replacement procedures (when possible) for each of the systems listed above.

Before assuming that an emissions control system is malfunctioning, check the fuel and ignition systems carefully. The diagnosis of some emission control devices requires specialized tools, equipment and training. If

1.6a The Vehicle Emission Control Information (VECI) label contains information such as the types of emission control systems installed on the engine and the idle speed and ignition timing specifications; the vacuum hose routing diagram indicates important emission-control devices and components, and it shows how they're connected together by vacuum hoses. Look for the VECI label on the upper radiator crossmember on 4.9L models . . .

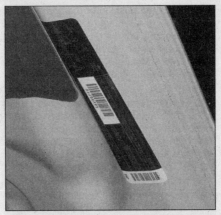

1.6b . . . or on the left edge (driver's side) of the hood on 4.6L models

2.1 Digital multimeters can be used for testing all types of circuits; because of their high impedance, they are much more accurate than analog meters for measuring low-voltage computer circuits

2.2 Scanners like the Actron Scantool and the AutoXray XP240 are powerful diagnostic aids - programmed with comprehensive diagnostic information, they can tell you just about anything you want to know about your engine management system

checking and servicing become too difficult or if a procedure is beyond your ability, consult a dealer service department or other repair shop. Remember, the most frequent cause of emissions problems is simply a loose or broken wire or vacuum hose, so always check the hose and wiring connections first.

This doesn't mean, however, that emissions control systems are particularly difficult to maintain and repair. You can quickly and easily perform many checks and do most of the regular maintenance at home with common tune-up and hand tools. **Note:** *Because of a Federally mandated warranty which covers the emissions control system components, check with your dealer about warranty coverage before working on any emissions-related systems. Once the warranty has expired, you may wish to perform some of the component checks and/or replacement procedures in this Chapter to save money.*

Pay close attention to any special precautions outlined in this Chapter. It should be noted that some illustrations of the various systems might not *exactly* match the system installed on your vehicle because of changes made by the manufacturer during production or from year-to-year.

A Vehicle Emissions Control Information (VECI) label **(see illustrations)** is attached to the underside of the hood. This label contains important emissions specifications and adjustment information. Part of this label, the Vacuum Hose Routing Diagram, provides a vacuum hose schematic with emissions components identified. When servicing the engine or emissions systems, the VECI label and the vacuum hose routing diagram in your particular vehicle should always be checked for up-to-date information.

2   On-Board Diagnostic (OBD) system and trouble codes

On-Board Diagnostics (OBD) system (1995 and earlier models)

Diagnostic tool information
Refer to illustrations 2.1 and 2.2

1   A digital multimeter is necessary for checking fuel injection and emission related components **(see illustration)**. A digital volt-ohmmeter is preferred over the older style analog multimeter for several reasons. The analog multimeter cannot display the volts-ohms or amps measurement in hundredths and thousandths increments. When working with electronic circuits which are often very low voltage, this accurate reading is most important. Another good reason for the digital multimeter is the high impedance circuit. The digital multimeter is equipped with a high resistance internal circuitry (10 million ohms). Because a voltmeter is hooked up in parallel with the circuit when testing, it is vital that none of the voltage being measured should be allowed to travel the parallel path set up by the meter itself. This dilemma does not show itself when measuring larger amounts of voltage (9 to 12 volt circuits) but if you are measuring a low voltage circuit such as the oxygen sensor signal voltage, a fraction of a volt may be a significant amount when diagnosing a problem. Obtaining the diagnostic trouble codes is one exception where using an analog voltmeter is necessary.

2   Hand-held scanners are the most powerful and versatile tools for analyzing engine management systems used on later model vehicles **(see illustration)**. Early model scanners handle codes and some diagnostics for many OBD-I systems. Each brand scan tool must be examined carefully to match the year, make and model of the vehicle you are working on. Often interchangeable cartridges are available to access the particular manufacturer (Ford, GM, Chrysler, etc.). Some manufacturers will specify by continent (Asia, Europe, USA, etc.).

OBD system general description

3   All vehicles described in this manual are equipped with an On-Board Diagnostic (OBD-I) system. The OBD-I system consists of several on-board computers, known as the Electronic Control Module (PCM) and the Body Control Module (BCM) and information sensors, which monitor various functions of the engine and send data to the PCM. Based on the data and the information programmed into the computer's memory, the PCM generates output signals to control various engine functions via control relays, solenoids and other output actuators.

4   The PCM, which is located in the right front corner of the passenger compartment, under the right end of the dash, is the "brain" of the electronic engine control system and is interlinked with the BCM to control various engine and body subsystems. It receives data from a number of sensors and other electronic components (switches, relays, etc.). Based on the information it receives,

6

the PCM generates output signals to control various relays, solenoids and other actuators. The PCM is specifically calibrated to optimize the emissions, fuel economy and driveability of the vehicle.

5   Both computers have self-diagnostic capabilities that can be accessed through the Electronic Climate Control Panel and the Data Link Connector (DLC) with the use of a scan tool.

Information sensors

6   **A/C selector switch -** During air conditioning operation, the PCM controls the air conditioning clutch control relay to delay clutch engagement after the air conditioning is turned ON to allow the IAC valve to adjust the idle speed of the engine to compensate for the additional load.

7   **Camshaft position (CMP) sensor -** The CMP sensor provides information on camshaft position and the speed to the PCM. The PCM uses this information to trigger the fuel injectors in the proper sequence.

8   **Crankshaft position (CKP) sensor -** The CKP sensor provides a signal to the ignition control module which the PCM uses to determine crankshaft position and the engine speed. The PCM and the Ignition control module use this information to control ignition and fuel injection timing.

9   **Engine coolant temperature (ECT) sensor -** The ECT monitors engine coolant temperature and sends the PCM a voltage signal that affects PCM control of the fuel mixture, ignition timing, and EGR operation.

10   **Intake Air Temperature (IAT) sensor -** The IAT provides the PCM with intake air temperature information. The PCM uses this information along with the MAP or MAF sensor to calculate the quantity of air flowing into the engine. This sensor may also be referred to as the Manifold Air temperature (MAT) sensor.

11   **Knock sensor (KS) -** The knock sensor is a piezoresistive microphone that detects the sound of engine detonation, or "pinging". The PCM uses the input signal from the knock sensor to recognize detonation and retard spark advance to avoid engine damage.

12   **Oxygen sensors (O2) -** The O2 sensor generates a voltage signal that varies with the difference between the oxygen content of the exhaust and the oxygen in the surrounding air.

13   **Manifold Absolute Pressure (MAP) sensor -** This sensor is used to monitor intake manifold pressure and ambient barometric pressure. The PCM uses this input signal along with the IAT sensor signal to control fuel injector pulse width (On time) and ignition timing.

14   **Mass airflow (MAF) sensor -** The MAF sensor measures the molecular mass of the intake airflow entering the engine. The MAF sensor, along with the IAT sensor, provide mass airflow and air temperature information for the most precise fuel metering.

15   **Park Neutral Position (PNP) switch -** The PNP switch is mounted on the transaxle and senses the position of the gear selector as chosen by the driver. Depending on the gear selector position, current is routed through the switch contacts and back to the PCM. The PCM and BCM use this signal for a number of engine and transaxle control operations.

16   **Power steering pressure (PSP) switch -** The PSP sensor is used to detect excessive line pressure in the power steering system. The PCM uses this input signal to adjust the idle speed under increased engine loads during low-speed vehicle maneuvers.

17   **Throttle Position Sensor (TPS) -** The TPS senses throttle movement and position, then transmits a voltage signal to the PCM. This signal enables the PCM to determine when the throttle is closed, in a cruise position, or wide open.

18   **Vehicle speed sensor (VSS) -** The vehicle speed sensor provides information to the PCM to indicate vehicle speed.

Output actuators

19   **Body Control Module (BCM) -** The BCM receives input signals from various sensors and switches such as the vehicle speed sensor, park neutral position switch to control various vehicle functions. The BCM is a separate control module from the PCM although both control modules are interlinked to share information, which gives the self diagnostic system greater control capabilities.

20   **EGR and EVAP vacuum control solenoids -** The EGR and EVAP control solenoids are controlled by the PCM to help regulate the opening of the vacuum-operated EGR valve and to help control the purging of the EVAP system.

21   **Fuel injectors -** The PCM opens the fuel injectors individually in firing order sequence. The PCM also controls the time the injector is open, called the "pulse width." The pulse width of the injector (measured in milliseconds) determines the amount of fuel delivered. For more information on the fuel delivery system and the fuel injectors, including injector replacement, refer to Chapter 4.

22   **Fuel pump relay -** The fuel pump relay is activated by the PCM with the ignition switch in the Start or Run position. When the ignition switch is turned on, the relay is activated to supply initial line pressure to the system. Refer to Chapter 12 or your owner's manual for more information on relay location. For more information on fuel pump check and replacement, refer to Chapter 4.

23   **Idle Air Control (IAC) valve -** The IAC valve controls the amount of air to bypass the throttle plate when the throttle valve is closed or at idle position. The IAC valve opening and the resulting airflow is controlled by the PCM.

24   **Idle Speed Control (ISC) motor -** The ISC motor is mounted to throttle body and is actuated by the PCM to control engine idle speed under varying conditions. The ISC motor also contains a throttle switch (ON/OFF). The position of the switch tells the PCM whether or not to send idle speed commands to the ISC motor.

25   **Ignition Control Module (ICM) -** The ICM amplifies the current generated by the distributor pick-up coil and intermittently grounds the primary circuit to the ignition coil which generates high voltage in the secondary circuit, thus sending spark from the ignition coil to the distributor spark plug wires. The ICM also sends a crankshaft reference signal to the PCM, which determines proper ignition timing. Refer to Chapter 5 for more information on the Ignition Control Module.

26   **Torque Converter Clutch (TCC) solenoid -** The TCC solenoid is located in the transaxle and is controlled by the PCM. The TCC solenoid when actuated increases line pressure to the torque converter clutch thereby reducing the converter slippage and improving fuel economy.

Obtaining and clearing OBD system codes

Refer to illustrations 2.28a, 2.28b, 2.28c and 2.29

27   The PCM will illuminate the CHECK ENGINE light (also known as the SERVICE ENGINE SOON light) on the dash if it recognizes a component fault for two consecutive drive cycles. It will continue to set the light until the codes are cleared or the PCM does not detect any malfunction for three or more consecutive drive cycles. **Note:** *Some diagnostic trouble codes will not set the CHECK ENGINE or SERVICE ENGINE SOON light, it is always a good idea to access the self diagnostic system and look for any trouble codes which may exist that have not set the CHECK ENGINE light.*

28   The diagnostic codes for OBD-I systems can be extracted from the PCM using two methods. The first method requires accessing the computer's self-diagnostic mode with the use of the Electronic Climate Control Panel. To extract the diagnostic trouble codes using this method proceed as follows:

2.28a Simultaneously press the OFF and WARMER buttons on the climate control panel to enter the diagnostic service mode (1995 and earlier models)

ENTERING SERVICE MODE	Turn ignition key to the ON position. Simultaneously press the OFF and WARMER buttons on the electronic climate control panel for three seconds.
SEGMENT CHECK	Visually inspect that "-1.8.8" illuminates on the electronic climate control panel and that "8.8.8" illuminates on the fuel data center after the OFF and WARMER buttons are pressed for three seconds.
DIAGNOSTIC TROUBLE CODE DISPLAY (ECM TROUBLE CODES)	After the service mode has been entered all ECM diagnostic trouble codes will automatically be displayed. ".. E" designates the start of the ECM history codes. ". E . E" designates the start of the ECM current codes. Write down all trouble codes as they're being displayed, if any trouble codes are missed turn the ignition key OFF and restart the procedure.
DIAGNOSTIC TROUBLE CODE DISPLAY (BCM TROUBLE CODES)	After the ECM trouble codes, the BCM trouble codes will automatically be displayed. ".. F" designates the start of the BCM history codes. ". F . F" designates the start of the BCM current codes. Write down all trouble codes as they're being displayed, if any trouble codes are missed turn the ignition key OFF and restart the procedure.
SYSTEM READY MODE	After all diagnostic trouble codes have been displayed or if no codes are present , the fuel data center will display a ".7.0" this indicates that the system is ready for further instructions or testing.
CLEARING CODES	Enable to clear codes, the fuel data center must first display a system ready mode (".7.0"). To clear ECM codes, simultaneously press the OFF and HI buttons on the electronic climate control panel until "E.0.0" is displayed. To clear BCM codes, simultaneously press the OFF and LO buttons on the electronic climate control panel until "F.0.0" is displayed.

2.28b Trouble code extraction procedure - quick-reference chart (1994 and 1995 DeVille models)

ENTERING SERVICE MODE	Turn ignition key to the ON position. Simultaneously press the OFF and WARMER buttons on the electronic climate control panel for three seconds.
SEGMENT CHECK (NON-CRT MODELS)	Visually inspect that "-1.8.8" illuminates on the electronic climate control panel and all the lights on the instrument panel cluster illuminate after the OFF and WARMER buttons are pressed for three seconds.
DIAGNOSTIC TROUBLE CODE DISPLAY	After the service mode has been entered all diagnostic trouble codes will automatically be displayed. Write down all trouble codes as they're being displayed, if any trouble codes are missed turn the ignition key OFF and restart the procedure.
SYSTEM LEVEL MODE (ECM or BCM)	To select a system level, press the fan LO button to scroll to the desired system level, then press the fan HI button to enter your selection. A system level must be selected before the computer can proceed to the next menu.
CLEARING CODES	To clear codes, press the fan LO button to scroll to the "CLEAR CODES" menu, then press the fan HI button to enter your selection. A "CODES CLEAR" message should appear for approximately three seconds.

2.28c Trouble code extraction procedure - quick-reference chart (1992 through 1995 Seville models)

6

DeVille models

a) Turn the ignition key ON (engine not running). **Note:** *Before you begin the code extraction process, be sure to obtain a pad of paper and a pencil to write down* any stored trouble codes as they're displayed.

b) Simultaneously press the OFF and WARMER buttons on the electronic climate control panel until *"-1.8.8"* illuminates on the climate control panel and *"8.8.8"* illuminates on the fuel data center (**see illustrations 2.28a and 2.28b**). **Note:** *If all of the panel segments do not illuminate, it will be necessary to remove* the affected display panel and have it serviced at a dealer service department or other qualified repair facility. Burnt out or broken panel segments will lead to incorrect trouble code displays, thereby leading to misdiagnosis of a particular system or component.

c) After the segment check has been performed, *"8.8.8"* will be displayed on the fuel data center for approximately two more seconds, this indicates the beginning of the diagnostic trouble codes.

d) PCM trouble codes will now be displayed numerically from the lowest denomination to the highest on the fuel data center in two separate passes. The first pass will contain the PCM history codes and the second pass will contain the PCM current codes. All PCM trouble codes will begin with an *"E"* prefix.

e) The display *". E"* designates the start of PCM history codes (first pass).

f) The display *". E . E"* designates the start of PCM current codes (second pass).

g) If no PCM codes are present, the self diagnostic system will bypass the PCM code symbols (*". E"* or *". E . E"*) and begin to display the BCM codes.

h) After the PCM trouble codes, the self diagnostic system will now begin to display the BCM trouble codes numerically from the lowest denomination to the highest on the fuel data center in two separate passes. The first pass will contain the BCM history codes and the second pass will contain the BCM current codes. All BCM trouble codes will begin with an *"F"* prefix.

i) The display *". F"* designates the start of BCM history codes (first pass).

j) The display *". F. F"* designates the start of BCM current codes (second pass).

k) When all PCM and BCM codes are finished being displayed or if no codes are present *".7.0"* will be displayed. This code indicates a system ready status and the beginning of a switch test mode for various components within the self diagnostic system. **Note:** Because of the complexity of the remaining OBD system, all further testing of the self diagnostic system is considered beyond the scope of the home mechanic and should be performed by a dealer service department or other qualified repair facility.

l) To clear PCM trouble codes, simultaneously press the OFF and HI buttons on the electronic climate control panel until "E.0.0" is displayed.

m) To clear BCM trouble codes, simultaneously press the OFF and LO buttons on the electronic climate control panel until "F.0.0" is displayed.

n) To exit the self diagnostic system at any time, press the "AUTO" button and turn the ignition key OFF.

Seville models

a) Turn the ignition key ON (engine not running). **Note:** Before you begin the code

extraction process, be sure to obtain a pad of paper and a pencil to write down any stored trouble codes as they're displayed.

b) Simultaneously press the OFF and WARMER buttons on the electronic climate control panel until *"-1.8.8"* illuminates on the climate control panel and all the lights illuminate on the instrument panel cluster **(see illustrations 2.28a and 2.28c). Note:** If all of the panel segments do not illuminate, it will be necessary to remove the affected display panel and have it serviced at a dealer service department or other qualified repair facility. Burnt out or broken panel segments will lead to incorrect trouble code displays, thereby leading to misdiagnosis of a particular system or component.

c) After the segment check has been performed, PCM trouble codes will now be displayed numerically from the lowest denomination to the highest on the climate control panel or the instrument panel cluster.

d) All PCM trouble codes will begin with an *"EO"* prefix and will be followed by the suffix *"C "* (current) or *"H"* (history). Suffix *"C"* (current) after the trouble code indicates that the fault was still present the last time the PCM performed a self diagnostic check. Suffix *"H"* (history) after the trouble code indicates that the fault was not present the last time the PCM performed a self diagnostic check.

e) If no PCM codes are present, the self diagnostic system will display a "NO PCM CODES" message or a "NO X CODE" message.

f) After the PCM trouble codes, the self diagnostic system will now begin to display the BCM trouble codes numerically from the lowest denomination to the highest. All BCM trouble codes will begin with a *"B"* prefix and again will be followed by the suffix *"C "* (current) or *"H"* (history) as described in above.

g) If no BCM codes are present, the self diagnostic system will display a "NO BCM CODES" message or a "NO X CODE" message.

h) When all PCM and BCM codes are finished being displayed the self diagnostic system will display codes for other subsystems such as the CRT, instrument panel cluster and the SIR system. **Note 1:** Because of the complexity of the remaining OBD system, All further trouble code diagnosis and system testing on the CRT, instrument panel and SIR systems is considered beyond the scope of this manual and should be performed by a dealer service department or other qualified repair facility. **Note 2:** If a "NO X DATA" message appears on the display screen at any time during the trouble code extraction process it signifies that the BCM lost communication with that particular system and cannot

retrieve any codes until the communication line or circuit is fixed.

i) To clear trouble codes, you must first select the system level to be cleared. Press the fan LO button on the climate control panel until the system to be cleared (*"PCM"* or *"BCM"*) is displayed, then press the fan HI button to select (enter) the system.

j) Second you must select the test type. Again press the fan LO button until the *"CLEAR CODES"* menu is displayed, then press the fan HI button to select (enter) the test type. A *"CODES CLEAR"* message should appear for three seconds. **Note 1:** This procedure must be performed for each system level to be cleared. Example: clearing both the PCM and the BCM codes requires performing this procedure twice, once for the PCM system codes and a second time for the BCM system codes. **Note 2:** On models equipped with a CRT display it will be necessary to press the NO button on the "SERVICE MODE" page to scroll through the system levels and the test types and then press the YES button to select (enter) the system levels and *"CLEAR CODES"* menu.

29   The second method uses a special SCAN tool that is programmed to interface with the OBD-I system by plugging into the DLC **(see illustration).** When used, the SCAN tool has the ability to diagnose in-depth driveability problems and it allows data to be retrieved from the PCM stored memory. If the tool is not available and intermittent driveability problems exist, have the vehicle checked at a dealer service department or other qualified repair shop.

All models

30   Always clear the codes from the PCM before a new electronic emission control component is installed onto the engine. The PCM will often store trouble codes during sensor malfunctions. The PCM will also record new trouble codes if a new sensor is

2.29 The Data Link Connector (DLC) is located to the left or right of the steering column, depending on the model year of the vehicle (1995 and earlier models)

allowed to operate before the parameters from the old sensor have been erased. Clearing the codes will allow the computer to relearn the new operating parameters relayed by the new component. During the computer relearning process, the engine may experience a rough idle or slight driveability changes. This period of time, however, should last no longer than 15 to 20 minutes. **Caution:** *Do not disconnect the battery from the vehicle to clear the codes. This will erase stored operating parameters from the memory and cause the engine to run rough for a period of time while the computer relearns* the information. If necessary, have the codes cleared by a dealer service department or other qualified repair facility. **Note:** *If using an OBD SCAN tool, scroll the menu for the function that describes "CLEARING CODES" and follow the prescribed method for that particular SCAN tool.*

OBD trouble codes (1992 through 1995 models)

Code	Code definition
12	No distributor signal (4.9L models) or ignition reference signal (4.6L models)
13	Right (rear) oxygen sensor not ready
14	Shorted engine coolant temperature sensor or circuit
15	Open engine coolant temperature sensor or circuit
16	System voltage out of range
17	Left (front) oxygen sensor not ready
19	Shorted fuel pump circuit
20	Open fuel pump circuit
21	Shorted Throttle Position Sensor (TPS) or circuit
22	Open Throttle Position Sensor (TPS) or circuit
23	Electronic Spark Timing (EST) or ignition control signal problem
24	Vehicle Speed Sensor (VSS) or circuit
25	24X reference signal low
26	Shorted throttle switch signal or Throttle Position Sensor (TPS) circuit
27	Open throttle switch signal or Throttle Position Sensor (TPS) circuit
28	Transaxle pressure switch or circuit problem
29	Transaxle shift "B" solenoid problem (1st, 3rd, 4th gear)
31	Shorted Manifold Absolute Pressure (MAP) sensor signal
32	Open Manifold Absolute Pressure (MAP) sensor signal
33	Extended travel brake switch input circuit problem
34	Manifold Absolute Pressure (MAP) sensor signal out of range or too high
35	Ignition ground voltage out of range
36	EGR valve pintle position out of range
37	Shorted Manifold Air Temperature (MAT) or Intake Air Temperature (IAT) signal
38	Open Manifold Air Temperature (MAT) or Intake Air Temperature (IAT) signal
39	Torque Converter Clutch (TCC) engagement problem
40	Power steering pressure switch signal open
41	No camshaft position sensor signal from ignition control module
42	Left (front) oxygen sensor signal lean
43	Left (front) oxygen sensor signal rich

6

OBD trouble codes (1992 through 1995 models) (continued)

Code	Code definition
44	Right (rear) oxygen sensor signal lean
45	Right (rear) oxygen sensor signal rich
46	Left-to-right (front-to-rear) cylinder bank fueling difference
47	Body Control Module (BCM)-to-Powertrain Control Module (PCM) data problem
48	Exhaust Gas Recirculation (EGR) system malfunction
51	PROM or MEM-CAL problem
52	PCM Keep-Alive-Memory reset
53	Distributor signal or reference signal interrupt from Ignition Control Module
55	Closed throttle angle out of range
56	Transaxle input speed sensor circuit problem
57	Shorted transaxle temperature sensor circuit
58	PASS-Key control problem
60	Transaxle not in drive (cruise control)
61	Vent solenoid problem (cruise control)
62	Vacuum solenoid problem (cruise control)
63	Difference between set speed and actual speed detected (cruise control)
64	Vehicle acceleration too high (cruise control)
65	Servo Position Sensor (SPS) signal problem (cruise control)
66	Engine rpm out of range or too high (cruise control)
67	Set/Coast or Resume/Accel switch or signal shorted (cruise control)
68	Cruise control servo position out of range
69	Traction control active while in cruise control
70	Intermittent Throttle Position Sensor (TPS) signal
71	Intermittent Manifold Absolute Pressure (MAP) signal
73	Intermittent Engine Coolant Temperature (ECT) sensor signal
74	Intermittent Manifold Absolute Temperature (MAT) sensor signal
75	Intermittent Vehicle Speed Sensor (VSS) signal
76	Transaxle pressure control solenoid circuit malfunction
80	Fuel system rich (1992 and 1993 models; 1994 4.9L models)
80	Throttle Position (TP) sensor idle learn not complete (1994 and 1995 4.6L models)
81	CAM-to-4X reference correlation problem
83	24X reference signal too high
85	Idle throttle angle too high
86	Undefined gear ratio - transaxle pressure control
88	Torque Converter Clutch (TCC) not disengaging
89	Long shift - transaxle pressure control
90	TCC brake switch input circuit problem
91	PRNDL switch or Transmission Range (TR) switch signal problem

Code	Code definition
92	Heated windshield request problem
93	Traction control system PWM link failure
94	Transaxle shift "A" solenoid problem (1st, 3rd, 4th gear)
95	Engine stall detected
96	Torque converter overstressed
97	Park or Neutral shift to Drive or Reverse at high rpm or at high throttle angle
98	High rpm Park or Neutral shift to Drive or Reverse under Idle Speed Control range
99	Control servo not applied in cruise control
102	Shorted Brake Booster Vacuum (BBV) sensor
103	Open Brake Booster Vacuum (BBV) sensor
105	Brake Booster Vacuum (BBV) too low
106	Brake light switch input circuit problem
107	Powertrain or Body Control Module (PCM)/(BCM)
108	Programmable Read-Only Memory (PROM) problem
109	PCM keep-alive memory reset
110	Alternator L-terminal circuit problem
112	Total EEPROM failure
117	Shift "A"/Shift "B" circuit output open or shorted
119	Open or shorted fuel injector
131	Active knock sensor failure
132	Knock sensor circuit failure
137	Loss of ABS/TCS data

On-Board Diagnostics II (OBD-II) system (1996 and later models)

Scan tool information

Refer to illustration 2.32

31   Hand-held scanners are the most powerful and versatile tools for analyzing engine management systems used on later model vehicles **(see illustration 2.2)**. Early model scanners handle codes and some diagnostics for many systems. Each brand scan tool must be examined carefully to match the year, make and model of the vehicle you are working on. Often, interchangeable cartridges are available to access the particular manufacturer (Ford, GM, Chrysler, Toyota etc.). Some manufacturers will specify by continent (Asia, Europe, USA, etc.). **Note:** *An aftermarket generic scanner should work with any model covered by this manual. However, some early OBD-II models, although technically classified as OBD-II compliant by the manufacturer and by the federal government, might not be fully compliant with all SAE standards for OBD-II. Some generic scanners are unable to extract all the codes from these early OBD-II models. Before purchasing a* *generic scan tool, contact the manufacturer of the scanner you're planning to buy and verify that it will work properly with the OBD-II system you want to scan. If necessary, of course, you can always have the codes extracted by a dealer service department or an independent repair shop with a professional scan tool.*

32   With the arrival of the Federally mandated On-Board Diagnostics-II (OBD-II) system, a specially designed scanner has been developed. Several tool manufacturers have released OBD-II scan tools for the home mechanic **(see illustration)**. Ask the parts salesman at a local auto parts store for additional information concerning dates and costs.

OBD II system general description

33   All 1996 and later models are equipped with the OBD-II system. This system consists of an on-board computer known as the Powertrain Control Module (PCM), and information sensors, which monitor various functions of the engine and send data to the PCM. This system incorporates a series of diagnostic monitors that detect and identify fuel injection and emissions control systems faults and store the information in the computer memory. This updated system also tests sensors and output actuators, diagnoses drive cycles, freezes data and clears codes.

34   This powerful diagnostic computer must be accessed using the new OBD-II scan tool and 16 pin Data Link Connector (DLC) located under the driver's dash area. The PCM, which is located inside its own special

6

2.32 Trouble code readers like the Actron OBD-II diagnostic tester simplify the task of extracting the trouble codes (1996 and later models)

housing inside the forward section of the air filter housing, is the "brain" of the electronically controlled fuel and emissions system. It receives data from a number of sensors and other electronic components (switches, relays, etc.). Based on the information it receives, the PCM generates output signals to control various relays, solenoids (i.e. fuel injectors) and other actuators. The PCM is specifically calibrated to optimize the emissions, fuel economy and driveability of the vehicle.

35   It isn't a good idea to attempt diagnosis or replacement of the PCM or emission control components at home while the vehicle is under warranty. Because of a Federally mandated warranty which covers the emissions system components and because any owner-induced damage to the PCM, the sensors and/or the control devices may void this warranty, take the vehicle to a dealer service department if the PCM or a system component malfunctions.

Information sensors

36   The PCM receives inputs from various information sensors and switches and uses the information it receives to control the operation of the engine in an appropriate and optimal manner. The following list provides a brief description of the function and location of each of the important information sensors.

37   **Camshaft Position (CMP) sensor -** The CMP sensor is one of two sensors (the CKP sensor is the other) that the PCM uses for cylinder identification and fuel injection synchronization. The CMP sensor is located on the right (passenger side) end of the rear cylinder head.

38   **Crankshaft Position (CKP) sensor -** The CKP sensor, which provides information on crankshaft position and engine speed to the PCM, is also used (along with the CMP sensor) by the PCM to determine which spark plug to fire and which cylinder to inject with fuel. The CKP sensors (there are two of them) are located on the front of the engine block, just above and to the left of the oil filter.

39   **Engine Coolant Temperature (ECT) sensor –** The ECT sensor monitors engine coolant temperature and sends the PCM a voltage signal that affects PCM control of the fuel mixture, ignition timing and EGR operation. The ECT sensor is located right below the throttle body.

40   **Intake Air Temperature (IAT) sensor -** The IAT sensor is used by the PCM to calculate air density, one of the variables it must determine in order to calculate injector pulse width and adjust ignition timing. The IAT sensor, which is an integral component of the Mass Air Flow (MAF) sensor, is located on the air intake duct.

41   **Knock sensor -** The knock sensors monitor engine "knock" (pre-ignition or detonation) and then signals the PCM when knock occurs, so that the PCM can retard ignition timing accordingly. The knock sensor is located below the intake manifold, on the inner wall of the rear cylinder head.

42   **Manifold Absolute Pressure (MAP) sensor –** The MAP sensor measures the intake manifold vacuum that draws the air/fuel mixture into the combustion chambers. The PCM uses this information to help it calculate injector pulse width and spark advance. The MAP sensor is located on top of the throttle body.

43   **Oxygen sensors -** The oxygen sensors generate a voltage signal that varies in accordance with the difference between the oxygen content of the exhaust and the oxygen in the surrounding air. There are two oxygen sensors: an upstream, or pre-converter, oxygen sensor, and a downstream, or post-converter, oxygen sensor. The PCM uses the data from the upstream sensor to calculate the injector pulse width. The downstream oxygen sensor monitors the content of the exhaust gases as they exit the downstream catalytic converter. This information is used by the PCM to predict catalyst deterioration and/or failure. The upstream sensors are located on the exhaust manifolds, just ahead of the manifold flanges. The downstream sensor is located on the intermediate exhaust pipe, right behind the catalytic converter.

44   **Power steering pressure switch -** The power steering pressure switch signals the PCM to increase the flow of air through the Idle Air Control (IAC) motor to prevent engine stalling when power steering pump pressure is excessive during, for example, parking maneuvers. The power steering pressure switch is located on top of the rack-and-pinion steering gear assembly.

45   **Throttle Position (TP) Sensor -** The TP sensor, which is located on the throttle body, produces a variable voltage signal in proportion to the opening angle of the throttle valve. This signal, which is monitored by the PCM, enables the PCM to calculate throttle position.

46   **Vehicle Speed Sensor (VSS) -** The VSS provides information to the PCM to indicate vehicle speed. The PCM uses this information to adjust the idle air control motor to maintain MAP values within an acceptable range during deceleration and to maintain an acceptable engine speed when the engine is idling. The VSS is also used to operate the speedometer and as an input for the cruise control system. The VSS is located on top of the transaxle.

Output actuators

47   Based on the information it receives from the information sensors described above, the PCM adjusts fuel injector pulse width, idle speed, ignition spark advance, ignition coil dwell and EVAP canister purge operation. It does so by controlling the output actuators. The following list provides a brief description of the function and location of each of the important output actuators.

48   **AIR relays -** The PCM uses the two AIR relays to control the two AIR pumps that pump air into the exhaust system. The AIR relays are located at the right rear corner of the engine compartment.

49   **AIR vacuum solenoid -** The PCM uses the AIR vacuum solenoid to allow or block vacuum supply to the AIR check valves. The AIR vacuum solenoid is located on the rear valve cover, right in front of the rear AIR check valve assembly.

50   **Exhaust Gas Recirculation (EGR) valve solenoid -** The PCM controls the flow of exhaust gases with a solenoid inside the EGR valve, which is located at the left end of the rear cylinder head. When the PCM energizes the solenoid, it raises a pintle valve, which allows exhaust gases to travel from the exhaust crossover pipe into the exhaust manifolds.

51   **Fuel injectors -** The PCM opens the fuel injectors sequentially (in firing order sequence). The PCM also controls the "pulse width," the interval of time during which each injector is open. The pulse width of an injector (measured in milliseconds) determines the amount of fuel delivered. For more information on the fuel delivery system and the fuel injectors, including injector replacement, refer to Chapter 4.

52   **Fuel pump relay -** When energized by the PCM, the fuel pump relay connects battery voltage to the fuel pump. The fuel pump relay provides battery voltage to the fuel pump. The fuel pump relay is located inside the fuse and relay box in the engine compartment. For more information about the fuel pump relay, refer to Chapter 4.

53   **Ignition coils -** The ignition coils are triggered by the PCM. The ignition coils are mounted on the valve cover. Refer to Chapter 5 for more information on the ignition coils.

54   **Idle air control (IAC) motor -** The IAC motor, which is mounted on the throttle body, allows a certain amount of air to bypass the throttle plate when the throttle valve is closed or at idle position. The IAC motor is controlled by the PCM.

Obtaining OBD-II system trouble codes

Refer to illustration 2.56

55   The PCM will illuminate the CHECK ENGINE light (also called the Malfunction Indicator Light) on the dash if it recognizes a

2.56 The 16-pin Data Link Connector (DLC) is located under the left side of the dash (1996 and later models)

component fault for two consecutive drive cycles. It will continue to set the light until the PCM does not detect any malfunction for three or more consecutive drive cycles.

56 The diagnostic codes for the OBD-II system can be extracted from the PCM by plugging a generic OBD-II scan tool **(see illustration 2.32)** into the PCM's data link connector **(see illustration)**, which is located under the left side of the dash.

57 Plug the scan tool into the 16-pin data link connector (DLC), and then follow the instructions included with the scan tool to extract all the diagnostic codes.

OBD-II "P-Zero" trouble codes (1996 and later models)

Code	Code definition
P0030	Heated oxygen sensor heater control circuit (Bank 1, sensor 1)
P0036	Heated oxygen sensor heater control circuit (Bank 1, sensor 2)
P0101	Mass Air Flow (MAF) sensor or MAF system performance problem
P0102	Mass Air Flow (MAF) sensor circuit - low frequency detected
P0103	Mass Air Flow (MAF) sensor - high frequency detected
P0105	Insufficient activity in MAP sensor circuit
P0106	Manifold Absolute Pressure (MAP) system or sensor performance fault
P0107	Manifold Absolute Pressure (MAP) sensor circuit low voltage
P0108	Manifold Absolute Pressure (MAP) sensor circuit high voltage
P0111	Intake Air Temperature (IAT) sensor circuit performance
P0112	Intake Air Temperature (IAT) sensor circuit low voltage
P0113	Intake Air Temperature (IAT) sensor circuit high voltage
P0117	Engine Coolant Temperature (ECT) sensor circuit low voltage
P0118	Engine Coolant Temperature (ECT) sensor circuit high voltage
P0120	Throttle Position (TP) sensor system performance
P0121	Throttle Position (TP) sensor insufficient activity
P0122	Throttle Position (TP) sensor circuit low voltage
P0123	Throttle Position (TP) sensor circuit high voltage
P0125	Engine Coolant Temperature (ECT) sensor takes too long to enter closed loop
P0130	Heated oxygen sensor circuit, closed loop performance (Bank 1, Sensor 1)
P0131	Heated oxygen sensor circuit, low voltage (Bank 1, Sensor 1)
P0132	Heated oxygen sensor circuit, high voltage (Bank 1, Sensor 1)
P0133	Heated oxygen sensor, slow response (Bank 1, Sensor 1)
P0134	Heated oxygen sensor, insufficient activity (Bank 1, Sensor 1)
P0135	Heated oxygen sensor, heater circuit fault (Bank 1, Sensor 1)
P0137	Heated oxygen sensor circuit, low voltage (Bank 1, Sensor 2)
P0138	Heated oxygen sensor circuit, high voltage (Bank 1, Sensor 2)
P0139	Heated oxygen sensor, slow response (Bank 1 Sensor 2)
P0140	Heated oxygen sensor circuit, insufficient activity (Bank 1, Sensor 2)
P0141	Heated oxygen sensor, heater circuit fault (Bank 1, Sensor 2)
P0143	Heated oxygen sensor circuit, low voltage (Bank 1, Sensor 3)
P0144	Heated oxygen sensor circuit, high voltage (Bank 1, Sensor 3)
P0146	Heated oxygen sensor circuit, insufficient activity (Bank 1, Sensor 3)
P0147	Heated oxygen sensor, heater circuit fault (Bank 1, Sensor 3)

6

OBD-II "P-Zero" trouble codes (1996 and later models) (continued)

Code	Code definition
P0151	Heated oxygen sensor circuit, low voltage (Bank 2, Sensor 1)
P0152	Heated oxygen sensor circuit, high voltage (Bank 2, Sensor 1)
P0153	Heated oxygen sensor, slow response (Bank 2, Sensor 1)
P0154	Heated oxygen sensor circuit, insufficient activity (Bank 2, Sensor 1)
P0155	Heated oxygen sensor, heater circuit fault (Bank 2, Sensor 1)
P0171	Fuel trim system lean (Bank 1)
P0172	Fuel trim system rich (Bank 2)
P0174	Fuel trim system lean (Bank 1)
P0175	Fuel trim system rich (Bank 2)
P0201	Injector 1 control circuit
P0202	Injector 2 control circuit
P0203	Injector 3 control circuit
P0204	Injector 4 control circuit
P0205	Injector 5 control circuit
P0206	Injector 6 control circuit
P0207	Injector 7 control circuit
P0208	Injector 8 control circuit
P0230	Fuel pump relay control circuit
P0231	Fuel pump feedback circuit, low voltage
P0232	Fuel pump feedback circuit, high voltage
P0300	Engine misfire detected
P0322	Ignition Control (IC) module 4X reference circuit - no frequency
P0325	Knock sensor module circuit
P0326	Knock sensor circuit, excessive spark retard
P0327	Knock sensor circuit, low voltage
P0335	Crankshaft Position (CKP) sensor circuit
P0336	Crankshaft Position (CKP) sensor "A" performance
P0340	Ignition Control (IC) module cam reference circuit, no frequency (1996 through 1999 models)
P0340	Camshaft Position (CMP) sensor circuit (2000 and later models)
P0341	Camshaft Position (CMP) sensor performance
P0342	Camshaft Position sensor circuit
P0351	Ignition coil 1 control circuit
P0352	Ignition coil 2 control circuit
P0353	Ignition coil 3 control circuit
P0354	Ignition coil 4 control circuit
P0355	Ignition coil 5 control circuit
P0356	Ignition coil 6 control circuit
P0357	Ignition coil 7 control circuit
P0358	Ignition coil 8 control circuit

Code	Code definition
P0371	Ignition Control (IC) module 24X reference circuit, too many pulses
P0372	Ignition Control (IC) module 24X reference circuit, missing pulses
P0401	Exhaust Gas Recirculation (EGR) system, insufficient flow
P0403	Exhaust Gas Recirculation (EGR) solenoid control circuit
P0404	Exhaust Gas recirculation (EGR) valve, open position performance
P0405	Exhaust Gas Recirculation (EGR) valve position sensor circuit, low voltage
P0410	Secondary Air Injection (AIR) system
P0412	Secondary Air Injection (AIR) solenoid relay control circuit, Bank 1
P0418	Secondary Air Injection (AIR) pump relay control circuit, Bank 1
P0419	Secondary Air Injection (AIR) pump relay control circuit, Bank 2
P0420	Three Way Catalyst (TWC) system, low efficiency
P0440	Evaporative Emission (EVAP) system
P0441	Evaporative Emission (EVAP) system, no flow during purge cycle
P0442	Evaporative Emission (EVAP) system, small leak detected
P0443	Evaporative Emission (EVAP) purge solenoid valve 1 control circuit
P0446	Evaporative Emission (EVAP) vent solenoid vale control system
P0449	Evaporative Emission (EVAP) vent solenoid control circuit
P0452	EVAP system fuel tank pressure sensor, low voltage
P0453	EVAP system fuel tank pressure sensor, high voltage
P0461	Fuel level sensor performance
P0462	Fuel level sensor circuit, low voltage
P0463	Fuel level sensor circuit, high voltage
P0480	Cooling fan relay 1 control circuit
P0481	Cooling fan relay 2 control circuit
P0506	Low idle speed
P0507	High idle speed
P0532	Air Conditioning (A/C) refrigerant pressure sensor circuit, low voltage
P0533	Air Conditioning (A/C) refrigerant pressure sensor circuit, high voltage
P0550	Power Steering Pressure (PSP) switch circuit, low voltage
P0560	Low system voltage
P0563	High system voltage
P0601	Powertrain Control Module (PCM) memory problem
P0602	Powertrain Control Module (PCM) not programmed
P0603	Powertrain Control Module (PCM) long-term memory reset
P0606	Powertrain Control Module (PCM) internal performance problem
P0615	Starter relay control circuit
P0621	Alternator L-terminal circuit problem
P0622	Alternator F-terminal circuit problem
P0650	Malfunction Indicator Light (MIL) control circuit problem

6

3.3 To detach the knee bolster trim panel from the dash on 4.9L models, remove these fasteners

3.4a On some 4.9L models, the PCM is mounted vertically and attached to the heater box . . .

3.4b . . . and on others, it's mounted horizontally and attached to the firewall; in either case, simply remove the mounting nut and disengage the PCM from its mounting bracket

3.4c After removing the PCM from its mounting bracket, unplug all electrical connectors (these connectors are usually color-coded to match their corresponding receptacles, and are equipped with a different number of terminals, so it's impossible to mix them up)

3.7 The MEM-CAL chip is located in the upper part of the PCM, under this cover

3   Powertrain Control Module (PCM) - replacement

Warning: *The models covered by this manual are equipped with Supplemental Inflatable Restraint systems (SIR), more commonly known as airbags. Always disable the airbag system before working in the vicinity of the impact sensors, steering column or instrument panel to avoid the possibility of accidental deployment of the airbag, which could cause personal injury (see Chapter 12).*
Caution 1: *To prevent damage to the PCM, the ignition switch must be turned to OFF when disconnecting or connecting the PCM connectors.*
Caution 2: *To avoid electrostatic discharge damage to the PCM, handle the PCM only by its case. Do not touch the electrical terminals during removal and installation. Ground yourself to the vehicle with an anti-static ground strap (available at computer supply stores).*
Note: *The PCM is a highly reliable component and rarely requires replacement. Because the PCM is the most expensive component in the On-Board Diagnostic sys-*

tem, have a dealer service department or a competent independent repair shop verify *that it has failed before you assume that it's defective.*

4.9L models

Refer to illustrations 3.3, 3.4a, 3.4b, 3.4c, 3.7, 3.8 and 3.9

1   The PCM is located at the right front corner of the passenger compartment, under the dash.
2   Disconnect the cable from the negative terminal of the battery (see Chapter 5).
3   Remove the right knee bolster trim panel from the underside of the dashboard **(see illustration)**.
4   Remove the PCM retaining nut **(see illustrations)** and then disengage the PCM from its mounting bracket and pull it out so that you can disconnect the electrical connectors **(see illustration)**. (It's not necessary to remove the PCM mounting bracket to remove the PCM from the vehicle.)
5   Carefully remove the PCM without disturbing the electrical connectors and PCM

wiring harness.
6   If you're replacing the PCM, remove the old memory calibration (MEM-CAL) chip and install it in the new PCM. New PCMs do NOT include new MEM-CAL chips. Use care not to damage the MEM-CAL chip or the PCM when working on these delicate electronic components.
7   Remove the screws and detach the access cover from the PCM to allow access to the MEM-CAL chip **(see illustration)**.
8   Using two fingers, carefully push both

3.8 Spread the retaining tabs apart to release the MEM-CAL chip

3.9 Carefully align the MEM-CAL with the notches in the seat, then press down on the edges of the MEM-CAL carrier until the unit snaps into place

3.14 To detach the PCM cover from the air cleaner housing, remove these three screws

retaining clips back away from the MEM-CAL and lift the unit straight out of the ECM **(see illustration)**.

9   Be sure to use the alignment notches in the seat area of the ECM when sliding the MEM-CAL back in place. Press only on the ends of the PROM assembly until it snaps back into place **(see illustration)**. Install the cover.

10   Installation is the reverse of removal.

4.6L models

Refer to illustrations 3.14 and 3.15

11   The PCM is located in the engine compartment, inside the forward part of the air filter housing.

12   Disconnect the negative battery cable (see Chapter 5).

13   Remove the air intake duct and the upper half of the air cleaner housing (see Section 9 in Chapter 4).

14   Remove the PCM housing cover screws **(see illustration)** and remove the cover.

15   Disconnect the electrical connectors from the PCM **(see illustration)** and lift the PCM from the lower air filter housing.

16   Installation is the reverse of removal.

4   Camshaft Position (CMP) sensor - replacement

4.6L models

Refer to illustrations 4.3 and 4.5

1   The CMP sensor is located on the right (passenger) end of the rear cylinder head.

2   Disconnect the cable from the negative battery terminal (see Chapter 5).

3   Disconnect the CMP sensor electrical connector **(see illustration)**.

4   Remove the CMP sensor retaining bolt and remove the CMP sensor.

5   Remove and inspect the CMP sensor O-ring **(see illustration)** for wear or damage. If it's worn or damaged, replace it.

6   Coat the new O-ring with clean engine oil, then install it on the CMP sensor.

7   Installation is the reverse of removal. Tighten the CMP sensor retaining bolt to the torque listed in this Chapter's Specifications.

4.9L models

Refer to illustration 4.11

8   The CMP sensor is located inside the distributor.

3.15 To unplug the electrical connectors from the PCM on 4.6L models, remove these retaining bolts (the connectors are usually color-coded to match their corresponding receptacles, and are equipped with a different number of terminals, so it's impossible to mix them up)

9   Disconnect the cable from the negative battery terminal (see Chapter 5).

10   Remove the distributor cap and position it aside, then remove the rotor (see Chapter 5).

11   Disconnect the electrical connector

6

4.3 To remove the CMP sensor, unplug the electrical connector and remove the sensor retaining bolt (4.6L models)

4.5 Inspect the CMP sensor O-ring; if it's cracked, torn or deteriorated, replace it; be sure to coat the new O-ring with clean engine oil before installing it on the CMP sensor (4.6L models)

4.11 On 4.9L models, the CMP sensor is located inside the distributor housing; to remove the CMP sensor, unplug the electrical connector and remove the two mounting screws

5.4a To remove a CKP sensor, unplug the electrical connector and remove the sensor retaining bolt ("A" CKP sensor)

5.4b The "B" CKP sensor, which is located right above the "A" sensor, is removed exactly the same way as the "A" sensor

5.6 Inspect the CKP sensor O-ring; if it's cracked, torn or deteriorated, replace it; be sure to coat the new O-ring with clean engine oil before installing it on the CKP sensor

from the CMP sensor (see illustration).
12   Remove the CMP sensor mounting screws and remove the CMP sensor from the distributor.
13   Installation is the reverse of removal.

5   Crankshaft Position (CKP) sensors - replacement

Refer to illustrations 5.4a, 5.4b and 5.6
Note: *The following procedure applies only to 4.6L models.*
1   The two CKP sensors are located on the front of the block, just above and to the left of the oil filter. The following procedure applies to either sensor.
2   Disconnect the cable from the negative battery terminal (see Chapter 5).
3   Raise the front of the vehicle and place it securely on jackstands.
4   Disconnect the CKP sensor electrical connector **(see illustrations)**.
5   Remove the CKP sensor retaining bolt and remove the CKP sensor.

6   Remove and inspect the CKP sensor O-ring **(see illustration)** for wear or damage. If it's worn or damaged, replace it.
7   Coat the new O-ring with clean engine oil and install it on the CKP sensor.
8   Installation is the reverse of removal. Tighten the CKP sensor retaining bolt to the torque listed in this Chapter's Specifications.

6   Engine Coolant Temperature (ECT) sensor - replacement

Refer to illustrations 6.1 and 6.6
Warning: *Do NOT perform this procedure until the engine is completely cool.*
1   On 4.9L models, the ECT sensor **(see illustration)** is located on the thermostat housing, which is located behind the distributor. On 4.6L models, the ECT sensor **(see illustration)** is located on the backside of the engine (the side facing toward the firewall), below the EGR valve.
2   Disconnect the cable from the negative battery cable (see Chapter 5).

3   Drain some of the engine coolant to minimize coolant loss when the ECT sensor is removed (see Chapter 1).
4   Disconnect the electrical connector from the ECT sensor **(see illustration 6.1a or 6.1b)**.
5   Unscrew the ECT sensor from the thermostat housing. If you didn't remove any coolant, be prepared for some coolant to run out when the sensor is removed.
6   Before installing the new ECT sensor, wrap the threads with Teflon sealing tape to prevent leakage and thread corrosion **(see illustration)**. (Even if you're planning to install the old ECT sensor, it's a good idea to remove any old thread sealant and rewrap the threads with new Teflon tape.)
7   Install the ECT sensor and tighten it to the torque listed in this Chapter's Specifications. Installation is otherwise the reverse of removal.
8   Check the coolant level as described in Chapter 1, adding as necessary. Start the engine and allow it to reach normal operating temperature, then check for coolant leaks. Check the coolant level in the expansion tank after the engine has warmed up and then cooled down again.

6.1a On 4.9L engines, the ECT sensor is located on the thermostat housing; to remove the ECT sensor, unplug the electrical connector and unscrew the sensor

6.1b On 4.6L engines, the ECT sensor is located below the EGR valve; to remove the ECT sensor, unplug the electrical connector and unscrew the sensor

6.6 Before installing the ECT sensor, wrap the threads of the sensor with Teflon tape to prevent coolant leaks

7.1 On 4.9L models, the IAT sensor is located on the intake manifold, next to the alternator (removed for clarity in this photo); to remove the IAT sensor, unplug the electrical connector and unscrew the sensor from the manifold

9.1 On 4.9L models, the MAP sensor is mounted on a bracket located between the throttle body and the rear valve cover

7 Intake Air Temperature (IAT) sensor - replacement

Refer to illustration 7.1

Note: *The following procedure applies to the IAT sensor on 4.9L models. On 4.6L models, the IAT sensor is integrated into the Mass Air Flow (MAF) sensor (see Section 10).*

1 The IAT sensor is located on the intake manifold, adjacent to the alternator **(see illustration)**.
2 Disconnect the cable from the negative battery terminal (see Chapter 5).
3 Disconnect the electrical connector from the IAT sensor **(see illustration 7.1)**.
4 Unscrew the IAT sensor.
5 Before installing the new IAT sensor, wrap the threads with Teflon sealing tape to prevent air leaks **(see illustration 6.6)**. (Even if you're planning to install the old IAT sensor, it's a good idea to remove any old thread sealant and rewrap the threads with new Teflon tape.)
6 Install the IAT sensor and tighten it to the torque listed in this Chapter's Specifications. Installation is otherwise the reverse of removal.

8 Knock sensor - replacement

Note: *The following procedure applies only to 4.6L models.*

1 The knock sensor is located underneath the intake manifold, on the inner wall of the rear cylinder head.
2 Remove the intake manifold (see Chapter 2B).
3 Unplug the knock sensor electrical connector.
4 Unscrew the knock sensor.
5 Installation is the reverse of removal. Be sure to tighten the knock sensor to the torque listed in this Chapter's Specifications.

9 Manifold Absolute Pressure (MAP) sensor - replacement

4.9L models

Refer to illustrations 9.1 and 9.5

1 The MAP sensor **(see illustration)** is mounted on a bracket located between the

throttle body and the rear valve cover.
2 Disconnect the cable from the negative battery terminal (see Chapter 5).
3 Disconnect the vacuum hose from the MAP sensor.
4 Disconnect the electrical connector from the MAP sensor.
5 Remove the MAP sensor mounting screws **(see illustration)** and remove the MAP sensor.
6 Installation is reverse of removal.

4.6L models

Refer to illustrations 9.7 and 9.10

7 The MAP sensor **(see illustration)** is located on the top of the intake manifold, near the throttle body.
8 Disconnect the cable from the negative battery terminal (see Chapter 5).
9 Disconnect the MAP sensor electrical connector.
10 Remove the accelerator cable bracket bolts **(see illustration)** and lift up the bracket.
11 Remove the MAP sensor from the throttle body.
12 Installation is the reverse of removal.

6

9.5 To remove the MAP sensor on a 4.9L model, disconnect the vacuum hose, unplug the electrical connector and remove the mounting screws

9.7 On 4.6L models, the MAP sensor is located on top of the throttle body; to remove it, unplug the electrical connector, detach the accelerator cable bracket from the throttle body (see next illustration) and pull the sensor off the throttle body

9.10 To detach the accelerator cable bracket from the throttle body, remove these bolts

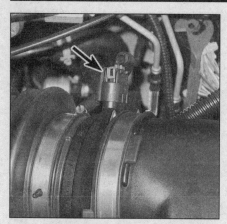

10.1 The MAF/IAT sensor is located on the air intake duct, next to the air cleaner

10.4 To remove the MAF/IAT sensor, loosen the hose clamp screws and detach the sensor from the air cleaner housing and from the air intake duct

10   Mass Air Flow/Intake Air Temperature (MAF/IAT) sensor - replacement

Refer to illustrations 10.1 and 10.4
Note: *The following procedure applies only to 4.6L models.*
1   The MAF/IAT sensor **(see illustration)** is located on the air intake duct, at the air filter housing.
2   Disconnect the cable from the negative battery terminal (see Chapter 5).
3   Disconnect the electrical connector from the MAF/IAT sensor.
4   Loosen the clamp screws **(see illustration)** that retain the MAF/IAT sensor to the air filter housing and air intake duct. Detach the sensor from the housing and duct.
5   Installation is the reverse of removal.

11   Oxygen sensors - replacement

Refer to illustrations 11.1a and 11.1b
1   The oxygen sensors, which are located in the exhaust system, monitor the oxygen content of the exhaust gas stream. On 4.9L models, there are two oxygen sensors. The sensor for the front cylinder head is in the exhaust pipe just below the front exhaust manifold flange and the sensor for the rear head is in the exhaust pipe just below the rear exhaust manifold flange. On 4.6L models, there are three oxygen sensors. The two upstream sensors are located on the front and rear exhaust manifolds **(see illustration)**. The downstream sensor is located behind the catalytic converter **(see illustration)**.
2   How does an oxygen sensor work? The oxygen content in the exhaust reacts with each oxygen sensor to produce a voltage output from 100 millivolts (high oxygen, lean mixture) to 900 millivolts (low oxygen, rich mixture). The ECM monitors this voltage output to determine the ideal air/fuel mixture. The ECM alters the air/fuel mixture ratio by controlling the pulse width (open time) of fuel injectors. A mixture of 14.7 parts air to 1 part fuel is the ideal ratio for minimizing exhaust emissions,

thus allowing the catalytic converter to operate at maximum efficiency. It is this ratio of 14.7 to 1 which the ECM and the oxygen sensor attempt to maintain at all times.
3   The oxygen sensor must be hot to operate properly (approximately 600-degrees F). During the initial warm-up period, the ECM operates in open loop mode - that is, it controls fuel delivery in accordance with a programmed default value instead of feedback information from the oxygen sensor.
4   The proper operation of the oxygen sensor depends on four conditions:
a) *Electrical* - The low voltages and low currents generated by the sensor depend upon good, clean connections which should be checked whenever a malfunction of the sensor is suspected or indicated.
b) *Outside air supply* - The sensor is designed to allow air circulation to the internal portion of the sensor. Whenever the sensor is removed and installed or replaced, make sure the air passages are not restricted.

11.1a On 4.6L models, the upstream oxygen sensors are located on the exhaust manifolds; this is the upstream sensor for the front exhaust manifold (they're also located on the exhaust manifolds on 4.9L engines)

c) *Proper operating temperature* - The ECM will not react to the sensor signal until the sensor reaches approximately 600-degrees F. This factor must be taken into consideration when evaluating the performance of the sensor.
d) *Unleaded fuel* - The use of unleaded fuel is essential for proper operation of the sensor. Make sure the fuel you are using is of this type.
5   In addition to observing the above conditions, special care must be taken whenever the sensor is serviced.
a) *The oxygen sensor has a permanently attached pigtail and connector which should not be removed from the sensor. Damage or removal of the pigtail or connector can adversely affect operation of the sensor.*
b) *Grease, dirt and other contaminants should be kept away from the electrical connector and the louvered end of the sensor.*
c) *Do not use cleaning solvents of any kind on the oxygen sensor.*
d) *Do not drop or roughly handle the sensor.*
e) *The silicone boot must be installed in the correct position to prevent the boot from being melted and to allow the sensor to operate properly.*

Replacement

Refer to illustrations 11.8a, 11.8b, 11.8c, 11.8d and 11.9
Note: *Because the oxygen sensor is located in the exhaust pipe, it may be too tight to remove when the engine is cold. If you find it difficult to loosen, start and run the engine for a minute or two, then shut it off. BUT, if you do so, be careful not to burn yourself when removing the oxygen sensor.*
6   Disconnect the cable from the negative terminal of the battery (see Chapter 5).
7   Some of the oxygen sensors on the vehicles covered by this manual are easier to

11.1b On 4.6L models, the downstream oxygen sensor is located in the intermediate pipe behind the catalytic converter (on 4.9L models, there is no downstream oxygen sensor)

11.8a This is the electrical connector for the front upstream oxygen sensor on a 4.6L model; on later models like this one, each oxygen sensor electrical connector is secured by this lock tab

11.8b To unlock a late-model oxygen sensor electrical connector, pull out the lock tab (front upstream sensor connector shown, other connectors similar)

11.8c This is the electrical connector for the rear upstream oxygen sensor on a 4.6L model: The sensor, which is on top of the rear exhaust manifold, is difficult to reach, or even see, but the connector is located near the left rear corner of the rear cylinder head valve cover

remove and install from above, with the vehicle on the ground. Some are buried beneath hoses, cables and wiring harnesses, and are easier to remove from underneath the vehicle. Before raising the vehicle try to locate the oxygen sensor from above, if possible. If you can't see it from above, raise the vehicle and place it securely on jackstands.

8   Disconnect the oxygen sensor electrical

connector (see illustrations). Because of the high temperatures in which an oxygen sensor must operate, the connector is rarely anywhere near the actual sensor. First, locate the oxygen sensor, then trace the pigtail lead to the connector.

9   Note the position of the silicone boot, if equipped, and then, using an oxygen sensor socket, carefully unscrew the sensor from the exhaust manifold or exhaust pipe (see illus-

tration). **Caution:** *Excessive force may damage the threads.*

10   Use anti-seize compound on the threads of the new (or old) oxygen sensor to facilitate future removal. The threads of a new sensor will already be coated with this compound, but if an old sensor is removed and reinstalled, recoat the threads.

11   Install the sensor and tighten it to the torque listed in this Chapter's Specifications.

12   Reconnect the electrical connector of the pigtail lead to the main engine wiring harness.

13   Lower the vehicle and reconnect the cable to the negative terminal of the battery.

11.8d On 1996 and later 4.6L models, which are equipped with a downstream oxygen sensor (A) behind the catalytic converter, the sensor pigtail lead and electrical connector are protected by this small shield; to remove the shield, drill out the rivets (use self-tapping sheetmetal screws to reattach the shield when you've completed the installation of the new sensor)

12   Power Steering Pressure (PSP) switch - replacement

Refer to illustration 12.1a and 12.1b

1   The Power Steering Pressure (PSP) switch is mounted on the steering gear **(see illustrations)**.

2   Disconnect the cable from the negative battery terminal (see Chapter 5).

6

11.9 Use a special oxygen sensor socket (available at most auto parts stores) to unscrew the oxygen sensor

12.1a Typical steering gear-mounted Power Steering Pressure (PSP) switch on a 4.9L model

12.1b Typical steering gear-mounted Power Steering Pressure (PSP) switch on a 4.6L model

13.4a TP sensor electrical connector and terminal guide (4.9L models)

13.4b To detach the TP sensor from the throttle body on a 4.6L model, unplug the electrical connector and then remove the sensor mounting screws

13.5 To detach the TP sensor from the throttle body on a 4.9L model, unplug the electrical connector and then remove the TP sensor mounting screws

3   Raise the front of the vehicle and place it securely on jackstands.
4   Disconnect the electrical connector from the PSP switch.
5   Position a suitable drain pan below the switch to catch any fluid draining from the steering gear.
6   Using a wrench, unscrew the switch from the steering gear.
7   Before installing the PSP switch, wrap the threads with Teflon tape to prevent leaks.
8   Installation is the reverse of removal.
9   Bleed air from the power steering system (see Chapter 10).
10   Add power steering fluid as required (see Chapter 1).

13   Throttle Position (TP) sensor - replacement

Refer to illustrations 13.4a, 13.4b, 13.5 and 13.6

1   Disconnect the cable from the negative battery terminal (see Chapter 5).
2   On 4.9L models, remove the air intake duct from the throttle body (see Chapter 4).
3   On 4.6L models, the Idle Air Control (IAC) valve is right above the TP sensor, so

it's a good idea to unplug the IAC valve electrical connector (see Section 15) and set it aside so that it's out of the way. (There are also some hoses and pipes in front of the TP sensor on 4.6L models, but if you're careful, you'll be able to remove the TP sensor mounting screws without having to remove any of them.)
4   Unplug the electrical connector from the TP sensor **(see illustrations)**.
5   Remove the two TP sensor mounting screws **(4.6L models, see illustration 13.4; 4.9L models, see illustration)** and then remove the TP sensor.
6   Remove and discard the old TP sensor O-ring, if equipped **(see illustration)**.
7   Installation is the reverse of removal. If you're installing the TP sensor on a 4.9L model, adjust the sensor before tightening the TP sensor screws.

TP sensor adjustment (4.9L models)

8   Remove the air cleaner assembly (see Chapter 4).
9   Loosen the TP sensor mounting screws.
10   Set the minimum idle speed adjustment

to specification (see Section 16).
11   Using a digital voltmeter at the TP sensor electrical connector **(see illustration 13.4a)**, backprobe the SIG terminal (dark blue wire) with the positive probe and the GND terminal (black or black and pink wire) with the ground probe. Be very careful not to damage the wiring harness. With the ignition key ON (engine not running) and the throttle fully closed, the voltage should read between 0.45 to 0.55 volts.
12   If the readings are incorrect, rotate the TP sensor body until the correct voltage is attained and tighten the mounting screws.

14   Vehicle Speed Sensor (VSS) - replacement

Refer to illustrations 14.1 and 14.4
1   The VSS **(see illustration)** is located on top of the transaxle.
2   Disconnect the cable from the negative battery cable (see Chapter 5).
3   Raise the vehicle and place it securely on jackstands.
4   Disconnect the VSS electrical connector **(see illustration)**.
5   Remove the VSS retaining bolt.

13.6 If the TP sensor is equipped with an O-ring, remove and discard it; to prevent air leaks, use a new O-ring even if you're installing the old TP sensor

14.1 The Vehicle Speed Sensor (VSS) is located on top of the transaxle

14.4 To remove the VSS, unplug the electrical connector and remove the VSS retaining bolt (not visible in this photo)

15.1 The Idle Air Control (IAC) valve is located on the front of the throttle body; to detach it from the throttle body, unplug the electrical connector and remove the retaining screws

15.5 Remove and discard the old IAC valve O-ring; coat the O-ring with a little engine oil to protect it during installation of the IAC valve

16.1 Typical Idle Speed Control (ISC) motor (A) and electrical connector (B) on a 4.9L model

6   Pull the VSS straight up to remove it from the transaxle. Remove and discard the old O-ring.
7   Apply a little clean engine oil to the new O-ring and install it on the VSS.
8   Install the VSS and tighten the retaining bolt to the torque listed in this Chapter's Specifications.
9   Reconnect the VSS electrical connector.
10   Lower the vehicle and reconnect the negative battery cable.

15   Idle Air Control (IAC) valve - replacement

Refer to illustrations 15.1 and 15.5
Note: *The following procedure applies only to 4.6L models.*
1   The IAC valve **(see illustration)** is located on the front of the throttle body.
2   Disconnect the cable from the negative battery terminal (see Chapter 5).
3   Disconnect the electrical connector

from the IAC valve.
4   Remove the IAC valve retaining screws, then remove the IAC valve from the throttle body.
5   Remove the IAC valve O-ring **(see illustration)**.
6   Install a new O-ring on the IAC valve. Use a little clean engine oil on the O-ring to protect it from damage during installation of the IAC valve.
7   Installation is otherwise the reverse of removal.

16   Idle Speed Control (ISC) motor - replacement and adjustment

Replacement

Refer to illustrations 16.1 and 16.3
Note: *The following procedure applies only to 4.9L models.*
1   The ISC motor **(see illustration)** is mounted on the throttle body.
2   Disconnect the electrical connector

from the ISC motor.
3   Remove the ISC mounting nuts **(see illustration)** and detach the ISC motor from the mounting bracket.
4   Installation is the reverse of removal. If the ISC motor is being replaced with a new one, perform a minimum idle speed adjustment.

Adjustment

Minimum idle speed adjustment

Refer to illustrations 16.9 and 16.11
5   Warm the engine to normal operating temperature.
6   Connect a tachometer in accordance with the tool manufacturer's instructions.
7   Set the ignition timing (see Chapter 1).
8   Shut off the engine, remove the air cleaner, disconnect the THERMAC vacuum hose (if equipped) and disable the charging system by grounding the green test connector located in the wiring harness at the rear of the alternator.
9   Using a pair of fused jumper wires, fully retract the ISC plunger by applying 12 volts to terminal C of the ISC motor connector and

16.3 To detach the ISC motor from its mounting bracket, remove these three nuts

16.9 ISC motor (A), electrical connector (B) and connector terminal guide (4.9L models)

6

16.11 Minimum idle speed screw (4.9L models)

16.14 With the ISC plunger at its fully-extended position, turn the plunger until the indicated voltage at the Throttle Position (TP) sensor is correct

17.1 Typical late-model catalytic converter (1) with a four-bolt flange ahead and a welded intermediate pipe (2) behind the catalyst and the downstream oxygen sensor (3) installed in the pipe; if your vehicle's catalyst is similar, you'll have to cut the intermediate pipe to replace the converter, or have the converter replaced by a muffler shop

grounding terminal D **(see illustration)**. **Note 1:** *Apply finger pressure to the to the ISC plunger while connecting terminal D to ground. Do not allow the battery voltage (12V) to contact terminal C any longer than necessary to retract the ISC plunger. Prolonged contact will cause damage to the motor.* **Note 2:** *It is very important to never connect a voltage source across terminals A and B, as it may damage the internal throttle contact switch.*

10   With the ISC motor fully retracted, the plunger should not be touching the throttle lever. If the plunger is contacting the throttle lever, turn the plunger inward (clockwise) until there is clearance between the two and the throttle lever is resting on the minimum idle screw. Check that the throttle lever is not binding and moves freely through its full range of motion.

11   Start the engine and check the minimum idle speed. It should be 500 to 550 rpm. If the minimum idle speed is out of specification, turn the minimum idle screw in the direction needed to bring the idle to the correct specification **(see illustration)**. Remove the ground wire from the alternator test connector.

Idle Speed Control (ISC) motor maximum extension adjustment

Refer to illustration 16.14

12   Check and adjust if necessary the Throttle Position (TP) sensor setting (see Section 13) with the minimum idle speed set to specification.

13   With the voltmeter still connected to the TP sensor, fully extend the ISC plunger by applying battery positive voltage to terminal D of the ISC connector and grounding terminal C **(see illustration 16.9)**. **Note:** *Do not allow battery voltage to contact terminal D any longer than necessary when extending the ISC plunger. Prolonged contact will cause damage to the motor.*

14   The TP sensor voltage should be approximately 1.1 to 1.2 volts with the ISC motor fully extended. Turn the ISC plunger as

necessary to achieve the correct specification **(see illustration)**.

15   Disconnect all the testing instruments, and reconnect the ISC motor connector. Turn the ignition key Off for at least 15 seconds, start the engine and check for proper operation of the ISC motor.

16   The adjustment procedure may set a diagnostic code in the On-Board Diagnostic system. If the CHECK ENGINE light comes on, erase the codes from the PCM memory (see Section 2).

17   Catalytic converter

General description

Refer to illustration 17.1

1   The catalytic converter **(see illustration)** is located in the exhaust system, under the vehicle. The catalytic converter is an emission control device that reduces pollutants in the exhaust gas stream. All catalysts used on the vehicles covered by this manual are the three-way type, which means that they reduce the three most prevalent, and most toxic, constituents of exhaust gas: hydrocarbons (HC), carbon monoxide (CO) and oxides of nitrogen (NOx). The three-way catalytic converter consists of two different catalysts in the same converter unit. The oxidation catalyst reduces HC and CO and the reduction catalyst reduces NOx.

Check

Note: *Because of a Federally-mandated extended warranty which covers emissions-related components such as the catalytic converter, check with a dealer service department before replacing the converter at your own expense.*

2   The test equipment for a catalytic converter is expensive and highly sophisticated. If you suspect that the converter on your vehicle is malfunctioning, take it to a dealer or authorized emissions inspection facility for

diagnosis and repair.

3   Whenever the vehicle is raised for servicing of underbody components, check the converter for leaks, corrosion, dents and other damage. Check the welds/flange bolts that attach the front and rear ends of the converter to the exhaust system. If damage is discovered, the converter should be replaced.

4   Although catalytic converters don't break too often, they can become plugged. The easiest way to check for a restricted converter is to use a vacuum gauge to diagnose the effect of a blocked exhaust on intake vacuum.

a) *Connect a vacuum gauge to an intake manifold vacuum source.*

b) *Warm the engine to operating temperature, place the transaxle in park and apply the parking brake.*

c) *Note and record the vacuum reading at idle.*

d) *Open the throttle until the engine speed is about 2000 rpm.*

e) *Release the throttle quickly and record the vacuum reading.*

f) *Perform the test three more times, recording the reading after each test.*

g) *If the reading after the fourth test is more than one in-Hg lower than the reading recorded at idle, the catalytic converter, muffler or exhaust pipes may be plugged or restricted.*

Replacement

Refer to illustration 17.7

Note: *Depending on the year and model, the following procedure might require the use of a cutting torch or a suitable cutting tool because, on some models, the exhaust pipe behind the catalytic converter must be cut to remove the catalyst. If you're unfamiliar with these types of tools, we recommend that you have the catalytic converter replaced by a*

17.7 On late-model vehicles, detach the front end of the catalytic converter from the front exhaust pipe by removing these four nuts

muffler shop or a dealer service department.

5   Raise the vehicle and place it securely on jackstands.

6   Disconnect the electrical connector from the post-converter oxygen sensor (see Section 11).

7   Remove the four flange nuts from the flange at the front of the converter **(see illustration)**. If there is a similar flange behind the converter, remove the fasteners from that flange and remove the catalyst. If the catalyst is clamped onto the exhaust system, loosen the clamp bolts and remove the catalyst. If the catalyst is an integral part of the exhaust system, cut the pipe behind the converter and remove the converter. If you're going to cut the exhaust pipe behind the converter, make sure that you have already obtained the new converter so that you know where to cut the pipe.

8   Installation is the reverse of removal.

18   Evaporative Emission Control (EVAP) system

General description and check

1   The Evaporative Emission Control (EVAP) system traps and stores fuel vapors from the fuel tank and the intake manifold.

2   The EVAP system consists of a charcoal-filled canister and the lines connecting the canister to the fuel tank, to the throttle body and to outside air. On 4.9L models, the canister **(see illustration 1.1a)** is located at the front right corner of the engine compartment. On 4.6L models, the canister is located under the vehicle, next to the fuel filter.

3   Fuel vapors are transferred from the fuel tank, and from the throttle body and intake manifold, to a canister where they are stored when the engine is not operating. When the engine is running, the fuel vapors are purged from the canister by intake air flow and consumed in the normal combustion process.

4   The PCM-controlled purge valve solenoid is located on top of the canister on 4.9L models and near the throttle body on 4.6L models. There's also a tank pressure sensor on later (OBD-II) models.

5   The EVAP system seldom fails, but on older vehicles, it might develop a leak, allowing raw fuel vapors to escape into the atmosphere. This is not only bad for the environment, but it wastes fuel. If you smell a strong fuel odor, the system is not functioning correctly. Poor idle, stalling and poor driveability can be caused by an inoperative purge valve, a damaged canister, split or cracked hoses or hoses connected to the wrong tubes.

6   Finding leaks on the EVAP system is difficult because there is a lot of plastic tubing and a lot of connections. Nevertheless, it's worth a try to raise the vehicle, put it on jackstands and inspect the tubing and connections for an obvious problem such as a disconnected line or a bad connection. If a visual inspection fails to pinpoint the source of the fuel odor, have the system pressure-checked by a dealer service department. **Warning:** *Do NOT try to pressure-test the EVAP system at home. A technician will pump the system full of an inert gas (nitrogen) and find out where it's escaping. Because of the explosive potential of fuel vapors, this is a dangerous procedure that should be carried out only by a dealer service department or other qualified repair shop.*

7   Once a dealer service department or other qualified repair shop has diagnosed the problem, replacing the canister and other components is easily performed at home.

Component replacement

4.9L models

EVAP canister

Refer to illustration 18.8

8   Disconnect the hoses and electrical connector from the canister **(see illustration)**.

9   Remove the canister mounting bolts **(see illustration 18.8)**. On some models, the canister is secured by a large clamp; to remove the canister on one of these models, simply loosen the clamp screw and pull the canister straight up.

10   Installation is the reverse of removal.

4.6L models

EVAP canister purge valve

Refer to illustration 18.11, 18.14 and 18.15

11   The EVAP canister purge valve, or purge solenoid **(see illustration)** is located on the back of the throttle body.

12   Remove the intake manifold service cover **(see illustration 2.2 in Chapter 4)**.

13   Disconnect the EVAP purge valve electrical connector **(see illustration 18.11)**.

18.8 A typical EVAP system charcoal canister on a 4.9L model

1   *Purge solenoid electrical connector*
2   *Purge line (upper line) - goes to throttle body*
3   *Fresh air inlet line (middle line) - brings fresh outside air into canister from body-mounted vent hose*
4   *Fuel vapor port line (lower line) - brings fuel vapors from fuel tank to canister*
5   *Purge valve solenoid*
6   *Canister mounting bolts (one bolt not visible in this photo)*

18.11 On 4.6L models, the EVAP canister purge valve is located on the upper rear part of the throttle body

1   *EVAP canister purge valve*
2   *Purge valve electrical connector*
3   *Canister purge line quick-connect fitting*

6

18.14 To disconnect the EVAP line quick-connect fitting, push the two locking tabs to the right (toward the firewall) (in this photo, the locking tab in the foreground, has already been unlocked)

18.15 To detach the EVAP canister purge valve from the throttle body, remove this bolt (you have to twist the throttle open to access this bolt)

18.18 The EVAP canister vent valve is located under the vehicle, near the left frame rail, behind the EVAP canister

18.20 To detach the EVAP canister vent valve from its mounting bracket, release the retaining tabs and slide the valve down (vent valve removed for clarity)

18.22 To disconnect the vent hose from the vent valve, squeeze these locking tangs together and pull off the hose fitting

14   Disconnect the EVAP canister purge hose from the purge valve **(see illustration)**.
15   Partially open the throttle and remove the EVAP purge valve retaining bolt **(see illustration)**.
16   Remove the EVAP canister purge valve.
17   Installation is the reverse of removal.

EVAP vent valve
Refer to illustration 18.18, 18.20 and 18.22
18   The EVAP vent valve **(see illustration)** is located under the vehicle, behind the EVAP canister, near the left frame rail.
19   Raise the rear of the vehicle and place it securely on jackstands.
20   Pry open the EVAP canister vent valve

retaining tabs and remove the EVAP canister vent valve from its retaining bracket **(see illustration)**.
21   Disconnect the EVAP canister vent valve electrical connector.
22   Squeeze the locking tangs together **(see illustration)** and disconnect the vent hose from the EVAP canister vent valve.
23   Remove the EVAP canister vent valve.
24   Installation is the reverse of removal.

18.25 On 4.6L models, the EVAP canister is located under the vehicle, next to the fuel filter

1   *Fuel filter*
2   *EVAP canister*
3   *EVAP vent hose*
4   *Fuel tank vapor hose*
5   *Purge hose*
6   *Canister mounting bolts*

18.27a To disconnect the vent hose from the EVAP canister, loosen the hose clamp and pull off the hose

18.27b To disconnect the fuel tank vapor hose from the EVAP canister, squeeze the locking tangs together and pull off the hose

18.27c To disconnect the purge hose from the EVAP canister, push the two locking tabs away from the canister and pull off the hose

18.28 To detach the EVAP canister mounting bracket, remove these three nuts

18.31 The fuel tank pressure sensor (1) is located on top of the fuel pump/fuel level sending unit module; to detach the pressure sensor from the module, spread the locking tangs (2) apart and lift off the sensor

EVAP canister

Refer to illustrations 18.25, 18.27a, 18.27b, 18.27c and 18.28

25   The EVAP canister (see illustration) is located under the vehicle, next to the fuel filter.

26   Raise the rear of the vehicle and place it securely on jackstands.

27   Disconnect the vent hose, the fuel tank vapor hose and the purge hose from the EVAP canister (see illustrations).

28   Remove the EVAP canister retaining nuts (see illustration) and remove the EVAP canister and canister mounting bracket as a single assembly.

29   Release the retaining tabs and detach the EVAP canister from its mounting bracket.

30   Installation is the reverse of removal.

Fuel tank pressure sensor

Refer to illustration 18.31

31   The fuel tank pressure sensor (see illustration) is located on top of the fuel pump/fuel level sending unit assembly.

32   Relieve the system fuel pressure (see Chapter 4).

33   Remove the spare tire cover, the jack and the spare tire.

34   Remove the carpeted rear compartment floor trim (see illustrations 5.19a and 5.1b in Chapter 4).

35   Remove the bolts from the fuel pump/fuel level sending unit assembly access

panel (see illustration 5.20a in Chapter 4).

36   Disconnect the fuel tank pressure sensor electrical connector.

37   Spread the fuel tank pressure sensor retaining clips (see illustration 18.31) apart and remove the sensor.

38   Installation is the reverse of removal.

19   Exhaust Gas Recirculation (EGR) system

General description

1   The EGR system meters exhaust gases into the intake manifold through passages cast into the manifold or through external pipes connecting the exhaust manifold, the EGR valve and the intake manifold. Once they're inside the manifold, the exhaust gases merge with the air/fuel mixture. When the air/fuel mixture is diluted by exhaust gases, it lowers combustion chamber temperatures, which reduces the level of oxides of nitrogen (NOx), which are a natural byproduct of high combustion temperatures. The amount of exhaust gases mixed with the air/fuel mixture is regulated by the PCM in response to engine operating conditions.

2   On 4.9L models, the EGR valve is vacuum-controlled. The PCM controls a vacuum control solenoid valve, which in turn allows a

vacuum signal to reach the EGR valve, or cuts it off when the PCM de-energizes the solenoid. The vacuum signal to the EGR valve is controlled by varying the "duty cycle" (on-time) of the solenoid valve in response to engine operating conditions.

3   On 4.6L models, the EGR valve is digital, i.e. under direct PCM control. The digital EGR valve, which meters exhaust gases into the intake manifold independently of intake manifold vacuum, is capable of controlling the amount of exhaust gases much more accurately than a vacuum-controlled EGR valve.

4   Common engine problems associated with the EGR system are rough idling or stalling at idle, rough engine performance during light throttle application and stalling during deceleration.

Check

Vacuum-controlled EGR valve (4.9L models)

Refer to illustration 19.6

5   With the engine cold, start it up and allow it to idle.

6   Manually lift the EGR diaphragm (see illustration) The engine should stall, or at

6

19.6 To test a vacuum-controlled EGR valve, push up on the diaphragm; if the diaphragm is stuck, or binds in the "up" position, replace the EGR valve (EGR valve removed for clarity)

19.13 To detach the vacuum-controlled EGR valve from a 4.9L engine, remove these bolts

19.19 Typical EGR valve vacuum solenoid installation details (4.9L models)

1   *Vacuum line*
2   *Electrical connector*
3   *Mounting bolt*
4   *EGR valve vacuum solenoid unit*

19.21 Typical digital EGR valve installation details (4.6L models)

1   *Electrical connector*
2   *Mounting nuts*
3   *EGR valve*

least the idle should drop considerably. **Warning:** *Be careful - the valve may be hot!*
7   If the EGR valve appears to be in proper operating condition, carefully check all hoses connected to the valve for breaks, leaks or kinks. Replace or repair the valve/hoses as necessary.
8   With the engine idling at normal operating temperature, disconnect the vacuum hose from the EGR valve and connect a vacuum pump. When vacuum is applied, the engine should stumble or die, indicating that the vacuum diaphragm is operating correctly. These models use a backpressure-type EGR valve. Backpressure must be created in the exhaust system before the vacuum pump will actuate the valve. To create backpressure, install a large socket into the tailpipe and clamp it to the pipe to prevent it from dropping out during the test. The 1/2 inch hole in the socket will allow the engine to idle but still create backpressure on the EGR valve. **Caution:** *Don't restrict the exhaust system any longer than necessary to perform this test.* Replace the EGR valve with a new one if the test does not affect the idle.
9   Check the operation of the EGR control solenoid. Check for vacuum to the solenoid. If vacuum exists, check for battery voltage to the solenoid.
10   Further testing of the EGR system, vacuum solenoid and the PCM will require a SCAN tool to access computer information that directly controls the EGR system. Have the vehicle checked by a dealer service department or other qualified repair facility.

Digital type (4.6L models)

11   Special electronic diagnostic equipment is needed to check this valve and should be left to a dealer service department or other qualified repair facility.

Component replacement

4.9L models

EGR valve

Refer to illustration 19.13

12   Disconnect the vacuum hose from the

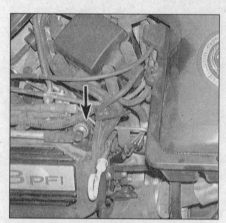

20.2a PCV valve location (4.9L models)

EGR valve.
13   Remove the nuts or bolts which secure the valve to the intake manifold or adapter **(see illustration)**.
14   Lift the EGR valve from the intake manifold.
15   Clean the mounting surfaces of the EGR valve. Remove all traces of gasket material.
16   Place the new EGR valve, with a new gasket, on the intake tube or adapter and tighten the attaching nuts or bolts.
17   Connect the vacuum signal hose or the electrical connector.

EGR vacuum solenoid

Refer to illustration 19.19

18   Remove the hoses from the EGR vacuum control solenoid, labeling them to ensure proper installation.
19   Remove the solenoid and replace it with the new one **(see illustration)**.
20   Installation is the reverse of removal.

4.6L models

EGR valve

Refer to illustration 19.21

21   The EGR valve **(see illustration)** is

20.2b PCV valve location (4.6L models); on some later models (such as the one shown here), the "dirty air" tube, which carries blow-by gases from the crankcase, through the PCV valve and to the throttle body, is routed under the intake manifold

located at the left end of the engine, behind the throttle body.
22   Disconnect the electrical connector from the EGR valve.
23   Remove the two EGR valve mounting nuts.
24   Remove the EGR valve.
25   Installation is the reverse of removal.

---

20   Positive Crankcase Ventilation (PCV) system

General description

Refer to illustrations 20.2a, 20.2b and 20.2c

1   The Positive Crankcase Ventilation (PCV) system reduces hydrocarbon emissions by circulating fresh air through the crankcase to pick up blow-by gases, which are then drawn by intake manifold vacuum

20.2c Typical "clean air" tube, between the valve cover and the throttle body (4.6L model shown)

21.6 The two AIR relays are located in the right rear corner of the engine compartment

21.8 To detach an AIR relay from its mounting bracket, slide it straight up

through the PCV valve to the throttle body or intake manifold to be burned in the engine.

2   The PCV system consists of the PCV valve, which regulates the flow of gases according to engine speed and manifold vacuum, and the two hoses (see illustrations). One hose directs fresh outside air from the air intake duct to the crankcase and the other directs crankcase gases from the crankcase, through the PCV valve and into the throttle body.

Check

3   It's easy to check the PCV system for correct operation. Inspect the PCV system regularly, because carbon and gunk deposited by blow-by gases will eventually clog the PCV valve, the "dirty" side system hose and the area inside the throttle body, behind the throttle plate. The common symptoms of a plugged or clogged PCV valve include a rough idle, stalling or a slow idle speed, oil leaks, oil in the air cleaner or sludge in the engine.

4   Refer to Chapter 1 for PCV valve checking and replacement procedures.

21   Secondary Air Injection (AIR) system

Note: The following section applies only to 4.6L models.

General description

1   The Secondary Air Injection (AIR) system helps reduce hydrocarbons and carbon monoxide levels in the exhaust by injecting air into the exhaust ports of each cylinder during cold engine operation. It also helps the catalytic converter to quickly reach its correct operating temperature during start-ups, which decreases tailpipe emissions when the engine is not yet fully warmed up.

2   The AIR system consists of two PCM-controlled air relays, two air pumps, two check valves, a vacuum solenoid and the

hoses, pipes and lines connecting these components.

3   When the AIR system is not operating, the vacuum-controlled check valves prevent air from getting into the exhaust manifolds and they also prevent exhaust gases from getting into the AIR system. The PCM controls the AIR system through the two relays. When the AIR system is operating, the PCM grounds one of the relays and it also grounds the vacuum solenoid. The vacuum solenoid directs vacuum to the check valves, which opens the valves. After a few seconds, the PCM grounds the second relay. When the PCM energizes the relays, they activate the air pumps, which force air through the system hoses, through the check valves and into the exhaust manifolds.

4   Because of the complexity of this system, it is difficult for the home mechanic to make an accurate diagnosis. If the system is malfunctioning, carefully inspect all hoses, vacuum lines, electrical wiring and connectors. Make sure that they are in good condition and that all connections are tight and clean.

5   If visual inspection fails to pinpoint the problem, have the AIR system checked out

by a dealer service department or other qualified repair shop.

Component replacement

AIR relays

Refer to illustrations 21.6 and 21.8
Note: The following procedure applies to either AIR relay.

6   The AIR relays (see illustration) are located in the right rear corner of the engine compartment, right behind the coolant reservoir

7   Disconnect the electrical connector from an AIR relay.

8   To detach an AIR relay from its mounting bracket, slide it straight up (see illustration) and remove it.

9   Installation is the reverse of removal.

AIR pumps

Left air pump

Refer to illustrations 21.10, 21.12, 21.13, 21.14, 21.15, 21.16a, 21.16b, 21.17a and 21.17b

10   The left AIR pump assembly (see illustration) is located in the lower left front corner of the vehicle. It pumps air into the exhaust manifold for the front cylinder head.

6

21.10 The left air pump, which pumps air into the exhaust manifold for the front cylinder head, is located at the lower left corner of the vehicle (splash shield removed)

1   Filter
2   Air inlet hose
3   AIR pump
4   Exhaust hose

21.12 To detach the splash shield, remove these fasteners

21.13 To disconnect the exhaust hose from the AIR pump, loosen this hose clamp and pull off the hose

11   Raise the front of the vehicle and place it securely on jackstands.

12   Remove the pop-fasteners from the splash shield **(see illustration)**, then remove the splash shield.

13   Loosen the exhaust hose clamp and disconnect the exhaust hose from the AIR pump **(see illustration)**.

14   Disconnect the filter/inlet hose from the AIR pump **(see illustration)**.

15   Disconnect the electrical connector from the AIR pump **(see illustration)**.

16   Loosen the two lower AIR pump-to-cradle bracket nuts **(see illustration)**, remove the upper AIR pump-to-cradle bolt **(see illustration)** and remove the AIR pump.

17   Remove the air inlet elbow pipe from the

21.14 Disconnect the inlet hose from the AIR pump

21.15 Unplug the AIR pump electrical connector

21.16a To detach the lower end of the AIR pump from the frame, loosen these two nuts . . .

21.16b . . . and to detach the upper end of the pump from the frame, remove the upper mounting bracket bolt (pump removed for clarity)

21.17a To detach the air inlet pipe/filter assembly from the AIR pump, squeeze these four tangs together and carefully disengage the inlet pipe/filter from each tang; do NOT try to simply pry the assembly off with a screwdriver or you will break the plastic tangs

21.17b Inspect this O-ring for cracks, tears and deterioration; if it's damaged (or missing), replace it

21.20a The right air pump, which pumps air into the exhaust manifold for the rear cylinder head, is located at the lower right corner of the vehicle (splash shield removed)

1   Filter
2   Air inlet hose
3   AIR pump
4   Air exhaust hose

21.20b The exhaust hoses and pipes between the right AIR pump and the exhaust manifold are routed along the lower right end of the engine; anytime you're servicing anything under the engine, be sure to inspect the exhaust hoses and pipes of both AIR pumps for cracks, tears and deterioration and replace as necessary

21.21 The rear check valve is mounted on a bracket bolted to the rear valve cover

1   Vacuum line   3   Check valve
2   Inlet hose   4   Mounting bracket nuts

pump and inspect the O-ring **(see illustrations)**. If the O-ring is cracked, torn, deteriorated or missing, replace it.

18   Make sure that the O-ring is in place on the bottom of the pump and then reattach the air inlet elbow pipe. Listen for an audible click to verify that the elbow pipe is fully attached to the pump.

19   Installation is the reverse of removal.

Right AIR pump

Refer to illustrations 21.20a and 21.20b

20   The right AIR pump assembly **(see illustrations)** is located in the lower right front corner of the vehicle. It pumps air into the exhaust manifold for the rear cylinder head. The replacement procedure for the right pump is virtually identical to the procedure for replacing the left pump (see Steps 11 through 19).

Check valves

Rear vacuum control check valve

Refer to illustrations 21.21, 21.24a and 21.24b

21   The rear vacuum control check valve **(see illustration)** is located on top of the rear valve cover.

22   Disconnect the vacuum line from the rear check valve.

23   Disconnect the air inlet hose from the rear check valve.

24   Before the rear check valve can be removed, the short section of corrugated **(see illustration)** that connects the check valve to the exhaust manifold pipe must be disconnected. The flange at the upper end of this corrugated pipe is connected to the underside of the check valve and mounting bracket by two nuts that are extremely difficult to access with the check valve installed. But raise the front of the vehicle and place it securely on jackstands, then go under the backside of the engine and, using a flashlight, locate the flange at the lower end of the corrugated pipe **(see illustration)** in the space between the engine and the firewall. The lower flange of the corrugated pipe is connected to a rigid pipe on the exhaust manifold by two bolts. The easier way to disconnect the corrugated pipe is to remove these two lower bolts and then disconnect the cor-

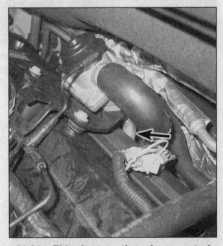

21.24a This short section of corrugated pipe routes air from the check valve to the exhaust manifold; it's attached to the underside of the check valve by two bolts that are difficult to access from above while the check valve is installed . . .

6

rugated pipe from the check valve and mounting bracket after removing the entire assembly from the engine compartment.

25   Remove the three check valve mounting bracket nuts and remove the rear check valve, mounting bracket and corrugated pipe as a single assembly.

26   Remove the two upper flange nuts and disconnect the upper end of the corrugated pipe from the check valve.

27   Detach the check valve from the mounting bracket.

28   When reassembling the check valve, mounting bracket and corrugated pipe, be sure to tighten the corrugated pipe flange bolts securely. After the assembly has been installed on the rear valve cover, reconnect the lower end of the corrugated pipe to the fixed pipe on the rear exhaust manifold and tighten the lower flange bolts securely.

29   Installation is otherwise the reverse of removal.

Front vacuum control check valve

Refer to illustration 21.30

30   The front vacuum control check valve **(see illustration)** is located to the left of the front cylinder head. Replacing this check

valve is essentially the same as replacing the rear check valve, except that the upper mounting flange of the corrugated pipe between the check valve and the front exhaust manifold is easier to access, so it's not necessary to disconnect the corrugated pipe at its lower end.

Vacuum control solenoid (located on the front of the bracket for the rear check valve)

Refer to illustration 21.31

31   The vacuum control solenoid **(see illustration)** is located on the rear valve cover. It's bolted to the rear check valve mounting bracket.

32   Disconnect the electrical connector from the vacuum control solenoid.

33   Disconnect the vacuum lines from the vacuum control solenoid.

34   Remove the vacuum control solenoid mounting bracket nut and remove the solenoid and bracket as a single assembly.

35   Separate the vacuum control solenoid from its mounting bracket.

36   Installation is the reverse of removal.

21.24b ... but the two bolts that attach the *lower* flange of the corrugated pipe to the rigid pipe of the exhaust manifold are easier to remove, from below (you can disconnect the corrugated pipe from the check valve after removing the check valve and mounting bracket from the engine compartment)

21.30 The front check valve is located to the left of the front cylinder head

1   *Vacuum line*
2   *Air inlet hose*
3   *Check valve*
4   *Corrugated pipe (directs air from the check valve to the exhaust manifold)*
5   *Corrugated pipe flange nuts*

21.31 The vacuum control solenoid is located on the rear valve cover, right in front of the rear vacuum control check valve

1   *Electrical connector*
2   *Vacuum line to rear vacuum control check valve*
3   *Vacuum line to front vacuum control check valve*
4   *Vacuum control solenoid mounting bracket nut*
5   *Vacuum control solenoid*

Chapter 7
Automatic transaxle

Contents

Specifications

General
Fluid type and capacity .... See Chapter 1

Torque specifications
Ft-lbs (unless otherwise indicated)
Subframe mounting bolts .... See Chapter 2C
Transaxle-to-engine bolts 55
Torque converter-to-driveplate bolts
4T60-E
  1994 and earlier models 46
  1995 models 44
4T80-E
  1994 and earlier models 35
  1995 and later models 44

1 General information

Refer to illustration 1.1

The vehicles covered by this manual are equipped with a four-speed Turbo Hydra-Matic automatic transaxle **(see illustration)**.

Two models of the Turbo Hydra-Matic automatic transaxles are used on these vehicles: the THM 4T60-E and the THM 4T80-E.

Due to the complexity of the clutches and the hydraulic control system, and because of the special tools and expertise required to perform an automatic transaxle overhaul, it should not be undertaken by the home mechanic. Therefore, the procedures in this Chapter are limited to general diagnosis, routine maintenance, adjustment and transaxle removal and installation.

If the transaxle requires major repair work, it should be left to a dealer service department or an automotive or transmission repair shop. If you've decided that the transaxle must be removed for overhaul or major repair work, several preliminary steps should be taken. Read all removal and installation procedures carefully prior to committing this job.

Transaxle removal involves removing the engine and transaxle as an assembly - this can only be preformed using a heavy-duty vehicle hoist, jackstands and a heavy-duty engine hoist. If all the necessary equipment is not available, have the engine/transaxle assembly removed by a professional automotive repair facility.

2 Diagnosis - general

Note: *Automatic transaxle malfunctions may be caused by five general conditions: poor engine performance, improper adjustments, hydraulic malfunctions, mechanical malfunctions or malfunctions in the computer or its signal network. Diagnosis of these problems*

1.1 An underside view of an automatic transaxle and its related components

1   Transaxle fluid pan
2   Torque converter cover brace
3   Subframe (engine cradle)

should always begin with a check of the easily repaired items: fluid level and condition (see Chapter 1) and shift linkage adjustment. Next, perform a road test to determine if the problem has been corrected or if more diagnosis is necessary. If the problem persists after the preliminary tests and corrections are completed, additional diagnosis should be done by a dealer service department or transmission repair shop. Refer to the Troubleshooting section at the front of this manual for information on symptoms of transaxle problems.

Preliminary checks

1   Drive the vehicle to warm the transaxle to normal operating temperature.
2   Check the fluid level as described in Chapter 1:

a) *If the fluid level is unusually low, add enough fluid to bring the level within the designated area of the dipstick, then check for external leaks (see below).*

b) *If the fluid level is abnormally high, drain off the excess, then check the drained fluid for contamination by coolant. The presence of engine coolant in the automatic transaxle fluid indicates that a failure has occurred in the internal radiator walls that separate the coolant from the transaxle fluid (see Chapter 3).*

c) *If the fluid is foaming, drain it and refill the transaxle, then check for coolant in the fluid or a high fluid level.*

3   Check the engine idle speed as described in Chapter 1. **Note:** *If the engine is malfunctioning, do not proceed with the preliminary checks until it has been repaired and runs normally.*
4   Check the shift cable (see Section 4). Make sure it's properly adjusted and operates smoothly.

Fluid leak diagnosis

5   Most fluid leaks are easy to locate visually. Repair usually consists of replacing a seal or gasket. If a leak is difficult to find, the following procedure may help.
6   Identify the fluid. Make sure it's transaxle fluid and not engine oil or brake fluid (automatic transaxle fluid is a deep red color).
7   Try to pinpoint the source of the leak. Drive the vehicle several miles, then park it over a large sheet of cardboard. After a minute or two, you should be able to locate the leak by determining the source of the fluid dripping onto the cardboard.
8   Make a careful visual inspection of the suspected component and the area immediately around it. Pay particular attention to gasket mating surfaces. A mirror is often helpful for finding leaks in areas that are hard to see.
9   If the leak still cannot be found, clean the suspected area thoroughly with a degreaser or solvent, then dry it.
10   Drive the vehicle for several miles at normal operating temperature and varying speeds. After driving the vehicle, visually inspect the suspected component again.
11   Once the leak has been located, the

cause must be determined before it can be properly repaired. If a gasket is replaced but the sealing flange is bent, the new gasket will not stop the leak. The bent flange must be straightened.
12   Before attempting to repair a leak, check to make sure that the following conditions are corrected or they may cause another leak. **Note:** *Some of the following conditions cannot be fixed without highly specialized tools and expertise. Such problems must be referred to a transmission repair shop or a dealer service department.*

Gasket leaks

13   Check the pan periodically. Make sure the bolts are tight, no bolts are missing, the gasket is in good condition and the pan is flat (dents in the pan may indicate damage to the valve body inside).
14   If the pan gasket is leaking, the vent may be plugged, the pan bolts may be too tight, the pan sealing flange may be warped, the sealing surface of the transaxle housing may be damaged, the gasket may be damaged or the transaxle casting may be cracked or porous. If sealant instead of gasket material has been used to form a seal between the pan and the transaxle housing, it may be the wrong type of sealant.

Seal leaks

15   If a transaxle seal is leaking, the vent may be plugged, the seal bore may be damaged, the seal itself may be damaged or improperly installed, the surface of the shaft protruding through the seal may be damaged or a loose bearing may be causing excessive shaft movement.
16   Make sure the dipstick tube seal is in good condition and the tube is properly seated. Periodically check the area around the speedometer gear or sensor for leakage. If transaxle fluid is evident, check the O-ring for damage.

Case leaks

17   If the case itself appears to be leaking, the casting is porous and will have to be repaired or replaced.

4.2 Using a flat-bladed screwdriver, carefully pry the cable from the shift lever ballstud

18   Make sure the oil cooler hose fittings are tight and in good condition.

Fluid comes out vent pipe or fill tube

19   If this condition occurs, the transaxle is overfilled, there is coolant in the fluid, the case is porous, the dipstick is incorrect, the vent is plugged or the drain-back holes are plugged.

3   Shift lever (floor shift models) - removal and installation

Warning: *The models covered by this manual are equipped with Supplemental Restraint Systems (SRS), more commonly known as airbags. Always disable the airbag system before working in the vicinity of any airbag system components to avoid the possibility of accidental deployment of the airbags, which could cause personal injury (see Chapter 12).*

1   Disconnect the cable from the negative battery terminal (see Chapter 5).
2   Remove the console trim plate (see Chapter 11).
3   If equipped, remove the anti-theft plate.
4   Remove the left side trim plate from the console (see Chapter 11).
5   Disconnect the shift cable from the shift lever by prying the cable end off the ballstud.
6   Disconnect the park/lock cable from the shift lever (see Section 5).
7   Remove the retaining nuts and lift the shifter lever assembly out of the vehicle.
8   To install the shift lever assembly, place the floor shift control assembly in position on the mounting studs and install the nuts.
9   Connect the shift and park/lock cables.
10   If equipped, install the anti-theft plate.
11   Install the console trim plates (see Chapter 11).
12   Reconnect the negative battery cable.

4   Shift cable - replacement and adjustment

Warning: *The models covered by this manual are equipped with Supplemental Restraint Systems (SRS), more commonly known as airbags. Always disable the airbag system before working in the vicinity of any airbag system components to avoid the possibility of accidental deployment of the airbags, which could cause personal injury (see Chapter 12).*

Floor shift models

Refer to illustrations 4.2, 4.3a and 4.3b
1   Position the shift lever into Neutral position.
2   Working in the engine compartment, remove the air filter housing (see Chapter 4), then disconnect the shift cable from the lever by carefully prying the cable end from the transaxle shift lever with a flat-bladed screwdriver **(see illustration)**.
3   To detach the shift cable from the

4.3a Remove the U-clip retainer . . .

4.3b . . . then squeeze the tangs (A) and
pull the cable from the bracket (B)

4.20 Using a flat-bladed screwdriver,
carefully pry the cable from control
lever ballstud

transaxle bracket, remove the U-clip retainer, then squeeze the tangs on the cable housing and pull the cable through the bracket **(see illustrations)**.

4   Working in the center console area in the passenger compartment, remove the console trim plate (see Chapter 11).

5   If equipped, remove the anti-theft plate.

6   Remove the clip at the cable housing end, then pry out the grommet from the front of the shift lever assembly and pull out the shift cable through the hole in the mount. You may have to pull back the carpeting to expose the cable. **Note:** *There are some later models that retain the shift cable to the shift lever assembly with a bolt.*

7   Disconnect the shift cable from the shift lever by prying the cable with a flat-bladed screwdriver.

8   Remove the grommet securing the cable to the firewall and remove the cable from the vehicle.

9   To install the shift cable, guide the new cable through the hole in the floor and install the grommet.

10   Connect the shift cable to the shift lever.

11   Place the shift control lever (inside the vehicle) in Neutral. Make sure it remains in the Neutral position until the shift cable is installed.

12   Attach the shift cable to the transaxle bracket.

13   Place the shift lever on the transaxle in

the Neutral position.

14   Connect the shift cable end to the shift lever on the transaxle, and install new cable-ties where needed.

15   Adjust the shift cable (see Steps 24 through 27).

16   The remainder of installation is the reverse of removal.

Column shift models

Refer to illustrations 4.20, 4.21a, 4.21b and 4.22

17   Working in the engine compartment, remove the air filter housing (see Chapter 4), then disconnect the shift cable from the lever on the transaxle.

18   To detach the shift cable from the transaxle bracket, remove the U-clip retainer then squeeze the tangs on the cable housing and pull the cable through the bracket.

19   Remove the lower sound insulator panel under the dash.

20   Disconnect the cable end from the shift control lever **(see illustration)**.

21   Remove the U-clip retainer then squeeze the tangs on the cable housing and remove the cable from the bracket **(see illustrations)**.

22   Pull the cable through the hole in the firewall to the engine side **(see illustration)**.

23   Installation is the reverse of removal. After installation, adjust the cable (see Steps 24 through 28).

4.21a Remove the U-clip retainer . . .

Adjustment

Refer to illustration 4.24

Note: *These models are equipped with a lock tab on the shift cable grommet at the transaxle bracket. This lock tab, when pressed and both levers are in the neutral position, locates the correct shift position and locks the cable in place.*

24   Using a screwdriver, lift the lock button tab on the cable **(see illustration)**.

25   The shift linkage must be adjusted so the engine starts only when the shift lever is positioned in Park or Neutral. First, position the shift lever in the Neutral position.

7

4.21b . . . then squeeze the tangs to
release the cable from the bracket

4.22 Squeeze the grommet with a pair of
pliers and remove the cable from
the engine side

4.24 Carefully lift the lock tab using a
flat-bladed screwdriver

26   Make sure the transaxle lever is correctly positioned in the Neutral detent.
27   Push the lock tab on the cable grommet assembly to lock the shift cable into place.
28   Check the shift lever for proper operation. It should operate smoothly, without binding. The engine should crank only when the lever is in Park or Neutral.

5   Park/lock cable (floor shift models) - removal and installation

Warning: *The models covered by this manual are equipped with Supplemental Restraint Systems (SRS), more commonly known as airbags. Always disable the airbag system before working in the vicinity of any airbag system components to avoid the possibility of accidental deployment of the airbags, which could cause personal injury (see Chapter 12).*

Removal

1   Disconnect the cable from the negative battery terminal (see Chapter 5).
2   Remove the driver's side kick panel and pull back the carpet near the lower end of the steering column.
3   Remove the steering column covers and the column reinforcement plate (see Chapter 11).
4   Place the shift lever in Park and the ignition switch in the Run position.
5   Insert a screwdriver blade into the slot in the ignition switch inhibitor, depress the cable latch and detach the cable.
6   Remove the console and radio trim panels (see Chapter 11).
7   Remove the cable from the shift control base.
8   Remove the park lock cable from the vehicle.

Installation

9   Make sure the cable lock button is in the UP position and the shift lever is in Park.
10   With the ignition key in the Run position (this is very important), snap the cable into the inhibitor housing. Do *not* attempt to insert the cable with the key in any other position.
11   Turn the ignition key to the Lock position.
12   Snap the end of the cable onto the shifter park/lock pin at the shift control base.
13   Push the nose of the cable connector forward to remove the slack.
14   With no load on the connector nose, snap down the cable connector lock button.
15   Check the operation of the park/lock cable as follows:
   a)   *With the shift lever in Park and the key in Lock, make sure the shift lever cannot be moved to another position and the key can be removed.*
   b)   *With the key in Run and the shift lever in Neutral, make sure the key cannot be turned to Lock.*
16   If it operates as described above, the

6.3 Remove the old seal using a seal removal tool

park/lock cable system is properly adjusted.
17   If the park/lock system doesn't operate as described, return the cable connector lock to the UP position and repeat the adjustment procedure. Push the cable connector down and recheck the operation.

6   Driveaxle oil seals - replacement

Refer to illustrations 10.3 and 10.6
1   Loosen the front wheel lug nuts and the driveaxle/hub nut. Raise the vehicle and support it securely on jackstands. Remove the wheel.
2   Remove the driveaxle(s) (see Chapter 8).
3   Pry out the seal and remove it from the transaxle housing **(see illustration)**.
4   Compare the new seal to the old one to make sure they're the same.
5   Coat the lips of the new seal with transaxle fluid.
6   Place the new seal in position and tap it into the bore with a hammer and a large socket or a piece of pipe that's the same diameter as the outside edge of the seal **(see illustration)**.
7   The remainder of installation is the reverse of removal.

7   Transaxle auxiliary oil cooler and lines - removal and installation

Auxiliary oil cooler

1   On some early models, an auxiliary oil cooler is provided for the automatic transaxle fluid. The cooler looks like a small radiator and is mounted in front of the engine radiator and air conditioning condenser, just behind the grille. Transaxle fluid flow comes from the transaxle to the auxiliary cooler through the transaxle fluid output line, and then from the auxiliary cooler to the standard cooler in the right-hand tank of the radiator.
2   To remove the cooler, place a drain pan under the cooler to catch the fluid and detach the lower fluid line from the cooler.
3   When no more fluid comes out, detach the upper fluid line.

6.6 Tap the new seal into place using a large socket or section of pipe and hammer - use a socket or section of pipe with a diameter slightly smaller than the outside diameter of the seal itself

4   Remove the mounting screws (at the upper radiator support, and the lower support bracket) and remove the cooler.
5   Installation is the reverse of removal.

Transaxle oil cooler lines

Refer to illustrations 7.8, 7.10, 7.11a, 7.11b, 7.12 and 7.14
6   If necessary, for better access to the lower cooler line on the front side of the transaxle, remove the air filter housing.
7   Place a drain pan under the cooler lines to catch the fluid.
8   Remove the retaining bolt for the upper cooler line bracket from the fan shroud **(see illustration)**.
9   On 1995 and earlier models, an open-end wrench to hold the stationary fittings on the radiator and a flare-nut wrench to unscrew the upper and lower cooler lines from the radiator side tank.
10   On 1996 and later models, unsnap the plastic collar from the quick-connect fittings, then pry off the quick-connect fitting retaining clips and remove the lines **(see illustration)**.
11   Remove the two bolts attaching the upper cooler line brackets to the transaxle **(see illustrations)**.

7.8 Remove the bolt securing the upper transaxle cooler line to the fan shroud

7.10 Use a small screwdriver to remove the quick-connect fitting clip

7.11a Remove the bolts retaining the upper transaxle cooler line bracket to the front . . .

7.11b . . . and to the side of the transaxle

12 Disconnect the upper transaxle cooler line from the rear of the transaxle **(see illustration)**.

13 Disconnect the lower cooler line from the transaxle **(see illustration).**

14 The remainder of installation is the reverse of removal, noting the following points:

  a) *Tighten all fasteners and fittings securely.*

  b) *On later models with quick/connect fittings, push the upper cooler line into the quick connect fitting until a audible Click is heard. Gently pull on the line to ensure a proper connection. Slide the plastic sleeve over the fitting.*

  c) *Check the transaxle fluid level as described in Chapter1.*

8 Park/Neutral Position (PNP) switch - replacement and adjustment

Replacement

Refer to illustration 8.6

1 Disconnect the cable from the negative battery terminal (see Chapter 5).

2 Remove the air filter housing (see Chapter 4).

3 Unplug the electrical connector for the Park/Neutral Position switch.

4 Detach the shift cable (see Section 4) and remove the lever from the transaxle.

5 If necessary, remove the fuel line and bracket.

6 Unscrew the switch retaining bolts and remove the switch **(see illustration).**

7 Installation is the reverse of removal. Be sure to adjust the switch before tightening the mounting bolts.

Adjustment

Refer to illustration 8.10

8 Place the shift lever in the Neutral position.

9 With the switch retaining bolts installed loosely, insert the tang on the switch assembly into the slot on the shift lever shaft.

10 Insert a 3/32-inch drill bit into the service adjustment hole **(see illustration)** and rotate the switch assembly until the drill bit drops into the carrier tang hole.

11 Tighten the switch retaining bolts securely.

12 Verify that the shifter operates correctly and the transaxle end of the cable functions in the range which corresponds to each position of the shift lever.

7.12 Detach the cooler line at the rear of the transaxle

9 Vacuum modulator (4T60-E transaxle) - check and replacement

Check

Refer to illustration 9.1

1 The vacuum modulator is located on the front (radiator) side of the transaxle. The modulator is connected to engine manifold vacuum to rapidly respond to changes in engine loading, and has an important effect

7

7.13 Use a flare-nut wrench on the tube nut and an open-end wrench on the fitting adapter when detaching the transaxle cooler lines from the transaxle

8.6 Remove the Park/Neutral Position switch mounting bolts

8.10 Insert a 3/32-inch drill bit into the service adjustment hole and rotate the switch assembly until the drill bit drops into the carrier tang hole

9.1 Disconnect the vacuum line from the modulator and attach a vacuum gauge

on shift quality. If your vehicle exhibits shifting problems such as slipping or shifts that are either too soft or too harsh, check the vacuum supply to the modulator **(see illustration)**. With the engine running, connect a vacuum gauge to the modulator's vacuum line. Anything less than normal engine vacuum here of 13 to 17 inches (idling hot in Drive with the brakes applied) could cause shifting problems. If vacuum is too low, find the engine problem, hose kink or hose leak that is causing the low vacuum signal.

2   Remove the modulator (see Steps 5 through 8), connect a hand-held vacuum pump to the vacuum connection on the modulator and apply 15 to 20 inches of vacuum while watching the plunger. If the plunger isn't drawn in as vacuum is applied, the modulator should be replaced. The modulator should be able to hold this vacuum for at least 30 seconds.

3   When the modulator is withdrawn from the transaxle, turn it so the vacuum pipe is down. If any oil, water or other fluid drips out, the modulator should be replaced. **Note:** *A vehicle with a modulator whose diaphragm has a leak may exhibit excessive smoking at the tailpipe, due to transaxle fluid being drawn into the engine and burned.*

4   The body of the modulator can be checked for leaks by coating the outside with soapy water and blowing (by mouth, no more than 6 psi) into the vacuum connector, using

9.7 Use a screwdriver to remove the O-ring from the transaxle

9.6 Vacuum modulator details

| A | Vacuum hose connection | B | Plunger |
| C | O-ring | | |

a short length of vacuum hose. Bubbles on the outside of the modulator or along the seam indicate a leak.

Replacement

Refer to illustrations 9.6, 9.7 and 9.8

5   Remove the air filter housing (see Chapter 4).

6   Disconnect the vacuum line, and remove the mounting bolt or stud, then withdraw the modulator **(see illustration)**.

7   Remove the O-ring from the modulator cavity, using a small screwdriver or hook **(see illustration)**.

8   Use a small magnet to remove the modulator valve from the transaxle **(see illustration)**. Inspect the valve for signs of abnormal wear or scoring.

9   Installation is the reverse of the removal procedure. Always use a new O-ring and make sure the modulator valve is installed the same way it came out.

---

10 Automatic transaxle - removal and installation

Note: *If the transaxle requires major repair work, it should be left to a dealer service department or an automotive or transmission repair shop. If you've decided that the*

9.8 A magnet can be used to reach in and extract the modulator valve

transaxle must be removed for overhaul or major repair work, several preliminary steps should be taken. Read all removal and installation procedures carefully prior to committing this job.
    Transaxle removal involves removing the engine and transaxle as an assembly, this procedure is described in Chapter 2C.

Removal

1   Drain the transaxle fluid (Chapter 1).
2   Refer to Chapter 2C, Section 7 to remove the engine/transaxle assembly, then separate the transaxle from the engine as described in that Section.

Installation

3   Installation is the reverse of removal, noting the following points:

a) *Prior to installation, make sure the torque converter is fully engaged in the transmission. To do this, rotate the converter while pushing it towards the transaxle. If it wasn't already fully in place, you'll feel it "clunk" into position as it engages with the input shaft and front pump. It may even "clunk" more than once. Lubricate the torque converter hub with multi-purpose grease.*

b) *Move the transaxle forward carefully until the dowel pins and the torque converter are engaged. Make sure the marks on the torque converter and drive plate are in alignment.*

c) *Install the transaxle-to-engine bolts. Tighten the bolts to the specified torque listed in this Chapter's Specifications.*

d) *Install the engine/transaxle assembly (see Chapter 2C).*

e) *Lower the vehicle. Install and adjust the shift cable (see Section 4).*

f) *Fill the transaxle with the recommended type and amount of fluid (Chapter 1), run the vehicle and check for fluid leaks.*

---

11 Automatic transaxle overhaul - general information

In the event of a fault occurring, it will be necessary to establish whether the fault is electrical, mechanical or hydraulic in nature, before repair work can be contemplated. Diagnosis requires detailed knowledge of the transaxle's operation and construction, as well as access to specialized test equipment, and so is deemed to be beyond the scope of this manual. It is therefore essential that problems with the automatic transaxle are referred to a dealer service department or other qualified repair facility for assessment.

Note that a faulty transaxle should not be removed before the vehicle has been assessed by a knowledgeable technician equipped with the proper tools, as troubleshooting must be performed with the transaxle installed in the vehicle.

Chapter 8
Driveaxles

Contents

Specifications

Driveaxles

Inner CV joint standard length (dimension A in **illustration 3.3u**)

2001 and earlier models	4.9 inches
2002 models	3.79 inches

Torque specifications

Ft-lbs

Driveaxle/hub nut

DeVille

1996 and earlier models	107
1997 models	118
1998 models	107
1999 and later models	118

Seville

1996 and earlier models	107
1997 and later models	118
Wheel lug nuts	See Chapter 1

8

1   General information

Power is transmitted from the transaxle to the front wheels by two driveaxles, which consist of splined axleshafts with constant velocity (CV) joints at each end. There are two types of inner CV joints used. Early models are equipped with inner tri-pot bearings with square bearing design that incorporate the bearings within a metal case. Later models are equipped with a "tri-pot" design using needle bearings and round bearing surfaces. Tri-pot bearings are identified by the tri-pot housing which will have three major indentations in it. Both the square and round tri-pot designs incorporate an inner stop-ring and outer retainer ring (clip) on the axleshaft. All outer CV joints are the double-offset type, and allow angular, but not axial, movement. The outer bearings are referred to as the ball-and-cage style CV joint design.

The CV joints are protected by rubber boots, which are retained by clamps so the joints are protected from water and dirt. The boots should be inspected periodically (see Chapter 1). Damaged CV joint boots must be replaced immediately or the joints can be damaged. Boot replacement involves removing the driveaxles (Section 2). It's a good idea to disassemble, clean, inspect and repack the CV joint whenever replacing a CV joint boot to make sure the joint isn't contaminated with moisture or dirt, which would cause premature failure of the CV joint.

The most common symptom of worn or damaged CV joints, besides lubricant leaks, are a clicking noise in turns, a clunk when accelerating from a coasting condition or vibration at highway speeds.

2 Driveaxles - removal and installation

Refer to illustrations 2.1, 2.6a, 2.6b, 2.7a, 2.7b and 2.9

Removal

1   Remove the wheel cover and loosen the hub nut **(see illustration)**. Loosen the wheel lug nuts, raise the front of the vehicle and support it securely on jackstands. Apply the parking brake and block the rear wheels to keep the vehicle from rolling off the jackstands. Remove the front wheel.

2   Remove the driveaxle/hub nut. To prevent the hub from turning, insert a screwdriver through the caliper and into the cooling vanes of the brake disc, then unscrew the nut and remove the washer.

3   Place a drain pan under the transaxle near the differential to catch any transaxle lubricant that may leak out when the driveaxle is removed.

4   Remove the brake caliper and disc and support the caliper out of the way with a piece of wire (see Chapter 9).

5   Remove the strut-to-steering knuckle

2.1 Loosen the driveaxle/hub nut with a long breaker bar

bolts and separate the strut from the steering knuckle (see Chapter 10).

6   Push the driveaxle out of the hub with a puller **(see illustration)**, then support the outer end of the driveaxle with a piece of wire to prevent damage to the inner CV joint **(see illustration)**.

7   Remove the driveaxle from the transaxle **(see illustrations)**.

2.6a A two-jaw puller works well for pushing the stub axle out of the hub

8   Support the CV joints and carefully remove the driveaxle from the vehicle.

Installation

9   Lubricate the differential seal with multipurpose grease, raise the driveaxle into position while supporting the CV joints and insert the splined end of the inner CV joint into the differential side gear. Seat the shaft in the

2.6b Support the outer end of the driveaxle with a piece of wire

2.7a Separate the passenger side driveaxle by gently tapping the inner joint from the transaxle

2.7b The driver's side driveaxle can be removed with a slide-hammer and driveaxle removal attachment

2.9 A large punch or screwdriver, positioned in the groove on the CV joint housing, can be used to seat the joint in the transaxle

3.3a Cut off the boot retaining clamps

3.3b Slide the housing off the spider assembly

3.3c Slide the boot towards the center of the driveaxle (square tri-pot bearing block design shown)

3.3d Mark the relationship of the tri-pot assembly to the outer race

3.3e Spread the ends of the stop-ring apart and slide it towards the center of the shaft

side gear (or onto the side gear shaft, depending on design) by positioning the end of a screwdriver in the groove in the CV joint and tapping it into position with a hammer **(see illustration)**.

10   Apply a light coat of multi-purpose grease to the outer CV joint splines, pull out on the steering knuckle and install the stub axle in the hub.

11   Reconnect the strut to the steering knuckle (see Chapter 10).

12   Install the brake disc and caliper (see Chapter 9).

13   Install the driveaxle/hub nut and washer. Lock the disc so it can't turn, using a screwdriver or punch inserted through the caliper into a disc cooling vane, and tighten the driveaxle/hub nut to approximately 70 ft-lbs. This is an initial torque setting. The final torque will be applied after the vehicle has been lowered to the ground.

14   Grasp the inner CV joint housing (not the driveaxle) and pull out to make sure the axle has seated securely in the transaxle.

15   Install the wheel and lug nuts and lower the vehicle.

16   Tighten the driveaxle/hub nut to the torque listed in this Chapter's Specifications. Tighten the wheel lug nuts to the torque listed in the Chapter 1 Specifications, then install

the wheel cover.

17   Check the transaxle lubricant level, adding as required (see Chapter 1).

3   Driveaxle boot - replacement

Note: *If the CV joint boots must be replaced, explore all options before beginning the job. Complete rebuilt driveaxles are available on an exchange basis, which eliminates much time and work. Whichever route you choose to take, check on the cost and availability of parts before disassembling the vehicle.*

1   Remove the driveaxle (see Section 2).

2   Place the driveaxle in a vise lined with rags to avoid damage to the axleshaft. Check the CV joint for excessive play in the radial direction, which indicates worn parts. Check for smooth operation throughout the full range of motion for each CV joint. If a boot is torn, disassemble the joint, clean the components and inspect for damage due to loss of lubrication and possible contamination by foreign matter.

Inner CV joint

Refer to illustrations 3.3a through 3.3w

Note: *Early models use a square tri-pot bear-*

ing design instead of the typical round bearing design on the inner CV joints. The square bearing type houses the bearings within a metal cage. Both the square and round tri-pot bearing designs incorporate an inner stop-ring and outer retainer (clip) on the driveaxle.

3   To replace the inner boot, refer to the accompanying photo sequence **(see illustrations 3.3a through 3.3w)**.

3.3f Slide the spider (or ball-and-cage) assembly back to expose the retaining ring and pry off the ring

8

3.3g Remove the spider from the driveaxle. Hold the bearings in place with your hand; even better, use tape or a cloth wrapped around the spider bearing assembly to retain them

3.3h If the spider sticks to the shaft, tap it off the axleshaft with a hammer and brass punch

3.3i Slide the stop-ring and the boot off the axleshaft

3.3j Clean all of the old grease out of the housing and spider assembly, then remove each bearing, one at time

3.3k On models with needle bearings, carefully disassemble each section of the spider assembly, clean the needle bearings with solvent and inspect the rollers, spider cross, bearings and housing for scoring, pitting and other signs of abnormal wear

3.3l Apply CV joint grease to hold the needle bearings in place and slide the bearing over them

3.3m On square tri-pot bearing assemblies, install the bearing blocks onto the posts of the spider, then turn them 90-degrees to lock them in place

3.3n Wrap the axleshaft splines with tape to avoid damaging the boot, then slide the small clamp and boot onto the axleshaft

3.3o Remove the tape and slide the stop-ring onto the axleshaft, past the groove in which it seats

3.3p Install the spider assembly with the recess in the counterbore facing the end of the driveaxle

3.3q Install the retaining ring, then slide the spider (or ball-and cage) assembly against it and install the stop-ring in its groove

3.3r Pack the housing with half of the grease furnished with the new boot and place the remainder in the boot - on square tri-pot bearing design, be sure to hold the bearing blocks in alignment so they can be inserted into the joint housing without cocking to the side

3.3s With the retaining clamps in place (but not tightened), install the joint housing

3.3t Seat the boot in the housing and axle seal grooves - a small screwdriver can make the job easier (make sure the boot isn't dimpled, stretched or out of shape)

3.3u Adjust the length of the joint to the dimension listed in this Chapter's Specifications

Outer CV joint

Refer to illustrations 3.4a through 3.4r

4   Refer to the accompanying photo sequence and perform the outer CV joint boot replacement procedure **(see illustrations 3.4a through 3.4r).**

3.3v Equalize the pressure inside the boot by inserting a *dull* screwdriver between the boot and the outer race . . .

3.3w . . . then secure the boot clamps with special pliers (available at most auto parts stores)

3.4a Cut off the band retaining the boot to the shaft, then slide the boot toward the center of the shaft

3.4b Using snap-ring pliers, spread the ears of the snap-ring apart, then slide the joint off the shaft and remove the old boot

3.4c Press down on the inner race far enough to allow a ball bearing to be removed - if it's difficult to tilt, gently tap the cage and inner race with a brass punch and hammer

3.4d Pry the balls out of the cage, one at a time

3.4e Tilt the inner race and cage 90-degrees, then align the windows in the cage (A) with the lands of the housing (B) and rotate the inner race up and out of the outer race

3.4f Align the inner race lands with the cage window and rotate the inner race out of the cage

3.4g After cleaning the components with solvent, check the inner race lands and grooves for pitting and score marks

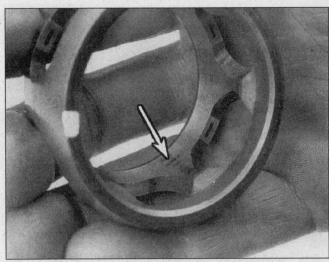

3.4h Check the cage for cracks, pitting and score marks - shiny spots are normal and don't affect operation

3.4i With the race and cage tilted 90-degrees, lower the assembly into the housing

3.4j Rotate the assembly by gently tapping with a hammer and brass punch . . .

3.4k . . . then press the balls into the cage windows, repeating until all of the balls are installed

8

3.4l Use needle-nose pliers to lower a
new snap-ring into the groove . . .

3.4m . . . then seat it into the groove with
snap-ring pliers

3.4n Apply grease through the splined
hole, then insert a wooden dowel (with a
diameter slightly less than that of the axle)
through the splined hole and push down -
the dowel will force the grease into the
joint - repeat until the bearing is
completely packed

3.4o Install the small clamp and the boot on the driveaxle and
apply grease to the inside of the axle boot until . . .

3.4p . . . the level is up to the end of the axle

3.4q Position the CV joint assembly on the driveaxle, aligning the
splines, then use a soft-face hammer to drive the joint onto the
driveaxle until the snap-ring is seated in the groove

3.4r Seat the inner end of the boot in the groove and install the
retaining clamp, then do the same on the other end of the boot -
equalize the pressure in the boot (see illustration 3.3v), then
tighten the boot clamps (see illustration 3.3w)

Chapter 9
Brakes

Contents

Specifications

General
Brake fluid type .... See Chapter 1

Disc brakes
Brake pad lining minimum thickness .... See Chapter 1

Disc (front)
Minimum thickness .... Refer to the dimension stamped into the disc
Runout (maximum) .... 0.002 inch

Disc (rear)
Minimum thickness .... Refer to the dimension stamped into the disc
Runout (maximum) .... 0.002 inch

Torque specifications
Ft-lbs (unless otherwise indicated)

Booster-to-firewall mounting nuts

DeVille
1999 and earlier models 20
2000 models 22
2001 and later models 27

Seville
1997 and earlier models 20
1998 through 2000 models 24
2001 and later models 17

Brake hose-to-caliper bolt 33

9

Torque specifications (continued)

	Ft-lbs (unless otherwise indicated)
Caliper mounting bolts	
Front	
DeVille	
1996 and earlier models	38
1997 and later models	63
Seville	
1996 and earlier models	38
1997 and later models	63
Rear	20
Caliper mounting bracket bolts	
Front	
1997 and later models	137
Rear	
1997 and earlier models	81
1998 and later models	94
Wheel lug nuts	See Chapter 1

1   General information

The vehicles covered by this manual are equipped with hydraulically operated front and rear brake systems. Both the front brakes and the rear brakes are disc type and are self adjusting.

Hydraulic system

The hydraulic system consists of two separate circuits. The master cylinder has separate reservoirs for the two circuits, and, in the event of a leak or failure in one hydraulic circuit, the other circuit will remain operative. On 1998 and earlier models, dual proportioning valves provide brake balance between the front and rear brakes.

Power brake booster

The power brake booster, utilizing engine manifold vacuum and atmospheric pressure to provide assistance to the hydraulically operated brakes, is mounted on the firewall in the engine compartment.

Parking brake

The parking brake operates the rear brakes only, through cable actuation. It's activated by a pedal mounted on the left side kick panel.

Service

After completing any operation involving disassembly of any part of the brake system, always test drive the vehicle to check for proper braking performance before resuming normal driving. When testing the brakes, perform the tests on a clean, dry, flat surface. Conditions other than these can lead to inaccurate test results.

Test the brakes at various speeds with both light and heavy pedal pressure. The vehicle should stop evenly without pulling to one side or the other.

Tires, vehicle load and wheel alignment are factors which also affect braking performance.

2   Anti-lock Brake System (ABS) - general information and speed sensor removal and installation

General information

Refer to illustrations 2.2a, 2.2b and 2.2c

1   The anti-lock brake system is designed to maintain vehicle steerability, directional stability and optimum deceleration under severe braking conditions on most road surfaces. It does so by monitoring the rotational speed of each wheel and controlling the brake line pressure to each wheel during braking. This prevents the wheels from locking up.

2   The ABS system has three main components - the wheel speed sensors, the electronic control unit (EBCM) and the hydraulic unit (BPMV) **(see illustrations)**. Four wheel speed sensors - one at each wheel - send a variable voltage signal to the control unit, which monitors these signals, compares

2.2a On 1998 and later models (and earlier models with traction control) the Electronic Brake Control Module (A) and the Brake Pressure Modulation Valve (B) are both mounted in the engine compartment (on earlier models without traction control the control module is mounted in the trunk, on the left side)

2.2b Front wheel sensor connector

2.2c Location of the rear wheel speed sensor

them to its program and determines whether a wheel is about to lock up. When a wheel is about to lock up, the control unit signals the hydraulic unit to reduce hydraulic pressure (or not increase it further) at that wheel's brake caliper. Pressure modulation is handled by electrically-operated solenoid valves.

3   If a problem develops within the system, an "ABS" warning light will glow on the dashboard. Sometimes, a visual inspection of the ABS system can help you locate the problem. Carefully inspect the ABS wiring harness. Pay particularly close attention to the harness and connections near each wheel. Look for signs of chafing and other damage caused by incorrectly routed wires. If a wheel sensor harness is damaged, the sensor must be replaced. **Warning:** *Do NOT try to repair an ABS wiring harness. The ABS system is sensitive to even the smallest changes in resistance. Repairing the harness could alter resistance values and cause the system to malfunction. If the ABS wiring harness is damaged in any way, it must be replaced.* **Cau-**

tion: *Make sure the ignition is turned off before unplugging or reattaching any electrical connections.*

Wheel speed sensor

4   Each wheel is equipped with a speed sensor, which is self-contained in each wheel bearing. The sensors are neither adjustable nor rebuildable. If a sensor malfunctions, the wheel bearing assembly must be replaced.

5   A wheel speed sensor measures wheel speed by monitoring the rotation of a toothed ring. As the teeth of the ring move through the magnetic field of the sensor, an AC voltage signal is generated. This signal frequency increases or decreases in proportion to the speed of the wheel. The EBCM monitors these signals for changes in wheel speed; if it detects the sudden deceleration of a wheel, i.e. wheel lockup, the EBCM activates the ABS system.

Diagnosis and repair

6   If a dashboard warning light comes on and stays on while the vehicle is in operation, the ABS system requires attention. Although special electronic ABS diagnostic testing tools are necessary to properly diagnose the system, you can perform a few preliminary checks before taking the vehicle to a dealer service department.

a) *Check the brake fluid level in the reservoir.*

b) *Verify that the computer electrical connectors are securely connected.*

c) *Check the electrical connectors at the hydraulic control unit.*

d) *Check the fuses.*

e) *Follow the wiring harness to each wheel and verify that all connections are secure and that the wiring is undamaged.*

7   If the above preliminary checks do not rectify the problem, the vehicle should be diagnosed by a dealer service department or other qualified repair shop. Due to the com-

plex nature of this system, all actual repair work must be done by a qualified automotive technician.

---

3   Disc brake pads - replacement

Warning: *Disc brake pads must be replaced on both front or rear wheels at the same time - never replace the pads on only one wheel. Also, the dust created by the brake system is harmful to your health. Never blow it out with compressed air and don't inhale any of it. An approved filtering mask should be worn when working on the brakes. Do not, under any circumstances, use petroleum-based solvents to clean brake parts. Use brake system cleaner only!*

1   Remove the cap from the brake fluid reservoir. Using a suction gun, remove approximately two-thirds of the fluid from the reservoir.

2   Loosen the wheel lug nuts, raise the front, or rear, of the vehicle and support it securely on jackstands.

3   Remove the front, or rear, wheels. Work on one brake assembly at a time, using the assembled brake for reference if necessary.

4   Inspect the brake disc carefully as outlined in Section 5. If machining is necessary, follow the information in that Section to remove the disc, at which time the calipers and pads can be removed as well.

Front pads

Refer to illustrations 3.5a and 3.5b

5   Wash the brake assembly with brake system cleaner **(see illustration)**, then push the piston back into the bore to provide room for the new brake pads. A C-clamp can be used to accomplish this **(see illustration)**. As the piston is depressed to the bottom of the caliper bore, the fluid in the master cylinder will rise. Make sure it doesn't overflow. If necessary, drain off some more of the fluid.

9

3.5a Before starting wash the brake disc and caliper assembly with brake cleaner

3.5b To make room for the new pads, use a C-clamp to depress the piston into its bore

3.6a Remove the two caliper mounting bolts (typical)

3.6b Remove the inner pad by snapping it out of the piston

1997 and earlier models

Refer to illustrations 3.6a through 3.6i

6   Follow the accompanying photos, beginning with **illustration 3.6a**, for the actual pad replacement procedure. Be sure to stay in order and read the caption under each illustration. **Note:** *It's a good idea to apply a thin layer of anti-squeal compound to the backing plates of the new pads. Allow the compound to dry before installing the pads.*

7   Proceed to Step 21.

3.6c Remove the outer brake pad

3.6d Inspect the caliper bolts and bushings (A) for damage and the contact surfaces (B) for corrosion

3.6e Suspend the caliper with a piece of wire whenever it's necessary to reposition it - DO NOT let it hang by the brake hose!

3.6f Lubricate the caliper mounting bolts with high-temperature brake grease

3.6g Be sure to bottom the caliper piston using a C-clamp

3.6h Snap the inner pad into the caliper piston

1998 and later models
Refer to illustrations 3.8a through 3.8j
8   Follow the accompanying photos, beginning with **illustration 3.8a**, for the actual pad replacement procedure. Be sure to stay in order and read the caption under each illustration. **Note:** *It's a good idea to apply a thin layer of anti-squeal compound to* the backing plates of the new pads. Allow the compound to dry before installing the pads.
9   Proceed to Step 21.

3.6i Install the outer brake pad in the caliper, making sure the locating lugs on the pad engage with the holes in the caliper, then place the caliper onto the mounting bracket

3.8a Remove the bottom caliper mounting bolt

3.8b Pivot the caliper up and support it and support it in this position for access to the brake pads

3.8c Remove the inner brake pad

9

3.8d Remove the outer brake pad

3.8e Remove the anti-rattle clips: inspect the clips for damage and replace as necessary (they should fit snugly)

3.8f Lubricate the smooth surface of the caliper mounting bolts with high-temperature grease

3.8g Install the upper anti-rattle clip . . .

3.8h . . . and the lower clip in the caliper mounting bracket - make sure they are fully seated

3.8i Install the outer pad . . .

Rear pads

Refer to illustrations 3.11, 3.12, 3.13a, 3.13b, 3.14, 3.15a, 3.15b, 3.16a, 3.16b, 3.17a, 3.17b and 3.18

10   Wash the brake assembly with brake system cleaner **(see illustration 3.5a).**

11   Remove the parking brake cable **(see illustration).**

12   Remove the lower caliper mounting bolt and pivot the caliper up for access to the brake pads **(see illustration).**

13   Remove the pads and retainers from the caliper mounting bracket **(see illustrations).**

14   Apply a thin coat of disc brake anti-

3.8j . . . and the inner pad in the caliper mounting bracket, then position the caliper into place. Install the caliper lower mounting bolt and tighten it to the torque listed in this Chapter's Specifications

3.11 Detach the parking brake cable from the notch in the parking brake lever and from the bracket

3.12 Remove the lower caliper mounting bolt and swing the caliper up

3.13a Remove the outer . . .

3.13b . . . and inner brake pads from the caliper bracket

3.13c Remove the upper and lower anti-rattle clips

3.14 A small amount of anti-squeal compound can be applied to the back of both new pads (let the compound "set up" a few minutes before installing them)

squeal compound, in accordance with the manufacturer's recommendations, on the backing plates of the new pads (see illustration).

15   Using a pair of needle-nose pliers, rotate

the piston to bottom it in its bore (see illustration). Make sure the cutouts in the piston are positioned at a 90-degree angle to the caliper mounting bolt holes (see illustration). The buttons on the back side of the brake

pads must engage with these alignment cutouts after the caliper has been installed onto the anchor plate.

3.15a Use a pair of needle-nose pliers with the tips engaged in the cutouts of the piston face to turn the piston into the cylinder bore

3.15b Make sure the cutouts in the end of the piston are positioned 90-degrees to the mounting bolts

9

3.16a Install the upper anti-rattle clip . . .

3.16b . . . and the lower anti-rattle clip in the caliper mounting bracket - make sure they are both fully seated

3.17a Install the inner pad . . .

16   Install the pad anti-rattle clips in the caliper mounting bracket **(see illustrations).**
17   Install the new pads to the caliper mounting bracket **(see illustrations).**
18   Slide the caliper off the upper guide pin, then lubricate the caliper upper guide pin and the smooth surface of the mounting bolt **(see illustration).**
19   Pivot the caliper down into position, making sure the tab on the inner brake pad mates with the cutout in the piston face. Install the mounting bolt and tighten it to the

3.17b . . . and install the outer pad

torque listed in this Chapter's Specifications.
20   Reconnect the parking brake cable. Proceed to the next step.

Front or rear pads

21   Install the wheel and lug nuts, lower the vehicle and tighten the lug nuts to the torque specified in Chapter 1.
22   Apply and release the brake pedal several times to bring the pads into contact with

3.18 Lubricate the caliper guide pin with high-temperature grease

the brake discs. Check the brake fluid level and add fluid, if necessary (see Chapter 1).
23   Check the operation of the brakes in an isolated area before driving the vehicle in traffic.
24   If you replaced the rear pads, check the operation of the parking brake.

4   Brake caliper - removal and installation

Warning: *Dust created by the brake system is harmful to your health. Never blow it out with compressed air and don't inhale any of it. An approved filtering mask should be worn when working on the brakes. Do not, under any circumstances, use petroleum-based solvents to clean brake parts. Use brake system cleaner only!*
Note: *Always replace the calipers in pairs - never replace just one of them.*

Front
Removal
Refer to illustrations 4.2a and 4.2b
1   Loosen - but don't remove - the lug nuts on the front wheels. Raise the front of the vehicle and place it securely on jackstands. Remove the front wheels.
2   Wash the brake assembly with brake

4.2a Location of the front caliper brake line banjo fitting bolt (A) and the brake caliper mounting bolts (B)

4.2b Using a short piece of rubber hose of the appropriate diameter, plug the brake line banjo fitting

4.11 Location of the rear caliper guide pin (A), mounting bolt (B) and the brake hose banjo fitting bolt (C)

5.2 Suspend the caliper with a piece of wire whenever it's necessary to reposition it - DO NOT let it hang by the brake hose!

system cleaner. Disconnect the brake line from the caliper and plug it to keep contaminants out of the brake system and to prevent losing any more brake fluid than is necessary (see illustrations). Note: *If you are simply removing the caliper for access to other components, don't disconnect the brake hose.*

3　Remove the caliper mounting bolts (see illustration 4.2a).

4　Detach the caliper from its mounting bracket.

Installation

5　Install the caliper by reversing the removal procedure. Remember to replace the sealing washers on either side of the brake line fitting with new ones. Tighten the caliper mounting bolts and the banjo bolt to the torque listed in this Chapter's Specifications.

6　Bleed the brake system (see Section 9).

7　Install the wheels and lug nuts and lower the vehicle. Tighten the wheel lug nuts to the torque listed in the Chapter 1 Specifications.

Rear

Removal

Refer to illustration 4.11

8　Loosen - but don't remove - the lug nuts on the rear wheels. Raise the rear of the vehicle and place it securely on jackstands. Remove the rear wheels.

9　Release the parking brake and detach the parking brake cable from the lever (see illustration 3.11).

10　Separate the parking brake cable from the bracket on the caliper.

11　Unscrew the banjo bolt and detach the brake line from the caliper (see illustration). Plug the fitting to prevent fluid loss and contamination (see illustration 4.2b). Note: *If you are simply removing the caliper for access to other components, don't disconnect the brake hose.*

12　Remove the caliper mounting bolt, then slide the caliper off the upper guide pin (see illustration 4.11).

Installation

13　Install the caliper by reversing the removal procedure. Remember to replace the sealing washers on either side of the brake line fitting with new ones. Tighten the caliper mounting bolts and the banjo bolt to the torque listed in this Chapter's Specifications.

14　Bleed the brake system (see Section 9).

15　Install the wheels and lug nuts. Lower the vehicle and tighten the lug nuts to the torque listed in the Chapter 1 Specifications.

5　Brake disc - inspection, removal and installation

Refer to illustrations 5.2, 5.3, 5.4a, 5.4b, 5.5a, and 5.5b

Inspection

1　Loosen the wheel lug nuts, raise the front of the vehicle and support it securely on jackstands. Apply the parking brake and block the rear wheels to keep the vehicle from rolling off the jackstands. Remove the

wheel and install the lug nuts to hold the disc in place.

2　Remove the brake caliper as outlined in Section 4. You don't have to disconnect the brake hose. After removing the caliper bolts, suspend the caliper out of the way with a piece of wire - DO NOT let it hang by the hose (see illustration).

3　Visually inspect the disc surface for score marks and other damage. Light scratches and shallow grooves are normal and may not be detrimental to brake operation, but deep score marks require disc removal and refinishing by an automotive machine shop. Be sure to check both sides of the disc (see illustration). If pulsating has been felt during application of the brakes, suspect excessive disc runout.

4　To check disc runout, mount a dial indicator at a point about 1/2-inch from the outer edge of the disc (see illustration). Set the indicator to zero and turn the disc. The indicator reading should not exceed the specified allowable runout limit. If it does, the disc should be refinished by an automotive machine shop. Note: *The discs should be*

5.3 The brake pads on this vehicle were obviously neglected as they wore down completely and cut deep grooves into the disc - wear this severe will require replacement of the disc

5.4a Check for runout with a dial indicator - mount it with the indicator needle about 1/2-inch from the outer edge

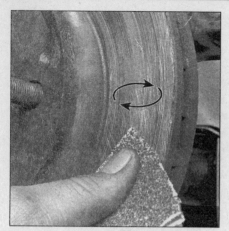

5.4b If you don't have the discs machined, at the very least be sure to break the glaze on the disc surface with sandpaper or emery cloth

5.5a The minimum wear thickness is cast into the inside of the disc (typical)

5.5b Measure the thickness of the disc at several points with a micrometer

resurfaced, regardless of the dial indicator reading, to impart a smooth finish and ensure perfectly flat brake pad surfaces (which will eliminate pedal pulsations. At the very least, if you don't have the discs resurfaced, remove the glaze with sandpaper or emery cloth using a swirling motion **(see illustration)**.

5.6a Front caliper mounting bracket bolts

5   The disc must not be machined to a thickness less than the specified minimum thickness, which is cast into the inside of the disc **(see illustration)**. The disc thickness can be checked with a micrometer **(see illustration)**.

Removal

Refer to illustrations 5.6a and 5.6b
6   Unbolt the caliper mounting bracket **(see illustrations)**. Remove the lug nuts that were put on to hold the disc in place and remove the disc from the hub. If you're removing a rear disc, you'll also have to remove the two bolts and detach the caliper mounting bracket from the rear knuckle.

Installation

7   Install the caliper mounting bracket and tighten the bolts to the torque listed in this Chapter's Specifications. Place the disc in position over the threaded studs.
8   Install the caliper and brake pad assembly over the disc and position it on the steering knuckle (refer to Section 4 for the caliper installation procedure, if necessary). Tighten the caliper bolts to the torque listed in this

Chapter's Specifications.
9   Install the wheel, then lower the vehicle to the ground and tighten the lug nuts to the torque listed in the Chapter 1 Specifications. Depress the brake pedal a few times to bring the brake pads into contact with the disc. Bleeding of the system won't be necessary unless the brake hose was disconnected from the caliper. Check the operation of the brakes carefully before driving the vehicle in traffic.

6   Master cylinder - removal and installation

Caution: *Before starting this procedure, have some plugs ready to cap the metal lines that connect the master cylinder to the hydraulic actuator. Failure to do so will allow air into the ABS actuator and can allow dirt and moisture to enter the ABS system.*

Removal

Refer to illustrations 6.1, 6.3 and 6.7
1   The master cylinder is located in the

5.6b Rear caliper mounting bracket bolts

6.1 Brake master cylinder

6.3 Disconnect the fluid level sensor connector

6.7 Remove the two master cylinder mounting nuts

engine compartment, on the left (driver's) side **(see illustration)**. Remove the air filter housing on models where it would obstruct master cylinder removal (see Chapter 4).

2   Remove as much fluid as you can from the reservoir with a syringe, such as an old turkey baster. **Warning:** *If a baster is used, never again use it for the preparation of food.* Reinstall the reservoir cap.

3   Detach the cable from the negative battery terminal (see Chapter 5). Unplug the fluid level sensor switch connector **(see illustration)**.

4   Place rags under the line fittings and prepare caps or plastic bags to cover the ends of the lines once they're disconnected. **Caution:** *Brake fluid will damage paint. Cover all painted parts and be careful not to spill fluid during this procedure.*

5   Loosen the fittings at the ends of the brake lines where they enter the master cylinder. To prevent rounding off the flats on the fittings, use a flare-nut wrench.

6   Pull the brake lines away from the master cylinder and plug the ends to prevent contamination.

7   Remove the two mounting nuts **(see illustration)** and detach the master cylinder from the vehicle.

Installation

Refer to illustration 6.9

8   Bench bleed the new master cylinder before installing it. Mount the master cylinder in a vise, with the jaws of the vise clamping on the mounting flange.

9   Attach a pair of master cylinder bleeder tubes to the outlet ports of the master cylinder **(see illustration)**.

10   Fill the reservoir with brake fluid of the recommended type (see Chapter 1).

11   Slowly push the pistons into the master cylinder (a large Phillips screwdriver can be used for this) - air will be expelled from the pressure chambers and into the reservoir. Because the tubes are submerged in fluid, air can't be drawn back into the master cylinder when you release the pistons.

12   Repeat the procedure until no more air bubbles are present.

13   Remove the bleed tubes, one at a time, and install plugs in the open ports to prevent fluid leakage and air from entering. Install the reservoir cap.

14   Install the master cylinder over the studs on the power brake booster and tighten the attaching nuts only finger tight at this time.

15   Thread the brake line fittings into the master cylinder. Since the master cylinder is

still a bit loose, it can be moved slightly in order for the fittings to thread in easily. Do not strip the threads as the fittings are tightened.

16   Tighten the mounting nuts securely, then the brake line fittings.

17   Fill the master cylinder reservoir with fluid, then bleed the master cylinder and the brake system as described in Section 9. To bleed the master cylinder on the vehicle, have an assistant depress the brake pedal and hold the pedal to the floor. Loosen the fitting nut to allow air and fluid to escape. Repeat this procedure on both fittings at the master cylinder until the fluid is clear of air bubbles. **Caution:** *Have plenty of rags on hand to catch the fluid - brake fluid will ruin painted surfaces. After the bleeding procedure is completed, rinse the area under the master cylinder with clean water.*

18   Test the operation of the brake system carefully before placing the vehicle into normal service. **Warning:** *Do not operate the vehicle if you are in doubt about the effectiveness of the brake system.*

7   Power brake booster - removal and installation

Refer to illustrations 7.4, 7.5 and 7.6

1   Power brake booster units should not be disassembled. They require special tools not normally found in most automotive repair stations or shops. They are fairly complex and because of their critical relationship to brake performance it is best to replace a defective booster unit with a new or rebuilt one.

2   Unbolt the brake master cylinder from the booster as described in Section 7. **Note:** *Depending on the vehicle, it may not be necessary to disconnect the brake lines.*

3   Taking care not to kink the brake lines, move the master cylinder forward to provide clearance for booster removal. If there is not enough slack in the lines to allow the master cylinder to be positioned far enough forward for booster removal, the brake lines will have to be removed from the master cylinder,

6.9 The best way to bench bleed the master cylinder before installing it on the vehicle is with a pair of bleeder tubes that direct fluid into the reservoir during bleeding

9

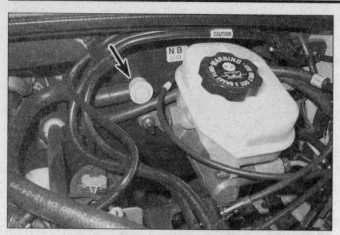

7.4 Carefully disconnect the vacuum hose fitting from the grommet in the booster

7.5 Remove the retaining clip from the pushrod clevis pin . . .

4   Disconnect the vacuum hose fitting from the power brake booster **(see illustration).**

5   Working under the dash, locate the pushrod clevis pin connecting the booster to the brake pedal **(see illustration)** and remove the retaining clip (and spacer, if applicable) and slide the pushrod off its peg on the brake pedal.

6   Remove the mounting nuts holding the brake booster to the firewall **(see illustration).**

7   Slide the booster straight out from the firewall until the studs clear the holes and remove the booster from the engine compartment.

8   Installation is the reverse of removal.

9   If the fluid lines were detached from the master cylinder, bleed the hydraulic system (see Section 9).

---

8   Brake hoses and lines - inspection and replacement

Refer to illustration 8.2

Flexible hoses

1   Raise the vehicle and support it securely on jackstands. Check the flexible hoses that connect the steel brake lines to the front and rear brake assemblies. Look for cracks, chafing of the outer cover, leaks, blisters and other damage. The hoses are an important part of the brake system and the inspection should be thorough. A light and mirror will be helpful to see into restricted areas. If a hose exhibits any of the above conditions, replace it with a new one.

2   Using an open-end wrench on the hose fitting and a flare-nut wrench on the line fitting, disconnect the brake line from the hose fitting, being careful not to bend the frame bracket or brake line **(see illustration).**

3   Use pliers to remove the U-clip from the female fitting at the bracket, then remove the hose from the bracket.

4   At the caliper end of the hose, remove the bolt from the fitting block, then remove the hose and the copper gaskets on either side of the fitting block.

5   When installing the hose, always use new copper gaskets on either side of the fitting block and lubricate all bolt threads with clean brake fluid before installation.

6   With the fitting flange engaged with the caliper locating ledge, attach the hose to the caliper.

7   Without twisting the hose, install the female fitting in the hose bracket. It'll fit the bracket in only one position.

8   Install the U-clip retaining the female fitting to the frame bracket.

9   Attach the brake line to the hose fitting, then tighten the fitting using the two wrenches as described in Step 2.

10   When the brake hose installation is complete, there shouldn't be any kinks in the hose. Make sure the hose doesn't contact any part of the suspension. Check it by turning the wheels to the extreme left and right positions. If the hose makes contact, remove the hose and correct the installation as necessary.

11   After installation, check the master cylinder fluid level and add fluid as necessary. Bleed the brake system (see Section 9) and test the brakes carefully before driving the vehicle in traffic.

Metal brake lines

12   When replacing brake lines, be sure to buy the correct replacement parts. Don't use copper or any other tubing for brake lines.

7.6 . . . then remove the booster-to-firewall fasteners (3 shown)

8.2 Using an open-end wrench on the flexible hose side of the fitting (A), loosen the tube nut (B) with a flare-nut wrench and remove the U-clip (C) from the hose fitting

9.8 When bleeding the brakes, a hose is connected to the bleeder valve at the caliper and submerged in brake fluid - air will be seen as bubbles in the container of in the tube (all air must be expelled before continuing to the next wheel)

10.2 Brake light switch

13 Auto parts stores and brake supply houses carry various lengths of prefabricated brake line. These sections can be bent with a tubing bender.

14 When installing the new line, make sure it's securely supported in the brackets with plenty of clearance between moving or hot components.

15 After installation, check the master cylinder fluid level and add fluid as necessary. Bleed the brake system as outlined in the next Section and test the brakes before driving the vehicle in traffic.

9 Brake hydraulic system - bleeding

Refer to illustration 9.8

Warning: *Wear eye protection when bleeding the brake system. If you get fluid in your eyes, rinse them immediately with water and seek medical attention.*

Note: *Bleeding the brakes is necessary to remove air that manages to find its way into the system when its been opened during removal and installation of a hose, line, caliper or master cylinder.*

1 It'll probably be necessary to bleed the system at all four brakes if air has entered the system due to low fluid level, or if the brake lines have been disconnected at the master cylinder.

2 If a brake line was disconnected at only one wheel, then only that caliper or wheel cylinder must be bled.

3 If a brake line is disconnected at a fitting located between the master cylinder and any of the brakes, that part of the system served by the disconnected line must be bled.

4 Remove any residual vacuum from the power brake booster by applying the brake several times with the engine off.

5 Remove the master cylinder reservoir cover and fill the reservoir with brake fluid. Reinstall the cover. **Note:** *Check the fluid*

level often during the bleeding procedure and add fluid as necessary to prevent the level from falling low enough to allow air bubbles into the master cylinder.

6 Have an assistant on hand, as well as a supply of new brake fluid, an empty, clear plastic container, a length of plastic, rubber or vinyl tubing to fit over the bleeder valve and a wrench to open and close the bleeder valve.

7 Beginning at the first wheel in the bleeding sequence, loosen the bleeder valve slightly, then tighten it to a point where it's snug but can still be loosened quickly and easily. The bleeding sequence differs depending on model and year.

  a) *On 1999 and earlier DeVille models, bleed the left front wheel, the right front wheel, the left rear wheel and right rear wheel in that order, and perform the same procedure.*

  b) *On 2000 and later DeVille models, bleed the right rear wheel, the left front wheel, the left rear wheel and the right front wheel in that order, and perform the same procedure.*

  c) *On 1997 and earlier Seville models, bleed the left front wheel, the right front wheel, the left rear wheel and the right rear wheel in that order, and perform the same procedure.*

  d) *On 1998 through 2000 Seville models, bleed the right rear wheel, the left rear wheel, the right front wheel and the left front wheel in that order, and perform the same procedure.*

  e) *On 2001 and later Seville models, bleed the right rear wheel, the left front wheel, the left rear wheel and the right front wheel in that order, and perform the same procedure.*

8 Place one end of the tubing over the bleeder valve and submerge the other end in brake fluid in the container **(see illustration)**.

9 Have your assistant depress the brake pedal, then hold the pedal down firmly.

10 While the pedal is held down, open the bleeder valve just enough to allow fluid to flow out of the valve. Watch for air bubbles to exit the submerged end of the tube. When the fluid slows after a couple of seconds, close the valve and have your assistant release the pedal.

11 Repeat Steps 9 and 10 until no more air is seen leaving the tube, then tighten the bleeder valve and proceed to the next wheel in the bleeding sequence (see Step 7). Be sure to check the fluid in the master cylinder reservoir frequently.

12 Never use old brake fluid. It contains moisture which can boil, rendering the brakes useless.

13 Refill the master cylinder with fluid at the end of the operation.

14 Check the operation of the brakes. The pedal should feel firm when depressed. If necessary, repeat the entire procedure.

Warning: *If you do not have a firm brake pedal at the end of the bleeding procedure, or the ABS light on the instrument panel does not go out, or you have any doubts as to the effectiveness of the brake system, DO NOT drive the vehicle. Have it towed to a dealer service department or other qualified repair shop for diagnosis.*

10 Brake light switch - removal and installation

9

Refer to illustration 10.2

Removal

1 Remove the drivers side under-dash cover.

2 Locate the switch at the top of the brake pedal bracket **(see illustration)**.

3 Twist the switch counter clockwise and remove it from the bracket.

4 Disconnect the electrical connector from the switch.

Installation

5   Connect the electrical connectors to the switch.

6   Push the new switch into the clip until the switch plunger is fully depressed into the switch barrel.

7   Rotate the switch clockwise until the switch locks into position and travel has stopped. No further adjustment will be required.

8   Make sure the brake lights are functioning properly.

9   The remainder of installation is the reverse of removal.

11   Parking brake - adjustment

1   Apply and release the parking brake pedal firmly (approximately 125 lbs of pressure on the pedal) six times.

2   Raise the vehicle and support it securely on jackstands.

3   Check the parking brake pedal assembly for full release by turning the ignition to On and noting whether the BRAKE warning light is off. If it's on even though the brake appears to be released, operate the pedal release lever and pull down on the front parking brake cable to remove slack from the assembly. Check both rear wheels to make sure they still turn freely.

4   Check the parking brake levers on both rear calipers. Levers should be against the stops on the back of the caliper housing. Check for cable binding if levers are not resting against the stops. This is the OFF position for the parking brake system.

5   Tighten the parking brake cable at the adjuster until the either lever starts to move off its stop.

6   Back off the cable adjuster until the lever that moved off its stop comes back to rest against its top. Both levers should now touch equally.

7   Activate the parking brake several times and check adjustment.

8   Release the parking brake and verify that both wheels rotate freely.

9   Lower the vehicle.

Chapter 10
Suspension and steering systems

Contents

Specifications

Torque specifications

Front suspension

Ft-lbs (unless otherwise indicated)

Balljoint-to-steering knuckle*
  DeVille
    1994 through 1999 models ... 38
    2000 and later models ... 88 in-lbs (then tighten an additional 150-degrees)
  Seville
    1992 through 1997 models ... 38
    1998 and later models ... 88 in-lbs (then tighten an additional 150-degrees)
Balljoint-to-control arm nuts (replacement balljoint)
  DeVille (1998 and earlier models) ... 50
  Seville (1997 and earlier models) ... 50
Control arm
  Brake reaction rod (front portion of control arm)-to-frame nut
    (1996 and earlier models) ... 58
  Front pivot bolt/nut
    DeVille
      1997 through 1999 models ... 93
      2000 and later models ... 116
    Seville
      1997 models ... 93
      1998 and later models ... 116

10

*If necessary, tighten the nut an additional amount to allow insertion of the cotter pin, on models so equipped (don't loosen the nut to insert the cotter pin).

Torque specifications

Front suspension (continued)

Control arm
  Rear pivot bolt/nut
    DeVille

1994 and 1995 models	103
1996 models	100
1997 and later models	116

    Seville

1992 models	91
1993 through 1995 models	103
1996 models	100
1997 and later models	116

Hub and bearing-to-knuckle
  DeVille

1994 through 1999 models	70
2000 and later models	96

  Seville

1992 through 1998 models	70
1999 and later models	96

Stabilizer bar
  Link nut
    DeVille

1994 and 1995 models	156 in-lbs
1996 through 1999 models	41
2000 and later models	156 in-lbs

    Seville

1992	48
1993 through1995 models	156 in-lbs
1996 and 1997 models	41
1998 and later models	156 in-lbs

  Bracket bolts
    DeVille

1994 and 1995 models	18
1996 through 1999 models	33
2000 and later models	24

    Seville

1992 through 1995 models	18
1996 and 1997 models	33
1998 and 1999 models	28
2000 and later models	24

Struts
  Strut-to-steering knuckle bolts/nuts
    DeVille

1994 through 1997 models	136
1998 and 1999 models	140
2000 and later models	108

    Seville

1992 models	140
1993 through 1996 models	136
1997 models	140
1998 models	125
1999 models	136
2000 and later models	108

  Strut upper mounting nuts/bolts
    DeVille

1994 through 1999 models	18
2000 and later models	30

    Seville

1992 through 1997 models	18
1998 and 1999 models	35
2000 and later models	33

Subframe mounting bolts

1998 and earlier DeVille, 1997 and earlier Seville	76
1999 and later DeVille, 1998 and later Seville	141

Rear suspension

Control arm mounting nuts (to frame and rear knuckle)	
Upper control arm	
DeVille (1994 through 1999 models)	42
Seville (1993 through 1997 models)	42
Lower control arm	
DeVille	
1994 through 1999 models	75
2000 and later models	78
Seville	
1993 through 1997	75
1998 and later models	78
Control arm-to-knuckle pivot bolt (1992 Seville models)	59
Inner control arm pivot bolt (1992 Seville models)	66
Toe link	
Deville	
1994 through 1999 models	
Inner bolt/nut	42
Outer bolt	55
2000 and later models	
Inner nut	59
Outer nut	22 (then tighten an additional 180-degrees)
Seville	
1993 through 1997 models	
Inner bolt/nut	42
Outer bolt	55
1998 models	
Inner bolt/nut	59
Outer nut	88 in-lbs (then tighten an additional 270-degrees)
1999 models	
Inner bolt/nut	59
Outer nut	36
2000 and later models	
Inner bolt/nut	55
Outer nut	55
Rear suspension support bolts (1998 and later Seville/2000 and later DeVille)	
Large bolts	141
Small (bracket) bolts	63
Hub/bearing mounting bolts	
DeVille	
1994 through 1999 models	52
2000 and later models	50
Seville	
1992 through 1998 models	52
1999 and later models	50
Leaf spring retainer bolts (1992 Seville models)	21
Stabilizer bar	
Bracket bolt	
DeVille	
1994 through 1999 models	44
2000 and later models	24
Seville	
1992 through 1997 models	44
1998 and later models	24
Link nut	
DeVille	
1994 and 1995 models	38
1996 through 1999 models	44
2000 and later models	132 in-lbs
Seville	
1992 through 1997 models	44
1998 and 1999 models	132 in-lbs
2000 and later models	108 in-lbs
Struts (1992 Seville)	
Strut upper mounting nut	65
Strut-to-control arm pinch bolt	40

Torque specifications

Ft-lbs (unless otherwise indicated)

Rear suspension (continued)

Shock absorbers
  Upper mounting nut
    DeVille
      1994 through 1999 models 55
      2000 and later models.. 18
    Seville
      1993 through 1997 models 55
      1998 and later models.. 18
  Lower mounting bolt/nut
    Deville
      1994 through 1999 models 75
      2000 and later models.. 18
    Seville
      1993 through 1997 models 75
      1998 and later models.. 18

Steering

Airbag module-to-steering wheel screws... 27 in-lbs
Intermediate shaft pinch bolt
  1999 and earlier models.. 35
  2000 and later models.. 33
Power steering pump mounting bolts
  DeVille
    1994 through 1999 models.. 18
    2000 and later models 37
  Seville
    1992 through 1997 models.. 18
    1998 and later models 37
Tie-rod end-to-steering knuckle nut*.. 35
Steering column mounting fasteners... 15 to 20
Steering gear mounting bolts
  DeVille
    1994 through 1999 models.. 50
    2000 and later models 70
  Seville
    1992 through 1997 models.. 50
    1998 and later models 89
Steering wheel nut 30

If necessary, tighten the nut an additional amount to allow insertion of the cotter pin, on models so equipped (don't loosen the nut to insert the cotter pin).

---

1   General information

Refer to illustrations 1.1a, 1.1b, 1.3 and 1.4

Suspension

The front suspension is a MacPherson strut design. The steering knuckles are located by control arms which are mounted to the subframe. The lower end of the steering knuckle pivots on a balljoint attached to the outer end of the control arm. The control arms are connected by a stabilizer bar, which reduces body lean during cornering **(see illustrations)**.

The rear suspension on the 1992 Seville is fully independent with a transversely mounted leaf spring. This single leaf is constructed of durable, lightweight composite material. The rear knuckle pivots on the end of the control arm and is supported laterally by a shock absorber/strut assembly.

The rear suspension on 1993 through 1997 Sevilles and 1994 through 1999 DeVilles is fully independent with each suspension knuckle supported by a lower control

arm, an upper control arm, a coil spring and dampened by a telescopic-type shock absorber. A rear suspension toe link, attached to the end of the trailing arm and the suspension crossmember, alters the toe setting during cornering maneuvers. A stabilizer bar minimizes body roll **(see illustration)**.

The rear suspension on 1998 and later Sevilles and 2000 and later DeVilles is a trailing-type control arm and coil spring design, dampened by a telescopic type shock absorber. A rear suspension toe link, attached to the end of the trailing arm and the suspension crossmember, alters the toe setting during cornering maneuvers. As with the other suspension designs, a stabilizer bar is connected to both trailing arms to reduce body roll **(see illustration)**.

Steering

All vehicles covered by this manual have power rack-and-pinion steering systems. The components making up the system are the steering wheel, steering column, rack-and-pinion assembly, tie-rods and tie-rod ends. The power steering system has a belt-driven

pump to provide hydraulic pressure.

In the power steering system, the motion of turning the steering wheel is transferred through the column to the pinion shaft in the rack-and-pinion assembly. Teeth on the pinion shaft are meshed with teeth on the rack, so when the shaft is turned, the rack is moved left or right in the housing. A rotary control valve in the rack-and-pinion unit directs hydraulic fluid under pressure from the power steering pump to either side of the integral rack piston, thereby reducing manual steering force. Depending on which side of the piston this hydraulic pressure is applied to, the rack will be forced either left or right, which moves the tie-rods, etc. If the power steering system loses hydraulic pressure it will still function manually, though with increased effort.

The steering column is a collapsible, energy-absorbing type, designed to compress in the event of a front end collision to minimize injury to the driver. The column also houses the ignition switch lock, key warning buzzer, turn signal controls, headlight dimmer control and windshield wiper controls.

1.1a Front suspension and steering components (1996 and earlier DeVille shown, 1996 and earlier Seville similar)

1	Tie-rod end	3	Control arm	5	Height sensor link	7	Strut/coil spring assembly
2	Tie-rod	4	Brake reaction rod	6	Stabilizer bar	8	Stabilizer bar link

1.1b Front suspension and steering components (2000 and later DeVille shown, 1998 and later Seville similar)

1	Strut/coil spring assembly	3	Control arm	5	Tie-rod	7	Stabilizer bar
2	Steering knuckle	4	Balljoint	6	Steering gear		

10

1.3 Rear suspension components (1999 and earlier DeVille shown, 1993 through 1997 Seville similar)

1 Rear suspension support	4 Upper control arm	6 Stabilizer bar
2 Lower control arm	5 Stabilizer bar link	7 Toe link
3 Coil spring		

1.4 Rear suspension components (2000 and later DeVille shown, 1998 and later Seville similar)

1 Toe link	4 Coil spring	7 Stabilizer bar bracket
2 Shock absorber	5 Control arm	8 Stabilizer bar
3 Hub and bearing assembly	6 Stabilizer bar link	9 Rear suspension support

The ignition and steering wheel can both be locked while the vehicle is parked. Due to the column's collapsible design, it's important that only the specified screws, bolts and nuts be used as designated and that they're tightened to the specified torque. Other precautions particular to this design are noted in appropriate Sections.

Precautions

Frequently, when working on the suspension or steering system components, you may come across fasteners which seem impossible to loosen. These fasteners on the underside of the vehicle are continually subjected to water, road grime, mud, etc., and can become rusted or "frozen," making them extremely difficult to remove. In order to unscrew these stubborn fasteners without damaging them (or other components), be sure to use lots of penetrating oil and allow it to soak in for a while. Using a wire brush to clean exposed threads will also ease removal of the nut or bolt and prevent damage to the threads. Sometimes a sharp blow with a hammer and punch is effective in breaking the bond between a nut and bolt threads, but care must be taken to prevent the punch from slipping off the fastener and ruining the threads. Heating the stuck fastener and surrounding area with a torch sometimes helps too, but isn't recommended because of the obvious dangers associated with fire. Long breaker bars and extension, or "cheater," pipes will increase leverage, but never use an extension pipe on a ratchet - the ratcheting mechanism could be damaged. Sometimes, turning the nut or bolt in the tightening (clockwise) direction first will help to break it loose. Fasteners that require drastic measures to unscrew should always be replaced with new ones.

Since most of the procedures that are dealt with in this Chapter involve jacking up the vehicle and working underneath it, a good pair of jackstands will be needed. A hydraulic floor jack is the preferred type of jack to lift the vehicle, and it can also be used to support certain components during various operations. **Warning 1:** *Never, under any circumstances, rely on a jack to support the vehicle while working on it. Also, whenever any of the suspension or steering fasteners are loosened or removed they must be inspected and, if necessary, replaced with new ones of the same part number or of original equipment quality and design. Torque specifications must be followed for proper reassembly and component retention. Never attempt to heat or straighten suspension or steering components. Instead, replace bent or damaged parts with new ones.*

Warning 2: *Whenever any of the suspension or steering fasteners are loosened or removed, they must be inspected and, if necessary, replaced with new ones of the same part number or of original equipment quality and design. Torque specifications must be followed for proper reassembly and component retention. Never attempt to heat or straighten any suspension or steering compo-*

2.2 Mark the position of the steering knuckle in the strut (this will help you get the camber setting close during reassembly)

nents. Instead, replace any bent or damaged part with a new one.
Note: *These vehicles have a combination of standard and metric fasteners on the various suspension and steering components, so it would be a good idea to have both types of tools available when beginning work.*

---

2 Strut/coil spring assembly (front) - removal, inspection and installation

---

Warning: *Always replace the struts and/or coil springs in pairs - never replace just one strut or one coil spring (this could cause dangerous handling peculiarities).*

Removal

Refer to illustrations 2.2, 2.3, 2.6 and 2.8

1   Apply the parking brake and block the rear wheels to keep the vehicle from rolling. Loosen the wheel lug nuts, raise the front of the vehicle and support it securely on jackstands. Remove the wheel.

2   Mark the relationship of the strut to the steering knuckle **(see illustration)**. This will help preserve alignment when the strut is reinstalled. **Note:** *If new struts are being installed, the front wheels will have to be aligned after the job has been completed.*

3   Remove the brake hose bracket and ABS wiring harness bracket from the strut **(see illustration)**.

4   Remove the strut-to-knuckle nuts **(see illustration 2.3)** and knock the bolts out with a soft-face hammer.

5   On 1999 and earlier DeVille models and 1997 and earlier Seville models, disconnect the stabilizer bar link from the strut.

6   Separate the strut from the steering knuckle **(see illustration)**. Be careful not to overextend the inner CV joint or stretch the brake hose.

7   If equipped, unplug the electrical connector from the strut.

8   Have an assistant support the strut

2.3 Strut lower mounting details

A   *Brake hose bracket*
B   *ABS sensor harness bracket*
C   *Strut-to-knuckle nuts/bolts*

2.6 Push in on the strut while pulling out on the top of the brake disc to separate the knuckle and strut

2.8 Strut upper mounting bolts

assembly. Remove the three strut upper mounting nuts or bolts **(see illustration)**. Remove the assembly out through the fenderwell.

Inspection

9   Check the strut body for leaking fluid, dents, cracks and other obvious damage

10

**3.4   After the spring has been compressed, remove the
damper shaft nut**

3.5a Remove the bearing cap . . .

which would warrant repair or replacement.

10   Check the coil spring for chips and cracks in the spring coating (this will cause premature spring failure due to corrosion). Inspect the spring seat for hardening, cracks and general deterioration.

11   If wear or damage is evident, replace the strut. Proceed to Section 3 for the strut/coil spring disassembly procedure.

Installation

12   Install the strut/coil spring assembly. Once the strut is in place in the strut tower, install the upper mounting nuts or bolts so the strut/coil spring assembly won't fall back through. This may require an assistant, since the strut is quite heavy and awkward. If equipped, reconnect the electrical connector to the strut.

13   Slide the steering knuckle into the strut flange and insert the two bolts, with the bolt heads pointing towards the front of the vehicle. Install the nuts, align the marks you made in Step 2 and tighten the nuts to the torque listed in this Chapter's Specifications.

14   On 1999 and earlier DeVilles and 1997 and earlier Sevilles, reconnect the stabilizer bar link to the strut and tighten the nut to the torque listed in this Chapter's Specifications.

15   Reconnect the brake hose and ABS harness brackets to the strut, tightening the bolts securely.

16   Install the wheel, lower the vehicle and tighten the lug nuts to the torque listed in the Chapter 1 Specifications.

17   Tighten the three upper mounting nuts or bolts to the torque listed in this Chapter's Specifications.

18   Have the front end alignment checked and, if necessary, adjusted.

---

3   Strut or coil spring (front) - replacement

Refer to illustrations 3.4, 3.5a, 3.5b, 3.6, 3.7a and 3.7b

Warning 1: *Disassembling a strut is a potentially dangerous job. Be very careful and follow the instructions closely or serious injury may result. Use only a high-quality spring compressor and carefully follow the manufacturer's instructions furnished with the tool. After removing the coil spring from the strut assembly, set it aside in a safe, isolated area.*

Warning 2: *Always replace the struts and/or coil springs in pairs - never replace just one strut or one coil spring (this could cause dangerous handling peculiarities).*

1   If the struts exhibit the telltale signs of wear (leaking fluid, loss of dampening capability) explore all options before beginning any work. Rebuilt or new strut assemblies (some complete with springs) may be available on an exchange basis which eliminates much time and work. Check on the cost and availability of parts before removing the strut.

2   Remove the strut and spring assembly following the procedure described in Section 2. Mount the strut assembly in a vise. Cushion the vise jaws with rags or blocks of wood.

3   Following the tool manufacturer's instructions, install the spring compressor (which can be obtained at most auto parts stores or equipment yards on a daily rental basis) on the spring and compress it sufficiently to relieve all pressure from the spring seat. This can be verified by wiggling the spring seat.

4   Loosen the damper shaft nut while using the proper tool to hold the shaft stationary **(see illustration)**.

5   Lift the bearing cap, upper spring seat and upper insulator off the damper shaft **(see illustrations)**. Inspect the bearing in the spring seat for smooth operation and replace it if necessary.

6   Carefully remove the compressed spring assembly **(see illustration)** and set it in a safe place. **Warning:** *Don't position your head near the end of the spring!*

7   Assemble the new strut beginning with the lower spring insulator and spring, then the upper spring insulator **(see illustration)**, spring seat and bearing cap. Position the

**3.5b . . . and the upper spring seat and
insulator from the damper shaft**

**3.6 Remove the compressed spring
assembly - be EXTREMELY CAREFUL
when handling the spring!**

**3.7a Install the upper spring seat with the
flat facing the steering knuckle flange**

spring seat and bearing cap with the flats facing the steering knuckle flange **(see illustration)**.

8   Install the damper shaft nut and tighten it to the torque listed in this Chapter's Specifications.

9   Install the strut and spring assembly as outlined in Section 2.

10   Have the front end alignment checked and, if necessary, adjusted.

---

4   Steering knuckle - removal and installation

Warning: *Dust created by the brake system is harmful to your health. Never blow it out with compressed air and don't inhale any of it. Do not, under any circumstances, use petroleum-based solvents to clean brake parts. Use brake system cleaner only.*

Removal

Refer to illustration 4.10

1   Remove the center cap from the wheel.

2   Apply the parking brake and block the rear wheels to keep the vehicle from rolling. Use a breaker bar and socket and loosen the driveaxle/hub nut with the weight of the vehicle on the wheel.

3   Loosen the wheel lug nuts slightly, raise the front of the vehicle and support it securely on jackstands placed under the frame. Remove the wheel and the driveaxle/hub nut.

4   Remove the brake caliper and the brake disc, and suspend the brake caliper using a piece of wire or rope.

5   Disconnect the electrical connector from the wheel speed sensor (see Chapter 9).

6   Remove the driveaxle/hub nut. Insert a prybar through the caliper inspection window and into the cooling vanes of the brake disc to hold the hub stationary while removing the nut. Pull the brake disc off the hub.

7   Mark the position of the strut to the steering knuckle **(see illustration 2.2)**. Remove the nuts, but don't drive out the bolts at this time.

8   Separate the tie-rod end from the steer-

3.7b The bearing cap must also be positioned with the flat facing the knuckle flange

ing knuckle arm (see Section 20) and the control arm balljoint from the steering knuckle (see Section 7).

9   Attach a puller to the hub flange and push the driveaxle out of the hub (see Chapter 8). Hang the driveaxle with a piece of wire to prevent damage to the inner CV joint. Remove the hub and bearing assembly, if necessary (see Section 5).

10   Support the knuckle and drive out the two strut-to-knuckle bolts with a soft-face hammer. Remove the steering knuckle from the strut **(see illustration)**.

Installation

11   Position the knuckle in the strut and insert the two bolts, with the bolt heads pointing towards the front of the vehicle. Tap the bolts into place and install the nuts, but don't tighten them at this time.

12   Install the driveaxle in the hub.

13   Connect the control arm and the tie-rod end to the steering knuckle and tighten the nuts to the torque values listed in this Chapter's Specifications. Install new cotter pins, on models so equipped.

14   Align the strut-to-knuckle marks and tighten the nuts to the torque listed in this Chapter's Specifications.

15   Reconnect the ABS speed sensor electrical connector.

16   Install the brake disc and caliper (see

Chapter 9).

17   Tighten the driveaxle/hub nut securely.

18   Install the wheel, lower the vehicle and tighten the lug nuts to the torque listed in the Chapter 1 Specifications.

19   Tighten the driveaxle/hub nut to the torque specified in Chapter 8.

20   Have the front end alignment checked and, if necessary, adjusted.

---

5   Hub and wheel bearing assembly (front) - removal and installation

---

Note: *The front hub and wheel bearing assembly is sealed-for-life and must be replaced as a unit.*

Removal

Refer to illustrations 5.6a, 5.6b, 5.7 and 5.8

1   Apply the parking brake and block the rear wheels to keep the vehicle from rolling. Remove the hubcap or wheel cover and loosen the driveaxle/hub nut.

2   Loosen the wheel lug nuts, raise the front of the vehicle and support it securely on jackstands. Remove the wheel.

3   Remove the brake caliper and hang it out of the way with a piece of wire (see Chapter 9). Disconnect the ABS speed sensor electrical connector.

4   Remove the driveaxle/hub nut. Insert a prybar through the caliper inspection window and into the cooling vanes of the brake disc to hold the hub stationary while removing the nut. Pull the brake disc off the hub.

5   Attach a puller to the hub flange and tighten it just enough to push the driveaxle in a little, breaking loose the splines from the hub.

6   Remove the hub retaining bolts. On early models the bolts are accessed through the opening in the hub flange **(see illustration)**. On later models they are accessed from the back side of the steering knuckle **(see illustration)**. The bolts on later models can be accessed without removing the driveaxle if you have the right tool setup (there's not much room to work), and can be loosened a little at a time as the hub and bearing assembly is withdrawn front the

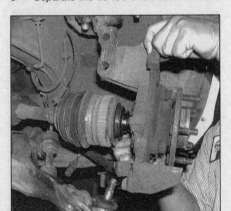

4.10 Separate the steering knuckle from the driveaxle and strut

5.6a On early models, unscrew the hub bolts through the flange

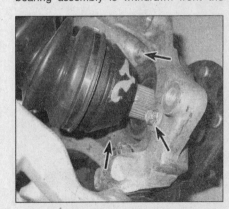

5.6b On later models, the hub bolts are accessed from the rear of the steering knuckle

5.7 If the driveaxle has been left in place, you'll probably have to push it out of the hub with a puller while you wiggle the hub out of the steering knuckle

5.10 If equipped, install a new O-ring on the wheel bearing assembly

steering knuckle. If your tool setup won't allow this, you'll have to remove the driveaxle (see Chapter 8).

7   Wiggle the hub and bearing assembly back-and-forth and pull it out of the steering knuckle (and off the driveaxle, if it was left in place), along with the brake disc shield, if equipped **(see illustration)**.

8   If the hub and bearing assembly is being

6.2 Remove the stabilizer bar link nut/bolt - note the arrangement of washers, bushings and spacer (2000 and later Deville models and 1998 and later Seville models)

5.8 Pry the seal out of the knuckle with a screwdriver (not all models are equipped with a seal)

replaced with a new one, it's a good idea to replace the dust seal in the back of the steering knuckle (if equipped). To replace the seal, disconnect the stabilizer bar and the balljoint from the control arm and pull the steering knuckle and strut assembly off the driveaxle stub shaft. If you can't pull the knuckle out far enough to clear the stub shaft, remove the driveaxle. Pry the seal out of the knuckle with a screwdriver **(see illustration)**.

Installation

Refer to illustrations 5.9 and 5.10

9   If removed, drive the new dust seal into the knuckle with a large socket or a seal driver and a hammer **(see illustration)**. Try not to cock the seal in the bore.

10   If equipped, install a new O-ring around the rear of the bearing and push it up against the bearing flange **(see illustration)**.

11   Clean the mating surfaces on the steering knuckle, bearing flange and knuckle bore. Lubricate the outside diameter of the bearing and the seal lips with high-temperature grease and insert the hub and bearing into the steering knuckle (and over the driveaxle, if it was left in place). Position the brake disc shield (on models so equipped) and install

6.3 Remove the two bolts from each stabilizer bar bushing clamp

5.9 Using a large socket, drive the new seal into place

the three bolts, tightening them to the torque listed in this Chapter's Specifications.

12   Install the driveaxle, if removed (see Chapter 8).

13   Attach the control arm to the steering knuckle, if it was separated (see Section 7).

14   Install the brake disc and caliper (see Chapter 9). Reconnect the ABS speed sensor electrical connector.

15   Install the driveaxle/hub nut and tighten it securely.

16   Install the wheel, lower the vehicle and tighten the lug nuts to the torque listed in the Chapter 1 Specifications.

17   Tighten the driveaxle/hub nut to the torque listed in the Chapter 8 Specifications.

6   Stabilizer bar (front) - removal and installation

Removal

Refer to illustrations 6.2 and 6.3

1   Loosen the lug nuts on both front wheels, raise the front of the vehicle and support it securely on jackstands. Apply the parking brake and block the rear wheels to keep the vehicle from rolling off the jackstands. Remove the front wheels.

2   Detach the stabilizer bar links from the struts or the control arms. On models where the links are connected to the control arms, note how the link bushings, spacers and washers are arranged **(see illustration)**. **Note:** *The stabilizer link on 2000 and later Deville models and 1998 and later Seville models is connected to the control arm; on earlier models the stabilizer link is attached to the strut housing.*

3   Remove the stabilizer bar bracket bolts **(see illustration)**.

4   If you're working on a 2000 and later DeVille or a 1998 and later Seville, detach the right-side tie-rod end from the steering knuckle (see Section 20).

5   If you're working on a 1999 and earlier DeVille or a 1997 and earlier Seville, detach the exhaust pipe from the rear exhaust manifold (see Chapter 2).

6   Turn the right-side steering knuckle to the left.

7   Slide the bar over the right steering

7.3 Remove the cotter pin and loosen the nut from the balljoint stud

7.4 Separate the balljoint from the steering knuckle

7.6 Remove the control arm pivot bolts/nuts - 2000 DeVille shown

knuckle, then pull down until the bar clears the frame.

8   Inspect the bushings for wear and damage and replace them if necessary.

Installation

9   Maneuver the stabilizer bar into position.

10   Loosely install the bushings and clamps.

11   Center the bar in the vehicle and connect the stabilizer bar to the links. Tighten the fasteners to the torque listed in this Chapter's Specifications.

12   The remainder of installation is the reverse of removal. Install the wheels and lower the vehicle. Tighten the lug nuts to the torque specified in Chapter 1.

7   Control arm (front) - removal and installation

Removal

Refer to illustrations 7.3, 7.4 and 7.6

1   Loosen the wheel lug nuts, raise the front of the vehicle and support it securely on jackstands. Apply the parking brake and block the rear wheels to keep the vehicle from rolling off the jackstands. Remove the wheel.

2   If you're working on a 2000 and later DeVille or a 1998 and later Seville, detach the stabilizer bar link(s) from the control arm(s). If only one control arm is being removed, disconnect only that end of the stabilizer bar. If both control arms are being removed, disconnect both ends (see Section 6).

3   Remove the cotter pin and loosen the balljoint stud-to-steering knuckle nut **(see illustration)**.

4   Using a balljoint separator (available at most auto parts stores) positioned between the control arm and steering knuckle, separate the balljoint from the knuckle **(see illustration)**. If the proper balljoint separator is not available, try striking the steering knuckle boss with a hammer to jar the balljoint stud loose. If that doesn't work, use a "picklefork" type balljoint separator, but note that the use of this tool will almost surely damage the balljoint boot. **Caution:** *When removing the balljoint from the knuckle, be careful not to*

8.3a Check for movement between the balljoint and steering knuckle when prying up

overextend the inner CV joint or it may be damaged. Remove the nut from the ballstud.

5   On models so equipped, detach the road sensing suspension position sensor from the control arm.

6   Remove the control arm-to-frame fasteners and detach the control arm **(see illustration)**. On 1996 and earlier models, remove the pivot bolt from the rear of the control arm and the brake reaction rod nut and bushing from the front.

7   The control arm bushings are replaceable, but special tools and expertise are necessary to do the job. Carefully inspect the bushings for hardening, excessive wear and cracks. If they appear to be worn or deteriorated, take the control arm to a dealer service department or suspension repair shop.

Installation

8   Position the control arm in the suspension support and install the fasteners. Do not tighten them completely at this time.

9   Insert the balljoint stud into the steering knuckle boss, install the nut and tighten it to the torque listed in this Chapter's Specifications. If necessary, tighten the nut a little more if the cotter pin hole doesn't line up with an opening on the nut. Install a new cotter pin.

10   On 2000 and later DeVille models or 1998 and later Seville models, install the stabilizer bar-to-control arm bolt, spacer, bushings and washers and tighten the nut to the torque listed in this Chapter's Specifications.

8.3b With the prybar positioned between the steering knuckle boss and the balljoint, pry down and check for play in the balljoint - if there's any play, replace the balljoint

11   On models so equipped, connect the road sensing suspension position sensor to the control arm.

12   Using a floor jack, raise the outer end of the control arm to simulate normal ride height, then tighten the control arm fasteners to the torque listed in this Chapter's Specifications. **Caution:** *If the bolts aren't tightened with the control arm raised to simulate normal ride height, control arm bushing damage may occur.*

13   Install the wheel and lower the vehicle. Tighten the lug nuts to the torque listed in the Chapter 1 Specifications.

8   Balljoints - check and replacement

Check

Refer to illustrations 8.3a and 8.3b

1   Apply the parking brake and block the rear wheels to keep the vehicle from rolling. Raise the front of the vehicle and support it securely on jackstands.

2   Visually inspect the rubber seal for damage, deterioration and leaking grease. If any of these conditions are noticed, the balljoint should be replaced.

3   Place a large prybar under the balljoint and attempt to push the balljoint up. Next,

10

8.8 Center-punch the rivets then drill out the rivet heads - use progressively larger drill bits until the rivet heads are removed (be careful not to distort the hole in the control arm)

8.11 Replacement balljoint details (typical) - be sure to tighten the bolts to the torque specified on the instruction sheet or in this Chapter's Specifications

1   *Replacement balljoint*
2   *Bolt*
3   *Grease fitting*
4   *Nut*
5   *Castle nut*
6   *Cotter pin*

position the prybar between the steering knuckle and control arm and pry down **(see illustrations)**. If any movement is seen or felt during either of these checks, a worn out balljoint is indicated.

4   Have an assistant grasp the tire at the top and bottom and move the top of the tire in-and-out. Touch the balljoint stud nut. If any looseness is felt, suspect a worn-out balljoint stud or a widened hole in the steering knuckle boss. If the latter problem exists, the steering knuckle should be replaced as well as the balljoint.

5   Separate the control arm from the steering knuckle (see Section 7). Using your fingers (don't use pliers), try to twist the stud in the socket. If the stud turns, replace the balljoint.

Replacement

Refer to illustrations 8.8 and 8.11
Note: *This procedure applies to 1998 and earlier DeVille models and 1997 and earlier Seville models only. The balljoint on all other models is not replaceable separately; if it's worn out, the entire control arm must be replaced.*

6   Apply the parking brake and block the rear wheels to keep the vehicle from rolling. Loosen the wheel lug nuts, raise the front of the vehicle and support it securely on jackstands. Remove the wheel.

7   Loosen the balljoint nut and separate the balljoint from the steering knuckle **(see illustration 7.4)**. Temporarily insert the balljoint stud back into the steering knuckle (loosely). This will hold the assembly stationary while drilling out the rivets.

8   Using a 1/8-inch drill bit, drill a pilot hole into the center of each balljoint-to-control arm rivet **(see illustration)**. Be careful not to drill through and damage the CV joint boot in the process.

9   Using a 1/2-inch drill bit, drill the head off each rivet. Work slowly and carefully to avoid deforming the holes in the control arm.

10   Pull the control arm and balljoint down to remove the balljoint stud from the steering knuckle, then dislodge the balljoint from the

control arm.

11   Position the new balljoint on the control arm and install the bolts (supplied in the balljoint kit) from the bottom of the control arm **(see illustration)**. Tighten the bolts to the torque specified in the new balljoint instruction sheet or in this Chapter's Specifications.

12   Insert the balljoint into the steering knuckle, install the castellated nut, tighten it to the torque listed in this Chapter's Specifications and install a new cotter pin. It may be necessary to tighten the nut further to align the cotter pin hole with an opening in the nut, which is acceptable. Never loosen the castle nut to allow cotter pin insertion.

13   Install the wheel, lower the vehicle and tighten the lug nuts to the torque listed in the Chapter 1 Specifications.

9   Strut (rear, 1992 Seville models) - removal and installation

Refer to illustration 9.9
Warning: *Always replace the struts in pairs - never replace just one strut (this could cause dangerous handling peculiarities).*

1   Loosen the rear wheel lug nuts.
2   Block the front wheels. Raise the rear of the vehicle and support it securely on jackstands placed under the frame.
3   Remove the rear wheels.
4   Remove the rear brake caliper and suspend it with a piece of wire or rope (see Chapter 9).
5   Install two of the wheel lug nuts onto the hub to retain the brake disc.
6   Disconnect the stabilizer bar from the strut (see Section 17).
7   If you're removing the left-side strut, detach the electronic level control (ELC) height sensor link from the control arm. Also disconnect the Computer Controlled Ride (CCR) electrical connector from the top of the strut. Also, on both the ELC and CCR systems, disconnect the air line from the strut **(see illustration 10.2)**.
8   Place a floor jack under the control arm

and raise the jack slightly to support the control arm. **Warning:** *The control arm must be supported by the floor jack before removing any strut fasteners or the control arm will be forced down by spring pressure, possibly causing serious injury or damage. The floor jack must remain in place under the control arm until the strut in reinstalled.*

9   Remove the strut upper mounting nut and insulator **(see illustration)**.

10   Loosen the knuckle-to-control arm pivot bolt. Slowly lower the control arm slightly with the floor jack and pull the strut upper mounting stud out of the suspension support.

11   Pivot the strut and knuckle outward and remove the strut lower pinch bolt. Note how the tang on the strut fits into the knuckle slot.

12   Installation is the reverse of removal. Tighten the fasteners to the torque values listed in this Chapter's Specifications. Refer to Chapter 9 for the torque specifications for the brake caliper mounting bolts.

13   When reconnecting the air lines to the struts, lubricate the fittings with slight amount of petroleum jelly. **Note:** *Before lowering the vehicle, turn the ignition key to the On position and let the Electronic Level Control system pressurize for approximately 45 seconds.*

14   Install the wheels and lug nuts. Lower the vehicle and tighten the lug nuts to the torque listed in the Chapter 1 Specifications.

9.9 Strut upper mounting nut (1992 Seville models)

10.2 To disconnect the air line from the shock absorber, remove this clip and pull the line off the fitting

10.5 Shock absorber lower mounting bolts (2000 and later DeVille models and 1998 and later Seville models)

10.7 Shock absorber upper mounting nuts (2000 and later DeVille models and 1998 and later Seville models)

10 Shock absorber (rear, 1993 and later Seville models, all DeVille models) - removal and installation

Refer to illustrations 10.2, 10.5 and 10.7

Warning: *Always replace the shock absorbers in pairs - never replace just one of them (this could cause dangerous handling peculiarities).*

1   Loosen the rear wheel lug nuts, raise the rear of the vehicle and support it securely on jackstands. Remove the wheel.

2   Disconnect the air line at the shock absorber **(see illustration)**.

3   Support the lower control arm with a floor jack placed under the outer end of the control arm. **Warning:** *The jack must remain in this position until the shock absorber is installed.*

4   If equipped with road-sensing suspension, disconnect the electrical connector from the shock absorber.

5   If you're working on a 1999 or earlier DeVille or a 1997 or earlier Seville, remove the nut and bolt securing the shock absorber to the lower control arm. If you're working on a 2000 or later DeVille or a 1998 or later Seville, remove the two bolts securing the shock absorber to the control arm **(see illustration)**.

6   If you're working on a 1999 or earlier DeVille or a 1997 or earlier Seville, remove the upper mounting nut, retainer and insulator.

7   If you're working on a 2000 or later DeVille or a 1998 or later Seville, open the trunk and pull back the carpet. Remove the dust cover and unscrew the upper mounting nuts **(see illustration)**.

8   Remove the shock absorber.

9   Installation is the reverse of removal, noting the following points:

a) *Tighten the mounting fasteners to the torque listed in this Chapter's Specifications.*

b) *Before lowering the vehicle, turn the*

ignition key to the On position and let the Electronic Level Control system pressurize for approximately 45 seconds.

c) *Lower the vehicle and tighten the lug nuts to the torque listed in the Chapter 1 Specifications.*

11 Leaf spring (rear, 1992 Seville models) - removal and installation

Due to the special tool required to perform this procedure, this job should be entrusted to a professional mechanic. The tool is generally unavailable to the public, and it is dangerous to attempt this job without the proper tool.

12 Coil spring (rear, 1993 and later Seville models and all DeVille models) - removal and installation

Warning: *Always replace the coil springs in pairs - never replace just one of them (this could cause dangerous handling peculiarities).*

1999 and earlier DeVille models, 1997 and earlier Seville models

Refer to illustration 12.6

Removal

1   Loosen the rear wheel lug nuts.

2   Block the front wheels.

3   Raise the rear of the vehicle and support it securely on jackstands placed under the frame.

4   Remove the rear wheels.

5   If you're removing the left-side coil spring, detach the ELC height sensor link from the control arm.

6   Install a suitable interior style spring compressor through the bottom of the control arm and onto the coil spring in accordance with the tool manufacturer's instructions **(see illustration)**. **Note:** *This tool is available at most auto parts stores and equipment rental yards.* Compress the spring enough to relieve all pressure from the spring seats. Stop at this point and be sure to not compress the spring any more than necessary. When you can wiggle the spring, it is compressed enough.

7   Detach the rear stabilizer bar link from the control arm (see Section 17).

8   Detach the lower end of the shock absorber from the control arm (see Section 10). Also detach the air line from the shock absorber (see Section 10).

9   Place a floor jack under the inside edge of the control arm, positioning it so it doesn't interfere with the spring compressor. Raise the jack just enough to support the control arm.

10   Paint alignment marks to indicate the position of the coil spring pigtail in the insulator slot. The coil spring must be oriented in the same position when it is reassembled.

12.6 A typical aftermarket internal-type spring compressor tool: The hooked arms grip the upper coils of the spring, the plate is inserted below the lower coils, and, when the nut on the threaded rod is turned, the spring is compressed

10

12.20 When installing the right-side coil spring, the pigtail at the top of the spring must be pointing toward the front of the vehicle (and when installing the left spring, it must be pointing to the rear)

11   Remove the control arm pivot bolts and detach the control arm from the frame cross-member (see Section 15).
12   Slowly lower the jack and remove the spring and insulators. Carefully remove the spring compressor from the spring.

Installation

13   Installation is the reverse of removal, noting the following points:
a) Replace the insulators if they're damaged or worn.
b) Be sure to position each insulator in the correct position in the control arm and the upper body in alignment with the end of the coil spring pigtail.
c) Before tightening the control arm pivot bolts, raise the outer end of the control arm to simulate normal ride height.
d) Tighten all suspension fasteners to the torque listed in this Chapter's Specifications.
e) Tighten the wheel lug nuts to the torque listed in the Chapter 1 Specifications.

2000 and later DeVille models, 1998 and later Seville models

Refer to illustration 12.20

Removal

14   Loosen the rear wheel lug nuts, raise the rear of the vehicle and support it securely on jackstands. Block the front wheels and remove the rear wheel.
15   Detach the stabilizer bar link from the control arm (see Section 17).
16   Support the lower control arm with a floor jack placed under the end of the control arm. **Warning:** *The jack must remain in this position until the shock absorber is installed.*
17   Detach the shock absorber from the control arm (see Section 10).
18   Detach the toe link from the control arm (see Section 16).
19   Slowly lower the floor jack until the control arm comes to rest against the suspension support. Remove the coil spring.

Installation
20   Installation is the reverse of removal, noting the following points:
a) When installing the coil spring, make sure the insulator is in place on the control arm.
b) If you're installing the left coil spring, the pigtail at the upper end of the spring must be pointing to the rear; if you're installing the right coil spring, the pigtail must be pointing forward **(see illustration)**.
c) Tighten all suspension fasteners to the torque listed in this Chapter's Specifications.
d) Tighten the wheel lug nuts to the torque listed in the Chapter 1 Specifications.

---

13   Hub and wheel bearing assembly (rear) - removal and installation

---

Refer to illustration 13.6
Note: *The rear hub and bearing assembly is sealed for life and must be replaced as a unit.*
1   Loosen the rear wheel lug nuts.
2   Block the front wheels.
3   Raise the rear of the vehicle and support it securely on jackstands placed under the frame.
4   Remove the rear wheel.
5   Remove the rear brake caliper, mounting bracket and brake disc (see Chapter 9). Hang the caliper with a piece of wire - don't let it hang by the brake hose.
6   Rotate the hub to align one of the holes in the flange with each of the mounting bolts and remove the bolts **(see illustration)**. Remove the hub and bearing assembly.
7   Installation is the reverse of removal. Be sure tighten the bolts to the torque listed in this Chapter's Specifications. Tighten the brake fasteners to the torque values listed in the Chapter 9 Specifications.

---

14   Knuckle (rear) - removal and installation

Note: *This procedure applies to 1999 and earlier DeVille models and 1997 and earlier Seville models only.*

Removal

1   Loosen the rear wheel lug nuts.
2   Block the front wheels.
3   Raise the rear of the vehicle and support it securely on jackstands.
4   Remove the rear wheels.
5   Detach the Electronic Level Control (ELC) height sensor link from the control arm (if applicable).
6   Remove the rear brake caliper (see Chapter 9) and suspend it from the body using wire or a piece of rope. Do NOT disconnect the brake hose.
7   Remove the rear brake disc (see Chapter 9) and the hub and bearing assembly (see

13.6 To remove the rear hub and bearing assembly, rotate the hub flange until one of the holes in the flange is aligned with a mounting bolt

Section 13). Also detach the ABS wheel speed sensor electrical connector (and detach the harness from the knuckle, if applicable).

1992 Seville models

8   Remove the strut (see Section 9).
9   Remove the nut and pivot bolt and detach the knuckle from the control arm.
10   Separate the knuckle from the control arm.
11   Proceed to Step 16.

1993 through 1997 Seville models/1994 through 1999 DeVille models

12   Support the outer end of the control arm with a floor jack. Raise the jack just enough to take the force of the coil spring off the knuckle. **Warning:** *The jack must remain in this position throughout the entire procedure.*
13   Detach the toe link from the knuckle (see Section 16).
14   Remove the upper control arm-to-knuckle nut and bolt.
15   Remove the lower control arm-to-knuckle nut and bolt, then separate the knuckle from the control arms.

Installation

16   Installation is the reverse of removal, noting the following points:
a) Tighten all suspension fasteners to the torque listed in this Chapter's Specifications, but before tightening the knuckle-to-control arm bolts and toe link-to-control arm bolt, raise the outer end of the lower control arm with the floor jack to simulate normal ride height.
b) Before lowering the vehicle, turn the ignition key to the On position and let the Electronic Level Control system pressurize for approximately 45 seconds.
c) Tighten the lug nuts to the torque listed in the Chapter 1 Specifications.

15 Control arm(s) (rear) - removal and installation

1992 Seville models

Note: *Replacement of the bushings in the rear control arms requires a number of special tools. If a bushing must be replaced, take the control arm to a dealer service department or other properly equipped repair facility.*

Removal

1 Loosen the rear wheel lug nuts. Block the front wheels, then raise the rear of the vehicle and support it securely on jackstands placed under the frame.
2 Detach the height sensor link from the control arm.
3 Disconnect the stabilizer bar from the strut (see Section 17).
4 Remove the rear brake caliper (see Chapter 9) and suspend it from the body using wire or a piece of rope. Also remove the brake disc.
5 Disconnect the rear ABS wheel speed sensor (see Chapter 9).
6 Loosen, but do not remove the knuckle pivot bolt on the outer end of the control arm. Support the control arm using a floor jack positioned toward the outer end of the control arm.
7 Remove the upper strut mounting nut and insulator. Slowly lower the control arm and detach the strut upper mounting stud from the suspension support.
8 Support the knuckle and remove the control arm-to-knuckle pivot bolt. Remove the strut, knuckle and hub as an assembly.
9 Slowly lower the jack to relieve spring pressure.
10 Remove the control arm pivot bolts.
11 Remove the control arm from the vehicle.

Installation

12 Install the control arm and strut, knuckle and hub assembly, but do not fully tighten the fasteners at this time.
13 Using a floor jack, raise the outer end of the control arm to simulate normal ride height, then tighten the strut upper mounting

bolt, knuckle pivot bolt and control arm pivot bolts to the torque listed in this Chapter's Specifications. **Caution:** *If the bolts aren't tightened with the control arm raised to simulate normal ride height, control arm bushing damage may occur.*
14 The remainder of installation is the reverse of removal.
15 Install the wheel and lug nuts, lower the vehicle and tighten the lug nuts to the torque listed in this Chapter's Specifications.

1993 through 1997 Seville models/1994 through 1999 DeVille models

Lower control arm

Removal

16 Loosen the rear wheel lug nuts. Block the front wheels, then raise the rear of the vehicle and support it securely on jackstands placed under the frame.
17 Remove the coil spring (see Section 12).
18 Remove the toe link (see Section 16).
19 Remove the knuckle-to-lower control arm nut and bolt, then detach the control arm from the knuckle.

Installation

20 Installation is the reverse of removal, noting the following points:
a) *Tighten all suspension fasteners to the torque listed in this Chapter's Specifications, but before tightening the knuckle-to-control arm bolts, control arm inner pivot bolts and toe link bolts, raise the outer end of the lower control arm with the floor jack to simulate normal ride height.*
b) *Before lowering the vehicle, turn the ignition key to the On position and let the Electronic Level Control system pressurize for approximately 45 seconds.*
c) *Tighten the lug nuts to the torque listed in the Chapter 1 Specifications.*

Upper control arm

Removal

21 Loosen the rear wheel lug nuts. Block

the front wheels, then raise the rear of the vehicle and support it securely on jackstands placed under the frame. Remove the wheel.
22 Disconnect the ELC height sensor link.
23 Remove the road sensing suspension position sensor and bracket.
24 Remove the knuckle-to-upper control arm nut and bolt and the upper control arm nut and bolt, then detach the control arm from the vehicle.

Installation

25 Installation is the reverse of removal, noting the following points:
a) *Tighten all suspension fasteners to the torque listed in this Chapter's Specifications, but before tightening the knuckle-to-control arm bolts and the control arm inner pivot bolts, raise the outer end of the lower control arm with a floor jack to simulate normal ride height.*
b) *Before lowering the vehicle, turn the ignition key to the On position and let the Electronic Level Control system pressurize for approximately 45 seconds.*
c) *Tighten the lug nuts to the torque listed in the Chapter 1 Specifications.*

1998 and later Seville models/2000 and later DeVille models

Refer to illustrations 15.35 and 15.37

Removal

26 Loosen the rear wheel lug nuts. Block the front wheels, then raise the rear of the vehicle and support it securely on jackstands placed under the unibody frame members (not under the suspension support). Remove the wheel.
27 Remove the exhaust system (see Chapter 4).
28 Remove the coil springs (see Section 12).
29 Remove the brake calipers and support them with lengths of wire (see Chapter 9). Also remove the brake discs and disconnect the electrical connectors from the wheel speed sensors.
30 Detach all wiring harnesses and air lines from the suspension support.
31 Detach the Electronic Level Control (ELC) link(s) from the control arm(s).
32 Remove the hub and bearing assembly, if necessary (see Section 13).
33 Remove the toe link from the suspension arm to be removed (see Section 16).
34 Remove the stabilizer bar link from the suspension arm to be removed (see Section 17).
35 Place a floor jack under the front and rear portions of the suspension support. Remove the bolts from the front part of the suspension support (see illustration).
36 Remove the two bolts from the rear part of the suspension support, then carefully lower the jacks. Remove the suspension support from under the vehicle.

15.35 Suspension support mounting bolts - 1998 and later Seville models/2000 and later DeVille models

15.37 Control arm pivot bolts (1998 and later Seville models/2000 and later DeVille models)

16.7 Before loosening the toe link-to-suspension support nut, mark the position of the adjusting cam to the suspension support

16.8 Use a small puller to separate the toe link ballstud from the control arm (loosening, but not removing the nut will prevent the link from separating violently)

37 Remove the control arm pivot bolts and detach the control arm from the suspension support **(see illustration)**.

38 Installation is the reverse of removal, noting the following points:

a) *Tighten all suspension fasteners to the torque listed in this Chapter's Specifications, but before tightening the control arm pivot bolts, raise the end of the lower control arm with a floor jack to simulate normal ride height.*

b) *Tighten the brake caliper bolts to the torque listed in the Chapter 9 Specifications.*

c) *Before lowering the vehicle, turn the ignition key to the On position and let the Electronic Level Control system pressurize for approximately 45 seconds.*

d) *Tighten the lug nuts to the torque listed in the Chapter 1 Specifications.*

16 Toe link - removal and installation

1 Loosen the rear wheel lug nuts.
2 Block the front wheels.
3 Raise the vehicle and place it securely on jackstands.
4 Remove the wheel.

1997 and earlier Seville models/1999 and earlier DeVille models

5 Remove the fasteners from each end of the toe link. **Warning:** *The manufacturer states that the toe link-to-knuckle bolt is not reusable and must be replaced with a new one.*
6 Installation is the reverse of removal, noting the following points:

a) *Tighten the mounting fasteners to the torque listed in this Chapter's Specifications.*

b) *Tighten the wheel lug nuts to the torque listed in the Chapter 1 Specifications.*

c) *Have the rear wheel alignment checked and, if necessary, adjusted.*

1998 and later Seville models/2000 and later DeVille models

Refer to illustrations 16.7 and 16.8

7 Mark the position of the toe adjusting cam at the inner end of the toe link **(see illustration)**.
8 Loosen the to link-to-control arm nut, then pop the ballstud out of the control arm using a puller **(see illustration)**. Remove the nut and separate the toe link from the control arm.
9 Remove the exhaust system (see Chapter 4).
10 Remove the two bolts from the rear of the suspension support and lower the rear of the support **(see illustration 15.35)**.
11 To detach the inner end of the link from the suspension support, remove the nut, cam washer and bolt, then detach the link **(see illustration 16.7)**.
12 Installation is the reverse of removal, noting the following points:

a) *Before tightening the link-to-suspension support nut, align the marks you made on the toe adjusting cam and suspension support.*

b) *Tighten all suspension fasteners to the torque listed in this Chapter's Specifications.*

c) *Tighten the wheel lug nuts to the torque listed in the Chapter 1 Specifications.*

d) *Have the rear wheel alignment checked and, if necessary, adjusted.*

17 Stabilizer bar (rear) - removal and installation

Refer to illustration 17.7

1 Loosen the rear wheel lug nuts.
2 Block the front wheels.
3 Raise the rear of the vehicle and place it

securely on jackstands.
4 Remove the rear wheels.
5 If you're working on a 1992 Seville, detach the stabilizer bar from the struts.
6 If you're working on a 1993 through 1997 Seville or a 1994 through 1999 DeVille, detach the stabilizer bar links from the control arms.
7 If you're working on a 1998 or later Seville or a 2000 or later DeVille, detach the stabilizer bar link bolt/bushing assembly from each control arm **(see illustration)**. Note how the bushings and washers are arranged.
8 Remove the stabilizer bar clamp bolts and remove the stabilizer bar.
9 If you're replacing the stabilizer bar and/or the bracket bushings, bend the end of the clamp open and remove the bushings. Note how the bushings are positioned; when they are reinstalled, the slits must be facing the same way.
10 Installation is the reverse of removal. Tighten the fasteners to the torque listed in this Chapter's Specifications.
11 Tighten the wheel lug nuts to the torque listed in the Chapter 1 Specifications.

17.7 Rear stabilizer bar mounting details - 1998 and later Seville/2000 and later DeVille

A *Stabilizer bar link bolt/nut*
B *Bracket bolt*

18.3 Remove the airbag module screws from behind the steering wheel (1998 and earlier Seville models and 1999 and earlier DeVille models)

18.4 On later models, the airbag is secured by spring clips that engage four posts on the airbag; to release them, insert two screwdrivers into the slots and twist, then repeat on the other side

18.5 Lift the airbag module off and disconnect the electrical connectors (the number on your vehicle may differ); to detach the airbag connector, flip up the locking tab, then pull the connector straight off

18 Steering wheel - removal and installation

Warning 1: *These models have airbags. Always disable the airbag system before working in the vicinity of the impact sensors, steering column or instrument panel to avoid the possibility of accidental deployment of the airbag, which could cause personal injury (see Chapter 12).*

Warning 2: *Do not use a memory saving device to preserve the PCM's memory when working on or near airbag system components.*

Steering wheel removal and installation

Refer to illustrations 18.3, 18.4, 18.5, 18.7 and 18.8

1 Park the vehicle with the wheels pointing straight ahead. Disconnect the cable from the negative terminal of the battery (see Chapter 5).

2 Disable the airbag system (see Chapter 12).

3 On 1998 and earlier Seville models and 1999 and earlier DeVille models, remove the screws that secure the airbag module to the steering wheel **(see illustration)**.

4 On 1999 and later Seville models and 2000 and later DeVille models, remove the steering column covers (see Chapter 11). Detach the airbag module by inserting a pair of screwdrivers into the slots in the backside of the steering wheel, then twist the screwdrivers to spread the retaining springs, which will release the airbag retaining posts **(see illustration)**. There are four retaining posts; free one side, then the other.

5 Lift the airbag module carefully away from the steering wheel and disconnect the electrical connectors **(see illustration)**.

6 Remove the airbag module. **Warning:** *When carrying the airbag module, keep the*

18.7 Mark the relationship of the steering wheel to the steering shaft

driver's side of it away from your body, and when you set it down (in an isolated area), have the driver's side facing up.

7 Remove the steering wheel nut, then mark the relationship of the steering wheel to the shaft **(see illustration)**.

8 Install a steering wheel puller (available at most auto parts stores) and turn the center bolt until the wheel is free **(see illustration)**. On early models (steering wheels with two threaded holes in the hub), a traditional bolt-type steering wheel puller can be used. On later models, no threaded holes are provided; a steering wheel puller with special leg attachments, which engage with two holes in the steering wheel hub, must be used. **Caution:** *Never strike the steering wheel or the steering shaft in an attempt to remove the steering wheel.*

9 Remove the puller and lift the steering wheel off the shaft, feeding the wiring harness through the hole in the wheel.

10 Installation is the reverse of removal, noting the following points:

18.8 Use a steering wheel puller to remove the steering wheel (be sure to use the proper type; this is an early model, with threaded holes in the hub. Later models don't have threaded holes)

a) *Make sure the airbag clockspring is centered before installing the steering wheel (see Steps 16 through 19).*

b) *When installing the steering wheel, align the marks on the shaft and the steering wheel hub.*

c) *Tighten the steering wheel nut to the torque listed in this Chapter's Specifications.*

d) *On 1998 and earlier Seville models and 1999 and earlier DeVille models, tighten the airbag retaining screws to the torque listed in this Chapter's Specifications.*

e) *On 1999 and later Seville models and 2000 and later DeVille models, install the airbag module on the steering wheel and push it into place until the retaining posts engage with the retaining springs.*

f) *Enable the airbag system (see Chapter 12).*

10

18.13 To remove the clockspring from the steering shaft, remove this snap-ring

18.16 To center the clockspring on 1998 and earlier models, depress the spring lock and rotate the hub in the direction of the arrow on the housing until it stops, then turn it in the opposite direction 2-1/2 turns and release the spring lock

18.18 On later model clocksprings with a centering window, the clockspring is centered when the window (A) appears yellow and the two arrows (B) are aligned

Clockspring replacement and centering procedure

Refer to illustrations 18.13, 18.16, 18.18 and 18.22
Warning: *The airbag clockspring assembly is a ribbon-like mechanism which allows electrical current to flow to the airbag module regardless of steering wheel position. If the clockspring becomes uncentered, it may break when the vehicle is returned to service.*
Note: *It is not necessary to remove the clockspring unless repairs to the steering column are required. The clockspring does not have to be centered unless the center hub of the clockspring was moved while the steering wheel was off or the clockspring was removed from the steering column. Follow the centering procedure if the clockspring was removed and the alignment was changed.*
11   On some models it may be necessary to remove the steering column covers (see Chapter 11).
12   Make sure the front wheels are pointed straight ahead.
13   Remove the snap-ring retaining the clockspring to the steering shaft **(see illustration)**.
14   Remove the clockspring from the steering column.
15   Carefully withdraw the clockspring harness and connector through the steering column. Working on the harness connector at the base of the steering column, attach a piece of wire or string to the connector and gently withdraw the assembly. Allow the wire to be drawn up through the column and out the top (face). Disconnect the wire from the harness connector and allow the wire to remain in position until the clockspring is installed. This extra step will make the installation of the clockspring harness through the steering column quicker and easier.

1998 and earlier models

Note: *On 1994 and earlier models there are two different styles of clocksprings; one winds-up clockwise and the other winds-up counterclockwise. 1995 through 1998 models use a similar style clockspring, but only*

winds-up clockwise.
16   On models with a spring lock tab on the back, hold the clockspring assembly with the bottom side facing up, depress the spring lock and rotate the hub in the direction of the arrow until it stops **(see illustration)**. The arrow is stamped onto the back of the clockspring assembly. The clockspring should wind up tight against the center hub (don't apply too much force, though).
17   Rotate the hub in the opposite direction 2-1/2 turns and then release the spring lock to secure the locking tab. proceed to Step 20.

1999 and later models

Note: *On 1999 and later models, two style clocksprings are used; one type has a window on the front face and no spring lock tab on the back. The other type does not have a window but does have a spring lock tab.*
18   If your clockspring has a window on the front and no spring lock tab on the back,

18.22 On early models, when properly installed, the clockspring will be centered with the marks aligned (A) and the tab fitted between the projections on the top of the steering column (B)

hold it face up and turn the hub clockwise until it stops (don't apply excessive force). Now slowly turn the hub counterclockwise at least two turns until the window turns yellow and the arrows on the hub and the housing are in alignment **(see illustration)**. Proceed to Step 20.
19   If your clockspring does not have a window on the front, turn it over and depress the spring lock on the back, then rotate the hub in the direction of the arrow on the housing until it stops (don't apply too much force). Now turn the hub 2-1/2 turns in the opposite direction and release the spring lock tab. Proceed to the next Step.

All models
20   Before installing the clockspring onto the steering column, make sure the block tooth on the steering shaft is at the 12 o'clock position, the wheels straight ahead and the ignition in LOCK.
21   Pull the clockspring harness through the steering column using the wire or string.
22   Seat the clockspring on the steering column and install the snap-ring. On early models, the tab should be at the top of the clockspring and the arrows on the face of the clockspring should be aligned **(see illustration)**. On later models, **see illustration 18.18** for proper alignment.
23   Install the steering wheel and the airbag as described earlier in this Section.
24   Enable the airbag system (see Chapter 12).

19   Steering column - removal and installation

Refer to illustrations 19.6, 19.7 and 19.9
Warning 1: *These models are equipped with airbags. Always disable the airbag system before working in the vicinity of any airbag system component to avoid the possibility of accidental deployment of the airbag(s), which could cause personal injury (see Chapter 12).*

19.6 Remove this cover from the lower end of the steering column

19.7 Mark the steering shaft to the intermediate shaft, then remove the nut and pinch bolt

19.9 Steering column mounting fasteners

Warning 2: *Do not use a memory saving device to preserve the PCM's memory when working on or near airbag system components.*

Removal

1   Park the vehicle with the wheels in the straight-ahead position. Disconnect the cable from the negative terminal of the battery (see Chapter 5, Section 1). Disable the airbag system (see Chapter 12).
2   Remove the steering column covers (see Chapter 11).
3   Remove the steering wheel and the airbag clockspring (see Section 18).
4   Remove the lower instrument panel trim (under the steering column), the knee bolster and the heater/air conditioning duct (see Chapter 11).
5   Detach the shift cable and shift interlock cable from the ignition lock cylinder, if equipped (see Chapter 7).
6   Remove the cover from the lower part of the steering column, on models so equipped **(see illustration)**.
7   Mark the relationship of the steering column shaft to the intermediate shaft, then remove the pinch bolt **(see illustration)**.
8   Mark and disconnect any electrical connectors that would interfere with removal.

9   Remove the steering column mounting nuts **(see illustration)**, then guide the column out from the instrument panel.

Installation

10   Guide the column into position, connecting the steering shaft with the intermediate shaft. Be sure to align the marks made in Step 7.
11   Install the mounting fasteners, tightening them to the torque listed in this Chapter's Specifications.
12   Install the pinch bolt and tighten it to the torque listed in this Chapter's Specifications.
13   The remainder of installation is the reverse of the removal procedure. Refer to Section 18 for the clockspring, steering wheel and airbag module installation details.

20   Tie-rod ends - removal and installation

Refer to illustrations 20.3a, 20.3b and 20.4

Removal

1   Loosen the wheel lug nuts. Apply the parking brake, raise the front of the vehicle

and support it securely on jackstands. Remove the front wheel.
2   Remove the cotter pin (if equipped) and loosen the nut on the tie-rod end stud.
3   Hold the tie-rod with a pair of locking pliers or wrench and loosen the jam nut enough to mark the position of the tie-rod end in relation to the threads **(see illustrations)**.
4   Disconnect the tie-rod from the steering knuckle arm with a puller **(see illustration)**. Remove the nut and detach the tie-rod.
5   Unscrew the tie-rod end from the tie-rod.

Installation

6   Thread the tie-rod end on to the marked position and insert the tie-rod stud into the steering knuckle arm. Tighten the jam nut securely.
7   Install the nut on the stud and tighten it to the torque listed in this Chapter's Specifications. On models that use a castle nut, install a new cotter pin. If the hole for the cotter pin doesn't line up with one of the slots in the nut, turn the nut an additional amount until it does.
8   Install the wheel and lug nuts. Lower the vehicle and tighten the lug nuts to the torque

20.3a Loosen the jam nut . . .

20.3b . . . then mark the relationship of the tie-rod end to the tie-rod

20.4 Separate the tie-rod end from the steering knuckle with a puller

10

21.2 The steering gear boot inner clamp (A) must be cut off; the outer clamp (B) can be removed with pliers

22.5 Remove the pinch bolt from the intermediate shaft universal joint

22.7 Detach the power steering fluid lines from the steering gear

listed in the Chapter 1 Specifications.
9   Have the alignment checked and, if necessary, adjusted.

21 Steering gear boots - replacement

Refer to illustration 21.2
1   Remove the tie-rod ends (see Section 20).
2   Cut off the inner boot clamp and discard it. Using pliers, squeeze the tangs and slide the outer boot clamp off the boot **(see illustration)**.
3   Detach the boot from the vent cross tube (if equipped) and slide the boots off the tie-rod.
4   Before installing the new boots, wrap the threads on the ends of the tie-rods with a layer of tape so the small ends of the new boots aren't damaged during installation.
6   Loosely install the inner boot clamp on each boot.
7   Slide the new boots onto the tie-rod and secure them on the steering gear. Connect the breather tube, if equipped.
8   Using the appropriate boot clamp pliers, tighten the inner boot clamp. Slide the outer clamp onto the boot.
9   Install the tie-rod ends and connect them to the steering knuckle (see Section 20).
10   Have the front end alignment checked and, if necessary, adjusted.

22 Steering gear - removal and installation

Refer to illustrations 22.5, 22.7 and 22.11
Warning 1: *Always disable the airbag system before working in the vicinity of any airbag system components to avoid the possibility of accidental deployment of the airbag, which could cause personal injury (see Chapter 12).*
Warning 2: *Make sure the steering shaft is*

not turned while the steering gear is removed or the airbag clockspring could become damaged. To prevent the shaft from turning, place the ignition key in the LOCK position or thread the seat belt through the steering wheel and clip it into place.
1   Disconnect the cable from the negative terminal of the battery (see Chapter 5).
2   Loosen the front wheel lug nuts.
3   Apply the parking brake and block the rear wheels to keep the vehicle from rolling. Raise the front of the vehicle and place it securely on jackstands.
4   Remove the front wheels.
5   Remove the steering column intermediate shaft pinch bolt at the steering gear **(see illustration)**. Separate the shaft from the steering gear.
6   Disconnect any electrical connectors from the steering gear.
7   Detach the power steering line fittings from the steering gear **(see illustration)**. Be sure to mark the positions of the lines if there is any chance of confusion.
8   Detach the tie-rod ends from the steering knuckles (see Section 20).
9   Support the rear of the subframe with a floor jack. Loosen, but do not remove, the

22.11 Steering gear mounting bolts (2000 DeVille shown)

rear subframe-to-body bolts. Slowly lower the jack for access to the steering gear mounting bolts. **Caution:** *Don't lower the subframe any farther than necessary.*
10   Remove the heat shield, if equipped.
11   Remove the steering gear mounting bolts **(see illustration)**.
12   Slide the steering gear assembly out the left wheel well to remove it.
13   Installation is the reverse of removal. Tighten the fasteners to the torque listed in this Chapter's Specifications.
14   Bleed the steering system (see Section 24).
15   Have the front end alignment checked and, if necessary, adjusted.

23 Power steering pump - removal and installation

Removal

1   Disconnect the cable from the negative battery terminal (see Chapter 5).
2   Remove the pump drivebelt (see Chapter 1).
3   Remove the external reservoir, if equipped. **Note:** *Models with a 4.9L engine are equipped with an external reservoir that must be removed to gain access to the power steering pump. A one-piece adapter is used to link the pump with the reservoir. The adapter is equipped with internal O-rings. Be sure to install new O-rings into the adapter before installing the adapter onto the power steering pump.*
4   Detach the hydraulic lines from the pump.
5   Remove the pump mounting bolts and detach the pump from the engine.

Installation

6   Installation is the reverse of removal.
7   Fill the reservoir with the recommended fluid (see Chapter 1) and bleed the system, following the procedure described in the next Section.

25.3 Use a press tool to push the stud out of the flange

1   Hub flange
2   Lug nut on stud
3   Press tool

25.4 Install four washers and a lug nut on the stud, then tighten the nut to draw the stud into place

1   Hub flange
2   Spacer/washers

24 Power steering system - bleeding

1   Following any operation in which the power steering fluid lines have been disconnected, the power steering system must be bled to remove air and obtain proper steering performance.

2   With the front wheels turned all the way to the left, check the power steering fluid level and, if low, add fluid until it reaches the Cold mark on the dipstick.

3   Start the engine and allow it to run at fast idle. Recheck the fluid level and add more if necessary to reach the Cold mark on the dipstick.

4   Bleed the system by turning the wheels from side-to-side, without hitting the stops. This will work the air out of the system. Don't allow the reservoir to run out of fluid.

5   When the air is worked out of the system, return the wheels to the straight ahead position and leave the engine running for several minutes before shutting it off. Recheck the fluid level.

6   Road test the vehicle to be sure the steering system is functioning normally with no noise.

7   Recheck the fluid level to be sure it's up to the Hot mark on the dipstick while the engine is at normal operating temperature. Add fluid if necessary.

25 Wheel studs - replacement

Refer to illustrations 25.3 and 25.4
Note: *This procedure applies to both the front and rear wheel studs.*
1   Remove the brake disc (see Chapter 9).
2   Install a lug nut part way onto the stud being replaced.
3   Push the stud out of the hub flange with a press tool (**see illustration**).

4   Insert the new stud into the hub flange from the back side and install four flat washers and a lug nut on the stud (**see illustration**).
5   Tighten the lug nut until the stud is seated in the flange.
6   Reinstall the brake disc. Tighten the caliper mounting bolts to the torque listed in the Chapter 9 Specifications.

26 Wheels and tires - general information

Refer to illustration 26.1
All vehicles covered by this manual are equipped with metric-size steel belted radial tires (**see illustration**). The use of other size or type tires may affect the ride and handling

26.1 Metric tire size code

10

of the vehicle. Don't mix different types of tires, such as radials and bias belted, on the same vehicle, since handling may be seriously affected. Tires should be replaced in pairs on the same axle, but if only one tire is being replaced, be sure it's the same size, structure and tread design as the other.

Because tire pressure affects handling and wear, the tire pressures should be checked at least once a month or before any extended trips (see Chapter 1).

Wheels must be replaced if they're bent, dented, leak air, have elongated bolt holes, are heavily rusted, out of vertical symmetry or if the lug nuts won't stay tight. Wheel repairs by welding or peening aren't recommended.

Tire and wheel balance is important to the overall handling, braking and performance of the vehicle. Unbalanced wheels can adversely affect handling and ride characteristics as well as tire life. Whenever a tire is installed on a wheel, the tire and wheel should be balanced by a shop with the proper equipment.

27   Wheel alignment - general information

Refer to illustration 27.1

Wheel alignment refers to the adjustments made to the wheels so they're in proper angular relationship to the suspension and the ground **(see illustration)**. Wheels that are out of proper alignment not only affect steering control, but also increase tire wear.

Getting the proper wheel alignment is a very exacting process, one in which complicated and expensive machines are necessary to perform the job properly. Because of this, you should have a technician with the proper equipment perform these tasks. We will, however, attempt to give you a basic idea of what's involved with front end alignment so you can better understand the process and deal intelligently with the shop that does the work.

Toe is the relationship between the front-to-rear alignment of the wheels and the centerline of the vehicle. The purpose of a toe specification is to ensure parallel rolling of the wheels. In a vehicle with zero toe, the distance between the front edges of the wheels will be the same as the distance between the rear edges of the wheels. A small amount of initial toe-in is normally desired because centrifugal force is attempting to push the wheels out as the vehicle is moving. Incorrect toe-in will cause the tires to wear improperly by making them scrub against the road surface.

On the front wheels, toe-in adjustment is controlled by the length of the tie-rod. The tie-rod end may be threaded in-or-out on the inner tie-rod to lengthen or shorten the overall length of the tie-rod assembly. Rear wheel toe adjustments differ according to suspension design. On 1992 Seville models, the toe

CAMBER ANGLE (FRONT VIEW)

CASTER ANGLE (SIDE VIEW)

27.1 Wheel alignment details

*A minus B = C
  (degrees camber)
D = degrees caster
E minus F = toe-in
  (measured in inches)
G = toe-in (expressed
  in degrees)*

TOE-IN (TOP VIEW)

adjustment is made by loosening the control arm pivot bolts and changing the position of the lower control arm. By prying between the rear inner bolt and the rear support assembly the toe specification can be adjusted in or out. On 1997 and earlier Seville models and 1999 and earlier DeVille models, the toe adjustment is made by loosening the inner toe link bolt and prying in or out, as necessary. On 1998 and later Seville models and 2000 and later DeVille models the toe adjustment in made by loosening the inner toe link nut and turning the bolt one way or the other, which turns an adjustment cam to pull the control arm inward or push it outward.

Camber is the tilting of the wheels from vertical when viewed from the front or rear of the vehicle. When the wheels tilt out at the top, the camber is said to be positive (+). When the wheels tilt in at the top, the camber is negative (-). The amount of tilt is measured in degrees from the vertical and this measurement is called the camber angle. This angle affects the amount of tire tread which contacts the road and compensates for changes in the suspension geometry when

the vehicle is cornering or traveling over an undulating surface.

Camber, on the front suspension, is adjusted by loosening the strut-to-knuckle bolts/nuts and altering the relationship between the strut and knuckle. On 1993 through 1997 Seville models and 1994 through 1999 DeVille models, the camber on the rear suspension is adjusted by loosening the lower control arm pivot bolts and moving the control arm in or out. Rear camber is not adjustable on other models.

Caster is the tilting of the top of the front steering axis from the vertical. A tilt toward the rear is positive caster and a tilt toward the front is negative caster. Caster affects the straight-line steerability of the vehicle. Incorrect caster settings may cause the vehicle to pull to one side or the other. Caster is adjustable on the front end by loosening the strut upper mounting nuts or bolts and moving the top of the strut towards the front or rear of the vehicle, as necessary (on some early models the holes may have to be elongated with a file). Caster is not adjustable on the rear of these vehicles.

Chapter 11 Body

Contents

1   General information

Warning: *These models are equipped with a Supplemental Inflatable Restraint (SIR) system (more commonly known as airbags). Always disable the airbag system before working in the vicinity of any airbag system component to avoid the possibility of accidental deployment of the airbag, which could cause personal injury (see Chapter 12).*

These models feature a "unibody" construction, using a floor pan with front and rear subframes which support the body components, front and rear suspension systems and other mechanical components.

Certain body components are particularly vulnerable to accident damage and can be unbolted and repaired or replaced. Among these parts are the body moldings, front fenders, doors, bumpers, the hood, trunk lid and all glass.

Only general body maintenance practices and body panel repair procedures within the scope of the do-it-yourselfer are included in this Chapter.

2   Body - maintenance

1   The condition of your vehicle's body is very important, because the resale value depends a great deal on it. It's much more difficult to repair a neglected or damaged body than it is to repair mechanical components. The hidden areas of the body, such as the wheel wells, the frame and the engine compartment, are equally important, although they don't require as frequent attention as the rest of the body.

2   Once a year, or every 12,000 miles, it's a good idea to have the underside of the body steam cleaned. All traces of dirt and oil will be removed and the area can then be inspected carefully for rust, damaged brake lines, frayed electrical wires, damaged cables and other problems. The front suspension components should be greased after completion of this job.

3   At the same time clean the engine and the engine compartment with a steam cleaner or water-soluble degreaser.

4   The wheel wells should be given close attention, since undercoating can peel away

11

and stones and dirt thrown up by the tires can cause the paint to chip and flake, allowing rust to set in. If rust is found, clean down to the bare metal and apply an anti-rust paint.

5   The body should be washed about once a week. Wet the vehicle thoroughly to soften the dirt, then wash it down with a soft sponge and plenty of clean soapy water. If the surplus dirt is not washed off very carefully, it can wear down the paint.

6   Spots of tar or asphalt thrown up from the road should be removed with a cloth soaked in solvent.

7   Once every six months, wax the body and chrome trim. If a chrome cleaner is used to remove rust from any of the vehicle's plated parts, remember that the cleaner also removes part of the chrome, so use it sparingly.

3   Vinyl trim - maintenance

Don't clean vinyl trim with detergents, caustic soap or petroleum-based cleaners. Plain soap and water works just fine, with a soft brush to clean dirt that may be ingrained. Wash the vinyl as frequently as the rest of the vehicle. After cleaning, application of a high-quality rubber and vinyl protectant will help prevent oxidation and cracks. The protectant can also be applied to weatherstripping, vacuum lines and rubber hoses, which often fail as a result of chemical degradation, and to the tires.

4   Upholstery and carpets - maintenance

1   Every three months, remove the floormats and clean the interior of the vehicle (more frequently if necessary). Use a stiff whiskbroom to brush the carpeting and loosen dirt and dust, and then vacuum the upholstery and carpets thoroughly, especially along seams and crevices.

2   Dirt and stains can be removed from carpeting with basic household or automotive carpet shampoos available in spray cans. Follow the directions and vacuum again, then use a stiff brush to bring back the "nap" of the carpet.

3   Most interiors have cloth or vinyl upholstery, either of which can be cleaned and maintained with a number of material-specific cleaners or shampoos available in auto supply stores. Follow the directions on the product for usage, and always spot-test any upholstery cleaner on an inconspicuous area (bottom edge of a back seat cushion) to ensure that it doesn't cause a color shift in the material.

4   After cleaning, vinyl upholstery should be treated with a protectant. **Note:** *Make sure the protectant container indicates the product can be used on seats - some products may make a seat too slippery.* **Caution:** *Do not use protectant on vinyl-covered steering wheels.*

5   Leather upholstery requires special

care. It should be cleaned regularly with saddlesoap or leather cleaner. Never use alcohol, gasoline, nail polish remover or thinner to clean leather upholstery.

6   After cleaning, regularly treat leather upholstery with a leather conditioner, rubbed in with a soft cotton cloth. Never use car wax on leather upholstery.

7   In areas where the interior of the vehicle is subject to bright sunlight, cover leather seating areas of the seats with a sheet if the vehicle is to be left out for any length of time.

5   Body repair

Repair of scratches

1   If the scratch is superficial and does not penetrate to the metal of the body, repair is very simple. Lightly rub the scratched area with a fine rubbing compound to remove loose paint and built up wax. Rinse the area with clean water.

2   Apply touch-up paint to the scratch, using a small brush. Continue to apply thin layers of paint until the surface of the paint in the scratch is level with the surrounding paint. Allow the new paint at least two weeks to harden, then blend it into the surrounding paint by rubbing with a very fine rubbing compound. Finally, apply a coat of wax to the scratch area.

3   If the scratch has penetrated the paint and exposed the metal of the body, causing the metal to rust, and a different repair technique is required. Remove all loose rust from the bottom of the scratch with a pocket knife, then apply rust inhibiting paint to prevent the formation of rust in the future. Using a rubber or nylon applicator, coat the scratched area with glaze-type filler. If required, the filler can be mixed with thinner to provide a very thin paste, which is ideal for filling narrow scratches. Before the glaze filler in the scratch hardens, wrap a piece of smooth cotton cloth around the tip of a finger. Dip the cloth in thinner and then quickly wipe it along the surface of the scratch. This will ensure that the surface of the filler is slightly hollow. The scratch can now be painted over as described earlier in this Section.

Repair of dents

See photo sequence

4   When repairing dents, the first job is to pull the dent out until the affected area is as close as possible to its original shape. There is no point in trying to restore the original shape completely as the metal in the damaged area will have stretched on impact and cannot be restored to its original contours. It is better to bring the level of the dent up to a point, which is about 1/8-inch below the level of the surrounding metal. In cases where the dent is very shallow, it is not worth trying to pull it out at all.

5   If the back side of the dent is accessible, it can be hammered out gently from behind

using a soft-face hammer. While doing this, hold a block of wood firmly against the opposite side of the metal to absorb the hammer blows and prevent the metal from being stretched.

6   If the dent is in a section of the body which has double layers, or some other factor makes it inaccessible from behind, a different technique is required. Drill several small holes through the metal inside the damaged area, particularly in the deeper sections. Screw long, self tapping screws into the holes just enough for them to get a good grip in the metal. Now pulling on the protruding heads of the screws with locking pliers can pull out the dent.

7   The next stage of repair is the removal of paint from the damaged area and from an inch or so of the surrounding metal. This is easily done with a wire brush or sanding disk in a drill motor, although it can be done just as effectively by hand with sandpaper. To complete the preparation for filling, score the surface of the bare metal with a screwdriver or the tang of a file or drill small holes in the affected area. This will provide a good grip for the filler material. To complete the repair, see the subsection on *filling and painting.*

Repair of rust holes or gashes

8   Remove all paint from the affected area and from an inch or so of the surrounding metal using a sanding disk or wire brush mounted in a drill motor. If these are not available, a few sheets of sandpaper will do the job just as effectively.

9   With the paint removed, you will be able to determine the severity of the corrosion and decide whether to replace the whole panel, if possible, or repair the affected area. New body panels are not as expensive as most people think and it is often quicker to install a new panel than to repair large areas of rust.

10   Remove all trim pieces from the affected area except those which will act as a guide to the original shape of the damaged body, such as headlight shells, etc. Using metal snips or a hacksaw blade, remove all loose metal and any other metal that is badly affected by rust. Hammer the edges of the hole on the inside to create a slight depression for the filler material.

11   Wire brush the affected area to remove the powdery rust from the surface of the metal. If the back of the rusted area is accessible, treat it with rust inhibiting paint.

12   Before filling is done, block the hole in some way. This can be done with sheet metal riveted or screwed into place, or by stuffing the hole with wire mesh.

13   Once the hole is blocked off, the affected area can be filled and painted. See the following subsection on *filling and painting.*

Filling and painting

14   Many types of body fillers are available, but generally speaking, body repair kits which contain filler paste and a tube of resin

hardener are best for this type of repair work. A wide, flexible plastic or nylon applicator will be necessary for imparting a smooth and contoured finish to the surface of the filler material. Mix up a small amount of filler on a clean piece of wood or cardboard (use the hardener sparingly). Follow the manufacturer's instructions on the package, otherwise the filler will set incorrectly.

15   Using the applicator, apply the filler paste to the prepared area. Draw the applicator across the surface of the filler to achieve the desired contour and to level the filler surface. As soon as a contour that approximates the original one is achieved, stop working the paste. If you continue, the paste will begin to stick to the applicator. Continue to add thin layers of paste at 20-minute intervals until the level of the filler is just above the surrounding metal.

16   Once the filler has hardened, the excess can be removed with a body file. From then on, progressively finer grades of sandpaper should be used, starting with a 180-grit paper and finishing with 600-grit wet-or-dry paper. Always wrap the sandpaper around a flat rubber or wooden block, otherwise the surface of the filler will not be completely flat. During the sanding of the filler surface, the wet-or-dry paper should be periodically rinsed in water. This will ensure that a very smooth finish is produced in the final stage.

17   At this point, the repair area should be surrounded by a ring of bare metal, which in turn should be encircled by the finely feathered edge of good paint. Rinse the repair area with clean water until all of the dust produced by the sanding operation is gone.

18   Spray the entire area with a light coat of primer. This will reveal any imperfections in the surface of the filler. Repair the imperfections with fresh filler paste or glaze filler and once more smooth the surface with sandpaper. Repeat this spray-and-repair procedure until you are satisfied that the surface of the filler and the feathered edge of the paint are

perfect. Rinse the area with clean water and allow it to dry completely.

19   The repair area is now ready for painting. Spray painting must be carried out in a warm, dry, windless and dust free atmosphere. These conditions can be created if you have access to a large indoor work area, but if you are forced to work in the open, you will have to pick the day very carefully. If you are working indoors, dousing the floor in the work area with water will help settle the dust, which would otherwise be in the air. If the repair area is confined to one body panel, mask off the surrounding panels. This will help minimize the effects of a slight mismatch in paint color. Trim pieces such as chrome strips, door handles, etc., will also need to be masked off or removed. Use masking tape and several thickness of newspaper for the masking operations.

20   Before spraying, shake the paint can thoroughly, then spray a test area until the spray painting technique is mastered. Cover the repair area with a thick coat of primer. The thickness should be built up using several thin layers of primer rather than one thick one. Using 600-grit wet-or-dry sandpaper, rub down the surface of the primer until it is very smooth. While doing this, the work area should be thoroughly rinsed with water and the wet-or-dry sandpaper periodically rinsed as well. Allow the primer to dry before spraying additional coats.

21   Spray on the top coat, again building up the thickness by using several thin layers of paint. Begin spraying in the center of the repair area and then, using a circular motion, work out until the whole repair area and about two inches of the surrounding original paint is covered. Remove all masking material 10 to 15 minutes after spraying on the final coat of paint. Allow the new paint at least two weeks to harden, then use a very fine rubbing compound to blend the edges of the new paint into the existing paint. Finally, apply a coat of wax.

Major damage

22   Major damage must be repaired by an auto body shop specifically equipped to perform unibody repairs. These shops have the specialized equipment required to do the job properly.

23   If the damage is extensive, the body must be checked for proper alignment or the vehicle's handling characteristics may be adversely affected and other components may wear at an accelerated rate.

24   Due to the fact that all of the major body components (hood, fenders, etc.) are separate and replaceable units, any seriously damaged components should be replaced rather than repaired. Sometimes the components can be found in a auto salvage or wrecking yard that specializes in used vehicle components, often at considerable savings over the cost of new parts.

6   Hinges and locks - maintenance

Once every 6000 miles, or every six months, the hinges and latch assemblies on the doors, hood and trunk should be given a few drops of light oil or lock lubricant. The door latch strikers should also be lubricated with a thin coat of grease to reduce wear and ensure free movement. Lubricate the door and trunk locks with spray-on graphite lubricant.

7   Windshield and fixed glass - replacement

Replacement of the windshield and fixed glass requires the use of special fast setting adhesive/caulk materials. These operations should be left to a dealer or a shop specializing in glass work.

8   Hood support struts - replacement

Refer to illustrations 8.2a and 8.2b
1   Open the hood and support it securely.
2   Detach the clips from the upper and lower ends of the strut with a screwdriver and remove the strut **(see illustrations)**.
3   Installation is the reverse of removal.

9   Radiator support cover - removal and installation

Warning: *These models are equipped with a Supplemental Inflatable Restraint (SIR) system (more commonly known as airbags). Always disable the airbag system before working in the vicinity of any airbag system component to avoid the possibility of accidental deployment of the airbag, which could cause personal injury (see Chapter 12).*

11

8.2a Pry the retaining clip off the upper end . . .

8.2b . . . and the lower end of the strut, then detach the strut from the mounting studs

These photos illustrate a method of repairing simple dents. They are intended to supplement *Body repair - minor damage* in this Chapter and should not be used as the sole instructions for body repair on these vehicles.

1   If you can't access the backside of the body panel to hammer out the dent, pull it out with a slide-hammer-type dent puller. In the deepest portion of the dent or along the crease line, drill or punch hole(s) at least one inch apart . . .

2   . . . then screw the slide-hammer into the hole and operate it. Tap with a hammer near the edge of the dent to help 'pop' the metal back to its original shape. When you're finished, the dent area should be close to its original contour and about 1/8-inch below the surface of the surrounding metal

3   Using coarse-grit sandpaper, remove the paint down to the bare metal. Hand sanding works fine, but the disc sander shown here makes the job faster. Use finer (about 320-grit) sandpaper to feather-edge the paint at least one inch around the dent area

4   When the paint is removed, touch will probably be more helpful than sight for telling if the metal is straight. Hammer down the high spots or raise the low spots as necessary. Clean the repair area with wax/silicone remover

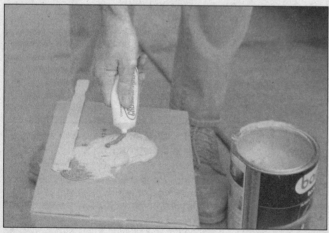

5   Following label instructions, mix up a batch of plastic filler and hardener. The ratio of filler to hardener is critical, and, if you mix it incorrectly, it will either not cure properly or cure too quickly (you won't have time to file and sand it into shape)

6   Working quickly so the filler doesn't harden, use a plastic applicator to press the body filler firmly into the metal, assuring it bonds completely. Work the filler until it matches the original contour and is slightly above the surrounding metal

7 Let the filler harden until you can just dent it with your fingernail. Use a body file or Surform tool (shown here) to rough-shape the filler

8 Use coarse-grit sandpaper and a sanding board or block to work the filler down until it's smooth and even. Work down to finer grits of sandpaper - always using a board or block - ending up with 360 or 400 grit

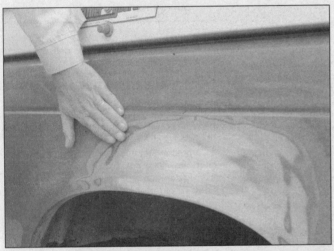

9 You shouldn't be able to feel any ridge at the transition from the filler to the bare metal or from the bare metal to the old paint. As soon as the repair is flat and uniform, remove the dust and mask off the adjacent panels or trim pieces

10 Apply several layers of primer to the area. Don't spray the primer on too heavy, so it sags or runs, and make sure each coat is dry before you spray on the next one. A professional-type spray gun is being used here, but aerosol spray primer is available inexpensively from auto parts stores

11 The primer will help reveal imperfections or scratches. Fill these with glazing compound. Follow the label instructions and sand it with 360 or 400-grit sandpaper until it's smooth. Repeat the glazing, sanding and respraying until the primer reveals a perfectly smooth surface

12 Finish sand the primer with very fine sandpaper (400 or 600-grit) to remove the primer overspray. Clean the area with water and allow it to dry. Use a tack rag to remove any dust, then apply the finish coat. Don't attempt to rub out or wax the repair area until the paint has dried completely (at least two weeks)

9.1 Radiator support cover retainer locations

9.2 Press the center of the plastic retainer pin with a screwdriver to release it, then lift retainer out

Removal

Refer to illustrations 9.1 and 9.2

1   Open the hood and locate the cover panel retainers **(see illustration)**.
2   Detach the retainers by pressing the centers in and lifting them out **(see illustration)**.
3   Once all the retainers are removed, lift the panel out.

Installation

4   Place the panel in position, insert the retainers then press the centers firmly into place to lock them in place.

10   Radiator grille - removal and installation

Refer to illustration 10.2
Warning: *These models are equipped with a*

Supplemental Inflatable Restraint (SIR) system (more commonly known as airbags). Always disable the airbag system before working in the vicinity of any airbag system component to avoid the possibility of accidental deployment of the airbag, which could cause personal injury (see Chapter 12).
1   Open the hood.
2   On models with hood-mounted grilles, remove the retaining bolts/nuts and detach the grille/bracket assembly as a unit **(see illustration)**.
3   Remove the screws/nuts and separate the grille from the bracket.
4   On body-mounted grilles, remove the radiator support cover for access.
5   Remove the grille retaining screws or plastic retainers.
6   Rotate the top of the grille out and lift it from the vehicle.
7   Installation is the reverse of removal.

11   Hood - removal, installation and adjustment

Note: *The hood is somewhat awkward to remove and install, at least two people should perform this procedure.*

Removal and installation

1   Open the hood, then place blankets or pads over the fenders and cowl area of the body. This will protect the body and paint as the hood is lifted off.
2   Disconnect any cables or wires that will interfere with removal.
3   Make marks or scribe a line around the hood hinge to ensure proper alignment during installation **(see illustration 11.11)**.
4   Support the hood and detach the support struts (see Section 8).
5   Have an assistant support one side of the hood while you support the other, then remove the hinge-to-hood bolts and lift off the hood.
6   Installation is the reverse of removal. Align the hinge bolts with the marks made in Step 3.

10.2 Hood-mounted grille retainer locations

11.10 Mark the hood latch location, then loosen the bolts and move the hood latch to adjust the hood closed position

11.11 Mark the hinge location before loosening the nuts/bolts to adjust the hood position forward or rearward

11.12 Screw the hood bumpers in or out to adjust the hood flush with the fenders

12.2 Use needle-nose pliers to pry out the cable retainer from the hood latch assembly, then disengage the cable

Adjustment

Refer to illustrations 11.10, 11.11 and 11.12

7   Side-to-side adjustment of the hood is done by moving the hinge plate slot after loosening the bolts or nuts.

8   Scribe or draw a line around the entire hinge plate so you can determine the amount of movement.

9   Loosen the bolts or nuts and move the hood into correct alignment. Move it only a little at a time. Tighten the hinge bolts and carefully lower the hood to check the position.

10   If necessary after installation, the entire hood latch assembly can be adjusted up-and-down as well as from side-to-side on the radiator support so the hood closes securely and flush with the fender. Scribe or draw a line or mark around the hood latch mounting bolts to provide a reference point, then loosen them and reposition the latch assembly, as necessary **(see illustration)**. Following adjustment, retighten the mounting bolts.

11   To adjust the hood fore-and-aft, loosen the hinge bracket bolts, move the bracket as necessary and tighten the bolts **(see illustration)**.

12   Finally, adjust the hood bumpers on the radiator support so the hood, when closed, is flush with the fenders **(see illustration)**. Don't forget the bumper located on the cowl for adjusting the rear edge of the hood.

13   The hood latch assembly, as well as the hinges, should be periodically lubricated with white, lithium-base grease to prevent binding and wear.

12   Hood latch and release cable - removal and installation

Warning: *These models are equipped with a Supplemental Inflatable Restraint (SIR) system (more commonly known as airbags). Always disable the airbag system before working in the vicinity of any airbag system component to avoid the possibility of acci-*

dental deployment of the airbag, which could cause personal injury (see Chapter 12).

Latch

Refer to illustration 12.2

1   Scribe a line around the latch to aid alignment when installing, then remove the retaining bolts securing the hood latch to the radiator support **(see illustration 11.10)**. Remove the latch.

2   Disconnect the hood release cable by disengaging the cable from the latch assembly **(see illustration)**.

3   Installation is the reverse of removal. **Note:** *Adjust the latch so the hood engages securely when closed and the hood bumpers are slightly compressed.*

Cable

Refer to illustration 12.6

4   Disconnect the hood release cable from the latch assembly as described in step 2.

5   Attach a piece of thin wire or string to the end of the cable and unclip all remaining cable retaining clips. **Note:** *It may be necessary on some vehicles to remove the air cleaner assembly (see Chapter 4) to allow access for release cable removal.*

6   Working in the passenger compartment, remove the driver's side kick panel (if neces-

12.6 Remove the screws from the handle, then detach the cable and pull it rearward into the passenger compartment

sary) and detach the cable from the hood release lever **(see illustration)**.

7   On some models it will be necessary to remove the inner fender splash panel for access and detach the cable from the clips. Pull the cable and grommet rearward into the passenger compartment until you can see the wire or string. Ensure that the new cable has a grommet attached then remove the wire or string from the old cable and fasten it to the new cable.

8   With the new cable attached to the wire or string, pull the wire or string back through the firewall until the new cable reaches the latch assembly.

9   Working in the passenger compartment, reinstall the new cable into the hood release lever. It may be necessary to use pliers to crimp the retaining clip, which secures the cable to the release lever.

10   The remainder of the installation is the reverse of removal. **Note:** *Push on the grommet with your fingers from the passenger compartment to seat the grommet in the firewall correctly.*

13   Bumpers - removal and installation

Warning: *These models are equipped with a Supplemental Inflatable Restraint (SIR) system (more commonly known as airbags). Always disable the airbag system before working in the vicinity of any airbag system component to avoid the possibility of accidental deployment of the airbag, which could cause personal injury (see Chapter 12).*

Front bumper

Refer to illustrations 13.3, 13.5a, 13.5b and 13.6

1   On 1997 and earlier Seville models and 1999 and earlier DeVille models, disable the airbag system (see Chapter 12).

2   If necessary to provide working room, raise the front of the vehicle and support it securely on jackstands. Open the hood.

11

13.3 Remove the fasteners and detach the air deflector

13.5a Remove the fasteners along the top of the front bumper cover

13.5b Remove the nuts retaining the rear edges of the front bumper cover

13.6 Remove the front bumper bolts/nuts (it may be necessary to use a ratchet, long extension and a socket)

3   Remove the air deflector **(see illustration)**.
4   Working in the front wheel opening, remove the inner fender splash shield-to-bumper cover fasteners, then detach any retaining screws securing the inner fender-well extension panels to the bumper. If equipped, disconnect the cornering or side marker lamp electrical connectors.
5   Remove the fasteners, separate the bumper cover from the fenders, then pull the bumper assembly straight out and away from the vehicle to remove **(see illustrations)**.

6   Working under the front of the vehicle, remove the retaining nuts and bolts securing the bumper to the bumper energy absorbers **(see illustration)**.
7   Installation is the reverse of removal.

Rear bumper

Refer to illustrations 13.9, 13.10 and 13.11
8   If necessary to provide working room, apply the parking brake, raise the rear of the vehicle, support it securely on jackstands and remove the rear wheels.

9   Working inside the trunk compartment, peel back the trunk finishing panels and remove the nuts and securing the bumper cover **(see illustration)**.
10   Working in the wheel wells, remove the bumper cover-to-body bolts **(see illustration)**.
11   Working under the vehicle, remove the retaining nuts securing the bumper to the body **(see illustration)**. Pull the bumper assembly straight out and away from the vehicle to remove it.
12   Installation is the reverse of removal.

13.9 Working in the trunk compartment, remove the nuts securing the bumper cover

13.10 Remove the bolts securing the bumper cover to the body

13.11 Remove the rear bumper retaining bolts/nuts

14.4a Remove the retainers from the front of the inner fenderwell splash shield . . .

14.4b . . . and from the rear

14   Front fender - removal and installation

Refer to illustrations 14.4a, 14.4b, 14.7a and 14.7b

Warning: *These models are equipped with a Supplemental Inflatable Restraint (SIR) system (more commonly known as airbags). Always disable the airbag system before working in the vicinity of any airbag system component to avoid the possibility of accidental deployment of the airbag, which could cause personal injury (see Chapter 12).*

1   Remove the hood (see Section 11).
2   Remove the headlight housing (see Chapter 12).
3   Loosen the wheel lug nuts. Raise the vehicle, support it securely on jackstands and remove the front wheel.
4   Remove the inner fenderwell splash shield **(see illustrations)**.
5   Remove the fasteners securing the bumper cover to the fender.
6   Remove the rocker panel molding. On some models the molding is retained with bolts; on others it's retained by plastic push-in fasteners.
7   Remove the upper and lower bolts attaching the fender to the chassis **(see illustrations)**.
8   Open the door and remove the bolt near the top of the A-pillar, on models so equipped.
9   Carefully detach the fender. It's a good idea to have an assistant support the fender while it's being moved away from the vehicle to prevent damage to the surrounding body panels.
10   Installation is the reverse of removal.

15   Cowl cover - removal and installation

Refer to illustration 15.2a and 15.2b

1   Remove the windshield wiper arms (see Chapter 12).
2   Remove the fasteners securing the cowl cover **(see illustrations)**.
3   Lift the cover up, disconnect the windshield washer hoses, then remove the cover from the vehicle.
4   Installation is the reverse of removal.

14.7a Remove the upper . . .

14.7b . . . and the lower fender retaining bolts

15.2a Remove the left side . . .

15.2b . . . and right side retainers, then detach the cowl covers

11

16.1 Pull out the handle, remove the screw and pry out the inside door handle bezel

16.2a Pry out the armrest control switch with a screwdriver

16.2b Lift up on the control switch and disconnect the electrical connector

16.3a Remove the clip and detach the lock knob

16.3b Remove the screw from the lock knob opening

16.4a Insert a trim removal tool or a putty knife between the door and the trim panel and disengage the retaining clips

16 Door trim panel - removal and installation

Removal

Refer to illustrations 16.1, 16.2a, 16.2b, 16.3a, 16.3b, 16.4a, 16.4b and 16.6

1   Lower the window fully, then disconnect the cable from the negative terminal of the battery (see Chapter 5). On later models,

remove the screw and detach the inside door handle trim bezel (see illustration).

2   Use a screwdriver to carefully pry out the armrest switch control plate and disconnect the electrical connections (see illustrations).

3   Remove the lock knob in the unlocked (up) position, - on later models remove it by rotating it counterclockwise or detaching the lock clip with a screwdriver (see illustrations). On later models, remove the screw

from the lock knob opening

4   Insert a wide putty knife or a special trim panel removal tool between the trim panel and the head of the retaining clip to disengage the door panel retaining clips (see illustrations). Note: *Door trim panel retaining clips are approximately six to ten inches apart. Pry at the clip location only. Prying in between clips will result in distorted or damaged door trim panels.*

16.4b Door trim panel retaining clip locations

16.6 Remove the plastic fasteners and detach the watershield from the door

17.7 Remove the nuts and disconnect the door check link

17.8a On early models, remove the hinge-to-door bolts

17.8b On later models removing the bolt on each intermediate hinge will allow the door to be lifted off

5   Once all of the clips and screws are disengaged, detach the trim panel and remove the trim panel from the vehicle by gently pulling it up and out of the door.

6   For access to the inner door, remove the fasteners and detach the watershield **(see illustration)**.

7   To install the door panel, place it in position over the alignment dowels to make sure the retaining clips are lined up with their mating holes, then gently tap inward with the palm of your hand.

8   The remainder of the installation is the reverse of removal.

17   Door - removal, installation and adjustment

Removal and installation

Refer to illustrations 17.7, 17.8a and 17.8b

1   Raise the window completely and disconnect the negative cable from the battery (see Chapter 5).

2   Open the door all the way and support it on jacks or blocks covered with rags to prevent damaging the paint.

3   Remove the door trim panel and watershield as described in Section 16.

4   Unplug all electrical connections, ground wires and harness retaining clips from the door. **Note:** *It is a good idea to label all connections to aid the reassembly process.*

5   Working on the door side, detach the rubber conduit between the body and the door. Pull the wiring harness through the conduit hole and remove the wiring from the door.

6   Mark around the door hinges with a pen or a scribe to facilitate realignment during reassembly.

7   Disconnect the door check link **(see illustration)**.

8   Have an assistant hold the door, remove the hinge-to-door bolts and lift the door away from the vehicle **(see illustration)**. On later models, it will only be necessary to remove

the single fastener bolt on each intermediate hinge, then the door can be lifted off the hinge **(see illustration)**.

9   Installation is the reverse of removal.

Adjustment

Refer to illustration 17.12

10   Door-to-body alignment adjustments are made by loosening the hinge-to-body nuts/bolts then moving the door. Proper body alignment is achieved when the top of the doors are parallel with the roof section, the front door is flush with the fender, the rear door is flush with the rear quarter panel and the bottom of the doors are aligned with the lower rocker panel.

11   To adjust the door closed position, first check that the door latch is contacting the center of the latch striker. If not, remove the striker and add or subtract washers to achieve correct alignment.

12   Finally, adjust the latch striker as necessary (up-and-down or sideways) to provide positive engagement with the latch mechanism and the door panel is flush with the rear door or rear quarter panel **(see illustration)**.

18.2 Remove the latch retaining screws (arrows) from the end of the door, then detach the actuating rods and pull the latch assembly through the access hole

17.12 Adjust the door lock striker by loosening the mounting screws and gently tapping the striker in the desired direction

18   Door latch, lock cylinder and handles - removal and installation

Door latch

Refer to illustration 18.2

1   Raise the window and remove the door trim panel (see Section 16).

2   Remove the screws securing the latch to the door **(see illustration)**.

3   Working through the large access hole, position the latch as necessary to disengage the outside door handle and outside lock cylinder to latch rods and the inside handle to latch rod.

4   Position the latch as necessary to disengage the door lock actuator rod. Then remove the latch assembly from the door.

5   Installation is the reverse of removal.

Door lock cylinder and outside handle

Refer to illustrations 18.7, 18.9 and 18.10

6   To remove the lock cylinder, raise the window and remove the door trim panel and watershield as described in Section 16.

11

18.7 Detach the latch rod from the lock cylinder

18.14a On later models push the inside door handle actuator toward the end of the door and detach it . . .

18.14b . . . then use a screwdriver to slide the handle housing off the bracket and detach it

18.9 Remove the outside handle retaining nuts or bolts with a socket and extension working through the access holes in the door . . .

7   Working through the large access hole, disconnect the electrical connector then disengage latch rod from the clip on the lock cylinder **(see illustration)**.
8   To remove the lock cylinder on early models, remove the lock cylinder retaining nuts and remove the lock cylinder. On later models, remove the outside handle (see the next step) then remove the nuts and detach the lock cylinder.
9   Working through the access holes in the door, use a socket and extension to remove the outside door handle retaining nuts or bolts **(see illustration)**.
10   Push up on the retaining tabs (if equipped) and remove the outside handle **(see illustration)**.
11   Installation is the reverse of removal.

Inside handle

Refer to illustration 18.14a and 18.14b

12   Remove the door trim panel and watershield as described in Section 16.
13   Detach the actuating rods from the handle.
14   On early models, remove the bolts and

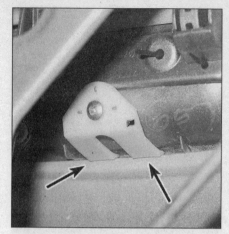

18.10 . . . then, on later models, detach the outside handle from the door by pushing up on the retaining tabs

nuts or drill out the rivets securing the inside handle. On later models use a screwdriver to push the actuator handle toward the end of the door to disengage it, then push on the handle mount in the same direction to slide it off the bracket on the inner door **(see illustration)**.
15   Installation is the reverse of removal.

---

19 Door window glass - removal and installation

Refer to illustrations 19.3. 19.4 and 19.7

1   Disconnect the negative cable from the battery (see Chapter 5).
2   Remove the door trim panel and watershield (Section 16).
3   On later models, remove the inner door handle (see Section 18) and the door control module **(see illustration)**.
4   On all models, pry the sealer strip out of door window glass opening **(see illustration)**.
5   On later models, remove the bolts and detach the window glass front run channel.
6   On later models remove the inner door

19.3 Disconnect the electrical connectors, remove the screws and detach the door electrical control module

19.4 Pry the sealer strip out of the door window opening

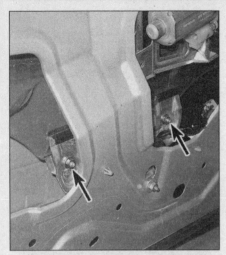

19.7 Loosen the window glass retainer bolts about four turns (later models)

20.4 On later models, the window regulator is held in place by bolts and nuts

handle assembly for access to the glass retainers (refer to Section 18).

7   Connect the battery, raise the glass to the top of the door, and tape it securely to window frame. On early models, drill out the glass retaining rivets and detach the glass from the window regulator. On later models, loosen the glass retainer bolts about four turns and detach them from the glass **(see illustration)**.

8   While supporting the glass, remove the tape and lower the glass slightly while tilting it downward at the front, then pull up at the rear and remove it from the door.

9   Install by inserting the glass into the door. On early models it may be necessary to connect the channel, making sure to engage the glass guide securely to the channel, before installing the new rivets. On later models, insert the glass, connect the retainers and tighten the bolts securely (but not excessively).

10   The remainder of installation is the reverse of removal.

20   Door window glass regulator - removal and installation

Refer to illustration 20.4

Removal

1   Disconnect the negative cable from the battery (see Chapter 5).

2   With the window glass in the full up position, remove the door trim panel and watershield (Section 16).

3   Secure the window glass in the up position with strong adhesive tape fastened to the glass and wrapped over the door frame.

4   On early models, punch out the center pins of the rivets that secure the window regulator and drill the heads of the rivets off with a 1/4-inch drill bit. **Caution:** *Be careful not to enlarge the holes in the door sheetmetal.* On later models, the regulator is held in place by bolts and nuts **(see illustration)**.

5   Unplug the electrical connector.

6   After removing the retaining rivets or

bolts/nuts, move the regulator until it is disengaged from the door. Lift the regulator from the door.

7   The window motor can be replaced if necessary on early models. This involves removing the bolts securing the motor to the regulator frame. The new motor should come with screws and nuts for attaching the motor to the regulator. **Warning:** *On early models, the regulator arms are under extreme spring tension and can cause serious injury if the motor is removed without locking the sector gear to the regulator frame. This can be done by inserting a bolt through one of the holes in the regulator frame and sector gear, then fastening it in place with a nut (if no holes are provided, drill through the sector gear and regulator frame).*

Installation

8   Place the regulator in position and engage in the door.

9   Secure the regulator to the door using new rivets and a riveting tool, or with bolts and nuts.

10   Install the window (see Section 19).

11   Plug in the electrical connector.

12   Install the water shield and door trim panel. Connect the negative battery cable.

21   Outside mirrors - removal and installation

Refer to illustrations 21.3 and 21.5

1   Disconnect the negative cable from the battery (see Chapter 5).

2   Remove the door trim panel and the watershield (see Section 16).

3   If equipped, detach the door window garnish from the window frame **(see illustration)**.

4   Disconnect the electrical connector from the mirror.

5   Remove the three mirror retaining nuts or bolts and detach the mirror from the vehi-

21.3 Pry out the two retainers and detach the window garnish piece

21.5 Remove the mirror retaining nuts

11

22.2 Detach the trunk lid cover for access to the retaining bolts

22.4 After marking their position, remove the trunk lid retaining bolts

22.9 Loosen the bolts and move the latch assembly as necessary to adjust the trunk lid flush with the quarter panels in the closed position

22.10 Adjust the trunk lid rubber bumpers so they're slightly compressed when the trunk lid is in the closed position

cle **(see illustration)**.

6   Installation is the reverse of removal.

22   Trunk lid - removal, installation and adjustment

Refer to illustrations 22.2 and 22.4
Note: *The trunk lid is heavy and somewhat awkward to remove and install - at least two people should perform this procedure.*

Removal and installation

1   Open the trunk lid and cover the edges of the trunk compartment with pads or cloths to protect the painted surfaces when the lid is removed.
2   Remove the covers (if equipped) from the hinge arms and disconnect any cables or wire harness connectors attached to the trunk lid that would interfere with removal **(see illustration)**.
3   Make alignment marks around the trunk lid hinge bolts.
4   While an assistant helps you support the lid, remove the hinge bolts from both sides and lift the trunk lid off the vehicle **(see illustration)**.
5   Installation is the reverse of removal.

Note: *When reinstalling the trunk lid, align the hinge bolts with the marks made during removal.*

Adjustment

Refer to illustrations 22.9 and 22.10
6   Fore-and-aft and side-to-side adjustment of the trunk lid is done by moving the trunk lid in relation to the hinge plate after loosening the bolts or nuts.
7   Scribe a line around the hinge bolt heads as described earlier in this Section so you can judge the amount of movement.
8   Loosen the bolts or nuts and move the trunk lid into correct alignment. Move it only a little at a time. Tighten the hinge bolts or nuts and carefully lower the trunk lid to check the alignment.
9   If necessary after installation, the entire trunk lid latch assembly can be adjusted up and down as well as from side to side on the trunk lid so the lid closes securely and is flush with the rear quarter panels. To do this, scribe a line around the trunk lid latch mounting bolts to provide a reference point. Then loosen the bolts and reposition the latch assembly as necessary **(see illustration)**. Following adjustment, retighten the mounting bolts.
10   Adjust the bumpers on the trunk lid, so

that the trunk lid is flush with the rear quarter panels when closed **(see illustration)**.
11   The trunk lid latch assembly, as well as the hinges, should be periodically lubricated with white lithium-base grease to prevent sticking and wear.

23   Trunk lid latch, striker and lock cylinder - removal and installation

Latch and latch striker

1   Unplug any electrical connectors and detach any cables from the latch assembly.
2   Remove the trunk lid latch bolts **(see illustration 22.9)**.
3   To access the striker, remove the plastic retaining nuts and clips securing the rear trunk finishing panel. On later models, it will be necessary to remove the rear bumper cover for access to the striker retaining nuts.
4   Remove the striker retaining bolts/nuts and detach the striker from the vehicle.
5   Installation is the reverse of removal.

23.8 Insert a screwdriver into the slot in the plastic collar and disconnect the release cable from the lock cylinder

23.9 Detach the lock cylinder retaining clip

24.4a Use needle-nose pliers to pry out the retainers and detach the solenoid

24.4b Pull the solenoid into the fuel door opening . . .

24.5 . . . then disconnect the electrical connector and remove the solenoid (later model DeVille shown)

Lock cylinder

Refer to illustrations 23.8 and 23.9

6   Remove the trunk lid trim panel.

7   On some models it may be necessary to remove the back-up light housing for access.

8   Disconnect the release cable **(see illustration)**.

9   Detach the retaining clip then push the lock cylinder out of the trunk lid and remove it from the vehicle **(see illustration)**.

10   Installation is the reverse of removal.

24   Fuel door actuator - removal and installation

Refer to illustrations 24.4a, 24.4b and 24.5

1   Open the trunk lid and remove the left side trim panel.

2   Open the fuel door.

3   Remove the retaining screw(s) and disconnect the actuating cable (if equipped), then remove the actuator.

4   Remove the fasteners and detach the solenoid **(see illustrations)**.

5   Disconnect the electrical connector and detach the assembly from the vehicle **(see illustration)**.

6   Installation is the reverse of removal.

25   Center console - removal and installation

Warning: *These models are equipped with a Supplemental Inflatable Restraint (SIR) system (more commonly known as airbags). Always disable the airbag system before working in the vicinity of any airbag system component to avoid the possibility of accidental deployment of the airbag, which could cause personal injury (see Chapter 12).*

1   Apply the parking brake lever and place the gear selector into the neutral position. Disconnect the cable from the negative terminal of the battery (see Chapter 5).

2   If equipped, pry out the shift lever knob retaining clip and remove the knob.

3   Pry out the gear selector trim bezel by disengaging the clips on the front edge. Then disconnect the electrical connectors and remove the bezel from the console assembly.

4   Remove the retaining screws securing the front half of the console.

5   Working in the console glove box, detach the retaining screws and nuts securing the rear half of the console.

6   Lift the console up and over the shift lever. Disconnect any electrical connections and remove the console from the vehicle.

7   Installation is the reverse of removal.

26   Dashboard trim panels - removal and installation

Warning: *These models are equipped with a Supplemental Inflatable Restraint (SIR) system (more commonly known as airbags). Always disable the airbag system before working in the vicinity of any airbag system component to avoid the possibility of accidental deployment of the airbag, which could*

26.2 Detach the cluster bezel from the clips in the dashboard and lift it off

cause personal injury (see Chapter 12).

Note: *On some models the instrument cluster and bezel are removed as a single unit (see Chapter 12 for the cluster removal procedure).*

Instrument cluster bezel

Refer to illustration 26.2

1   Disconnect the cable from the negative terminal of the battery (see Chapter 5). Remove the instrument panel dash pad (see Section 27) for access to the instrument cluster.

2   Remove the screws/nuts, grasp the bezel securely and detach any clips from the instrument panel **(see illustration)**.

3   Unplug any electrical connectors that interfere with removal.

4   Installation is the reverse of removal.

Steering column covers

Refer to illustrations 26.5 and 26.6

5   Remove the knee bolster trim panel (see Step 8), then remove the steering column cover retaining screws **(see illustration)**. Also remove the tilt lever.

6   Detach the lower half, then remove the

26.5 Remove the tilt lever and the steering column cover screws

11

**26.6 Some models also have another
screw securing the upper cover**

**26.8 Grasp the knee bolster and detach it
from the dashboard**

**26.9 Remove these screws and detach
the filler panel**

26.10 Remove the knee bolster bolts

**26.12 Use a screwdriver or hooked tool to
detach the upper center grille panel,
then lift it off**

**26.13a Remove the screws and detach
the lower center panel**

screw securing the upper half **(see illustration)**.
7   Installation is the reverse of removal.

Driver's knee bolster trim panel

Refer to illustrations 26.8, 26.9 and 26.10

8   Detach the knee bolster clips by pulling
it straight down and back **(see illustration)**.
9   Remove the lower steering column filler
panel **(see illustration)**.
10   Remove the fasteners and detach the

knee bolster **(see illustration)**.
11   Installation is the reverse of removal.

Center trim panels

*Refer to illustrations 26.12, 26.13a and
26.13b*

12   Detach the upper trim panel on models
so equipped, using a screwdriver or a hooked

tool **(see illustration)**.
13   Remove the lower trim panel bolts or
screws, then lower the panel from the dash
and disconnect the electrical connectors
(see illustrations).
14   Installation is the reverse of removal.

Passenger's knee bolster

Refer to illustration 26.15

15   To remove the bolster by grasping it
securely and pulling straight back **(see illustration)**.
16   Installation is the reverse of the removal
procedure.

**26.13b Rotate the panel back and
disconnect the electrical connectors**

**26.15 Grasp the knee bolster securely
and detach it from the dashboard by
pulling out**

**26.17 Remove the screws and detach the
glove box**

27.2 Use screwdrivers to press on the clips and detach the air vent grilles

27.3a Use a socket wrench with an extension and work though the grille openings to remove the bolts that retain the dash pad to the instrument panel

27.3b Remove the remaining dash pad bolts

Glove box

Refer to illustration 26.17

17   To remove the glove box, simply remove the screws and detach the glove box from the instrument panel **(see illustration)**.

18   Installation is the reverse of the removal procedure.

27   Instrument panel dash pad - removal and installation

Refer to illustrations 27.2, 27.3a, 27.3b, 27.4, 27.5 and 27.7

Warning: *These models are equipped with a Supplemental Inflatable Restraint (SIR) system (more commonly known as airbags). Always disable the airbag system before working in the vicinity of any airbag system component to avoid the possibility of accidental deployment of the airbag, which could cause personal injury (see Chapter 12).*

1   Disconnect the negative cable from the battery (see Chapter 5).

2   Detach and remove the air vent grilles and remove the dashboard trim piece **(see illustration)**.

3   Remove the screws retaining the rear edge of the pad **(see illustrations)**.

4   Use a screwdriver to carefully pry out the windshield pillar molding pieces at each

end of the pad **(see illustration)**.

5   Carefully pry the up on the rear edge of the defroster grille and detach it from the dash pad **(see illustration)**. Disconnect the electrical connectors and remove the grille.

6   Remove the screws along the front edge of the trim pad.

7   Lift up the rear edge of the trim pad, then lift the pad off the instrument panel **(see illustration)**.

8   Installation is the reverse of removal.

28   Seats - removal and installation

Warning: *Some of the models covered by this manual are equipped with side-impact airbags located in the seat backs. Some are also equipped with seat belt pre-tensioners, which are pyrotechnic (explosive) devices which tighten the seat belts during an impact of sufficient force. Be sure to disarm the airbag system when working in the vicinity of any of the airbag system or seat belt pre-tensioner components (see Chapter 12).*

Front seat

Refer to illustrations 28.2a and 28.2b

1   Position the seat all the way forward or all the way to the rear to access the front seat retaining bolts.

2   Detach the trim covers and remove the

27.4 Use a screwdriver to remove the windshield trim pieces

27.5 Detach the defroster grille from the clips and rotate it up and out of the dash cover

27.7 Lift the rear of the pad and remove it from the instrument panel

28.2a Detach the covers and remove the retaining bolts at the front . . .

11

28.2b ... and rear of the seat

28.5 Use a screwdriver to detach the two seatback release clips

28.6 Push in on the two clips at the base of the rear seat cushion, then lift it up

retaining nuts **(see illustrations)**.
3   Tilt the seat upward to access the underside, then disconnect any electrical connectors and lift the seat from the vehicle.
4   Installation is the reverse of removal.

Rear seat

Refer to illustrations 28.5 and 28.6
5   Insert a screwdriver between the rear shelf and the seatback and detach the two clips, then lift the seat back out of the vehicle **(see illustration)**.
6   Remove the seat cushion by pushing in on the two clips at the base and then lifting the seat cushion up and out of the vehicle **(see illustration)**.
7   Installation is the reverse of removal.

29   Instrument panel - removal and installation

Refer to illustrations 29.8, 29.9 and 29.12
Warning: *These models are equipped with a Supplemental Inflatable Restraint (SIR) system (more commonly known as airbags). Always disable the airbag system before working in the vicinity of any airbag system component to avoid the possibility of accidental deployment of the airbag, which could*

cause personal injury (see Chapter 12).
Note: *It is not necessary, but it is suggested to remove both front seats to allow additional working space and lessen the chance of damage to the seats during this procedure.*
1   Disconnect the negative battery cable.
2   Remove the center console (see Section 25).
3   Remove the knee bolsters (see Section 26).
4   Remove the dashboard right and left end trim panels.
5   Disconnect the electrical connectors at both ends of the instrument panel.
6   Remove the instrument panel dash pad (see Section 27).
7   Remove the steering column mounting nuts/bolts, disconnect the intermediate shaft (see Chapter 10) and lower the column.
8   Disconnect the column shift and tilt column cables and electrical connectors. **(see illustration)**.
9   Remove the instrument panel center bracket bolts **(see illustration)**.
10   Remove the glove box (see Section 26). Remove the passenger airbag module (see Chapter 12). **Warning:** *Carry the airbag with the trim cover side FACING AWAY from your body to minimize injury if the airbag module accidentally deploys. Store the airbag module*

29.8 Disconnect the shift cables and electrical connectors

aside in a safe, isolated location with the trim cover side facing UP.
11   Remove the nuts along the top of the instrument panel that attach it to the cowl.
12   Remove the nuts retaining the ends of the instrument panel **(see illustration)**.
13   Lift up the instrument panel and pull rearward then withdraw it from the vehicle.
14   Installation is the reverse of removal.

29.9 Remove the instrument panel center support bracket bolts

29.12 Remove the bolts at each end of the instrument panel

Chapter 12
Chassis electrical system

Contents

1 General information

The electrical system is a 12-volt, negative ground type. Power for the lights and all electrical accessories is supplied by a lead/acid-type battery, which is charged by the alternator.

This Chapter covers repair and service procedures for the various electrical components not associated with the engine. Information on the battery, alternator, distributor and starter motor can be found in Chapter 5. It should be noted that when portions of the electrical system are serviced, the negative battery cable should be disconnected from the battery to prevent electrical shorts and/or fires.

Warning: *These models are equipped with a Supplemental Inflatable Restraint (SIR) system (more commonly known as airbags). Always disable the airbag system before working in the vicinity of any airbag system component to avoid the possibility of accidental deployment of the airbag, which could cause personal injury (see Section 25).*

2 Electrical troubleshooting

Refer to illustration 2.15

A typical electrical circuit consists of an electrical component, any switches, relays, motors, fuses, fusible links or circuit breakers related to that component and the wiring and connectors that link the component to both the battery and the chassis. To help you pinpoint an electrical circuit problem; wiring diagrams are included at the end of this Chapter.

Before tackling any troublesome electrical circuit, first study the appropriate wiring diagrams to get a complete understanding of what makes up that individual circuit. Noting if other components related to the circuit are operating properly, for instance, can often narrow trouble spots, down. If several components or circuits fail at one time, chances are the problem is in a fuse or ground connection, because several circuits are often routed through the same fuse and ground connections.

Electrical problems usually stem from simple causes, such as loose or corroded connections, a blown fuse, a melted fusible link or a failed relay. Visually inspect the condition of all fuses, wires and connections in a problem circuit before troubleshooting the circuit.

If test equipment and instruments are going to be utilized, use the diagrams to plan ahead of time where you will make the necessary connections in order to accurately pinpoint the trouble spot.

The basic tools needed for electrical troubleshooting include a circuit tester or voltmeter (a 12-volt bulb with a set of test leads can also be used), a continuity tester, which includes a bulb, battery and set of test leads, and a jumper wire, preferably with a circuit breaker incorporated, which can be used to bypass electrical components. Before attempting to locate a problem with test instruments, use the wiring diagram(s) to decide where to make the connections.

Voltage checks

Voltage checks should be performed if a circuit is not functioning properly. Connect one lead of a circuit tester to either the negative battery terminal or a known good ground. Connect the other lead to a connector in the circuit being tested, preferably nearest to the battery or fuse. If the bulb of the tester lights, voltage is present, which means that the part of the circuit between the connector and the battery is problem free. Continue checking the rest of the circuit in the same fashion. When you reach a point at which no voltage is present, the problem lies between that point and the last test point with voltage. Most of the time the problem can be traced to a loose connection. **Note:** *Keep in mind that some circuits receive voltage only when the ignition key is in the Accessory or Run position.*

Finding a short

One method of finding shorts in a circuit is to remove the fuse and connect a test light or voltmeter in place of the fuse terminals. There should be no voltage present in the circuit. Move the wiring harness from side-to-side while watching the test light. If the bulb goes on, there is a short to ground somewhere in that area, probably where the insulation has rubbed through. The same test can be performed on each component in the circuit, even a switch.

Ground check

Perform a ground test to check whether a component is properly grounded. Disconnect the battery and connect one lead of a self-powered test light, known as a continuity tester, to a known good ground. Connect the other lead to the wire or ground connection being tested. If the bulb goes on, the ground is good. If the bulb does not go on, the ground is not good.

Continuity check

A continuity check is done to determine if there are any breaks in a circuit - if it is passing electricity properly. With the circuit off (no power in the circuit), a self-powered continuity tester can be used to check the circuit. Connect the test leads to both ends of the circuit (or to the "power" end and a good ground), and if the test light comes on the circuit is passing current properly. If the light doesn't come on, there is a break somewhere in the circuit. The same procedure can be used to test a switch, by connecting the continuity tester to the switch terminals. With the switch turned On, the test light should come on.

Finding an open circuit

When diagnosing for possible open circuits, it is often difficult to locate them by sight because the connectors hide oxidation or terminal misalignment. Merely wiggling a connector on a sensor or in the wiring harness may correct the open circuit condition. Remember this when an open circuit is indicated when troubleshooting a circuit. Intermittent problems may also be caused by oxi-

2.15 To backprobe a connector, insert a small, sharp probe (such as a T-pin) into the back of the connector alongside the desired wire until it contacts the metal terminal inside; connect your meter leads to the probes - this allows you to test a functioning circuit

dized or loose connections.

Electrical troubleshooting is simple if you keep in mind that all electrical circuits are basically electricity running from the battery, through the wires, switches, relays, fuses and fusible links to each electrical component (light bulb, motor, etc.) and to ground, from which it is passed back to the battery. Any electrical problem is an interruption in the flow of electricity to and from the battery.

Connectors

Most electrical connections on these vehicles are made with multi-wire plastic connectors. The mating halves of many connectors are secured with locking clips molded into the plastic connector shells. The mating halves of large connectors, such as some of those under the instrument panel, are held together by a bolt through the center of the connector.

To separate a connector with locking clips, use a small screwdriver to pry the clips apart carefully, then separate the connector halves. Pull only on the shell; never pull on the wiring harness as you may damage the individual wires and terminals inside the connectors. Look at the connector closely before trying to separate the halves. Often the locking clips are engaged in a way that is not immediately clear. Additionally, many connectors have more than one set of clips.

Each pair of connector terminals has a male half and a female half. When you look at the end view of a connector in a diagram, be sure to understand whether the view shows the harness side or the component side of the connector. Connector halves are mirror images of each other, and a terminal shown on the right side end view of one half will be on the left side end view of the other half.

It is often necessary to take circuit voltage measurements with a connector con-

nected. Whenever possible, carefully insert the test probes of your meter into the rear of the connector shell to contact the terminal inside. This kind of connection is called "backprobing" **(see illustration)**. When inserting a test probe into a male terminal, be careful not to distort the terminal opening. Doing so can lead to a poor connection and corrosion at that terminal later.

Troubleshooting a typical circuit

Most of your troubleshooting will center on discovering why something on the vehicle doesn't work, for example, a power window. A typical circuit will encompass a motor (or other device at the end of the circuit such as a light), a switch, a relay and a fuse.

Begin by checking for power and ground at the device end of the circuit, i.e. at the motor or light. Refer to the wiring diagrams at the end of this Chapter for the circuit diagram, terminals and wire colors. Disconnect the connector at the device and, on the harness side of the connector, clip a 12-volt test light to the ground side of the connector and probe the power side of the connector with the switch turned On. If the test light glows brightly, both power and ground circuits to the device are good.

If there is power at the connector on the device, but the device doesn't operate when the switch is turned On, disconnect the electrical connector at the device and ground the ground side terminal of the device with a jumper wire to a known-good chassis ground. Attach a fused jumper wire (the fuse should have a rating the same as the fuse that normally feeds that device) to the power supply terminal on the device. If it's doesn't operate, that device, motor or light is faulty.

If the device is OK, but the test light did not light at the connector, trace the circuit according to the wiring diagram and check the fuse that is the power source for the circuit. If the fuse is good, check for power at the relay that sends power to the device. If there is power to the relay, refer to Section 6 and test the relay. If the relay is good, check the continuity of wiring from the relay to the switch, and from the relay to the device.

In a process of elimination, you will find an open or short in the circuit, or a faulty switch.

---

3 Fuses - general information

Fuses

Refer to illustrations 3.1a, 3.1b and 3.3

Electrical circuits are protected by a combination of fuses and circuit breakers. Models covered by this manual have a fuse/relay panel in the engine compartment, as well as an electrical center or fuse/relay panel under the rear seat or in the trunk **(see illustrations)**.

Each of the fuses is designed to protect

3.1a A large underhood fuse/relay panel is located in the engine compartment on all models

3.1b Most models have a fuse block or an electrical center like this mounted under the rear seat or in the trunk

a specific circuit (or circuits), and the various circuits are identified on the fuse panel cover or the fuse panel itself.

Miniaturized fuses are employed in the fuse block. These compact fuses, with blade terminal design, allow fingertip removal and replacement. If an electrical component fails, always check the fuse first. The easiest way to check fuses is with a test light. Check for power at the exposed terminal tips of each fuse. If power is present on one side of the fuse but not the other, the fuse is blown. When removed, a blown fuse is easily identified through the clear plastic body. Visually inspect the element for evidence of damage (see illustration).

Be sure to replace blown fuses with the correct type. Fuses of different ratings are physically interchangeable, but only fuses of the proper rating should be used. Replacing a fuse with one of a higher or lower value than specified is not recommended. Each electrical circuit needs a specific amount of protection. The amperage value of each fuse is molded into the fuse body.

If the replacement fuse immediately fails, don't replace it again until the cause of the problem is isolated and corrected. In most cases, the cause will be a short circuit in the wiring caused by a broken or deteriorated wire.

4   Circuit breakers - general information

Circuit breakers protect components such as sunroof motors, power seat motors, power window motors and airbag inflator resistors.

On some models the circuit breaker resets itself automatically, so an electrical overload in a circuit-breaker-protected system will cause the circuit to fail momentarily, then come back on. If the circuit does not come back on, check it immediately. Once the condition is corrected, the circuit breaker will resume its normal function. Some circuit breakers must be reset manually. Most circuit breakers are located in the underhood or interior fuse/relay panels (see Section 3).

3.3 When a fuse blows, the element between the terminals melts - the fuse on the left is blown, the fuse on the right is good

Bad   Good

5   Relays - general information and testing

General information

1   Several electrical accessories in the vehicle, such as the fuel injection system, horns, starter, and fog lamps use relays to transmit the electrical signal to the component. Relays use a low-current circuit (the control circuit) to open and close a high-current circuit (the power circuit). If the relay is defective, that component will not operate properly. Most relays are mounted in the engine compartment and interior fuse/relay boxes (see illustrations 3.1a and 3.1b). If a faulty relay is suspected, it can be removed and tested using the procedure below or by a dealer service department or a repair shop. Defective relays must be replaced as a unit.

Testing

Refer to illustrations 5.2a and 5.2b

2   Most of the relays used in these vehicles are of a type often called "ISO" relays, which

5.2a Typical ISO relay designs, terminal numbering and circuit connections

Relay with internal resistor   Relay with internal diode

24053-12-5.2a HAYNES

12

5.2b Most relays are marked on the outside to easily identify the control circuit and power circuit - this one is of the four-terminal type

6.4 On later models turn signal/hazard flasher is located under the lest side of the steering column

7.3a Use a special tool (available at most auto parts stores) to depress the lock plate, then pry out the retaining ring (early models)

refers to the International Standards Organization. The terminals of ISO relays are numbered to indicate their usual circuit connections and functions. There are two basic layouts of terminals on the relays used in these vehicles **(see illustrations)**.

3   Two of the terminals are the relay control circuit and connect to the relay coil. The other relay terminals are the power circuit. When the relay is energized, the coil creates a magnetic field that closes the larger contacts of the power circuit to provide power to the circuit loads.

4   Terminals 85 and 86 are normally the control circuit. If the relay contains a diode, terminal 86 must be connected to battery positive (B+) voltage and terminal 85 to ground. If the relay contains a resistor, terminals 85 and 86 can be connected in either direction with respect to B+ and ground.

5   Terminal 30 is normally connected to the battery voltage (B+) source for the circuit loads. Terminal 87 is connected to the circuit leading to the component being controlled. If the relay has several alternate terminals for load or ground connections, they usually are numbered 87A, 87B, 87C, and so on.

6   Use an ohmmeter to check continuity through the relay control coil.

 a) *Connect the meter according to the polarity shown in the illustration for one check; then reverse the ohmmeter leads and check continuity in the other direction.*

 b) *If the relay contains a resistor, resistance should be indicated on the meter, and should be the same value with the ohmmeter in either direction.*

 c) *If the relay contains a diode, resistance should be higher with the ohmmeter in the forward polarity direction than with the meter leads reversed.*

 d) *If the ohmmeter shows infinite resistance in both directions, replace the relay.*

7   Remove the relay from the vehicle and use the ohmmeter to check for continuity between the relay power circuit terminals.

There should be no continuity between terminal 30 and 87 with the relay de-energized.

8   Connect a fused jumper wire to terminal 86 and the positive battery terminal. Connect another jumper wire between terminal 85 and ground. When the connections are made, the relay should click.

9   With the jumper wires connected, check for continuity between the power circuit terminals. Now, there should be continuity between terminals 30 and 87.

10   If the relay fails any of the above tests, replace it.

6   Turn signal/hazard flasher - check and replacement

Refer to illustration 6.4

Warning: *These models are equipped with a Supplemental Inflatable Restraint (SIR) system (more commonly known as airbags). Always disable the airbag system before working in the vicinity of any airbag system component to avoid the possibility of accidental deployment of the airbag, which could cause personal injury (see Section 25).*

1   On 1997 and earlier Sevilles and 1999 and earlier DeVilles, the turn signals and hazard flashers are controlled by two separate flasher units, located under the dash near the steering column and left kick panel. On 1998 and later Sevilles and 2000 and later DeVilles, the flashers have been combined into one unit, located under the dash by the steering column.

2   When the flasher unit is functioning properly, an audible click can be heard during its operation. If the turn signals fail on one side or the other and the flasher unit does not make its characteristic clicking sound (early models), or if a bulb on one side of the vehicle flashes much faster than normal but the bulb at the other end of the vehicle (on the same side) doesn't light at all (later models), a faulty turn signal bulb may be indicated.

3   If both turn signals fail to blink, the problem may be due to a blown fuse, a faulty

flasher unit, a broken switch or a loose or open connection. If a quick check of the fuse box indicates that the turn signal fuse has blown, check the wiring for a short before installing a new fuse.

4   To replace the flasher, remove the left side knee bolster and (if equipped) the close out panel (see Chapter 11) and disconnect the unit(s) from the electrical connector **(see illustration)**.

5   Make sure that the replacement unit is identical to the original. Compare the old one to the new one before installing it.

6   Installation is the reverse of removal.

7   Steering column switches - replacement

Warning: *These models are equipped with a Supplemental Inflatable Restraint (SIR) system (more commonly known as airbags). Always disable the airbag system before working in the vicinity of any airbag system component to avoid the possibility of accidental deployment of the airbag, which could cause personal injury (see Section 25).*

1   Disconnect the cable from the negative battery terminal (see Chapter 5) and disable the airbag system (see Section 25).

2   Remove the steering wheel (see Chapter 10).

Early models

Turn signal switch

Removal

Refer to illustrations 7.3a, 7.3b, 7.4, 7.5a, 7.5b, 7.7 and 7.10

3   Remove the airbag clockspring (see Chapter 10, Section 18); let the clockspring hang by the wiring harness. Remove the wave washer. Using a lock plate removal tool, depress the lock plate for access to the retaining ring **(see illustrations)**. Use a small screwdriver to pry the retaining ring out of the groove in the steering column and remove the lock plate.

7.3b Lift the lockplate out

7.4 Remove the hazard warning knob screw and the knob

7.5a Remove the cancel cam . . .

7.5b . . . and the spring

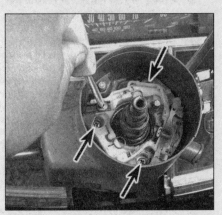

7.7 Remove the screw and the turn signal lever actuating arm (shown here with screwdriver), then remove the switch mounting screws - to get at the upper screw in this photo, the top of the switch must be clicked down

4   Use a small Phillips head screwdriver to remove the hazard warning knob **(see illustration)**.

5   Remove the turn signal cancel cam and the spring **(see illustrations)**.

6   Remove the turn signal lever actuating arm screw and remove the actuating arm.

7   Remove the turn signal switch mounting screws **(see illustration)**.

8   Remove the knee bolster panel below the steering column (see Chapter 11).

9   Locate the turn signal switch electrical connector and unplug it. Remove the wiring protector. **Note:** *On certain models it may be necessary to remove the terminals for the key reminder buzzer from the turn signal switch connector. To do this, insert a narrow pin into the electrical connector, from the side opposite the wire, depress the tang on the terminal and pull the wire out. Be sure the wires get installed into their proper positions upon reassembly.*

10   Attach a length of mechanic's wire to the electrical connector (this will aid in the installation of the new switch). Pull the wiring harness and electrical connector up through the steering column and remove the switch assembly **(see illustration)**. **Note:** *On some models it may be necessary to remove the steering column mounting bracket to provide clearance for the electrical connector.*

Installation

11   Attach the mechanic's wire to the electrical connector of the new switch. Slowly pull the wiring harness through the steering column. **Note:** *If the column mounting bracket was removed, install it and tighten the bracket-to-column bolts (see Chapter 10).*

12   Seat the turn signal switch on the column and install the turn signal switch mounting screws and lever actuating arm. Install the hazard knob.

13   Connect the switch electrical connector and reinstall the wiring protector.

14   Install the spring, cancel cam and the lock plate. Depress the lock plate and install the retaining ring.

15   If necessary, center the airbag clockspring as described in Chapter 10, Section 18. **Note:** *Make sure the front wheels are pointing straight ahead before installing the clockspring.*

16   Install the wave washer and the airbag clockspring. Pull the slack out of the clockspring lower wiring harness to keep it tight through the steering column, or it may be cut when the steering wheel is turned. Install the clockspring retaining snap-ring.

17   The remainder of installation is the reverse of removal.

Wiper/washer switch (column-mounted switch)

Removal

Refer to illustrations 7.20, 7.21, 7.22, 7.24 and 7.25

18   The wiper/washer functions are controlled by a switch mounted on the steering column under the column cover assembly.

7.10 Pull the turn signal switch out, carefully drawing the wiring harness through the steering column

12

7.20 Gently pry off the cover behind the multi-function lever

7.21 Disconnect the cruise-control electrical connector

7.22 To remove the multi-function lever, grasp it firmly and pull straight out

The multi-function lever controls the wiper switch. Only the cruise control switch is contained within the multi-function lever.

19   Refer to the procedure above and remove the turn signal switch. It isn't necessary to pull the switch wiring harness and connector out of the column, just let the switch hang from the column by the wires. Refer to Section 8 and remove the ignition key lock cylinder.

20   Remove the plastic cover behind the multi-function lever at the left side of the steering column **(see illustration)**.

21   Disconnect the cruise control wiring connector at the column, just below the tilt lever **(see illustration)**. If necessary, remove the tilt lever by turning it counterclockwise.

22   Grasp the multi-function lever and pull it straight out of the wiper switch/pivot assembly, fishing the cruise control wires out with it **(see illustration)**.

23   Disconnect the wiper switch wire connector at the base of the steering column near the turn signal switch connector. Attach a length of mechanics wire to the electrical connector (this will aid in the installation of

the new switch).

24   Remove the three screws and pull the steering column cover away from the column **(see illustration)**.

25   Remove the pivot pin from the cover assembly **(see illustration)**. Remove the wiper switch/pivot assembly and pull the wiring harness and connector through the lower steering column shroud.

Installation

26   Attach the mechanic's wire to the electrical connector of the new switch. Slowly pull the wiring harness through the steering column and install the switch/pivot assembly into the cover.

27   Insert the pivot pin through the switch and into the cover.

28   Connect the switch wire connector at the base of the steering column.

29   The remainder of the installation is the reverse of the removal procedure. Make sure the front wheels are pointing straight ahead and the airbag clockspring is centered (as described in Chapter 10, Section 18 before installing it.

Headlight dimmer switch

Refer to illustration 7.31

30   The dimmer switch is located on the side of the steering column, just below the ignition switch. If continuity tests reveal a problem with the dimmer switch, disconnect the negative battery cable and remove the trim panel and knee bolster from below the steering column (see Chapter 11).

31   Remove the nut from the stud, remove the screw and pull out the dimmer switch, disengaging it from the dimmer switch actuator rod **(see illustration)**.

32   Follow the dimmer switch wiring harness to the bulkhead connector at the base of the column.

33   Withdraw the dimmer switch and wiring harness.

34   Install the new dimmer switch leaving the nut/screw loose and adjust it as follows:

a)   *Insert a 3/32-inch drill bit into the adjustment hole provided on the dimmer switch.*

b)   *Slide the dimmer switch toward the actuating rod, removing all clearance between the switch and rod.*

7.24 Remove the three Torx screws and pull the cover off the steering column

7.25 Use needle-nose pliers to remove the pivot pin (A), then remove the wiper switch/pivot assembly (B) from the steering column cover

7.31 Remove the nut and screw securing the dimmer switch (A) to the steering column, and withdraw the switch from the actuator rod (B)

7.37 Remove the screws and detach the turn signal/multi-function switch (later model)

7.41 Pull straight out to detach the switch(es) from the steering wheel

c) *Tighten the nut/screw and remove the drill bit.*

35   The remainder of installation is the reverse of removal.

Later models

Turn signal switch/multi-function switch

Refer to illustration 7.37

36   Remove the steering column covers (see Chapter 11).
37   Remove the turn signal/multi-function switch retaining screws **(see illustration)**.
38   Detach the turn signal/multi-function switch and disconnect the electrical connectors.
39   Installation is the reverse of removal.

Steering wheel mounted switches

Refer to illustration 7.41

40   Disable and remove the airbag module (see Section 25).
41   Pull straight back to detach the switch from the steering wheel, then disconnect the electrical connector **(see illustration)**.
42   Installation is the reverse of removal.

8   Ignition switch and key lock cylinder - replacement

Warning: *These models are equipped with a Supplemental Inflatable Restraint (SIR) system (more commonly known as airbags). Always disable the airbag system before working in the vicinity of any airbag system component to avoid the possibility of accidental deployment of the airbag, which could cause personal injury (see Section 25).*

Early models

Lock cylinder

Refer to illustrations 8.4, 8.5, 8.6a and 8.6b

1   The lock cylinder is located on the upper right-hand side of the steering column.
2   Disconnect the negative battery cable (see Chapter 5). Refer to Section 25 and disable the airbag system.
3   Remove the steering wheel (see Chapter 10) and turn signal switch (see Section 7). **Note:** *The turn signal switch need not be fully removed provided that it can be slipped over the end of the shaft. Do not pull the harness out of the column.*

4   Insert the key and place the lock cylinder in the Run position. Using needle-nose pliers, remove the buzzer switch **(see illustration)**.
5   Remove the lock cylinder retaining screw **(see illustration)**.
6   Remove the lock cylinder by pulling the assembly straight out of the column **(see illustration)**. On models equipped with a PASS key security system, remove the PASS key wiring harness as follows:

a) *Note exactly how the wires are routed through the column and remove the wiring harness retaining clips and wire protector.*
b) *Follow the PASS key wires at the base of the steering column to the turn signal electrical connector, disconnect the electrical connector and remove the PASS key wire terminals from the connector by inserting a small screwdriver into the connector to depress the terminal retaining tab* **(see illustration)**.
c) *Tape the wire terminals to a length of mechanics wire and pull the wire harness and mechanics wire up through the steering column. Remove the terminals*

8.4 Pull the buzzer switch out of the column with needle-nose pliers

8.5 Remove the lock cylinder retaining screw

8.6a Pull the lock cylinder straight out of the steering column

12

8.6b To remove the PASS key wire harness terminals from the connector, insert a small screwdriver or pin into the front of the connector, depress the retaining tab (part of the terminal) and pull the wire and terminal out from the backside

8.13 After the steering column has been lowered, remove the ignition switch wiring cover screws - with the cover off remove the switch-to-column screws

from the mechanics wire but leave the mechanics wire in place.

7   Insert the ignition key into the new lock cylinder and install the lock cylinder, aligning the tab on the cylinder with the keyway in the steering column housing.

8   Push the lock all the way in and install the retaining screw. If equipped with a PASS key system, tape the wire terminals to the mechanics wire used in Step 6 and pull the wiring harness through the steering column. Route the wiring harness exactly as originally installed, insert the wiring terminals into the electrical connector at the base of the column and connect the connector. Install the retaining clips and wire protector. **Note:** *Make sure the PASS key wiring harness terminals are properly installed in the connector. If they are not properly installed, the vehicle will not start on completion of the procedure.*

9   Install the remaining components, referring to the appropriate Sections.

Ignition switch

Refer to illustration 8.13

10   The ignition switch is located on the lower portion of the steering column and is activated by a rod connected to the ignition lock cylinder. Disconnect the negative cable at the battery (see Chapter 5). Refer to Section 25 and disable the airbag system, if equipped.

11   Place the ignition switch in the Lock position. If the key lock cylinder has been removed, pull the actuating rod up until a definite stop can be felt, then move it down one detent.

12   Remove the trim panel under the steering column and the knee bolster. Remove the steering column bracket-to-instrument panel bolts or nuts and lower the steering column for access to the ignition switch.

13   Remove the ignition switch retaining screws and remove the ignition switch **(see illustration)**. Disconnect the ignition switch harness connector from the ignition switch.

14   Prior to installation make sure the igni-

tion switch is in the Lock position.

15   Connect the actuating rod to the switch.

16   Connect the electrical connector to the new switch.

17   Press the switch into position and install the screws.

18   Raise the steering column into position and install and tighten the bolts or nuts securely. Make sure the switch is actuated when the ignition key is turned to the Start position. If it doesn't, loosen the switch screws and adjust the position of the switch on the steering column.

Later models

Lock cylinder/ignition switch

Refer to illustrations 8.21a and 8.21b

19   Disconnect the negative battery cable (see Chapter 5). Refer to Section 25 and disable the airbag system.

20   On DeVille models, remove the steering column cover screws and raise the upper cover for access to the lock cylinder/ignition switch release pin access hole.

21   Lift the column cover up, insert a small

screwdriver or a pick with a bent tip, turn the lock cylinder to the Start position then push down on the pin while releasing the switch to Run to remove it **(see illustrations)**.

22   On Seville models, remove the radio and heater control for access to the release button on the side of the lock cylinder.

23   Turn the key to the Run position. Working through the radio opening, depress the release button and remove the lock cylinder.

24   On both models, install the lock cylinder by lining up the lock cylinder and switch assembly slot and locking tabs and with the key in place then insert the cylinder until it clicks into position.

---

9   Instrument panel switches - replacement

Refer to illustrations 9.4a, 9.4b, 9.5a, 9.5b and 9.5c

Warning: *These models are equipped with a Supplemental Inflatable Restraint (SIR) system (more commonly known as airbags).*

8.21a Turn the lock cylinder to the Start position while inserting a screwdriver or pick with a bent tip, push down on the release button . . .

8.21b . . . then turn the key to the Run position and remove the lock cylinder

9.4a Remove the mounting screws retaining the switch to the cluster bezel

9.4b Detach the switch from the bezel

Always disable the airbag system before working in the vicinity of any airbag system component to avoid the possibility of accidental deployment of the airbag, which could cause personal injury (see Section 25).

1   Disconnect the negative battery cable (see Chapter 5).

2   Refer to Chapter 11 and remove the instrument panel bezel.

3   On early models remove the screws and pull the switch pod out from the instrument panel. Pull the switch out far enough to disconnect the electrical connector on the back.

4   On later models the switches may be mounted in the cluster bezel and instrument panel. Detach the bezel (see Chapter 11) and remove the information center switches **(see illustrations)**.

5   The headlight switch is held in place by clips. Remove the instrument panel end cap for access, reach behind and detach it from the instrument panel, then disconnect the electrical connector **(see illustrations)**.

6   Installation is the reverse of the removal procedure.

9.5a Detach the instrument panel end cap

10   Instrument cluster - removal and installation

Refer to illustration 10.3

Warning: *These models are equipped with a Supplemental Inflatable Restraint (SIR) system (more commonly known as airbags). Always disable the airbag system before*

9.5b Reach behind the headlight switch and detach the clips from the instrument panel

working in the vicinity of any airbag system component to avoid the possibility of accidental deployment of the airbag, which could cause personal injury (see Section 25).

1   Disconnect the negative cable from the battery (see Chapter 5).

2   Remove the instrument cluster bezel (see Chapter 11).

3   Remove the instrument cluster screws, pull out the cluster and unplug the electrical connectors **(see illustration)**.

4   Installation is the reverse of removal.

11   Radio and speakers - removal and installation

Warning: *These models are equipped with a Supplemental Inflatable Restraint (SIR) system (more commonly known as airbags). Always disable the airbag system before working in the vicinity of any airbag system component to avoid the possibility of accidental deployment of the airbag, which could cause personal injury (see Section 25).*

12

9.5c Pull the headlight switch from the instrument panel and disconnect the electrical connector

10.3 Remove the mounting screws, pull the instrument cluster out for access and disconnect the electrical connectors

11.3a Remove the radio mounting screws

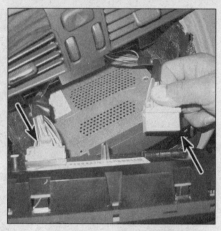

11.3b Disconnect the electrical connectors at the back of the radio

11.6 Disconnect the electrical connector (A) at the front speaker, then remove the mounting screws (B) (early model shown)

11.12 With the package shelf removed, you can remove the rear speaker mounting screws (early model)

12.1 Apply tape to the body around the antenna to ensure the paint isn't scratched, then remove the antenna base nut

12.3 Remove the antenna cable (A), disconnect the electrical connector at the antenna relay (B), and remove the bolts (C) securing the antenna assembly (early model)

Radio

Refer to illustrations 11.3a and 11.3b

1   Disconnect the negative battery cable (see Chapter 5).
2   Remove the radio bezel (early models) or on later models refer to Chapter 11 and detach the instrument panel center bezel.
3   Remove the retaining screws and pull the radio outward to access the backside, then disconnect the electrical connectors and the antenna lead and lift the radio out of the instrument panel **(see illustrations)**.
4   Installation is the reverse of removal.

Front speakers

Refer to illustration 11.6

5   Remove the front door trim panel (see Chapter 11).
6   Remove the speaker retaining screws. Disconnect the electrical connector and remove the speaker from the vehicle **(see illustration)**.
7   Installation is the reverse of removal.

Rear speakers

8   Refer to Chapter 11 and remove the rear seat, then remove the package shelf.

9   Remove the speaker retaining screws, leaving the plastic enclosure in place. On some models the speaker is held in place by clips instead of screws and on later models plastic retainers are used. Disconnect the electrical connector and remove the speaker from the vehicle.
10   Installation is the reverse of removal.

12 Antenna - removal and installation

Early models

Power antenna assembly

Refer to illustrations 12.1 and 12.3

1   Using a pair of snap-ring pliers or an antenna tool, remove the antenna base retaining nut. An antenna removal tool is available at most auto parts stores **(see illustration)**, and won't slip off and possibly scratch the body, like pliers or other tools.
2   Working in the trunk, pry out the plastic clips securing the passenger side trunk finishing panels to allow access to the antenna motor.

3   Detach the motor/base assembly retaining bolt(s). Disconnect the antenna lead and the electrical connector (if equipped) and remove the antenna motor/base assembly from the vehicle **(see illustration)**.
4   Installation is the reverse of removal.

12.7a Detach the cover and remove the seat belt retractor bolt and nut

12.7b Remove the left side assist handle

12.8 Carefully pry the left side quarter trim panel out, then lower the rear of the headliner for access to the antenna module

12.9 Disconnect the electrical connectors, remove the retaining bolt and lower the antenna module

Later models

AM/FM module

Refer to illustrations 12.7a, 12.7b, 12.8 and 12.9

5   Later models are equipped with an AM/FM antenna module mounted to the roof inside the vehicle on rear left side.

6   Remove the rear seat (see Chapter 11).

7   Remove the assist handle and left side rear seat belt retractor **(see illustration)**.

8   Detach the left side quarter trim panel and headliner for access to the antenna module **(see illustration)**.

9   Disconnect the antenna cables, remove the bolt and detach the antenna module from the vehicle **(see illustration)**.

10   Installation is the reverse of removal.

13   Headlight bulb - replacement

Refer to illustrations 13.4 and 13.5

Warning 1: *Halogen gas filled bulbs are under pressure and may shatter if the surface is scratched or the bulb is dropped. Wear eye protection and handle the bulbs carefully, grasping only the base whenever possible.*

Do not touch the surface of the bulb with your fingers because the oil from your skin could cause it to overheat and fail prematurely. If you do touch the bulb surface, clean it with rubbing alcohol.

Warning 2: *High Intensity Discharge (HID) headlight systems present on some 2001 and later Seville models produce very high voltage which could cause personal injury. Any work on an HID system should be left to a dealer service department or other repair shop.*

Note: *On later models the high and low beam headlight bulbs and turn signal bulbs are mounted in the headlight housing.*

1   Open the hood.

2   Remove the radiator support cover (see Chapter 11).

3   Remove the screws/nuts and pull the headlight housing out for access to the bulb holders (see Section 15).

4   Disconnect the electrical connector(s) from the headlight housing **(see illustration)**.

5   Remove the cover(s) for access to the bulb(s) **(see illustration)**.

6   Rotate the bulb holder(s) counterclockwise.

7   Without touching the glass with your bare fingers, insert the new bulb and holder

assembly into the headlight housing and rotate clockwise to lock it in place.

8   Reinstall the headlight housing and radiator support cover.

14   Headlights - adjustment

Refer to illustrations 14.1 and 14.3

Caution: *The headlights must be aimed correctly. If adjusted incorrectly they could blind the driver of an oncoming vehicle and cause a serious accident or seriously reduce your ability to see the road. The headlights should be checked for proper aim every 12 months and any time a new headlight is installed or front end body work is performed. It should be emphasized that the following procedure is only an interim step, which will provide temporary adjustment until the headlights can be adjusted by a properly equipped shop.*

1   Headlights have two spring loaded adjusting screws, one controlling up-and-down movement and one controlling left-and-right movement. Later models have a built-in aiming gauge. On later models, the adjuster must be set to zero before making

13.4 Disconnect the headlight housing electrical connector

13.5 Remove the headlight housing covers for access to the appropriate bulb right side shown)

A   High beam
B   Low beam
C   Turn signal

12

14.1 Before adjustment, set the headlight adjuster to zero (A) by turning the adjusting screw (B)

14.3 Headlight adjustment details

adjustments **(see illustration)**.

2   There are several methods of adjusting the headlights. The simplest method requires a large level area with a blank wall.

3   Position masking tape vertically on the wall in reference to the vehicle centerline and the centerlines of both headlights **(see illustration)**.

4   Position a horizontal tape line in reference to the centerline of all the headlights. **Note:** *It may be easier to position the tape on the wall with the vehicle parked only a few inches away.*

5   Adjustment should be made with the vehicle parked 25 feet from the wall, sitting level, the gas tank half-full and no unusually heavy load in the vehicle.

6   Starting with the low beam adjustment, position the high intensity zone so it is two inches below the horizontal line and two inches to the side of the headlight vertical line, away from oncoming traffic. Adjustment is made by turning the top adjusting screw clockwise to raise the beam and counterclockwise to lower the beam. The adjusting screw on the side should be used in the same manner to move the beam left or right.

7   With the high beams on, the high intensity zone should be vertically centered with the exact center just below the horizontal line. **Note:** *It may not be possible to position the headlight aim exactly for both high and low beams. If a compromise must be made, keep in mind that the low beams are the most used and have the greatest effect on safety.*

8   Have the headlights adjusted by a dealer service department or service station at the earliest opportunity.

---

15   Headlight housing - replacement

Refer to illustration 15.2

Warning: *High Intensity Discharge (HID) headlight systems present on some 2001 and later Seville models produce very high voltage which could cause personal injury. Any work on models with an HID system should be left*

to a dealer service department or properly equipped shop.

1   Remove the radiator support cover (see Chapter 11).

2   Remove the bolts/nuts securing the headlight assembly **(see illustration)**.

3   Pull the housing out and remove the headlight bulb(s) or disconnect the electrical connector.

4   Remove the housing from the vehicle.

5   Installation is the reverse of removal.

---

16   Bulb replacement

Warning: *Some bulbs may remain hot for up to twenty minutes after they're turned off. Be*

sure bulbs are off and cool before you touch them.

Front cornering light

Refer to illustrations 16.2a and 16.2b

1   Raise the vehicle and support it securely on jackstands.

2   From under the vehicle, disconnect the electrical connector then turn the bulb holder counterclockwise and pull it out of the housing **(see illustrations)**.

3   Pull the bulb straight out of the holder.

4   Installation is the reverse of removal.

Front park/turn lights

5   On early models, remove the screws and detach the light housing from the body.

15.2 Remove the bolts, then pull the headlight assembly straight forward to detach the retaining clip (later models)

16.2a Disconnect the cornering lamp electrical connector

16.2b Rotate the bulb holder counterclockwise and withdraw it from the housing

and remove the nuts holding the light housing in place, then withdraw the housing from the vehicle.

10   On later models, the light housing runs the full width of the vehicle. Remove the nuts securing the taillight panel to the body. Pull the taillight panel out **(see illustrations)**.

11   On all models, rotate the bulb holder(s) 1/8-turn counterclockwise and pull it out of the housing, then pull the bulb out **(see illustration)**.

High-mounted brake light

Refer to illustration 16.14

12   On early models, access to the high-mounted brake light is at the package shelf behind the rear seat. Lift the cover in the center of the package shelf and twist the bulb holders out to replace the bulbs.

13   On later models, remove the trunk inner trim panel.

14   Remove the nuts retaining the high-mount brake light housing to the trunk lid **(see illustration)**.

15   Pull the housing out of the trunk lid for access to the bulbs.

16   On all models, twist the bulb holder counterclockwise to remove it, then pull the

Rotate the bulb holder counterclockwise and withdraw it. Remove the bulb from the holder.

6   On later models, remove the headlight housing and remove the appropriate bulbs as described in Section 15.

7   Installation is the reverse of removal.

Rear turn signal, back-up and brake light/taillight bulbs

Refer to illustrations 16.10a, 16.10b and 16.11

8   Open the trunk.

9   On early models, detach the trim panel

16.10a Remove the taillight housing mounting nuts (later models)

16.10b Detach the taillight housing and lift it away from the body

16.11 Rotate the taillight assembly light bulb holders counterclockwise for access to the bulb(s) (back-up light shown)

16.14 Remove the nuts retaining the high-mounted brake light to the trunk lid

12

16.20a Use a screwdriver to push on the right side to detach the license plate light housing

16.20b Gently pry out on the clip and disconnect the electrical connector by pulling it straight up

16.21 Rotate the bulb holder counterclockwise to remove it

bulb straight out of the holder.
17   Installation is the reverse of removal.

License plate lights

Refer to illustrations 16.20a 16.20b and 16.21
18   On early models, remove the screws and detach the license plate pocket assembly.
19   Replace the bulbs and install the license plate pocket assembly.

20   On later models open the trunk lid and press on the right side of the license plate bulb housing to detach the tab, then lower the housing and disconnect the electrical connector **(see illustrations)**.
21   Rotate the holder, withdraw it from the housing then pull the bulb straight out **(see illustration)**.
22   Installation is the reverse of removal.

Instrument panel lights

Refer to illustration 16.24
23   To gain access to the instrument panel lights, the instrument cluster will have to be removed first (see Section 10).
24   Rotate the bulb counterclockwise and remove it from the instrument cluster **(see illustration)**.
25   Pull the bulb straight out of the holder.
26   Installation is the reverse of removal.

Dome lights

Refer to illustrations 16.27a and 16.27b
27   Carefully pry off the dome light housing, remove the screws, then detach the bulb holder housing and turn it over for access to the bulbs **(see illustrations)**.
28   Installation is the reverse of removal.

Courtesy lights

Refer to illustration 16.29
29   Carefully pull out on the courtesy light housing to release the clips, turn the switch counterclockwise to release the switch from the bezel, then rotate the housing out of the opening **(see illustration)**.

16.24 To remove an instrument cluster bulb, depress it and turn counterclockwise

16.27a Carefully pry the dome light housing off . . .

16.27b . . . disconnect the electrical connector, remove the screws and turn the light housing over for access to the bulbs

16.29 Detach the courtesy lamp housing

16.32 Pry the vanity light lens off with a screwdriver

16.33 Spread the terminals at the ends and remove the bulb

30   Lower the light housing and remove the bulb.

31   Installation is the reverse of removal.

Vanity lights

Refer to illustrations 16.32 and 16.33

32   Use a small screwdriver to pry off the light lens **(see illustration)**.

33   Spread the terminals at either end of the bulb and remove the bulb **(see illustration)**.

34   Installation is the reverse of removal.

17 Wiper motor - removal and installation

Refer to illustrations 17.1, 17.3 and 17.6

1   Mark the positions of the wiper arms on the windshield, then remove the nuts and detach the windshield wiper arms **(see illustration)**.

2   Remove the cowl covers (see Chapter 11).

3   Remove the wiper motor cover **(see illustration)**.

4   If necessary, rotate the linkage so the wiper arm is opposite the Park position for clearance.

5   Detach the wiper motor electrical harness grommet and push the harness down into the cowl plenum.

6   Remove the wiper motor/linkage retaining bolts **(see illustration)**.

7   Detach the wiper motor/linkage assembly from the cowl.

8   Detach the linkage drive link from the wiper motor arm.

9   Remove the bolts and detach the wiper motor from the wiper linkage assembly.

10   Installation is the reverse of removal.

18 Horn - check and replacement

Check

Refer to illustrations 18.3 and 18.8

Note: *Check the fuses before beginning electrical diagnosis.*

1   Disconnect the electrical connector from the horns.

17.1 Remove the wiper arm nuts after marking the positions of the wiper blades on the windshield

2   To test the horns, connect battery voltage and ground to the horn terminals with a pair of jumper wires. If either horn doesn't sound, replace it.

17.3 Remove the bolts/nuts and detach the wiper motor cover

17.6 Remove the bolts retaining the wiper motor/linkage assembly

12

18.3 Check for voltage at the horn while an assistant pushes the horn button

18.8 Use the current adjusting screw (arrow) to achieve a draw of 4.5 to 5.5 amps for proper horn operation

18.10 Disconnect the electrical connectors, unscrew the bolt and remove the horn assembly

3   If the horn does sound, check for voltage at the horn connector when the horn switch is depressed **(see illustration)**. If there's voltage at the connector, check for a bad ground at the horn.

4   If there's no voltage at the horn, check the relay (see Section 6).

5   If the relay is OK, check for voltage to the relay power and control circuits. If either of the circuits is not receiving voltage, inspect the wiring between the relay and the fuse panel.

6   If both relay circuits are receiving voltage, depress the horn switch and check the circuit from the relay to the horn switch for continuity to ground. If there's no continuity, check the circuit for an open. If there's no open circuit, replace the horn switch.

7   If there's continuity to ground through the horn switch, check for an open or short in the circuit from the relay to the switch.

8   If the horn works, but the tone is off, either weak or strained, check the current draw of the horn, using an ammeter during operation. Hook the ammeter between the horn connector and the terminal on the horn. A correctly operating horn should draw 4.5 to 5.5 amps. Use the adjusting screw on the

horn to achieve this draw **(see illustration)**.

Replacement

Refer to illustration 18.10

9   The horn on is located in the fenderwell. Raise the vehicle and support it securely on jackstands. Remove the front wheel and the fenderwell splash shield for access.

10   Disconnect the electrical connectors and remove the bracket bolts **(see illustration)**.

11   Installation is the reverse of removal. Make sure the area of the body is clean where the horn bracket attaches. This is the ground point for the horn.

19   Daytime Running Lights (DRL) - general information

The Daytime Running Lights (DRL) system used on some models illuminates the headlights whenever the engine is running. The only exception is with the engine running and the parking brake engaged. Once the parking brake is released, the lights will remain on as long as the ignition switch is on, even if the parking brake is later applied.

The DRL system supplies reduced power to the headlights so they won't be too bright for daytime use, while prolonging headlight life.

20   Rear window defogger - check and repair

1   The rear window defogger consists of a number of horizontal heating elements baked onto the inside surface of the glass. Power is supplied through a large fuse from the power distribution box in the engine compartment. The heater is controlled by the instrument panel switch.

2   Small breaks in the element can be repaired without removing the rear window.

Check

Refer to illustrations 20.5, 20.6 and 20.8

3   Turn the ignition switch and defogger switches to the ON position.

4   Using a voltmeter, place the positive probe against the defogger grid positive terminal and the negative probe against the ground terminal. If battery voltage is not indicated, check the fuse, defogger switch and related wiring. If voltage is indicated, but all or part of the defogger doesn't heat, proceed with the following tests.

5   When measuring voltage during the next two tests, wrap a piece of aluminum foil around the tip of the voltmeter positive probe and press the foil against the heating element with your finger **(see illustration)**. Place the negative probe on the defogger grid ground terminal.

6   Check the voltage at the center of each heating element **(see illustration)**. If the voltage is 5 to 6 volts, the element is okay (there

20.5 When measuring the voltage at the rear window defogger grid, wrap a piece of aluminum foil around the positive probe of the voltmeter and press the foil against the wire with your finger

20.6 To determine if a wire has broken, check the voltage at the center of each wire. If the voltage is 5 to 6 volts, the wire is unbroken; if the voltage is 10 to 12 volts, the wire is broken between the center of the wire and the ground side; if the voltage is 0 volts, the wire is broken between the center of the wire and the power side

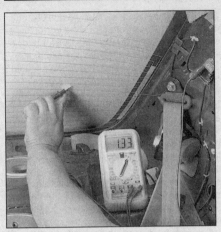

20.8 To find the break, place the voltmeter negative lead against the defogger ground terminal, place the voltmeter positive lead with the foil strip against the heat wire at the positive terminal end and slide it toward the negative terminal end - the point at which the voltmeter deflects from several volts to zero volts is the point at which the wire is broken

is no break). If the voltage is 0 volts, the element is broken between the center of the element and the positive end. If the voltage is 10 to 12 volts the element is broken between the center of the element and the ground side. Check each heating element.

7   If none of the elements are broken, connect the negative probe to a good chassis ground. The voltage reading should stay the same, if it doesn't the ground connection is bad.

8   To find the break, place the voltmeter negative probe against the defogger ground terminal. Place the voltmeter positive probe with the foil strip against the heating element at the positive side and slide it toward the negative side. The point at which the voltmeter deflects from several volts to zero is the point where the heating element is broken **(see illustration)**.

Repair

Refer to illustration 20.14

9   Repair the break in the element using a repair kit specifically for this purpose (available at most auto parts stores). The kit includes conductive plastic epoxy.

10   Before repairing a break, turn off the system and allow it to cool for a few minutes.

11   Lightly buff the element area with fine steel wool; then clean it thoroughly with rubbing alcohol.

12   Use masking tape to mask off the area being repaired.

13   Thoroughly mix the epoxy, following the kit instructions.

14   Apply the epoxy material to the slit in the masking tape, overlapping the undamaged area about 3/4-inch on either end **(see illustration)**.

20.14 To use a defogger repair kit, apply masking tape to the inside of the window at the damaged area, then brush on the special conductive coating

15   Allow the repair to cure for 24 hours before removing the tape and using the system.

---

21   Cruise control system - description

Refer to illustration 21.5

1   On early models the cruise control system maintains vehicle speed with a servo motor, located in the engine compartment, that is connected to the throttle linkage by a cable. The system models consists of the servo motor, brake switch, control switches, speed sensors and relays. On later models a module containing a controller and a stepper motor controls the throttle linkage through the cruise control cable. Some features of the system require special testers and diagnostic procedures that are beyond the scope of this manual. Listed below are some general procedures that may be used to locate common problems.

2   Locate and check the fuse (see Section 3).

3   The brake light switch deactivates the cruise control system. Have an assistant press the brake pedal while you check the

brake light operation.

4   If the brake lights do not operate properly, correct the problem and retest the cruise control.

5   Check the control cable between the cruise control servo/amplifier or module and the throttle linkage and adjust/replace as necessary. On early models, refer to Chapter 6 for the procedure to retract the plunger of the idle speed control motor, so that it doesn't touch the throttle linkage while you are adjusting the cruise control linkage. On later models the cable is self-adjusting and doesn't require adjustment **(see illustration)**.

6   The cruise control system uses a speed sensing device. The speed sensor is located in the transmission. To test the speed sensor, see Chapter 6.

7   Test drive the vehicle to determine if the cruise control is now working. Refer to Chapter 6 for the procedure to extract trouble codes from the vehicle. There are several cruise control-related trouble codes that may help you pinpoint the problem area. If there are no codes, or you can't locate the problem, don't use the cruise control until you can take it to a dealer service department or an automotive electrical specialist for further diagnosis.

---

22   Power window system - description and check

Caution: *The power window system will operate even when the ignition switch is Off. If the engine is shut off, the power windows can still operate for 10 minutes, or until one of the doors is opened. Do not operate the window switch when any part of your body is in the window opening, unless the battery has been disconnected.*

1   The power window system operates electric motors, mounted in the doors that lower and raise the windows. The system consists of the control switches, the motors, regulators, glass mechanisms and associated wiring.

2   The power windows can be lowered and raised from the master control switch by the driver or by remote switches located at the individual windows. Each window has a sep-

21.5 On later models, a module operates the cruise control system; the cable connects directly to the throttle linkage and doesn't require adjustment

12

arate motor that is reversible. The position of the control switch determines the polarity and therefore the direction of operation.

3   The circuit is protected by a fuse and a circuit breaker. Each motor is also equipped with an internal circuit breaker; this prevents one stuck window from disabling the whole system.

4   These procedures are general in nature, so if you can't find the problem using them, take the vehicle to a dealer service department or qualified repair facility.

5   If the power windows won't operate, always check the fuse and circuit breaker first. Refer to the wiring diagrams at the end of this Chapter to study the circuit in detail.

6   Check the wiring between the switches and fuse panel for continuity. Repair the wiring, if necessary.

7   Some models are equipped with an "express-down" module mounted near the driver's door window regulator. When equipped with this feature, a quick touch (less than 0.3 seconds) on the driver's window down button will lower the window a little. Touching the button for a longer period will send the window down all the way without the driver having to keep his finger on the button while driving.

8   If one of the passenger door windows is inoperative from the master control switch, try the other control switch at the window.

9   If the same window works from one switch, but not the other, check the switch for continuity.

10   If the switch tests OK, check for a short or open in the circuit between the affected switch and the window motor.

11   If one window is inoperative from both switches, remove the trim panel from the affected door and check for voltage at the switch and at the motor while the switch is operated.

12   If voltage is reaching the motor, disconnect the glass from the regulator (see Chapter 11). Move the window up and down by hand while checking for binding and damage. Also check for binding and damage to the regulator. If the regulator is not damaged and the window moves up and down smoothly, replace the motor. If there's binding or damage, lubricate, repair or replace parts, as necessary.

13   If voltage isn't reaching the motor, check the wiring in the circuit for continuity between the switches and motors. You'll need to consult the wiring diagram for the vehicle. If the circuit is equipped with a relay, check that the relay is grounded properly and receiving voltage.

14   Test the windows after you're done to confirm proper repairs.

23   Power door lock system - description and check

1   The power door lock system operates the door lock actuators mounted in each door. The system consists of the switches, actuators, and associated wiring. Diagnosis can usually be limited to simple checks of the wiring connections and actuators for minor faults that can be easily repaired.

2   Power door lock systems are operated by bi-directional solenoids or motors located in the doors. The lock switches have two operating positions: Lock and Unlock. On later models with keyless entry and theft-deterrent options, the switches activate a module that in turn connects voltage to the door lock solenoids or motors. Depending on which way the switch is activated, it reverses polarity, allowing the two sides of the circuit to be used alternately as the feed (positive) and ground side.

3   If you are unable to locate the trouble using the following general steps, consult a dealer service department or other qualified repair facility.

4   Always check the circuit protection first. Examine the wiring diagrams at the end of this Chapter.

5   Operate the door lock switches in both directions (Lock and Unlock) with the engine off. Listen for the faint click of the door lock relay operating.

6   If there's no click, check for voltage at the switches. If no voltage is present, check the wiring between the fuse block and the switches for shorts and opens.

7   If voltage is present but no click is heard, test the switch for continuity. Replace it if there's no continuity in both switch positions.

8   If the switch has continuity but the solenoid or motor doesn't click, check the wiring between the switch and solenoid for continuity. Repair the wiring if there's no continuity. Also check the wiring to and from the power door lock relay, usually located behind the driver's side kick panel.

9   If all but one lock solenoids operate, remove the trim panel from the affected door (see Chapter 11) and check for voltage at the solenoid while the lock switch is operated. One of the wires should have voltage in the lock position; the other should have voltage in the unlock position.

10   If the inoperative solenoid is receiving voltage but won't operate, replace the solenoid. **Note:** *It's common for wires to break in the portion of the harness between the body and door (opening and closing the door fatigues and eventually breaks the wires).*

24   Electric side view mirrors - description and check

Refer to illustration 24.6

1   Most electric rear view mirrors use two motors to move the glass; one for up-and-down adjustments and one for left-to-right adjustments. In addition, some models have electrically-heated glass defroster circuits, which are usually powered through the rear window defogger relay.

2   The control switch usually has a selector portion that sends voltage to the left or right side mirror. With the ignition ON but the engine OFF, roll down the windows and operate the mirror control switch through all functions (left-right and up-down) for both the left and right side mirrors.

3   Listen carefully for the sound of the electric motors running in the mirrors.

4   If the motors can be heard but the mirror glass doesn't move, there's probably a problem with the drive mechanism inside the mirror.

5   If the mirrors don't operate and no sound comes from the mirrors, check the fuse (see Chapter 1).

6   If the fuse is OK, remove the mirror control switch from its mounting without disconnecting the wires attached to it. On models where the power mirror switch is in the instrument panel, remove the switch from the instrument panel to probe the wires behind it. On models where the switch is in the driver's armrest, just pull up the switch panel. Turn the ignition ON and check for voltage at the switch **(see illustration)**. There should be voltage at one terminal. If there's no voltage at the switch, check for an open or short in the wiring between the fuse panel and the switch.

7   Locate the wire going from the switch to ground. Leaving the switch connected, connect a jumper wire between this wire and ground. If the mirror works normally with this wire in place, repair the faulty ground connection.

8   If the mirror still doesn't work, remove the cover and check the wires at the mirror for voltage with a test light. Check with ignition ON and the mirror selector switch on the appropriate side. Operate the mirror switch in all its positions. There should be voltage at one of the switch-to-mirror wires in each switch position (except the neutral "off" position).

9   If there's no voltage in any switch position, check the wiring between the mirror and control switch for opens and shorts.

10   If there's voltage, remove the mirror and test it off the vehicle with jumper wires. Replace the mirror if it fails this test (see Chapter 11).

25   Airbag system - general information and precautions

Description

Refer to illustrations 25.1a, 25.1b, 25.1c and 25.1d

1   The vehicle is equipped with a Supplemental Inflatable Restraint system (SIR), more commonly known as an airbag system. On some models the system also employs seat belt pre-tensioners. For the locations of the various SIR system components, refer to the accompanying diagrams **(see illustrations)**. **Warning:** *If your vehicle is ever involved in a flood, or the interior carpeting is soaked for*

1 Forward discriminating sensor
2 Right discriminating sensor
3 Arming sensor
4 Passenger's airbag module (1993 and later models)
5 Driver's airbag module and clockspring
6 Resistor module (1992 and 1993 models) (under instrument panel)
7 Diagnostic Energy Reserve Module (DERM) (under instrument panel)
8 Left discriminating sensor

25.1a Supplemental Inflatable Restraint system components - 1994 and earlier models

1 Forward discriminating sensor
2 Passenger's airbag module
3 Sensing and Diagnostic Module (SDM) (under driver's seat)
4 Driver's airbag module and clockspring

25.1b Supplemental Inflatable Restraint system components - 1995 and 1996 models

1 Forward discriminating sensor
2 Passenger's airbag module
3 Side impact airbag module and sensor (in door; DeVille only)
4 Seat belt pre-tensioner (1998 and 1999 Seville only)
5 Side impact sensor (on B-pillar; 1998 and 1999 Seville only)
6 Side impact airbag module (in seat back; 1998 and 1999 Seville only)
7 Side impact sensor (on B-pillar; 1998 and 1999 Seville only)
8 Seat belt pre-tensioner (1998 and 1999 Seville only)
9 Side impact airbag module and sensor (in door; DeVille only
10 Sensing and Diagnostic Module (SDM) (under driver's seat)
11 Driver's airbag module and clockspring

25.1c Supplemental Inflatable Restraint system components - 1997 through 1999 models

1 Forward discriminating sensor (2002 DeVille only)
2 Passenger's airbag module
3 Side impact airbag module (in seat back)
4 Seat belt pre-tensioner
5 Side impact sensor (on B-pillar)
6 Side impact airbag module (DeVille only)
7 Sensing and Diagnostic Module (SDM) (DeVille, under center console)
8 Sensing and Diagnostic Module (SDM) (Seville, under driver's seat)
9 Side impact airbag module (DeVille only)
10 Side impact sensor (on B-pillar)
11 Seat belt pre-tensioner
12 Side impact airbag module (in seat back)
13 Driver's airbag module and clockspring

25.1d Supplemental Inflatable Restraint system components - 2000 and later models

12

any reason, disconnect the battery and do not start the vehicle until the airbag system can be checked by your dealer. If the SIR system is subjected to flooding, the airbags could go off upon starting the vehicle, even without an accident taking place.

2   The SIR system consists of impact sensors, a resistor module (early models), airbag assemblies, seat belt retractors (some models) and a Diagnostic Energy Reserve Module (DERM) (early models) or Sensing and Diagnostic Module (SDM) (later models). The DERM or SDM is the heart of the system and determines when the airbag should be deployed and supply reserve energy to the SIR system, even if the crash destroys the vehicle's battery. It also monitors the rest of the system, records trouble codes, and turns on the AIRBAG warning light on the instrument panel if there is a problem with the system.

3   The airbag modules consist of a housing incorporating the cushion (airbag) and inflator unit. The inflator assembly is mounted on the back of the housing over a hole through which gas is expelled, inflating the bag almost instantaneously when an electrical signal is sent from the system. A specially wound coil (called a clockspring), located under the steering wheel, carries the signal to the driver's airbag module. The clockspring is a flat, ribbon-like electrically conductive tape wound in a plastic housing and connected to the steering column shaft. The coil transmits the electrical signal regardless of steering wheel position.

Operation

4   For the airbags to deploy, an accelerometer in the impact sensor(s) or Sensing and Diagnostic Module (SDM) must be activated by a collision of sufficient force. The control module compares the force of the collision to a value stored in its memory. If the control module determines the force is in excess of the value, the circuits to the airbag inflators are closed and the airbags inflate. If the battery is destroyed by the impact, or is too low to power the inflator, a back-up power unit inside the control module provides power.

Self-diagnosis system

5   A self-diagnosis circuit in the control module displays a light when the ignition switch is turned to the On position. If the system is operating normally, the light should flash a few times, then go out. If the light doesn't come on, or doesn't go out after six seconds, or if it comes on while you're driving the vehicle, there's a malfunction in the SIR system. Have it inspected and repaired as soon as possible. Do not attempt to troubleshoot or service the SIR system yourself. Even a small mistake could cause the SIR system to malfunction when you need it.

Servicing components near the SIR system

6   Nevertheless, there are times when you

need to remove the steering wheel, radio or service other components on or near the dashboard or near other airbag system components. At these times, you'll be working around components and wire harnesses for the SIR system. The SIR wiring harnesses are easy to identify because the connectors are all bright yellow. Except for the connectors mentioned in the following Steps, do not unplug the connectors for these wires. And do not use electrical test equipment on any airbag system component or wiring harness; it could damage a component or cause the airbag(s) to deploy. **ALWAYS DISABLE THE SIR SYSTEM BEFORE WORKING NEAR THE SIR SYSTEM COMPONENTS OR RELATED WIRING.**

Disabling the SIR system

Warning: *Any time you are working in the vicinity of airbag wiring or components, DISABLE THE SIR SYSTEM.*
Note: *Before you can disconnect an airbag module connector, you must remove the connector position assurance clip from the connector.*

7   With the ignition key OFF, refer to Section 3 and locate the SIR fuse, normally found in the fuse/relay panel located in the engine compartment on early models and either under the rear seat or in the trunk on later models. Remove the fuse.

Driver's airbag

8   Position the steering wheel with the front wheels pointing straight-ahead, turn the ignition switch to the Lock position and remove the key.

9   Remove the trim panel and driver's knee bolster below the steering column.

10   Disconnect the yellow airbag connector at the base of the steering column.

Passenger's airbag

11   Disconnect the yellow electrical connector for the airbag. This is reached either through a "trap door" in the back of the glove box, by removing the glove box, or by removing the passenger's side under-dash panel, depending on model and year.

Side-impact airbags

12   On models with door-mounted airbags, remove the door trim panel, then disconnect the yellow airbag electrical connector.

13   On models with seat-mounted airbags, disconnect the yellow airbag connector under the seat.

14   On models with rear side-impact airbags, remove the rear seat back (see Chapter 11), then disconnect the yellow airbag electrical connector.

Seat belt pre-tensioners

15   Disconnect the yellow airbag connector under the seat.

Enabling the system

16   Position the steering wheel with the front wheels pointing straight-ahead, turn the

ignition switch to the Lock position and remove the key.

17   Reconnect the airbag connector(s) and install the connector position assurance clip.

18   Install the SIR system fuse.

19   Turn the ignition key On and make sure the airbag system warning light flashes a few times, then goes out. **Warning:** *Keep your body away from the airbags when turning the key on for the first time after disabling the SIR system.*

Component removal and installation

Driver's airbag module and clockspring

20   Refer to Chapter 10, *Steering wheel - removal and installation*, for the driver's airbag module and clockspring removal and installation procedures.

Passenger's airbag

Refer to illustration 25.22

21   Disable the airbag system (see Step 6).

22   Remove the glove box (if not already done) (see Chapter 11).

23   Remove the mounting fasteners and gently remove the airbag unit from the instrument panel **(see illustration)**. **Warning:** *Carry the airbag module with the opening (bag or trim side) facing away from your body.*

24   Installation is the reverse of the removal procedure. Tighten the mounting fasteners securely.

25   Install the SIR system fuse.

26   Turn the ignition key On and make sure the airbag system warning light flashes a few times, then goes out. **Warning:** *Keep your body away from the airbags when turning the key on for the first time after disabling the SIR system.*

Side-impact airbags

Seat mounted airbags

27   On models with seat mounted airbags, this procedure should be left to a dealer service department or other qualified repair shop.

Door-mounted airbags

28   Disable the airbag system (see the **Warning** above).

29   Remove the door panel (see Chapter 11).

30   Disconnect the electrical connector, remove the mounting fasteners and detach the airbag. **Warning:** *Carry the airbag module with the opening (bag or trim side) facing away from your body.*

31   Installation is the reverse of the removal procedure. Tighten the mounting fasteners securely.

32   Install the SIR system fuse.

33   Turn the ignition key On and make sure the airbag system warning light flashes a few times, then goes out. **Warning:** *Keep your body away from the airbags when turning the key on for the first time after disabling the SIR system.*

Rear side impact airbags

34   Remove the rear seat back (see Chapter 11), then disconnect the yellow airbag electrical connector.

35   Remove the mounting fasteners and detach the airbag. **Warning:** *Carry the airbag module with the opening (bag or trim side) facing away from your body.*

36   Installation is the reverse of the removal procedure. Tighten the mounting fasteners securely.

37   Install the SIR system fuse.

38   Turn the ignition key On and make sure the airbag system warning light flashes a few times, then goes out. **Warning:** *Keep your body away from the airbags when turning the key on for the first time after disabling the SIR system.*

25.23 Passenger's side airbag mounting fasteners

---

26   Wiring diagrams - general information

Since it isn't possible to include all wiring diagrams for every year and model covered by this manual, the following diagrams are those that are typical and most commonly needed.

Prior to troubleshooting any circuits, check the fuse and circuit breakers (if equipped) to make sure they're in good condition. Make sure the battery is properly charged and check the cable connections (see Chapter 1).

When checking a circuit, make sure that all connectors are clean, with no broken or loose terminals. When unplugging a connector, do not pull on the wires. Pull only on the connector housings themselves.

Air conditioning and engine cooling fan system - 1994 and 1995 DeVille models (1 of 2) (1992 and 1993 Seville similar)

Air conditioning and engine cooling fan system - 1994 and 1995 DeVille models (2 of 2) (1992 and 1993 Seville similar)

Air conditioning and engine cooling fan system - 1996 through 1999 models (1 of 2) (except 1998 and 1999 Seville)

Air conditioning and engine cooling fan system 1996 through 1999 models - (2 of 2) (except 1998 and 1999 Seville)

12

Air conditioning and engine cooling fan system - 1998 and later Seville models (1 of 2)

Air conditioning and engine cooling fan system - 1998 and later Seville models (2 of 2)

12

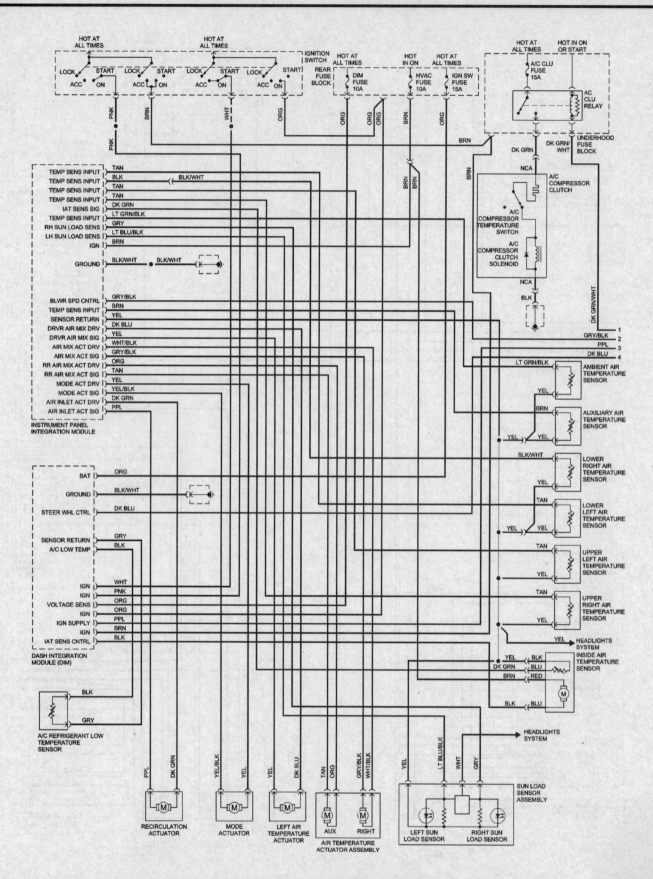

Air conditioning and engine cooling fan system - 2000 and later DeVille models (1 of 2)

Air conditioning and engine cooling fan system - 2000 and later DeVille models (2 of 2)

Starting and charging system - 1992 Seville models

Starting and charging system - 1993 Seville models

Starting and charging system - 1994 through 1996 models

Starting and charging system - 1998 and 1999 Seville models

Starting and charging system - 1997 through 1999 models (except 1998 and 1999 Seville)

Starting and charging system - 2000 and later models

Cruise control system - 1992 through 1995 models

Cruise control system - 1998 through 2000 Seville models

Cruise control system - 1996 through 1999 models (except 1998 and 1999 Seville)

Cruise control system - 2000 and later models (except 2000 Seville)

12

Power window system - 1992 through 1995 Seville models (1994 and 1995 DeVille similar)

Power window system - 1996 through 1999 models (except 1998 and 1999 Seville)

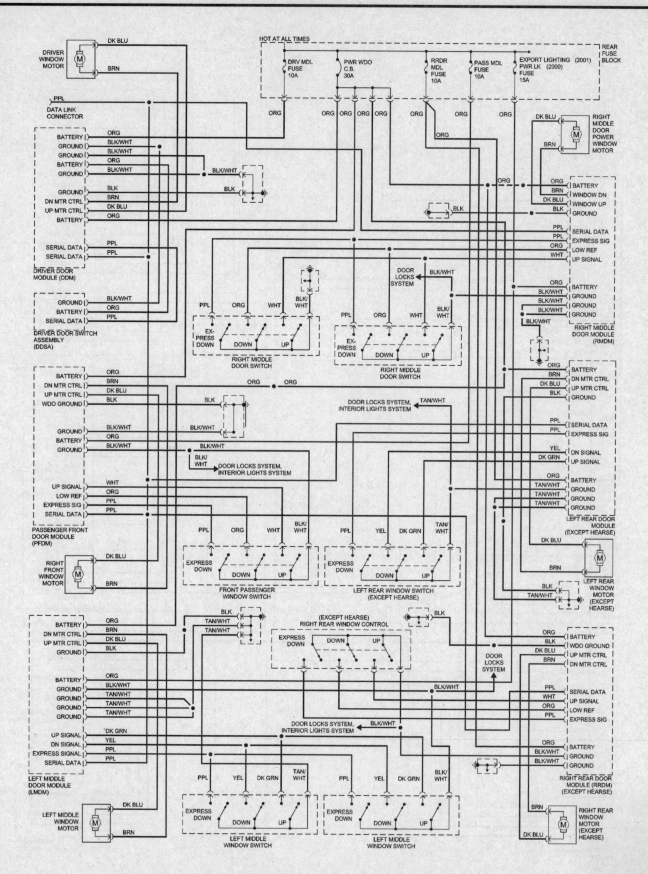

Power window system - 2000 and 2001 DeVille models (1998 and 1999 Seville similar)

Power window system - 2001 and later Seville

Power window system - 2000 DeVille (1 of 2)

Power window system - 2000 DeVille (2 of 2)

Exterior lights - 1992 through 1995 DeVille models (1 of 2)

Exterior lights - 1992 through 1995 DeVille models (2 of 2)

Exterior lights - 1992 through 1995 Seville models (1 of 2)

Exterior lights - 1992 through 1995 Seville models (2 of 2)

12

Exterior lights - 1996 through 1999 DeVille models (1 of 2)

Exterior lights - 1996 through 1999 DeVille models (2 of 2)

12

Exterior lights - 1996 and 1997 Seville models (1 of 2)

Exterior lights - 1996 and 1997 Seville models (2 of 2)

Exterior lights - 1998 and later Seville models (1 of 2)

Exterior lights - 1998 and later Seville models (2 of 2)

Exterior lights - 2000 and later DeVille models (1 of 2)

Exterior lights - 2000 and later DeVille models (2 of 2)

Power door lock system - 1994 and 1995 models (1992 and 1993 Seville similar)

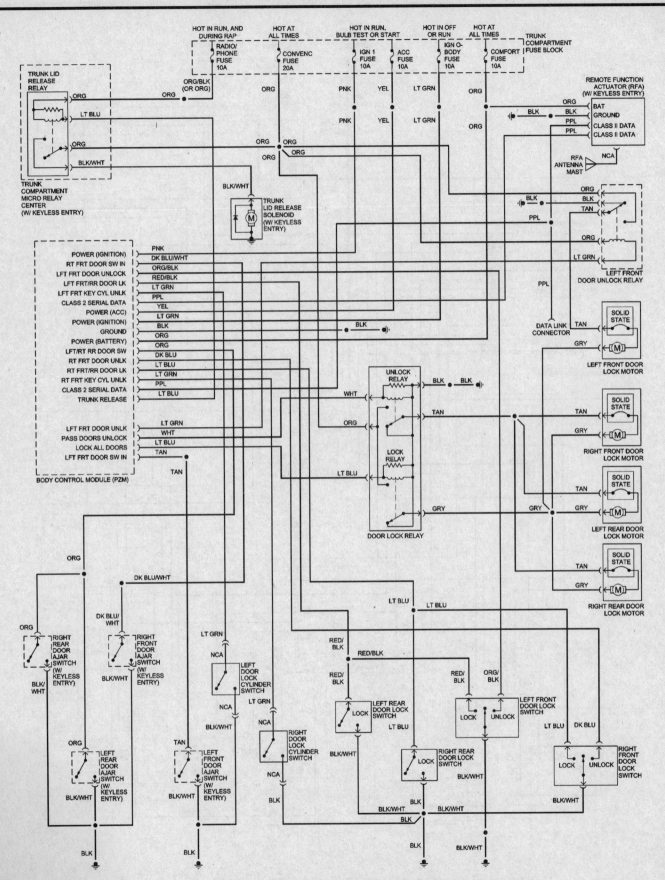

Power door lock system - 1996 and 1997 models

Power door lock system - 1998 and 1999 DeVille models

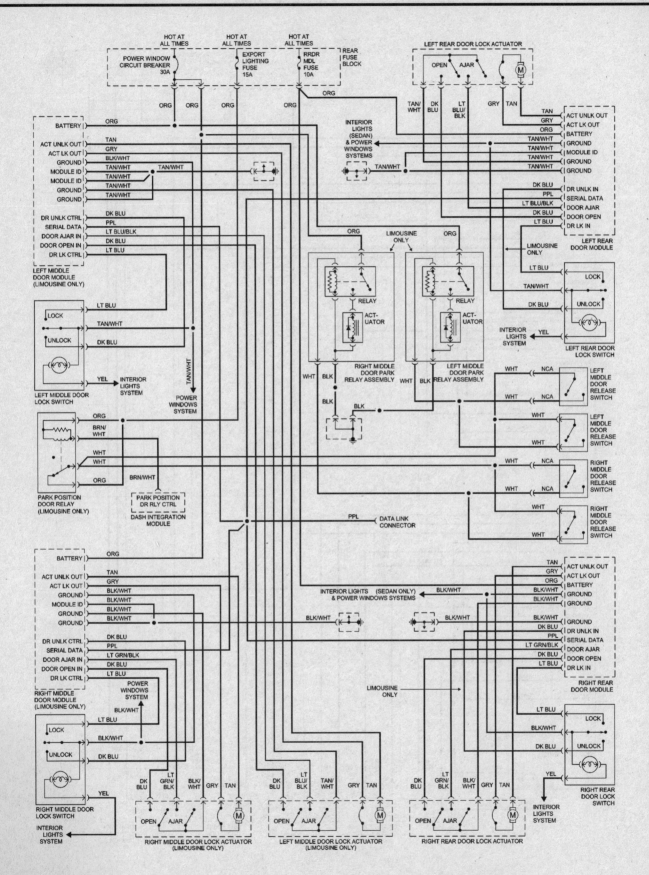

Power door lock system - 2000 and later models (1998 and 1999 Seville similar) (1 of 2)

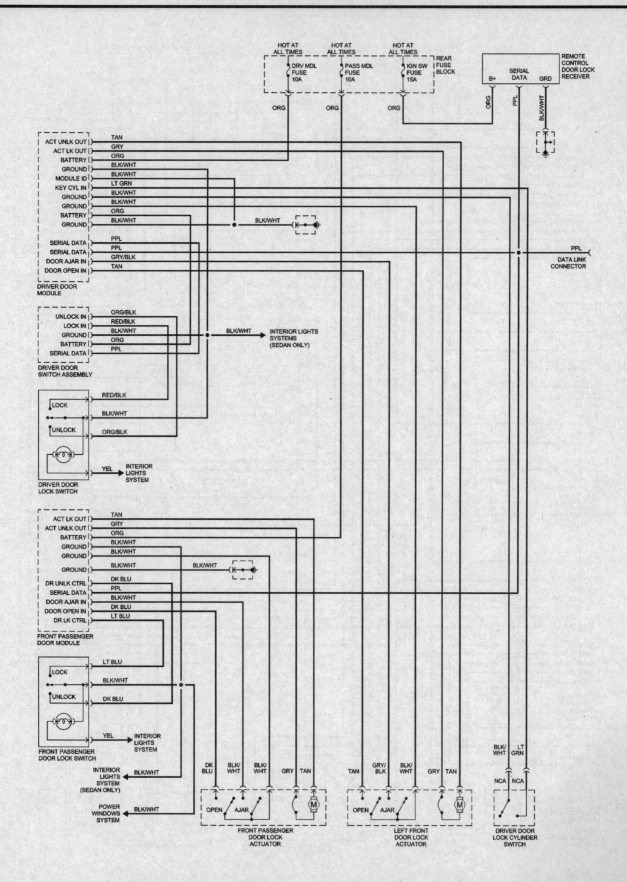

Power door lock system - 2000 and later models (1998 and 1999 Seville similar) (2 of 2)

Interior lights - 1992 through 1995 models

Interior lights - 1996 models

Interior lights - 1997 through 1999 models (except 1998 and 1999 Seville)

Interior lights - 2000 and later DeVille models (1 of 2)

Interior lights - 2000 and later DeVille models (2 of 2)

Interior lights - 1998 and later Seville models (1 of 2)

Interior lights - 1998 and later Seville models (2 of 2)

Headlight and foglight system - 1992 and 1993 models

Headlight and foglight system - 1994 and 1995 models

Headlight and foglight system - 1996 through 1999 DeVille models

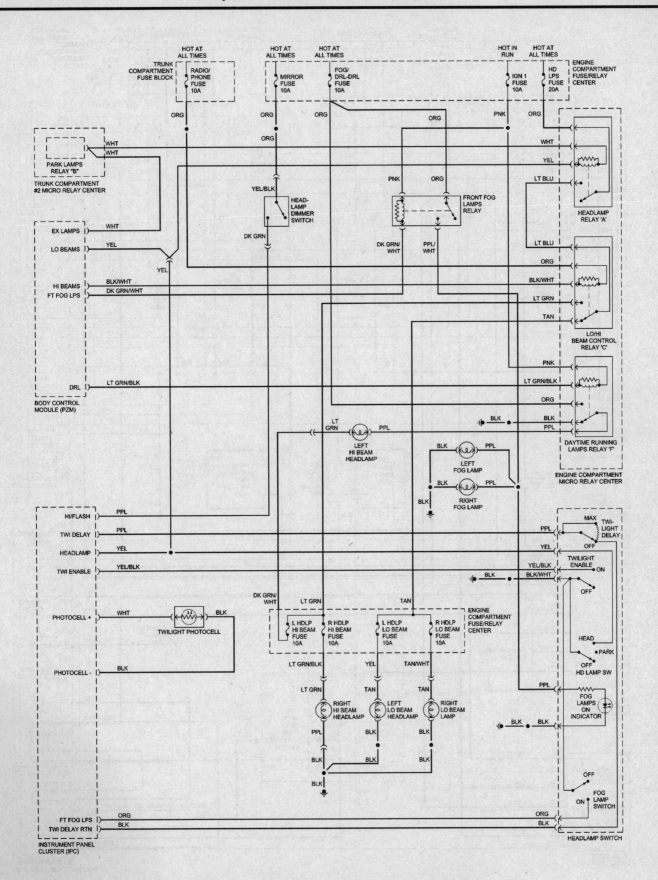

Headlight and foglight system - 1996 and 1997 Seville models

Headlight and foglight system - 1998 and later Seville models

Headlight and foglight system - 2000 and later DeVille models

Notes

Index

Haynes Automotive Manuals

NOTE: New manuals are added to this list on a periodic basis. If you do not see a listing for your vehicle, consult your local Haynes dealer for the latest product information.

ACURA
12020 **Integra** '86 thru '89 & **Legend** '86 thru '90
12021 **Integra** '90 thru '93 & **Legend** '91 thru '95

AMC
Jeep CJ - *see JEEP (50020)*
14020 **Mid-size models** '70 thru '83
14025 **(Renault) Alliance & Encore** '83 thru '87

AUDI
15020 **4000** all models '80 thru '87
15025 **5000** all models '77 thru '83
15026 **5000** all models '84 thru '88

AUSTIN-HEALEY
Sprite - *see MG Midget (66015)*

BMW
***18020** **3/5 Series** not including diesel or all-wheel drive models '82 thru '92
18021 **3-Series** incl. Z3 models '92 thru '98
18025 **320i** all 4 cyl models '75 thru '83
18050 **1500 thru 2002** except Turbo '59 thru '77

BUICK
***19010** **Buick Century** '97 thru '02
Century (front-wheel drive) - *see GM (38005)*
***19020** **Buick, Oldsmobile & Pontiac Full-size (Front-wheel drive)** '85 thru '02
Buick Electra, LeSabre and Park Avenue; **Oldsmobile** Delta 88 Royale, Ninety Eight and Regency; **Pontiac** Bonneville
19025 **Buick Oldsmobile & Pontiac Full-size (Rear wheel drive)**
Buick Estate '70 thru '90, Electra '70 thru '84, LeSabre '70 thru '85, Limited '74 thru '79 **Oldsmobile** Custom Cruiser '70 thru '90, Delta 88 '70 thru '85, Ninety-eight '70 thru '84 **Pontiac** Bonneville '70 thru '81, Catalina '70 thru '81, Grandville '70 thru '75, Parisienne '83 thru '86
19030 **Mid-size Regal & Century** all rear-drive models with V6, V8 and Turbo '74 thru '87
Regal - *see GENERAL MOTORS (38010)*
Riviera - *see GENERAL MOTORS (38030)*
Roadmaster - *see CHEVROLET (24046)*
Skyhawk - *see GENERAL MOTORS (38015)*
Skylark - *see GM (38020, 38025)*
Somerset - *see GENERAL MOTORS (38025)*

CADILLAC
21030 **Cadillac Rear Wheel Drive** all gasoline models '70 thru '93
Cimarron - *see GENERAL MOTORS (38015)*
DeVille - *see GM (38031 & 38032)*
Eldorado - *see GM (38030 & 38031)*
Fleetwood - *see GM (38031)*
Seville - *see GM (38030, 38031 & 38032)*

CHEVROLET
***24010** **Astro & GMC Safari Mini-vans** '85 thru '03
24015 **Camaro V8** all models '70 thru '81
24016 **Camaro** all models '82 thru '92
24017 **Camaro & Firebird** '93 thru '02
Cavalier - *see GENERAL MOTORS (38016)*
Celebrity - *see GENERAL MOTORS (38005)*
24020 **Chevelle, Malibu & El Camino** '69 thru '87
24024 **Chevette & Pontiac T1000** '76 thru '87
Citation - *see GENERAL MOTORS (38020)*
24032 **Corsica/Beretta** all models '87 thru '96
24040 **Corvette** all V8 models '68 thru '82
24041 **Corvette** all models '84 thru '96
10305 **Chevrolet Engine Overhaul Manual**
24045 **Full-size Sedans** Caprice, Impala, Biscayne, Bel Air & Wagons '69 thru '90
24046 **Impala SS & Caprice and Buick Roadmaster** '91 thru '96
Impala - *see LUMINA (24048)*
Lumina '90 thru '94 - *see GM (38010)*
***24048** **Lumina & Monte Carlo** '95 thru '03
Lumina APV - *see GM (38035)*
24050 **Luv Pick-up** all 2WD & 4WD '72 thru '82
Malibu '97 thru '00 - *see GM (38026)*
24055 **Monte Carlo** all models '70 thru '88
Monte Carlo '95 thru '01 - *see LUMINA (24048)*

24059 **Nova** all V8 models '69 thru '79
24060 **Nova and Geo Prizm** '85 thru '92
24064 **Pick-ups** '67 thru '87 - Chevrolet & GMC, all V8 & in-line 6 cyl, 2WD & 4WD '67 thru '87; Suburbans, Blazers & Jimmys '67 thru '91
24065 **Pick-ups** '88 thru '98 - Chevrolet & GMC, full-size pick-ups '88 thru '98, C/K Classic '99 & '00, Blazer & Jimmy '92 thru '94; Suburban '92 thru '99; Tahoe & Yukon '95 thru '99
***24066** **Pick-ups** '99 thru '03 - Chevrolet Silverado & GMC Sierra full-size pick-ups '99 thru '02, Suburban/Tahoe/Yukon/Yukon XL '00 thru '02
24070 **S-10 & S-15 Pick-ups** '82 thru '93, Blazer & Jimmy '83 thru '94,
***24071** **S-10 & S-15 Pick-ups** '94 thru '01, Blazer & Jimmy '95 thru '01, Hombre '96 thru '01
***24072** **Chevrolet TrailBlazer & TrailBlazer EXT, GMC Envoy & Envoy XL, Oldsmobile Bravada** '02 and '03
24075 **Sprint** '85 thru '88 & Geo Metro '89 thru '01
24080 **Vans** - Chevrolet & GMC '68 thru '96

CHRYSLER
25015 **Chrysler Cirrus, Dodge Stratus, Plymouth Breeze** '95 thru '00
10310 **Chrysler Engine Overhaul Manual**
25020 **Full-size Front-Wheel Drive** '88 thru '93
K-Cars - *see DODGE Aries (30008)*
Laser - *see DODGE Daytona (30030)*
25025 **Chrysler LHS, Concorde, New Yorker, Dodge** Intrepid, **Eagle** Vision, '93 thru '97
***25026** **Chrysler LHS, Concorde, 300M, Dodge** Intrepid, '98 thru '03
25030 **Chrysler & Plymouth Mid-size** front wheel drive '82 thru '95
Rear-wheel Drive - *see Dodge (30050)*
***25035** **PT Cruiser** all models '01 thru '03
***25040** **Chrysler Sebring, Dodge** Avenger '95 thru '02

DATSUN
28005 **200SX** all models '80 thru '83
28007 **B-210** all models '73 thru '78
28009 **210** all models '79 thru '82
28012 **240Z, 260Z & 280Z** Coupe '70 thru '78
28014 **280ZX** Coupe & 2+2 '79 thru '83
300ZX - *see NISSAN (72010)*
28016 **310** all models '78 thru '82
28018 **510 & PL521 Pick-up** '68 thru '73
28020 **510** all models '78 thru '81
28022 **620 Series Pick-up** all models '73 thru '79
720 Series Pick-up - *see NISSAN (72030)*
28025 **810/Maxima** all gasoline models, '77 thru '84

DODGE
400 & 600 - *see CHRYSLER (25030)*
30008 **Aries & Plymouth Reliant** '81 thru '89
30010 **Caravan & Plymouth Voyager** '84 thru '95
***30011** **Caravan & Plymouth Voyager** '96 thru '02
30012 **Challenger/Plymouth Saporro** '78 thru '83
30016 **Colt & Plymouth Champ** '78 thru '87
30020 **Dakota Pick-ups** all models '87 thru '96
***30021** **Durango** '98 & '99, **Dakota** '97 thru '99
30025 **Dart, Demon, Plymouth Barracuda, Duster & Valiant** 6 cyl models '67 thru '76
30030 **Daytona & Chrysler Laser** '84 thru '89
Intrepid - *see CHRYSLER (25025, 25026)*
***30034** **Neon** all models '95 thru '99
30035 **Omni & Plymouth Horizon** '78 thru '90
30040 **Pick-ups** all full-size models '74 thru '93
***30041** **Pick-ups** all full-size models '94 thru '01
30045 **Ram 50/D50 Pick-ups & Raider and Plymouth Arrow Pick-ups** '79 thru '93
30050 **Dodge/Plymouth/Chrysler** RWD '71 thru '89
30055 **Shadow & Plymouth Sundance** '87 thru '94
30060 **Spirit & Plymouth Acclaim** '89 thru '95
***30065** **Vans - Dodge & Plymouth** '71 thru '03

EAGLE
Talon - *see MITSUBISHI (68030, 68031)*
Vision - *see CHRYSLER (25025)*

FIAT
34010 **124 Sport Coupe & Spider** '68 thru '78
34025 **X1/9** all models '74 thru '80

FORD
10355 **Ford Automatic Transmission Overhaul**
36004 **Aerostar Mini-vans** all models '86 thru '97
36006 **Contour & Mercury Mystique** '95 thru '00
36008 **Courier Pick-up** all models '72 thru '82
***36012** **Crown Victoria & Mercury Grand Marquis** '88 thru '00
10320 **Ford Engine Overhaul Manual**
36016 **Escort/Mercury Lynx** all models '81 thru '90
36020 **Escort/Mercury Tracer** '91 thru '00
36022 **Ford Escape & Mazda Tribute** '01 thru '03
36024 **Explorer & Mazda Navajo** '91 thru '01
36025 **Ford Explorer & Mercury Mountaineer** '02 and '03
36028 **Fairmont & Mercury Zephyr** '78 thru '83
36030 **Festiva & Aspire** '88 thru '97
36032 **Fiesta** all models '77 thru '80
***36034** **Focus** all models '00 and '01
36036 **Ford & Mercury Full-size** '75 thru '87
36044 **Ford & Mercury Mid-size** '75 thru '86
36048 **Mustang V8** all models '64-1/2 thru '73
36049 **Mustang II** 4 cyl, V6 & V8 models '74 thru '78
36050 **Mustang & Mercury Capri** all models Mustang, '79 thru '93; Capri, '79 thru '86
***36051** **Mustang** all models '94 thru '03
36054 **Pick-ups & Bronco** '73 thru '79
36058 **Pick-ups & Bronco** '80 thru '96
***36059** **F-150 & Expedition** '97 thru '02, F-250 '97 thru '99 & Lincoln Navigator '98 thru '02
***36060** **Super Duty Pick-ups, Excursion** '97 thru '02
36062 **Pinto & Mercury Bobcat** '75 thru '80
36066 **Probe** all models '89 thru '92
36070 **Ranger/Bronco II** gasoline models '83 thru '92
***36071** **Ranger** '93 thru '00 & Mazda Pick-ups '94 thru '00
36074 **Taurus & Mercury Sable** '86 thru '95
***36075** **Taurus & Mercury Sable** '96 thru '01
36078 **Tempo & Mercury Topaz** '84 thru '94
36082 **Thunderbird/Mercury Cougar** '83 thru '88
36086 **Thunderbird/Mercury Cougar** '89 and '97
36090 **Vans** all V8 Econoline models '69 thru '91
***36094** **Vans** full size '92 thru '01
***36097** **Windstar Mini-van** '95 thru '03

GENERAL MOTORS
10360 **GM Automatic Transmission Overhaul**
38005 **Buick Century, Chevrolet Celebrity, Oldsmobile Cutlass Ciera & Pontiac 6000** all models '82 thru '96
***38010** **Buick Regal, Chevrolet Lumina, Oldsmobile Cutlass Supreme & Pontiac Grand Prix** (FWD) '88 thru '02
38015 **Buick Skyhawk, Cadillac Cimarron, Chevrolet Cavalier, Oldsmobile Firenza & Pontiac J-2000 & Sunbird** '82 thru '94
***38016** **Chevrolet Cavalier & Pontiac Sunfire** '95 thru '04
38020 **Buick Skylark, Chevrolet Citation, Olds Omega, Pontiac Phoenix** '80 thru '85
38025 **Buick Skylark & Somerset, Oldsmobile Achieva & Calais and Pontiac Grand Am** all models '85 thru '98
***38026** **Chevrolet Malibu, Olds Alero & Cutlass, Pontiac Grand Am** '97 thru '00
38030 **Cadillac Eldorado** '71 thru '85, **Seville** '80 thru '85, **Oldsmobile Toronado** '71 thru '85, **Buick Riviera** '79 thru '85
***38031** **Cadillac Eldorado & Seville** '86 thru '91, **DeVille** '86 thru '93, **Fleetwood & Olds Toronado** '86 thru '92, **Buick Riviera** '86 thru '93
38032 **Cadillac DeVille** '94 thru '02 & **Seville** - '92 thru '02
38035 **Chevrolet Lumina APV, Olds Silhouette & Pontiac Trans Sport** all models '90 thru '96
***38036** **Chevrolet Venture, Olds Silhouette, Pontiac Trans Sport & Montana** '97 thru '01
General Motors Full-size Rear-wheel Drive - *see BUICK (19025)*

GEO
Metro - *see CHEVROLET Sprint (24075)*
Prizm - '85 thru '92 *see CHEVY (24060)*, '93 thru '02 *see TOYOTA Corolla (92036)*

(Continued on other side)

* Listings shown with an asterisk (*) indicate model coverage as of this printing. These titles will be periodically updated to include later model years - consult your Haynes dealer for more information.

Haynes North America, Inc., 861 Lawrence Drive, Newbury Park, CA 91320-1514 • (805) 498-6703

Haynes Automotive Manuals (continued)

NOTE: New manuals are added to this list on a periodic basis. If you do not see a listing for your vehicle, consult your local Haynes dealer for the latest product information.

40030 Storm all models '90 thru '93
Tracker - see SUZUKI Samurai (90010)

GMC
Vans & Pick-ups - see CHEVROLET

HONDA
42010 Accord CVCC all models '76 thru '83
42011 Accord all models '84 thru '89
42012 Accord all models '90 thru '93
42013 Accord all models '94 thru '97
42014 Accord all models '98 thru '02
42020 Civic 1200 all models '73 thru '79
42021 Civic 1300 & 1500 CVCC '80 thru '83
42022 Civic 1500 CVCC all models '75 thru '79
42023 Civic all models '84 thru '91
42024 Civic & del Sol '92 thru '95
*42025 Civic '96 thru '00, CR-V '97 thru '00, Acura Integra '94 thru '00
42026 Civic '01 thru '04, CR-V '02 thru '04
42040 Prelude CVCC all models '79 thru '89

HYUNDAI
*43010 Elantra all models '96 thru '01
43015 Excel & Accent all models '86 thru '98

ISUZU
Hombre - see CHEVROLET S-10 (24071)
*47017 Rodeo '91 thru '02; Amigo '89 thru '94 and '98 thru '02; Honda Passport '95 thru '02
47020 Trooper & Pick-up '81 thru '93

JAGUAR
49010 XJ6 all 6 cyl models '68 thru '86
49011 XJ6 all models '88 thru '94
49015 XJ12 & XJS all 12 cyl models '72 thru '85

JEEP
50010 Cherokee, Comanche & Wagoneer Limited all models '84 thru '01
50020 CJ all models '49 thru '86
*50025 Grand Cherokee all models '93 thru '04
50029 Grand Wagoneer & Pick-up '72 thru '91
Grand Wagoneer '84 thru '91, Cherokee & Wagoneer '72 thru '83, Pick-up '72 thru '88
*50030 Wrangler all models '87 thru '00
50035 Liberty '02 thru '04

LEXUS
ES 300 - see TOYOTA Camry (92007)

LINCOLN
Navigator - see FORD Pick-up (36059)
*59010 Rear-Wheel Drive all models '70 thru '01

MAZDA
61010 GLC Hatchback (rear-wheel drive) '77 thru '83
61011 GLC (front-wheel drive) '81 thru '85
61015 323 & Protegé '90 thru '00
*61016 MX-5 Miata '90 thru '97
61020 MPV all models '89 thru '94
Navajo - see Ford Explorer (36024)
61030 Pick-ups '72 thru '93
Pick-ups '94 thru '00 - see Ford Ranger (36071)
61035 RX-7 all models '79 thru '85
61036 RX-7 all models '86 thru '91
61040 626 (rear-wheel drive) all models '79 thru '82
61041 626/MX-6 (front-wheel drive) all models '83 thru '91
61042 626 '93 thru '01, MX-6/Ford Probe '93 thru '97

MERCEDES-BENZ
63012 123 Series Diesel '76 thru '85
63015 190 Series four-cyl gas models, '84 thru '88
63020 230/250/280 6 cyl sohc models '68 thru '72
63025 280 123 Series gasoline models '77 thru '81
63030 350 & 450 all models '71 thru '80

MERCURY
64200 Villager & Nissan Quest '93 thru '01
All other titles, see FORD Listing.

MG
66010 MGB Roadster & GT Coupe '62 thru '80
66015 MG Midget, Austin Healey Sprite '58 thru '80

MITSUBISHI
68020 Cordia, Tredia, Galant, Precis & Mirage '83 thru '93
68030 Eclipse, Eagle Talon & Ply. Laser '90 thru '94
*68031 Eclipse '95 thru '01, Eagle Talon '95 thru '98
68035 Mitsubishi Galant '94 thru '03
68040 Pick-up '83 thru '96 & Montero '83 thru '93

NISSAN
72010 300ZX all models including Turbo '84 thru '89
72015 Altima all models '93 thru '04
72020 Maxima all models '85 thru '92
*72021 Maxima all models '93 thru '01
72030 Pick-ups '80 thru '97 Pathfinder '87 thru '95
*72031 Frontier Pick-up '98 thru '01, Xterra '00 & '01, Pathfinder '96 thru '01
72040 Pulsar all models '83 thru '86
Quest - see MERCURY Villager (64200)
72050 Sentra all models '82 thru '94
72051 Sentra & 200SX all models '95 thru '99
72060 Stanza all models '82 thru '90

OLDSMOBILE
73015 Cutlass V6 & V8 gas models '74 thru '88
For other OLDSMOBILE titles, see BUICK, CHEVROLET or GENERAL MOTORS listing.

PLYMOUTH
For PLYMOUTH titles, see DODGE listing.

PONTIAC
79008 Fiero all models '84 thru '88
79018 Firebird V8 models except Turbo '70 thru '81
79019 Firebird all models '82 thru '92
79040 Mid-size Rear-wheel Drive '70 thru '87
For other PONTIAC titles, see BUICK, CHEVROLET or GENERAL MOTORS listing.

PORSCHE
80020 911 except Turbo & Carrera 4 '65 thru '89
80025 914 all 4 cyl models '69 thru '76
80030 924 all models including Turbo '76 thru '82
80035 944 all models including Turbo '83 thru '89

RENAULT
Alliance & Encore - see AMC (14020)

SAAB
*84010 900 all models including Turbo '79 thru '88

SATURN
*87010 Saturn all models '91 thru '02
87020 Saturn all L-series models '00 thru '04

SUBARU
89002 1100, 1300, 1400 & 1600 '71 thru '79
89003 1600 & 1800 2WD & 4WD '80 thru '94

SUZUKI
90010 Samurai/Sidekick & Geo Tracker '86 thru '01

TOYOTA
92005 Camry all models '83 thru '91
92006 Camry all models '92 thru '96
*92007 Camry, Avalon, Solara, Lexus ES 300 '97 thru '01
92015 Celica Rear Wheel Drive '71 thru '85
92020 Celica Front Wheel Drive '86 thru '99
92025 Celica Supra all models '79 thru '92
92030 Corolla all models '75 thru '79
92032 Corolla all rear wheel drive models '80 thru '87
92035 Corolla all front wheel drive models '84 thru '92
92036 Corolla & Geo Prizm '93 thru '02
92040 Corolla Tercel all models '80 thru '82
92045 Corona all models '74 thru '82
92050 Cressida all models '78 thru '82
92055 Land Cruiser FJ40, 43, 45, 55 '68 thru '82
92056 Land Cruiser FJ60, 62, 80, FZJ80 '80 thru '96
92065 MR2 all models '85 thru '87
92070 Pick-up all models '69 thru '78
92075 Pick-up all models '79 thru '95
*92076 Tacoma '95 thru '00, 4Runner '96 thru '00, & T100 '93 thru '98
*92078 Tundra '00 thru '02 & Sequoia '01 thru '02
92080 Previa all models '91 thru '95

*92082 RAV4 all models '96 thru '02
92085 Tercel all models '87 thru '94

TRIUMPH
94007 Spitfire all models '62 thru '81
94010 TR7 all models '75 thru '81

VW
96008 Beetle & Karmann Ghia '54 thru '79
*96009 New Beetle '98 thru '00
96016 Rabbit, Jetta, Scirocco & Pick-up gas models '74 thru '91 & Convertible '80 thru '92
96017 Golf, GTI & Jetta '93 thru '98 & Cabrio '95 thru '98
*96018 Golf, GTI, Jetta & Cabrio '99 thru '02
96020 Rabbit, Jetta & Pick-up diesel '77 thru '84
96023 Passat '98 thru '01, Audi A4 '96 thru '01
96030 Transporter 1600 all models '68 thru '79
96035 Transporter 1700, 1800 & 2000 '72 thru '79
96040 Type 3 1500 & 1600 all models '63 thru '73
96045 Vanagon all air-cooled models '80 thru '83

VOLVO
97010 120, 130 Series & 1800 Sports '61 thru '73
97015 140 Series all models '66 thru '74
97020 240 Series all models '76 thru '93
97040 740 & 760 Series all models '82 thru '88
97050 850 Series all models '93 thru '97

TECHBOOK MANUALS
10205 Automotive Computer Codes
10210 Automotive Emissions Control Manual
10215 Fuel Injection Manual, 1978 thru 1985
10220 Fuel Injection Manual, 1986 thru 1999
10225 Holley Carburetor Manual
10230 Rochester Carburetor Manual
10240 Weber/Zenith/Stromberg/SU Carburetors
10305 Chevrolet Engine Overhaul Manual
10310 Chrysler Engine Overhaul Manual
10320 Ford Engine Overhaul Manual
10330 GM and Ford Diesel Engine Repair Manual
10340 Small Engine Repair Manual, 5 HP & Less
10341 Small Engine Repair Manual, 5.5 - 20 HP
10345 Suspension, Steering & Driveline Manual
10355 Ford Automatic Transmission Overhaul
10360 GM Automatic Transmission Overhaul
10405 Automotive Body Repair & Painting
10410 Automotive Brake Manual
10411 Automotive Anti-lock Brake (ABS) Systems
10415 Automotive Detaiing Manual
10420 Automotive Eelectrical Manual
10425 Automotive Heating & Air Conditioning
10430 Automotive Reference Manual & Dictionary
10435 Automotive Tools Manual
10440 Used Car Buying Guide
10445 Welding Manual
10450 ATV Basics

SPANISH MANUALS
98903 Reparación de Carrocería & Pintura
98905 Códigos Automotrices de la Computadora
98910 Frenos Automotriz
98915 Inyección de Combustible 1986 al 1999
99040 Chevrolet & GMC Camionetas '67 al '87 Incluye Suburban, Blazer & Jimmy '67 al '91
99041 Chevrolet & GMC Camionetas '88 al '98 Incluye Suburban '92 al '98, Blazer & Jimmy '92 al '94, Tahoe y Yukon '95 al '98
99042 Chevrolet & GMC Camionetas Cerradas '68 al '95
99055 Dodge Caravan & Plymouth Voyager '84 al '95
99075 Ford Camionetas y Bronco '80 al '94
99077 Ford Camionetas Cerradas '69 al '91
99088 Ford Modelos de Tamaño Mediano '75 al '86
99091 Ford Taurus & Mercury Sable '86 al '95
99095 GM Modelos de Tamaño Grande '70 al '90
99100 GM Modelos de Tamaño Mediano '70 al '88
99110 Nissan Camioneta '80 al '96, Pathfinder '87 al '95
99118 Nissan Sentra '82 al '94
99125 Toyota Camionetas y 4Runner '79 al '95

Over 100 Haynes motorcycle manuals also available

2-05

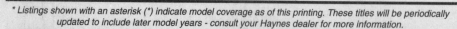

Haynes North America, Inc., 861 Lawrence Drive, Newbury Park, CA 91320-1514 • (805) 498-6703